via	Panama Canal	*
,,	Suez Canal	+
,,	Cape of Good Hope	C
,,	Straits of Magellan	M
,,	Kiel Canal	K

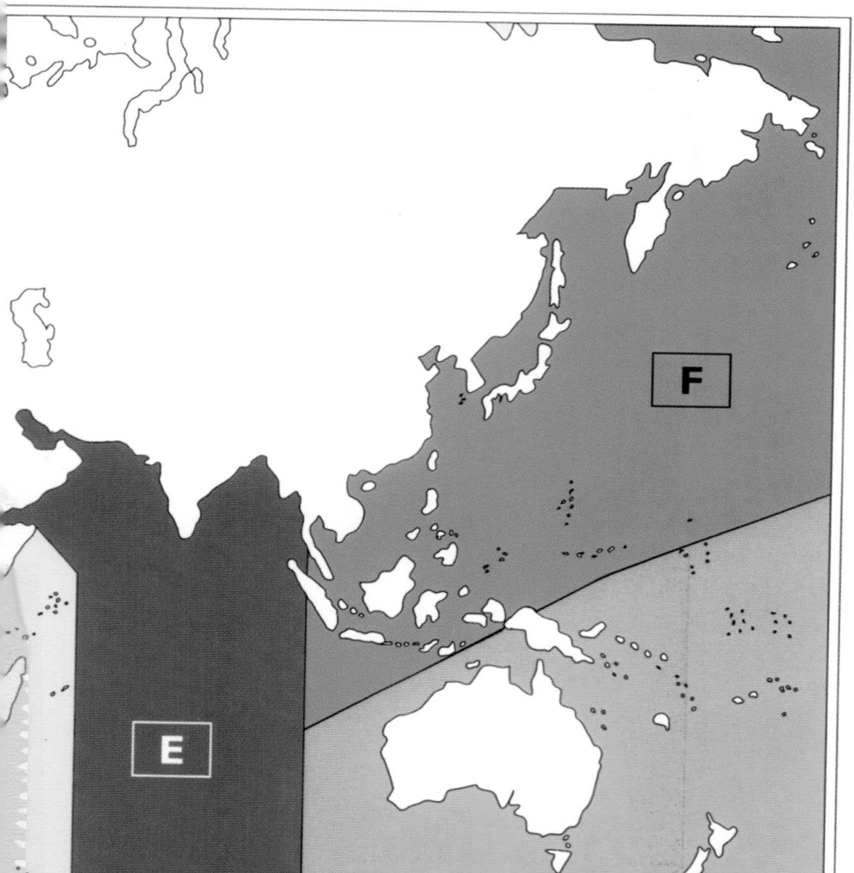

t meet at each of these points

dications are necessary:

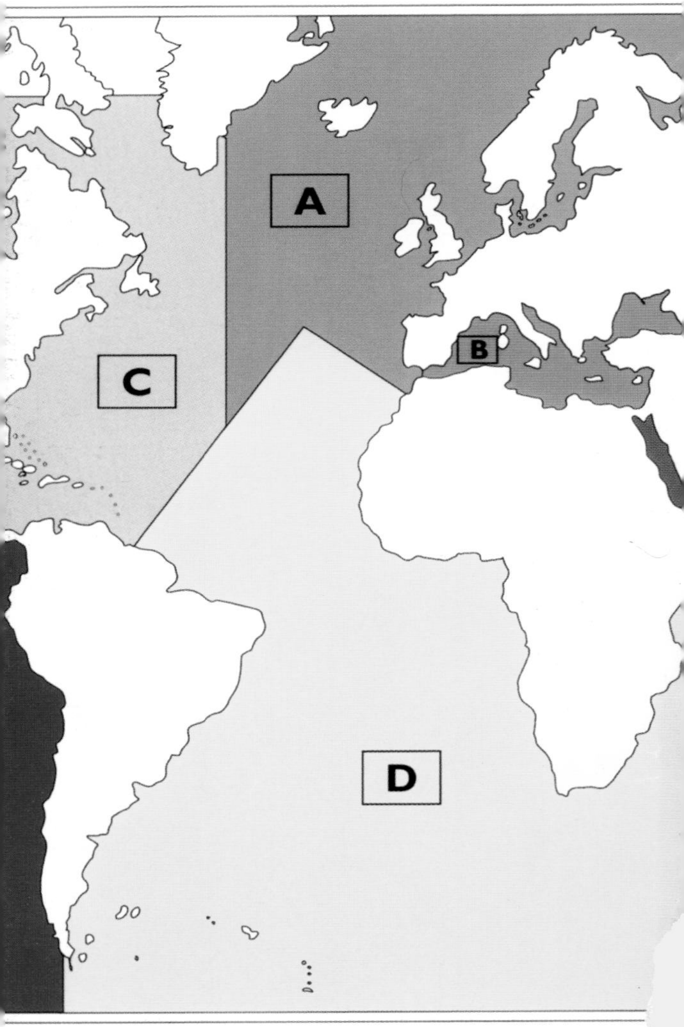

Area C **Area D** **Area E**

Gibraltar, Singapore, Honolulu and Panama (or Cristobal) can be found in b

Main routes used are indicated as follows, where

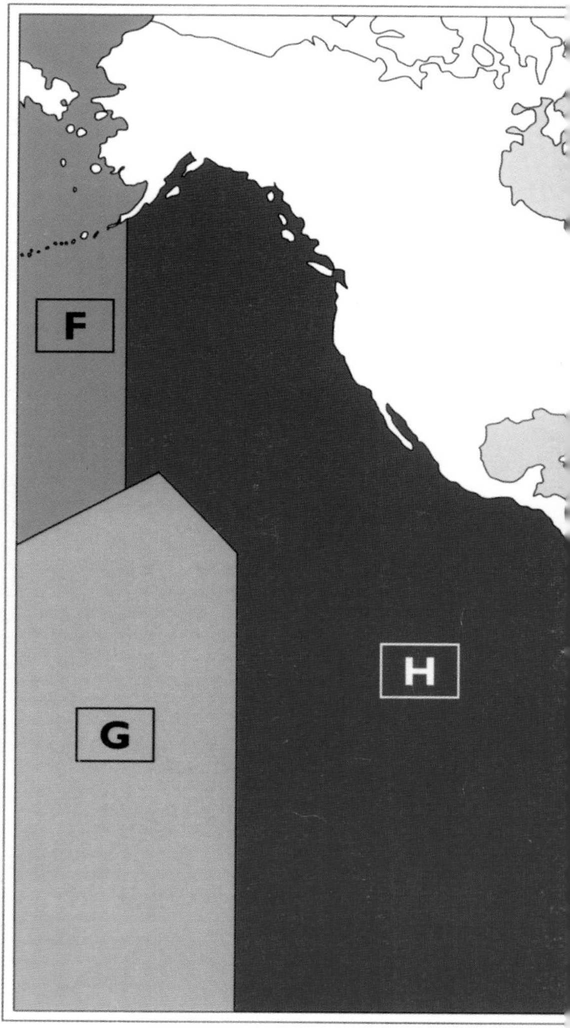

Area A **Area B**

Note:

Reed's Marine Distance Tables

Reed's Marine Distance Tables

10th edition

Compiled by
R W Caney, AICS and J E Reynolds, AICS
Revised by
Miranda Delmar-Morgan

ADLARD COLES NAUTICAL
London

Published by Adlard Coles Nautical
an imprint of A & C Black Publishers Ltd
38 Soho Square, London W1D 3HB
www.adlardcoles.com

First published by Thomas Reed Publications 1965
Second edition 1971
Third edition 1976
Fourth Edition 1978
Fifth Edition 1981
Sixth Edition 1988
Seventh Edition 1992
Eighth Edition 1995
Eighth Edition (Revised) 2000
Ninth edition published by Adlard Coles Nautical 2004
Tenth Edition 2007

ISBN 978 07136 8352 3

A CIP catalogue record for this book is available from the British Library.

This book is produced using paper that is made from wood grown in managed,
sustainable forests. It is natural, renewable and recyclable. The logging and
manufacturing processes conform to the environmental regulations of the
country of origin.

Typeset in Myriad 9.5pt on 10.5pt
Printed in Great Britain by
Martins the Printers, Berwick-upon-Tweed

Reed's Marine Distance Tables

10th edition

Compiled by
R W Caney, AICS and J E Reynolds, AICS
Revised by
Miranda Delmar-Morgan

ADLARD COLES NAUTICAL
London

Published by Adlard Coles Nautical
an imprint of A & C Black Publishers Ltd
38 Soho Square, London W1D 3HB
www.adlardcoles.com

First published by Thomas Reed Publications 1965
Second edition 1971
Third edition 1976
Fourth Edition 1978
Fifth Edition 1981
Sixth Edition 1988
Seventh Edition 1992
Eighth Edition 1995
Eighth Edition (Revised) 2000
Ninth edition published by Adlard Coles Nautical 2004
Tenth Edition 2007

ISBN 978 07136 8352 3

A CIP catalogue record for this book is available from the British Library.

This book is produced using paper that is made from wood grown in managed, sustainable forests. It is natural, renewable and recyclable. The logging and manufacturing processes conform to the environmental regulations of the country of origin.

Typeset in Myriad 9.5pt on 10.5pt
Printed in Great Britain by
Martins the Printers, Berwick-upon-Tweed

Note: While all reasonable care has been taken in the pu
of this book, neither the publisher nor the revisor take r
for the use of the methods or information in t

Contents

(for key see area map)

Preface

These tables give worldwide coverage of over 500 ports. They are divided into 'market areas' with the shipowner or broker in mind, and allow for quick and easy voyage estimating. They are also a handy reference for any master or navigator.

By making one simple reference, the user can calculate the shortest distance between all the major ports in the world. Eight key market areas (A–H) each have their own section from which distances to other market areas can be determined. The pull-out map shows the world divided into these market areas for clear and easy reference, and the new chartlets at the beginning of each section show every port included in that section. This provides a 'see at a glance' facility which can be verified by the index at the back of the book.

Mariners needing more localised distances can refer to the inter-area distances included at the end of each area section. The St Lawrence Seaway and Great Lakes are also included.

This tenth edition includes a new table with distances between major turning points around the globe.

Great circles are used where appropriate, and the shortest distance is usually the figure given in the tables. Traffic Separations Schemes are taken into account.

Every care has been taken in compiling the tables, but no responsibility for errors or omissions or their consequences is accepted by the publishers. It would be appreciated if users of these tables would draw attention to any errors or omissions, and suggestions for improving the work in the light of experience will be welcomed.

All distances except where otherwise stated are given in nautical miles and are based on the shortest or most usual routes taking into account shipping lanes. The main routes are signified where necessary, with the following symbols:

- * via the Panama Canal
- † via the Suez Canal
- C via the Cape of Good Hope
- M via the Straits of Magellan
- K via the Kiel Canal (except where all distances in a column are measured via the Kiel Canal, when this is noted in the column heading and the symbol K is omitted)

Key to abbreviations in the tables

BC	British Columbia, Canada
Ch	Chile
Col	Colombia
CR	Costa Rica
CW	Cape Wrath
DS	Dover Strait
G	Guyana
Guat	Guatemala
Mex	Mexico
NB	New Brunswick, Canada
NC	North Carolina, USA
NF	Newfoundland, Canada
NSW	New South Wales, Australia
NY	New York, USA
Oreg	Oregon, USA
PR	Puerto Rico
Tas	Tasmania
Vanc Is	Vancouver Island, Canada
Va	Virginia, USA

Acknowledgements

Grateful thanks are extended to Cdr R Porteous, RN, and to J C Bazley, Head of School of Professional Studies and J N Wilde, Senior Lecturer in Merchant Vessel Operations at Warsash Maritime Academy. Also to the Warsash Maritime Academy itself for the use of its facilities.

Area A

Distances between principal ports in the United Kingdom, North Europe (Gibraltar to Archangel inclusive) and the Baltic and White Seas.

and

Area B The Mediterranean Sea, Black Sea and the Adriatic.

Area C The East Coast of North America and Canada (including the Great Lakes and St Lawrence Seaway), the US Gulf and Central America (including the Gulf of Mexico and the Caribbean Sea).

Area D The East Coast of South America, the Atlantic islands, and West and East Africa.

Area E The Red Sea, The Gulf, the Indian Ocean and the Bay of Bengal.

Area F Malaysia, Indonesia, South East Asia, the China Sea and Japan.

Area G Australasia, New Guinea and the Pacific Islands.

Area H The West Coast of North and South America.

Area A Other ports in the UK, North Europe (from Gibraltar to Archangel inclusive) and the Baltic and White Seas.

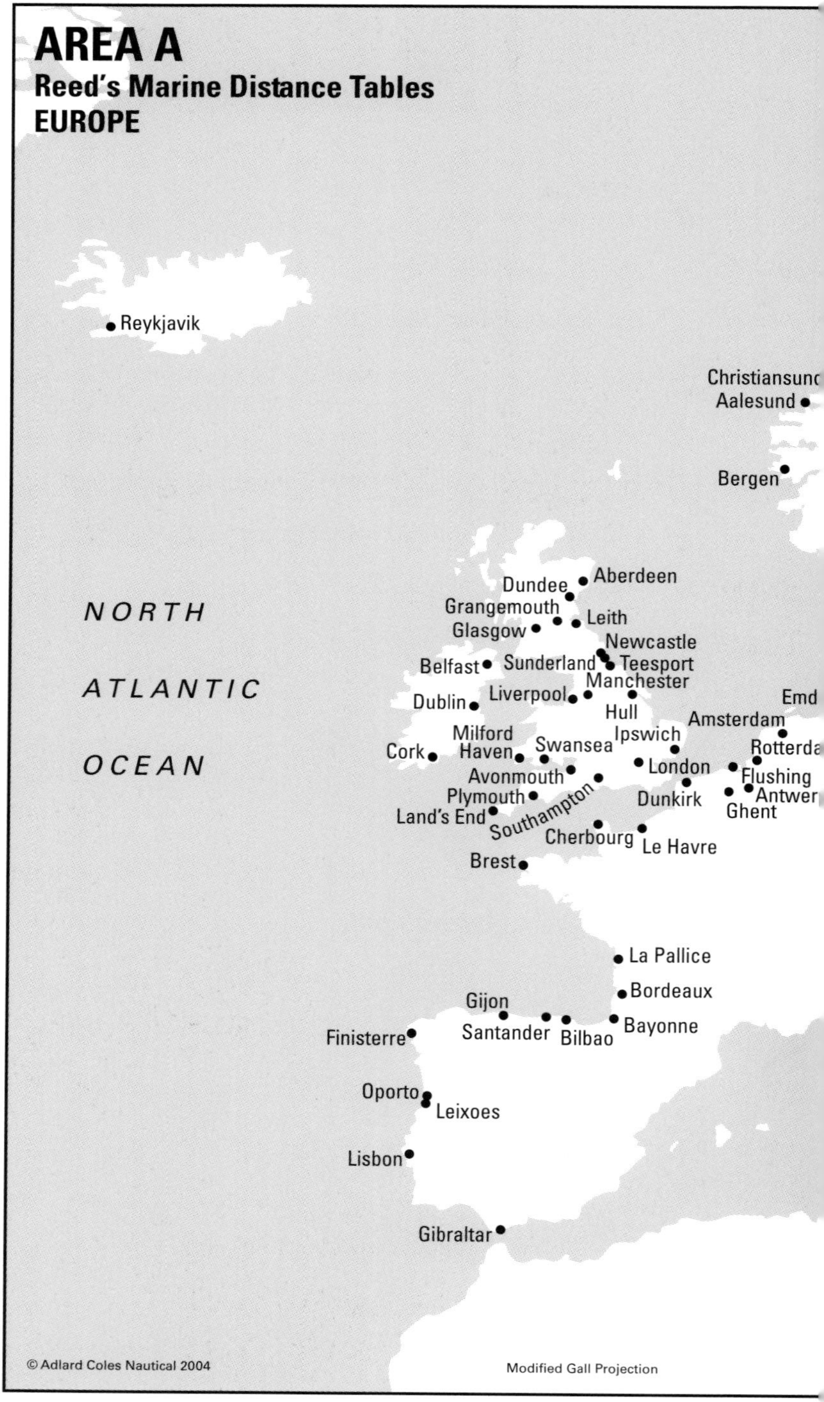
AREA A
Reed's Marine Distance Tables
EUROPE
NORTH
ATLANTIC
OCEAN
Reykjavik
Christiansunc
Aalesund
Bergen
Aberdeen
Dundee
Grangemouth
Leith
Glasgow
Newcastle
Belfast
Sunderland
Teesport
Manchester
Dublin
Liverpool
Emd
Hull
Amsterdam
Milford
Haven
Swansea
Ipswich
Rotterda
Cork
Avonmouth
London
Flushing
Plymouth
Southampton
Dunkirk
Antwer
Ghent
Land's End
Cherbourg
Le Havre
Brest
La Pallice
Bordeaux
Gijon
Santander
Bilbao
Bayonne
Finisterre
Oporto
Leixoes
Lisbon
Gibraltar
© Adlard Coles Nautical 2004
Modified Gall Projection

AREA A
Reed's Marine Distance Tables
EUROPE
Murmansk
Narvik
Lulea
Archangel
Trondheim
Vaasa
Hernosand
Turku
Kotka
Baltic
Sea
Helsinki
St Petersburg
Oslo
Stockholm
arvik
kaw
Gothenburg
Aalborg
Oskarshamn
Riga
Aarhus
sbjerg
Malmo
Klapeida
penhagen
Gdynia
iel
Rostock
Gdansk
Hamburg
Szczecin
remen
Black Sea
Mediterranean Sea
Awa Graphics

AREA B	AREA A	Aberdeen	Amsterdam	Antwerp	Archangel	Avonmouth	Belfast	Bergen	Bilbao
Alexandria		3449	3216	3181	5062	2981	3110	3620	2655
Algiers		2061	1828	1793	3695	1597	1725	2235	1270
Ancona		3187	2954	2919	4820	2698	2833	3360	2395
Barcelona		2176	1943	1908	3810	1674	1840	2350	1385
Beirut		3665	3430	3395	5310	3199	3340	3850	2885
Bourgas		3562	3329	3294	5195	3079	3225	3735	2770
Brindisi		2930	2697	2662	4565	2441	2595	3105	2140
Cagliari		2350	2115	2080	3995	1873	2025	2535	1570
Casablanca		1675	1445	1410	3306	1193	1327	1860	901
Constantza		3625	3392	3357	5257	3194	3287	3797	2832
Dubrovnik		3038	2781	2755	4655	2549	2681	3205	2256
Durres		3012	2780	2745	4660	2538	2690	3200	2235
Genoa		2506	2273	2238	4140	2035	2170	2680	1715
Gibraltar		1619	1369	1345	3225	1158	1292	1798	867
Haifa		3663	3430	3395	5310	3186	3340	3850	2885
Iskenderun		3688	3431	3405	5305	3199	3331	3855	2906
Istanbul		3433	3200	3165	5065	3001	3095	3605	2640
Izmir		3272	3039	3004	4905	2783	2935	3445	2480
Mariupol		3962	3730	3695	5605	3484	3635	4145	3180
Marseilles		2340	2107	2072	3975	1870	2005	2510	1550
Messina		2657	2424	2389	4290	2168	2320	2830	1865
Morphou Bay		3556	3323	3288	5190	3090	3220	3730	2765
Naples		2620	2387	2352	4253	2140	2283	2793	1828
Novorossiysk		3873	3640	3605	5505	3384	3535	4045	3080
Odessa		3778	3545	3510	5420	3344	3440	3950	2985
Palermo		2547	2314	2279	4180	2058	2210	2720	1755
Piraeus		3157	2924	2889	4790	2680	2820	3330	2365
Port Said		3557	3324	3289	5175	3100	3220	3730	2765
Poti		4033	3800	3765	5660	3539	3690	4200	3235
Rijeka		3297	3001	2975	4875	2769	2901	3470	2505
Sfax		2654	2367	2332	4235	2165	2265	2775	1872
Siracusa		2674	2417	2391	4291	2185	2317	2841	1892
Tarabulus (Libya)		2747	2514	2479	4380	2258	2410	2920	1955
Taranto		2878	2621	2595	4495	2389	2521	3045	2140
Thessaloniki		3355	3120	3085	5000	2888	3030	3540	2575
Trieste		3333	3041	3015	4915	2809	2941	3505	2540
Tunis		2425	2192	2157	4060	1977	2090	2600	1635
Valencia		2037	1804	1769	3670	1571	1700	2210	1245
Valletta		2631	2398	2363	4265	2165	2295	2805	1840
Venice		3324	3091	3056	4960	2819	2990	3500	2535

AREA B

AREA A	Bordeaux	Bremen	Brest	Cherbourg	Copenhagen (via Kiel Canal)	Cork	Dublin	Dunkirk
Alexandria	2807	3428	2720	2905	3600	2898	3015	3083
Algiers	1419	2040	1335	1520	2215	1510	1630	1695
Ancona	2545	3166	2460	2645	3340	2636	2742	2821
Barcelona	1534	2155	1450	1635	2330	1625	1745	1810
Beirut	3023	3644	2950	3135	3830	3114	3245	3300
Bourgas	2920	3541	2835	3020	3715	3011	3130	3196
Brindisi	2288	2909	2205	2390	3085	2379	2500	2564
Cagliari	1708	2330	1635	1820	2515	1800	1930	1984
Casablanca	995	1668	980	1170	1824	1128	1225	1317
Constantza	2983	3604	2900	3082	3777	3074	3198	3259
Dubrovnik	2400	2996	2337	2488	3187	2487	2590	2655
Durres	2373	2995	2300	2485	3180	2465	2595	2650
Genoa	1864	2485	1780	1965	2660	1955	2075	2140
Gibraltar	1013	1606	973	1117	1822	1131	1204	1255
Haifa	3023	3645	2950	3135	3830	3115	3245	3275
Iskenderun	3083	3646	3010	3138	3837	3175	3240	3305
Istanbul	2791	3412	2705	2890	3585	2882	3000	3067
Izmir	2630	3251	2545	2730	3425	2721	2840	2906
Mariupol	3320	3940	3297	3430	4125	3410	3540	3595
Marseilles	1698	2319	1615	1800	2495	1789	1910	1974
Messina	2015	2636	1930	2115	2810	2106	2225	2291
Morphou Bay	2823	3535	2830	3015	3710	3005	3125	3290
Naples	1978	2599	1893	2078	2773	2069	2188	2254
Novorossiysk	3231	3852	3202	3330	4025	3322	3440	3507
Odessa	3136	3757	3050	3235	3930	3227	3345	3412
Palermo	1905	2526	1820	2005	2700	1996	2115	2181
Piraeus	2515	3136	2430	2615	3310	2606	2725	2791
Port Said	2915	3536	2830	3015	3710	3006	3125	3191
Poti	3391	4012	3300	3485	4180	3482	3595	3667
Rijeka	2655	3216	2510	2755	3450	2746	2810	2875
Sfax	2016	2579	1953	2104	2803	2103	2206	2271
Siracusa	2036	2632	1973	2124	2823	2123	2226	2291
Tarabulus (Libya)	2105	2726	2020	2205	2900	2196	2315	2381
Taranto	2289	2836	2205	2328	3027	2327	2430	2495
Thessaloniki	2713	3335	2640	2825	3520	2805	2935	2990
Trieste	2691	3256	2605	2790	3485	2782	2850	2915
Tunis	1783	2404	1700	1885	2580	1874	1995	2059
Valencia	1395	2016	1310	1495	2190	1486	1605	1671
Valletta	1989	2610	1905	2090	2785	2080	2200	2265
Venice	2682	3303	2600	2785	3480	2773	2895	2958

AREA B

AREA A	Emden	Esbjerg	Finisterre	Flushing	Gdansk (via Kiel Canal)	Gibraltar	Gijon	Glasgow
Alexandria	3317	3400	2345	3115	3810	1800	2545	3198
Algiers	1933	2015	960	1730	2425	415	1160	1810
Ancona	3034	3140	2085	2855	3550	1540	2285	2936
Barcelona	2010	2130	1075	1845	2540	530	1275	1925
Beirut	3535	3630	2575	3345	4040	2030	2775	3430
Bourgas	3409	3515	2460	3230	3925	1915	2660	3311
Brindisi	2777	2885	1830	2600	3295	1285	2030	2679
Cagliari	2209	2315	1260	2030	2725	745	1460	2115
Casablanca	1556	1770	570	1359	2021	170	763	1420
Constantza	3530	3577	2522	3292	3987	2037	2722	3374
Dubrovnik	2959	3065	2010	2780	3475	1465	2210	2865
Durres	2874	2980	1925	2695	3390	1380	2125	2780
Genoa	2371	2477	1437	2174	2836	847	1632	2258
Gibraltar	1494	1600	560	1297	1959	–	755	1381
Haifa	3522	3630	2575	3345	4040	2000	2775	3430
Iskenderun	3651	3690	2635	3405	4100	2090	2835	3490
Istanbul	3337	3385	2330	3100	3795	1795	2530	3182
Izmir	3129	3225	2170	2940	3635	1685	2370	3021
Mariupol	3820	3925	2870	3640	4335	2325	3070	3710
Marseilles	2206	2295	1240	2010	2705	695	1440	2089
Messina	2504	2610	1555	2325	3020	1023	1755	2406
Morphou Bay	3426	3510	2455	3225	3930	1910	2655	3305
Naples	2476	2573	1518	2288	2983	973	1718	2369
Novorossiysk	3720	3825	2770	3540	4235	2295	2970	3622
Odessa	3680	3730	2675	3445	4140	2186	2875	3527
Palermo	2394	2500	1445	2215	2910	900	1645	2296
Piraeus	3016	3110	2055	2825	3520	1520	2255	2906
Port Said	3436	3510	2455	3225	3920	1925	2655	3306
Poti	3875	3980	2925	3695	4390	2380	3125	3782
Rijeka	3159	3250	2195	2965	3660	1650	2395	3046
Sfax	2447	2555	1500	2270	2965	1055	1695	2349
Siracusa	2594	2700	1645	2415	3110	1100	1845	2500
Tarabulus (Libya)	2594	2700	1645	2415	3110	1100	1845	2496
Taranto	2801	2885	1830	2600	3295	1285	2030	2680
Thessaloniki	3224	3320	2265	3035	3730	1720	2465	3120
Trieste	3204	3285	2230	3000	3695	1685	2430	3082
Tunis	2313	2380	1325	2095	2790	809	1525	2174
Valencia	1907	1990	935	1705	2400	390	1135	1786
Valletta	2501	2585	1530	2300	2995	1008	1730	2380
Venice	3211	3280	2225	2995	3690	1700	2425	3073

AREA B

AREA A	Gothenburg	Hamburg	Havre	Helsinki	Hernosand (via Kiel Canal)	Hull	Ipswich	Kiel (via Canal)
Alexandria	3600	3443	2985	4060	4115	3241	3099	3467
Algiers	2215	2055	1597	2675	2730	1853	1715	2079
Ancona	3340	3181	2723	3800	3865	2979	2815	3205
Barcelona	2330	2170	1712	2790	2845	1968	1792	2194
Beirut	3830	3660	3200	4290	4345	3457	3317	3683
Bourgas	3715	3556	3098	4175	4230	3354	3190	3580
Brindisi	3085	2924	2466	3545	3600	3733	2560	2948
Cagliari	2515	2345	1885	2975	3130	2142	1990	2363
Casablanca	1830	1669	1209	2310	2342	1489	1338	1702
Constantza	3777	3619	3161	4237	4292	3417	3252	3643
Dubrovnik	3265	3095	2635	3725	3780	2892	2740	3118
Durres	3180	3010	2550	3640	3695	2807	2655	3033
Genoa	2660	2500	2042	3120	3175	2298	2153	2524
Gibraltar	1779	1607	1147	2248	2280	1427	1276	1640
Haifa	3830	3660	3200	4290	4345	3457	3304	3683
Iskenderun	3890	3720	3260	4350	4405	3517	3433	3743
Istanbul	3585	3427	2969	4045	4100	3225	3119	3451
Izmir	3425	3266	2808	3885	3940	3064	2961	3290
Mariupol	4125	3956	3496	4585	4640	3752	3600	3980
Marseilles	2495	2334	1876	2955	3010	2132	1988	2358
Messina	2810	2651	2193	3270	3325	2449	2285	2675
Morphou Bay	3710	3550	3092	4170	4225	3348	3208	3574
Naples	2773	2614	2156	3233	3288	2412	2258	2638
Novorossiysk	4025	3867	3409	4485	4540	3665	3500	3891
Odessa	3930	3772	3314	4390	4445	3570	3462	3796
Palermo	2700	2541	2083	3160	3215	2339	2175	2565
Piraeus	3310	3151	2693	3770	3825	2949	2798	3175
Port Said	3710	3551	3093	4170	4225	3349	3218	3567
Poti	4180	4027	3569	4640	4695	3825	3655	4051
Rijeka	3450	3291	2833	3910	3965	3089	2941	3315
Sfax	2755	2594	2136	3215	3270	2392	2230	2618
Siracusa	2900	2730	2270	3360	3415	2527	2375	2753
Tarabulus (Libya)	2900	2741	2283	3360	3415	2539	2375	2765
Taranto	3085	2925	2467	3545	3600	2723	2583	2949
Thessaloniki	3520	3350	2890	3980	4035	3147	3006	3373
Trieste	3485	3327	2869	3945	4000	3125	2986	3351
Tunis	2580	2419	1961	3040	3095	2217	2095	2443
Valencia	2190	2031	1573	2650	2705	1829	1689	2055
Valletta	2785	2625	2167	3245	3300	2423	2283	2649
Venice	3480	3318	2860	3940	3995	3116	2993	3342

AREA B

AREA A	Klaipeda (via Kiel Canal)	Land's End	Leith	Leixoes	Lisbon	Liverpool	London	Lulea (via Kiel Canal)
Alexandria	3840	2822	3424	2277	2109	3079	3107	4277
Algiers	2455	1437	2036	893	721	1691	1719	2892
Ancona	3580	2562	3162	1994	1847	2817	2845	4017
Barcelona	2570	1552	2151	970	836	1806	1834	3007
Beirut	4070	3052	3640	2495	2330	3295	3320	4507
Bourgas	3955	2937	3537	2369	2222	3192	3220	4392
Brindisi	3325	2307	2905	1739	1590	2560	2588	3762
Cagliari	2755	1737	2325	1169	1010	1980	2005	3192
Casablanca	1682	1043	1662	479	324	1305	1363	2557
Constantza	4017	2999	3600	2490	2285	3255	3283	4454
Dubrovnik	3505	2487	3075	1919	1760	2730	2755	3942
Durres	3420	2402	2990	1834	1675	2645	2670	3857
Genoa	2900	1882	2481	1331	1166	2136	2164	3337
Gibraltar	2045	1022	1600	454	280	1270	1301	2495
Haifa	4070	3052	3640	2482	2325	3295	3320	4507
Iskenderun	4130	3112	3700	2544	2385	3335	3380	4567
Istanbul	3840	2817	3395	2249	2075	3065	3096	4262
Izmir	3665	2647	3247	2079	1932	2902	2930	4102
Mariupol	4365	3347	3936	2779	2621	3591	3616	4802
Marseilles	2740	1717	2295	1149	975	1965	1996	3172
Messina	3050	2032	2632	1464	1317	2287	2315	3487
Morphou Bay	3950	2932	3531	2364	2216	3186	3214	4387
Naples	3013	1995	2595	1436	1280	2250	2278	3450
Novorossiysk	4265	3247	3848	2679	2533	3503	3531	4702
Odessa	4170	3152	3752	2640	2438	3408	3436	4607
Palermo	2940	1922	2522	1354	1207	2177	2205	3377
Piraeus	3550	2532	3132	1976	1817	2787	2815	3987
Port Said	3970	2957	3525	2389	2215	3205	3236	4387
Poti	4420	3402	4008	2834	2693	3663	3691	4857
Rijeka	3690	2672	3272	2119	1957	2927	2955	4127
Sfax	2995	1977	2575	1409	1260	2230	2258	3432
Siracusa	3140	2122	2710	1554	1395	2365	2390	3577
Tarabulus (Libya)	3140	2122	2722	1554	1407	2377	2405	3577
Taranto	3325	2307	2906	1739	1591	2561	2589	3762
Thessaloniki	3760	2472	3330	2184	2015	2985	3010	4197
Trieste	3725	2707	3308	2164	1993	2963	2991	4162
Tunis	2820	1802	2400	1273	1085	2055	2083	3257
Valencia	2445	1422	2000	854	680	1670	1701	2867
Valletta	3025	2007	2606	1461	1291	2261	2289	3462
Venice	3720	2702	3299	2171	1984	2954	2982	4157

AREA B

AREA A	Milford Haven	Murmansk	Narvik	Newcastle	Oslo	Rostock (via Kiel Canal)	Rotterdam	St Petersburg (via Kiel Canal)
Alexandria	2920	4620	4240	3306	3667	3537	3179	4220
Algiers	1535	3235	2855	1918	2282	2152	1791	2835
Ancona	2660	4360	3980	3044	3407	3277	2917	3960
Barcelona	1650	3350	2970	2033	2397	2267	1906	2950
Beirut	3150	4850	4470	3520	3897	3767	3395	4450
Bourgas	3035	4735	4355	3419	3782	3652	3292	4335
Brindisi	2405	4105	3725	2787	3152	3022	2660	3705
Cagliari	1835	3535	3155	2205	2582	2452	2080	3135
Casablanca	1132	3019	2464	1570	1912	1782	1410	2461
Constantza	3097	4797	4417	3482	3844	3714	3355	4397
Dubrovnik	2585	4285	3905	2955	3332	3202	2830	3885
Durres	2500	4200	3820	2870	3247	3117	2745	2800
Genoa	1980	3680	3300	2363	2727	2597	2236	3280
Gibraltar	1120	2977	2427	1508	1850	1720	1348	2399
Haifa	3150	4850	4470	3520	3897	3767	3395	4450
Iskenderun	3210	4910	4530	3580	3957	3827	3455	4510
Istanbul	2905	4605	4225	3290	3652	3522	3163	4194
Izmir	2745	4445	4065	3129	3492	3362	3002	4045
Mariupol	3445	5145	4765	3816	4192	4062	3691	4745
Marseilles	1815	3515	3135	2197	2562	2432	2070	3094
Messina	2130	3830	3450	2514	2877	2747	2387	3430
Morphou Bay	3030	4730	4350	3413	3777	3647	3286	4330
Naples	2093	3793	3413	2477	2840	2710	2350	3393
Novorossiysk	3345	4045	4665	3730	4092	3962	3603	4645
Odessa	3250	4950	4570	3635	3997	3867	3508	4550
Palermo	2020	3720	3340	2404	2767	2637	2277	3320
Piraeus	2630	4330	3950	3014	3377	3247	2887	3930
Port Said	3030	4730	4350	3414	3777	3647	3287	4274
Poti	3500	5200	4820	3890	4247	4117	3763	4800
Rijeka	2770	4470	4090	3136	3517	3387	3027	4070
Sfax	2070	3775	3395	2457	2822	2692	2330	3375
Siracusa	2220	3920	3540	2590	2967	2837	2465	3520
Tarabulus (Libya)	2220	3920	3540	2604	2967	2837	2477	3520
Taranto	2405	4105	3725	2788	3152	3022	2661	3705
Thessaloniki	2840	4540	4160	3210	3587	3457	3085	4140
Trieste	2805	4505	4125	3190	3553	3422	3063	4105
Tunis	1900	3600	3220	2282	2647	2517	2155	3200
Valencia	1510	3210	3830	1894	2257	2127	1748	2799
Valletta	2105	3805	3425	2488	2852	2722	2361	3405
Venice	2800	4500	4120	3181	3547	3417	3065	4100

AREA B

AREA A	Skaw	Southampton	Stockholm (via Kiel Canal)	Sunderland	Szczecin (via Kiel Canal)	Teesport	Trondheim	Vaasä (via Kiel Canal)
Alexandria	3560	2996	3918	3316	3650	3306	3887	4153
Algiers	2175	1611	2533	1928	2265	1918	2502	2768
Ancona	3300	2736	3658	3054	3390	3044	3627	3893
Barcelona	2290	1726	2648	2043	2380	2033	2617	2883
Beirut	3790	3224	4148	3530	3880	3520	4117	4383
Bourgas	3675	3111	4033	3429	3765	3419	4002	4268
Brindisi	3045	2481	3403	2797	3135	2787	3372	3638
Cagliari	2475	1911	2833	2215	2565	2205	2802	3068
Casablanca	1795	1160	2185	1547	1904	1525	2120	2380
Constantza	3737	3173	4095	3492	3827	3482	4064	4330
Dubrovnik	3225	2661	3583	2965	3315	2955	3552	3818
Durres	3140	2576	3498	2880	3230	2870	3467	3733
Genoa	2620	2056	2978	2373	2710	2363	2947	3213
Gibraltar	1773	1119	2123	1485	1842	1504	2099	2357
Haifa	3790	3226	4148	3530	3880	3520	4017	4383
Iskenderun	3850	3286	4208	3590	3940	3580	4177	4443
Istanbul	3545	2981	3903	3300	3635	3290	3872	4138
Izmir	3385	2821	3743	3139	3475	3129	3712	3978
Mariupol	4085	3521	4443	3826	4175	3816	4412	4678
Marseilles	2455	1891	2813	2207	2545	2197	2782	3048
Messina	2770	2206	3128	2524	2860	2514	3097	3363
Morphou Bay	3670	3106	4028	3423	3760	3413	3997	4263
Naples	2733	2169	3091	2487	2823	2477	3060	3326
Novorossiysk	3985	3421	4343	3740	4075	3730	4312	4578
Odessa	3890	3326	4248	3645	3980	3635	4217	4483
Palermo	2660	2096	3018	2414	2750	2404	2987	3253
Piraeus	3270	2706	3628	3024	3360	3014	3597	3863
Port Said	3670	3106	4028	3424	3760	3414	3997	4263
Poti	4140	3576	4498	3900	4230	3890	4467	4733
Rijeka	3410	2846	3768	3146	3500	3154	3737	4003
Sfax	2715	2151	3073	2467	2805	2457	3042	3308
Siracusa	2860	2296	3218	2600	2950	2590	3187	3453
Tarabulus (Libya)	2860	2296	3218	2614	2950	2604	3187	3453
Taranto	3045	2481	3403	2798	3135	2788	3372	3638
Thessaloniki	3480	2916	3838	3220	3570	3210	3807	4073
Trieste	3445	2881	3803	3200	3535	3190	3772	4038
Tunis	2540	1976	2898	2292	2630	2282	2861	3133
Valencia	2173	1519	2523	1885	2242	1894	2499	2757
Valletta	2745	2181	3103	2498	2835	2488	3072	3338
Venice	3440	2836	3840	3202	3530	3181	3767	4033

^Special section on page 209 devoted to the St Lawrence Seaway and the Great Lakes.

AREA C

AREA A	Aberdeen	Amsterdam	Antwerp	Archangel	Avonmouth	Belfast	Bergen	Bilbao
Baie Comeau	2645	2895	2860	3920	2645	2490	2910	2760
Baltimore	3385	3610	3575	4645	3455	3230	3810	3440
Boston	2885	3110	3075	4015	3025	2730	3380	2920
Cartagena (Col)	4850	4620	4585	5610	4315	4445	4680	4240
Charleston	3535	3760	3725	4690	3580	3380	3935	3590
Churchill	2970	3339	3416	4163	3100	2873	3181	3357
Cienfuegos	4890	4660	4625	5620	4215	4485	4520	4185
Cristobal	5060	4830	4795	5820	4510	4655	4825	4450
Curacao	4590	4360	4325	5315	3970	4185	4385	3985
Duluth-Superior (^)	4165	4404	4380	5440	4165	4010	5430	4280
Galveston	5340	5110	5075	6161	4820	4950	5180	4755
Georgetown (G)	3735	3870	4100	5510	3830	3895	4285	3660
Halifax	2520	2745	2710	3665	2475	2365	2740	2580
Havana	4650	4420	4385	5315	4115	4215	4470	4045
Jacksonville	3725	3950	3915	4970	3730	3570	4090	3700
Key West	4590	4360	4325	5150	3990	4200	4395	4000
Kingston (Jamaica)	4590	4360	4325	5320	4010	4185	4325	3990
La Guiara	4530	4300	4265	5375	3950	4125	4390	4055
Maracaibo	4310	4435	4410	5420	4125	4090	4490	4110
Mobile	5100	4870	4835	5680	4585	4710	4940	4520
Montreal	2995	3245	3210	4270	2995	2840	3260	3110
Nassau (Bahamas)	3740	3959	3935	5042	3662	3585	3921	3749
New Orleans	5150	4920	4885	5730	4635	4760	4995	4570
New York	3085	3310	3275	4215	3185	2930	3545	3175
Norfolk (Va)	3245	3470	3435	4400	3335	3090	3690	3340
Nuevitas	3960	4225	4205	6130	3855	3780	4140	3820
Philadelphia	3235	3460	3425	4370	3330	3080	3685	3330
Port Au Prince	4465	4235	4200	5205	3880	4060	4220	3885
Portland (Maine)	2900	3090	3055	4110	2990	2745	3345	2940
Port of Spain	4300	4070	4035	5385	3780	3895	4200	3650
Puerto Limon	5210	4980	4945	6104	4580	4805	5336	4579
St John (NB)	2830	3020	2985	4065	2825	2675	3005	2885
St John's (NF)	1980	2260	2225	3270	1935	1825	2150	2085
San Juan (PR)	3755	3870	3850	5000	3560	3530	3935	3505
Santiago de Cuba	4490	4260	4225	5180	3885	4085	4195	3865
Santo Domingo	4310	4080	4050	5318	3767	3905	4135	3710
Tampa	4780	4550	4515	5440	4345	4390	4700	4280
Tampico	5480	5250	5215	6040	4945	5045	5300	4880
Veracruz	5440	5210	5175	6000	4905	5005	5260	4840
Wilmington (NC)	3694	3843	3819	4715	3309	3472	3875	3535

^Special section on page 209 devoted to the St Lawrence Seaway and the Great Lakes.

AREA C

AREA A	Bordeaux	Bremen	Brest	Cherbourg	Copenhagen	Cork	Dublin	Dunkirk
Baie Comeau	2770	3105	2610	2678	3215	2430	2605	2760
Baltimore	3450	3820	3320	3408	4115	3175	3415	3475
Boston	2950	3320	2875	2953	3685	2675	2985	2975
Cartagena (Col)	4480	4830	4195	4324	4985	4325	4275	4485
Charleston	3805	3970	3455	3552	4240	3325	3540	3625
Churchill	3365	3390	3100	3170	3400	2900	2973	3320
Cienfuegos	4625	4870	4410	4247	4825	4250	4175	4525
Cristobal	4695	5040	4420	4539	5130	4445	4480	4695
Curacao	4120	4570	3840	3985	4690	3975	3930	4225
Duluth-Superior (^)	4290	4625	4130	4198	4735	3950	4125	4280
Galveston	5045	5320	4665	4747	5480	4725	4780	4975
Georgetown (G)	3810	4345	3725	3841	4575	3660	3805	4000
Halifax	2585	2955	2450	2520	3045	2280	2440	2610
Havana	4355	4630	3955	4052	4775	4010	4075	4285
Jacksonville	3985	4160	3580	3753	4395	3515	3695	3815
Key West	4295	4570	3895	3991	4740	3975	4000	4225
Kingston (Jamaica)	4300	4570	3955	4050	4625	3950	3980	4225
La Guiare	4030	4510	3845	4020	4705	3915	3910	4156
Maracaibo	4180	4655	4010	4159	4795	3935	4085	4310
Mobile	4805	5080	4430	4550	5245	4485	4545	4735
Montreal	3120	3455	2960	3028	3565	2780	2955	3110
Nassau (Bahamas)	3849	4177	3622	3739	4225	3487	3637	3833
New Orleans	4855	5130	4480	4613	5300	4535	4595	4785
New York	3150	3520	3015	3183	3850	2875	3145	3175
Norfolk (Va)	3310	3680	3170	3314	3995	3035	3295	3335
Nuevitas	4010	4445	3730	3904	4445	3665	3815	4100
Philadelphia	3300	3670	3160	3266	3990	3025	3290	3325
Port Au Prince	4200	4445	3825	3927	4525	3825	3845	4100
Portland (Maine)	2930	3300	2740	2914	3650	2655	2950	2955
Port of Spain	3815	4260	3615	3786	4530	3685	3750	3935
Puerto Limon	4845	5190	4496	4623	5436	4570	4534	4845
St John (NB)	2860	3230	2645	2775	3310	2555	2785	2885
St John's (NF)	2160	2470	1930	1993	2455	1795	1895	2125
San Juan (PR)	3545	4090	3465	3636	4240	3370	3520	3745
Santiago de Cuba	4225	4470	3825	3936	4500	3850	3950	4125
Santo Domingo	3825	4290	3645	3781	4439	3570	3728	3945
Tampa	4485	4760	4190	4258	5005	4165	4365	4415
Tampico	5185	5460	4790	4880	5605	4840	4905	5115
Veracruz	5145	5420	4750	4842	5565	4800	4865	5075
Wilmington (NC)	3614	4061	3140	3488	4179	3329	3479	3717

^Special section on page 209 devoted to the St Lawrence Seaway and the Great Lakes.

AREA C

AREA A	Emden	Esbjerg	Finisterre	Flushing	Gdansk (via Kiel Canal)	Gibraltar	Gijon	Glasgow
Baie Comeau	3100	2954	2476	2915	3520	2810	2627	2535
Baltimore	3905	3799	3180	3705	4370	3445	3309	3275
Boston	3475	3344	2707	3275	3940	2945	2854	2775
Cartagena (Col)	4750	4794	3952	4550	5215	4125	4127	4545
Charleston	4030	3943	3313	3830	4495	3577	3471	3425
Churchill	3341	3287	3176	3370	3690	3657	3250	2920
Cienfuegos	4655	4683	3922	4460	5120	4300	4093	4585
Cristobal	4930	4981	4166	4735	5395	4340	4341	4755
Curacao	4410	4483	3591	4255	4875	3765	3765	4285
Duluth-Superior (^)	4620	4474	3996	4435	5040	4330	4149	4055
Galveston	5270	5111	4464	5070	5375	4810	4618	5045
Georgetown (G)	4250	4339	3352	4050	4715	3350	3518	3960
Halifax	2930	2867	2318	2745	3350	2625	2471	2410
Havana	4560	4487	3766	4365	5025	4120	3923	4310
Jacksonville	4180	4101	3466	3985	4645	3750	3624	3615
Key West	4410	4355	3705	4215	4875	4060	3862	4295
Kingston (Jamaica)	4430	4483	3714	4235	4895	3975	3886	4285
La Guiara	4375	4486	3550	4180	4840	3675	3736	4225
Maracaibo	4560	4642	3765	4360	5025	3910	3942	4125
Mobile	5030	4884	4234	4835	5495	4570	4391	4805
Montreal	3450	3304	2826	3265	3870	3160	2979	2885
Nassau (Bahamas)	4082	4117	3448	3885	4547	3640	3613	3620
New Orleans	5085	4956	4309	4890	5550	4620	4463	4855
New York	3635	3512	2875	3440	4100	3145	3022	2975
Norfolk (Va)	3780	3676	3057	3585	4245	3305	3186	3135
Nuevitas	4350	4340	3593	4153	4815	3815	3759	3815
Philadelphia	3780	3657	3050	3580	4240	3295	3167	3125
Port Au Prince	4325	4356	3583	4130	4790	3875	3754	4160
Portland (Maine)	3535	3177	2668	3240	3900	2925	2815	2790
Port of Spain	4200	4343	3338	4005	4665	3460	3527	3995
Puerto Limon	5039	5054	4285	4850	5490	4490	4456	4905
St John (NB)	3195	3122	2573	3085	3615	2855	2726	2720
St John's (NF)	2340	2291	1823	2210	2760	2200	1966	1870
San Juan (PR)	3995	4059	3199	3800	4460	3335	3382	3565
Santiago de Cuba	4305	4369	3608	4105	4770	3900	3779	4185
Santo Domingo	4202	4251	3410	4003	4667	3600	3584	3885
Tampa	4795	4627	3977	4595	5260	4250	4134	4485
Tampico	5395	5244	4594	5195	5860	4950	4751	5145
Veracruz	5355	5206	4556	5155	5820	4910	4713	5105
Wilmington (NC)	3966	3879	3251	3769	4431	3533	3409	3507

^Special section on page 209 devoted to the St Lawrence Seaway and the Great Lakes.

AREA C

	AREA A							
	Gothenburg	Hamburg	Havre	Helsinki	Hernosand	Hull	Ipswich	Kiel (via Canal)
Baie Comeau	3105	3120	2665	3755	3780	2920	2900	3180
Baltimore	4010	3835	3380	4655	4680	3630	3695	4030
Boston	3580	3335	2880	4225	4250	3135	3265	3600
Cartagena (Col)	4875	4845	4390	5500	5535	4645	4540	4875
Charleston	4135	3985	3530	4780	4805	3785	3820	4155
Churchill	3110	3390	3346	4000	4058	3215	4165	3415
Cienfuegos	4715	4885	4430	5365	5390	4685	4445	4780
Cristobal	5020	5055	4600	5670	5695	4855	4720	5060
Curacao	4580	4585	4130	5165	5255	4385	4200	4540
Duluth-Superior (^)	4625	4640	4185	5275	5300	4440	4420	4700
Galveston	5375	5335	4880	6020	6050	5135	5060	5395
Georgetown (G)	4115	4110	3655	5000	5035	4175	4040	4375
Halifax	2940	2970	2515	3585	3610	2770	2730	3010
Havana	4665	4645	4190	5315	5340	4445	4350	4685
Jacksonville	4285	4175	3720	4935	4960	3975	3970	4305
Key West	4595	4585	4130	5165	5195	4385	4200	4535
Kingston (Jamaica)	4520	4585	4130	5165	5195	4385	4220	4555
La Guiara	4585	4525	4070	5130	5160	4325	4165	4500
Maracaibo	4690	4675	4220	5315	5345	4490	4350	4685
Mobile	5135	5095	4640	5785	5810	4895	4820	5160
Montreal	3455	3470	3015	4105	4130	3270	3250	3530
Nassau (Bahamas)	4117	4197	3742	4765	4791	3985	3872	4208
New Orleans	5190	5145	4690	5840	5865	4945	4875	5210
New York	3740	3535	3080	4385	4415	3335	3425	3760
Norfolk (Va)	3885	3695	3240	4535	4560	3495	3570	3905
Nuevitas	4335	4465	4010	4985	5010	4280	4140	4475
Philadelphia	3880	3685	3230	4530	4555	3485	3565	3900
Port Au Prince	4415	4460	4005	5065	5090	4260	4115	4450
Portland (Maine)	3540	3315	2860	4190	4215	3115	3225	2565
Port of Spain	4395	4295	3840	4955	4990	4095	3990	4330
Puerto Limon	5111	5205	4750	5787	6044	5005	4826	5145
St John (NB)	3200	3245	2790	3850	3875	3045	3070	3275
St John's (NF)	2345	2485	2030	2995	3020	2285	2200	2420
San Juan (PR)	4130	4110	3655	4750	4780	3925	3785	4120
Santiago de Cuba	4395	4485	4030	5040	5065	4285	4095	4430
Santo Domingo	4331	4305	3850	4956	4988	4105	3992	4328
Tampa	4900	4775	4320	5545	5570	4575	4585	4920
Tampico	5500	5475	5020	6145	6170	5275	5185	5520
Veracruz	5460	5435	4980	6105	6130	5255	5145	5480
Wilmington (NC)	4071	4081	3626	4719	4745	3895	3656	4092

^Special section on page 209 devoted to the St Lawrence Seaway and the Great Lakes.

AREA C

AREA A	Klaipeda	Land's End	Leith	Leixoes	Lisbon	Liverpool	London	Lulea
Baie Comeau	3462	2504	2730	2631	2570	2630	2785	4005
Baltimore	4307	3234	3470	3239	3205	3375	3500	4905
Boston	3852	2779	2970	2776	2705	2875	3000	4475
Cartagena (Col)	5302	4150	4825	3979	3985	4425	4510	5750
Charleston	4451	3378	3620	3372	3370	3525	3650	5030
Churchill	3795	2986	3050	3247	3387	2930	3387	4240
Cienfuegos	5191	4073	4865	3958	4130	4465	4550	5615
Cristobal	5489	4365	5035	4193	4200	4635	4720	5920
Curacao	4993	3811	4565	3605	3625	4165	4220	5415
Duluth-Superior (^)	4982	4024	4250	4151	4090	4150	4305	5525
Galveston	5619	4573	5315	4523	4610	4925	5000	6270
Georgetown (G)	4950	3667	3815	3364	3375	3595	3800	4995
Halifax	3375	2346	2605	2469	2385	2480	2635	3840
Havana	4995	3878	4625	3820	3920	4195	4310	5565
Jacksonville	4609	3579	3810	3525	3550	3715	3840	5185
Key West	4860	3817	4565	3759	3860	4175	4250	5410
Kingston (Jamaica)	4991	3876	4565	3749	3805	4165	4250	5420
La Guiara	4994	3793	4505	3570	3535	4105	4190	5375
Maracaibo	5150	3985	4390	3781	3825	4155	4265	5560
Mobile	5392	4346	5075	4288	4370	4685	4760	6035
Montreal	3812	2854	3080	2981	2920	2980	3135	4355
Nassau (Bahamas)	4625	3565	3818	3503	3465	3709	3890	4404
New Orleans	5465	4418	5125	4368	4420	4735	4810	6090
New York	4020	2947	3170	2944	2905	3075	3200	4620
Norfolk (Va)	4184	3111	3300	3116	3065	3235	3360	4785
Nuevitas	4848	3730	4035	3641	3515	3885	4160	5235
Philadelphia	4165	3092	3320	3109	3055	3225	3350	4780
Port Au Prince	4864	3753	4440	3618	3705	4040	4125	5315
Portland (Maine)	3685	2740	2985	2737	2685	2855	2980	4440
Port of Spain	4851	3600	4275	3355	3320	3875	3960	5205
Puerto Limon	5562	4449	5185	4325	4350	4785	4870	6007
St John (NB)	3630	2601	2915	2687	2615	2755	2910	4100
St John's (NF)	2799	1821	2065	1905	1960	1995	2150	3245
San Juan (PR)	4567	3395	3830	3225	3185	3595	3805	4995
Santiago de Cuba	4877	3762	4465	3644	3730	4065	4150	5290
Santo Domingo	4759	3607	4285	3436	3430	3885	3970	5203
Tampa	5135	4089	4755	4031	4050	4365	4440	5795
Tampico	5752	4709	5455	4656	4750	5025	5140	6395
Veracruz	5714	4668	5415	4618	4710	4985	5100	6355
Wilmington (NC)	4387	3314	3772	3308	3319	3551	3774	4970

^Special section on page 209 devoted to the St Lawrence Seaway and the Great Lakes.

AREA C	AREA A	Milford Haven	Murmansk	Narvik	Newcastle	Oslo	Rostock	Rotterdam	St Petersburg
Baie Comeau		2550	3500	2935	3125	3140	3265	2855	3905
Baltimore		3279	4190	3825	3780	4040	4115	3570	4805
Boston		2824	3720	3320	3350	3610	3685	3070	4375
Cartagena (Col)		4215	5270	5105	4650	4910	4960	4580	5655
Charleston		3423	4455	3995	3905	4165	4240	3720	4930
Churchill		3080	3800	3510	3095	3350	3500	3330	4141
Cienfuegos		4124	5090	4920	4490	4745	4865	4620	5515
Cristobal		4429	5625	5225	4795	5055	5145	4790	5820
Curacao		3879	5250	4815	4355	4610	4625	4320	5315
Duluth-Superior (^)		4064	5020	4455	4645	4660	4785	4375	5425
Galveston		4623	6110	5330	5145	5405	5480	5070	6175
Georgetown (G)		3782	5725	5225	4255	4515	4460	4100	4910
Halifax		2386	3370	2905	2710	2970	3095	2705	3735
Havana		3928	5385	4885	4440	4700	4770	4380	5465
Jacksonville		3629	4540	4545	4060	4315	4390	3910	5085
Key West		3867	5260	4420	4365	4625	4620	4320	5315
Kingston (Jamaica)		3924	4875	4735	4290	4550	4640	4320	5320
La Guiara		3875	5165	5415	4360	4615	4585	4260	5280
Maracaibo		4053	6290	4925	4460	4720	4770	4415	5465
Mobile		4396	5875	5090	4910	5170	5245	4830	5936
Montreal		2894	3850	3285	3475	3490	3615	3205	4255
Nassau (Bahamas)		3615	5015	4320	3890	4149	4293	3936	4916
New Orleans		4468	5930	5185	4965	5220	5295	4880	5990
New York		2992	3845	3790	3510	3770	3845	3270	4540
Norfolk (Va)		3156	4330	3800	3660	3920	3990	3430	4685
Nuevitas		3778	5140	4370	4105	4365	4560	4205	5135
Philadelphia		3137	4040	3975	3655	3915	3985	3420	4680
Port Au Prince		3797	5175	4645	4190	4445	4535	4195	5215
Portland (Maine)		2785	3675	3285	3315	3575	2650	3050	4340
Port of Spain		3762	5500	4970	4165	4425	4415	4030	5105
Puerto Limon		4497	5732	5308	4860	5136	5230	4940	5925
St John (NB)		2641	3630	3100	2975	3235	3360	2980	4000
St John's (NF)		1849	2880	2350	2120	2380	2505	2220	3145
San Juan (PR)		3478	4900	4390	3905	4160	4205	3850	4900
Santiago de Cuba		3808	5175	4645	4165	4425	4515	4220	5190
Santo Domingo		3672	4869	4566	4104	4363	4413	4040	5107
Tampa		4139	5635	4850	4670	4930	5005	4510	5695
Tampico		4756	6235	5450	5270	5530	5605	5210	6295
Veracruz		4718	6195	5795	5230	5490	5565	5170	6255
Wilmington (NC)		3361	4300	4178	3844	4103	4177	3820	4870

^Special section on page 209 devoted to the St Lawrence Seaway and the Great Lakes.

AREA C

AREA A	Skaw	Southampton	Stockholm	Sunderland	Szczecin	Teesport	Trondheim	Vaasä
Baie Comeau	2962	2630	3630	2995	3400K	2985	2960	3712
Baltimore	3807	3345	4530K	3710	4250K	3700	3805	4557
Boston	3352	2845	4100K	3210	3820K	3200	3350	4102
Cartagena (Col)	4802	4355	5375K	4720	5095K	4710	4806	5552
Charleston	3951	3495	4655K	3860	4375K	3850	3949	4701
Churchill	3298	3205	3860	3090	3595	3121	3270	4045
Cienfuegos	4691	4395	5240	4760	5000K	4750	4689	5441
Cristobal	4989	4565	5545	4930	5280K	4920	4987	5739
Curacao	4493	4095	5040K	4430	4760K	4420	4503	5243
Duluth-Superior (^)	4483	4150	5150	5154	4920	4505	4480	5232
Galveston	5119	4845	5900K	5210	5615K	5200	5117	5869
Georgetown (G)	4450	3870	4875K	4240	4595K	4260	4492	5200
Halifax	2880	2480	3465	2845	3235K	2835	2873	3625
Havana	4495	4155	5190	4520	4910K	4510	4493	5245
Jacksonville	4109	3685	4810	4050	4530K	4040	4107	4859
Key West	4363	4095	5120	4460	4760K	4450	4361	5113
Kingston (Jamaica)	4491	4095	5045	4460	4780K	4450	4489	5241
La Guiara	4494	4035	5005K	4400	4725K	4390	4551	5244
Maracaibo	4650	4180	5190K	4460	4905K	4476	4654	5400
Mobile	4892	4605	5660K	4970	5380K	4960	4890	5642
Montreal	3312	2980	3980	3345	3750K	3335	3310	4062
Nassau (Bahamas)	4125	3702	4642	3897	4412K	3920	4123	4875
New Orleans	4964	4655	5715K	5020	5435K	5010	4962	5714
New York	3520	3045	4265	3410	3982K	3400	3518	4270
Norfolk (Va)	3684	3205	4410K	3570	4130K	3560	3682	4434
Nuevitas	4348	3970	4860	4105	4630K	4126	4346	5098
Philadelphia	3665	3195	4405K	3560	4125K	3550	3663	4415
Port Au Prince	4364	3970	4940	4335	4675K	4325	4362	5114
Portland (Maine)	3185	2825	3855	3190	3625K	3180	3183	3935
Port of Spain	4351	3805	4830K	4170	4550K	4160	4408	5101
Puerto Limon	4962	4715	5639	5080	5365	5070	5060	5812
St John (NB)	3130	2755	3725	3120	3570	3110	3128	3880
St John's (NF)	2299	1995	2870	2360	2640K	2350	2297	2049
San Juan (PR)	4067	3615	4625K	3900	4345K	3893	4124	4817
Santiago de Cuba	4377	3995	4920	4360	4650K	4350	4375	5127
Santo Domingo	4259	3815	4831	4180	4550K	4170	4263	5009
Tampa	4635	4285	5425	4650	5140K	4640	4633	5385
Tampico	5252	4985	6025	5350	5740K	5340	5250	6002
Veracruz	5214	4945	5985	5310	5700K	5300	5212	5964
Wilmington (NC)	3889	3586	4596	3842	4314K	3862	3884	4637

^Special section on page 214 devoted to distances within the Plate and Parana rivers.

AREA D

AREA A	Aberdeen	Amsterdam	Antwerp	Archangel	Avonmouth	Belfast	Bergen	Bilbao
Azores	1789	1556	1521	3280	1280	1439	1995	1089
Bahia Blanca	6890	6660	6625	8355	6260	6380	6855	6175
Beira †	7605	7375	7340	9155	7090	7225	7730	6800
Belem	4465	4235	4200	5805	3945	4080	4515	3700
Buenos Aires (^)	6670	6440	6405	8115	6135	6270	6810	5900
Cape Horn	7725	7465	7441	9262	7225	7341	7878	6941
Cape Town	6490	6260	6225	8050	5970	6100	6640	5680
Conakry	3295	3045	3021	4845	2805	2936	3474	2522
Dakar	2870	2640	2605	4420	2375	2510	3060	2095
Dar es Salaam †	6695	6465	6430	8323	6203	6334	6840	5909
Diego Suarez †	6795	6565	6530	8420	6302	6433	6939	6008
Douala	4835	4609	4585	6400	4354	4488	5038	4075
Durban C	7330	7100	7065	8775	6750	6880	7410	6500
East London C	7045	6815	6780	8525	6495	6630	7160	6250
Lagos	4580	4350	4315	6040	3935	4070	4660	3715
Las Palmas	2024	1791	1756	3670	1540	1674	2265	1258
Lobito	5370	5120	5095	6950	4900	5030	5545	4550
Luanda	5262	4890	4865	6800	4750	4888	5395	4400
Madeira	1799	1566	1531	3340	1320	1449	1990	1079
Maputo C	7630	7400	7365	9070	7045	7180	7710	6800
Mauritius †	7295	7065	7030	8915	6797	6928	7434	6503
Mogadiscio †	6035	5785	5770	7645	5575	5710	6215	5285
Mombasa †	6595	6365	6330	8175	6110	6242	6750	5815
Monrovia	3565	3335	3300	5120	3074	3208	3758	2795
Montevideo	6550	6320	6285	7990	6020	6155	6695	5775
Mozambique I †	7105	6875	6840	8704	6586	6717	7223	6292
Port Elizabeth C	6910	6680	6645	8400	6375	6510	7040	6125
Port Harcourt	4685	4455	4420	6270	4224	4358	4908	3945
Porto Alegre	6390	6160	6125	7905	5914	6008	6496	5679
Recife	4455	4225	4190	5945	3955	4090	4615	3715
Reunion Island †	7277	7029	7003	8887	6819	6950	7456	6425
Rio de Janeiro	5540	5310	5275	7015	5030	5160	5710	4790
Salvador	4840	4610	4575	6335	4304	4438	4926	4109
Santos	5175	5485	5450	7195	5200	5335	5860	4975
Sao Vicente Island	2844	2611	2576	4345	2350	2494	3030	2062
Takoradi	4185	3955	3920	5610	3585	3720	4290	3390
Tema	4285	4055	4020	5930	3770	3905	4475	3580
Tramandai	6240	6010	5975	7755	5709	5858	6346	5529
Vitoria (Brazil)	5290	5060	5025	6795	4764	4898	5386	4569
Walvis Bay	5865	5635	5600	7365	5245	5380	5920	5065

^Special section on page 214 devoted to distances within the Plate and Parana rivers.

AREA D

AREA A	Bordeaux	Bremen	Brest	Cherbourg	Copenhagen (via Kiel Canal)	Cork	Dublin	Dunkirk
Azores	1227	1768	1075	1259	2020	1220	1353	1423
Bahia Blanca	6270	6870	6160	6353	6970	6345	6295	6525
Beira †	6945	7585	6905	7049	7455	7055	7135	7240
Belem	3845	4445	3800	3913	4665	3920	3990	4100
Buenos Aires (^)	6050	6650	5930	6074	6835	6125	6180	6305
Cape Horn	7087	7659	7055	7172	7710	7118	7250	7351
Cape Town	5820	6470	5765	5896	6660	5940	6015	6125
Conakry	2663	3282	2600	2748	3498	2724	2848	2931
Dakar	2245	2850	2170	2315	3080	2320	2420	2505
Dar es Salaam †	6055	6675	6015	6159	6864	6145	6246	6330
Diego Suarez †	6154	6775	6114	6258	6963	6245	6341	6430
Douala	4223	4846	4152	4283	5062	4260	4400	4495
Durban C	6600	7310	6520	6677	7435	6780	6795	6965
East London C	6345	7025	6265	6421	7185	6495	6540	6680
Lagos	3855	4560	3785	3904	4680	4030	3980	4215
Las Palmas	1367	2003	1360	1444	2235	1474	1588	1658
Lobito	4750	5355	4685	4843	5570	4815	4945	5005
Luanda	4599	5206	4532	4710	5432	4668	4800	4865
Madeira	1177	1778	1085	1269	2010	1249	1363	1433
Maputo C	6895	7610	7265	6971	7730	7080	7090	7265
Mauritius †	6649	7275	6609	6753	7458	6745	6840	6930
Mogadiscio †	5430	6025	5390	5567	6240	5545	5620	5670
Mombasa †	5965	6575	5925	6067	6770	6045	6155	6230
Monrovia	2943	3545	2872	2999	3782	3015	3120	3200
Montevideo	5930	6530	5800	5977	6720	6005	6065	6185
Mozambique I †	6438	7085	6398	6542	7247	6555	6629	6740
Port Elizabeth C	6225	6840	6145	6299	7060	6360	6420	6545
Port Harcourt	4093	4665	4022	4147	4932	4135	4270	4320
Porto Alegre	5785	6370	5663	5834	6622	5800	5920	6025
Recife	3835	4430	3795	3907	4660	3910	4000	4090
Reunion Island †	6671	7264	6631	6775	7480	6800	6862	6913
Rio de Janeiro	4920	5520	4840	4976	5730	4995	5075	5175
Salvador	4220	4820	4093	4291	5052	4205	4350	4475
Santos	5095	5695	4990	5163	5920	5170	5245	5350
Sao Vicente Island	2222	2823	2130	2314	3000	2294	2408	2478
Takoradi	3525	4165	3485	3594	4315	3635	3630	3820
Tema	3685	4265	3605	3690	4495	3735	3815	3920
Tramandai	5620	6220	5513	5684	6472	5635	5770	5875
Vitoria (Brazil)	4670	5270	4553	4707	5512	4700	4810	4925
Walvis Bay	5190	5845	5120	5278	5940	5315	5294	5500

^Special section on page 214 devoted to distances within the Plate and Parana rivers.

AREA D

AREA A	Emden	Esbjerg	Finisterre	Flushing	Gdansk	Gibraltar	Gijon	Glasgow
Azores	1700	1793	805	1470	2156K	990	990	1534
Bahia Blanca	6640	6914	5806	6480	7105K	5585	6003	6640
Beira †	7425	7598	6482	7230	7890K	5960	6672	7355
Belem	4340	4451	3393	4140	4805K	3305	3586	4215
Buenos Aires (^)	6505	6635	5527	6355	6970K	5365	5722	6420
Cape Horn	7590	7676	6625	7383	8056K	6387	6818	7423
Cape Town	6335	6446	5347	6135	6800K	5190	5540	6240
Conakry	3170	3317	2199	2973	3635K	1916	2392	3025
Dakar	2755	2882	1766	2555	3220K	1570	1959	2620
Dar es Salaam †	6536	6708	5592	6339	7001K	5050	5782	6445
Diego Suarez †	6635	6807	5691	6438	7100K	5150	5881	6545
Douala	4734	4852	3734	4537	5199K	3467	3927	4577
Durban C	7105	7246	6128	6915	7575K	6030	6321	7080
East London C	6855	6990	5872	6660	7320K	5745	6065	6795
Lagos	4355	4473	3355	4155	4820K	3280	3548	4330
Las Palmas	1905	2048	930	1705	2370K	715	1124	1769
Lobito	5245	5412	4294	5045	5710K	3995	4487	5120
Luanda	5095	5279	4161	4895	5569K	3837	4354	4970
Madeira	1690	1832	715	1480	2155K	610	908	1544
Maputo C	7405	7540	6422	7210	7870K	6330	6615	7380
Mauritius †	7130	7302	6186	6933	7595K	5650	6376	7045
Mogadiscio †	5910	6156	4974	5715	6375K	4390	5131	5785
Mombasa †	6445	6616	5500	6245	6910K	4950	5690	6345
Monrovia	3454	3566	2448	3257	3919K	2265	2641	3315
Montevideo	6390	6538	5430	6195	6855	5245	5625	6300
Mozambique I †	6919	7091	5975	6722	7384K	5460	6165	6855
Port Elizabeth C	6735	6868	5750	6540	7200K	5610	5943	6660
Port Harcourt	4604	4716	3598	4407	5069K	3385	3791	4435
Porto Alegre	6294	6395	5287	6097	6759K	5085	5480	6097
Recife	4335	4467	3360	4135	4800K	3150	3553	4205
Reunion Island †	7152	7324	6208	6955	7617K	5658	6398	7039
Rio de Janeiro	5405	5539	4429	5205	5870K	4235	4622	5290
Salvador	4724	4848	3746	4527	5189K	3535	3939	4528
Santos	5590	5726	4616	5395	6055K	4410	4809	5465
Sao Vicente Island	2725	2862	1749	2525	3190K	1540	1942	2589
Takoradi	3985	4163	3045	3790	4450K	2885	3238	3935
Tema	4170	4259	3141	3970	4635K	2985	3334	4035
Tramandai	6144	6245	5137	5947	6609K	4935	5330	5950
Vitoria (Brazil)	5184	5270	4160	4987	5649K	3985	4353	5000
Walvis Bay	5615	5847	4729	5415	6080K	4565	4922	5615

^Special section on page 214 devoted to distances within the Plate and Parana rivers.

AREA D

AREA A	Gothenburg	Hamburg	Havre	Helsinki	Hernosand	Hull	Ipswich	Kiel (via Canal)
Azores	1975	1783	1325	2445K	2475K	1581	1450	1807
Bahia Blanca	6925	6885	6430	7395K	7425K	6685	6420	6910
Beira †	7710	7600	7145	6180K	8210K	7400	7210	7625
Belem	4625	4460	4005	5095	5125	4260	4120	4485
Buenos Aires (^)	6790	6665	6210	7260K	7290K	6465	6290	6690
Cape Horn	7884	7693	7235	8348K	8411K	7512	7381	7716
Cape Town	6620	6485	6030	7085K	7120K	6285	6115	6460
Conakry	3455	3068	2823	3924K	3956K	3103	2952	3296
Dakar	3040	2865	2410	3510K	3540K	2665	2535	2880
Dar es Salaam †	6821	6690	6235	7290K	7322K	6490	6318	6715
Diego Suarez †	6920	6790	6335	7389	7421K	6590	6417	6815
Douala	5019	4847	4387	5488K	5520K	4667	4516	4860
Durban C	7395	7325	6870	7860K	7895K	7125	6890	7235
East London C	7140	7040	6585	7610K	7640K	6840	6640	6980
Lagos	4640	4575	4120	5110K	5140K	4375	4140	4480
Las Palmas	2190	2018	1560	2660K	2695K	1816	1685	2042
Lobito	5530	5350	4895	6000K	6030K	5175	5025	5370
Luanda	5389	5217	4807	5858K	5888K	5037	4886	5230
Madeira	1975	1793	1335	2440K	2475K	1591	1460	1817
Maputo C	7690	7625	7170	8160K	8190K	7425	7185	7530
Mauritius †	7415	7290	6835	7884K	7916K	7090	6912	7315
Mogadiscio †	6195	5530	5575	6665K	6700K	5840	5695	6040
Mombasa †	6730	6590	6135	7200K	7230K	6390	6225	6615
Monrovia	3739	3560	3105	4208K	4240K	3320	3236	3580
Montevideo	6675	6545	6090	7145K	7180K	6345	6175	6570
Mozambique I †	7204	7100	6645	7673K	7705K	6900	6701	7125
Port Elizabeth C	7020	6905	6450	7490K	7520K	6705	6515	6860
Port Harcourt	4889	4680	4225	5358K	5390K	4480	4386	4730
Porto Alegre	6638	6385	5930	7048K	7080K	6185	6076	6410
Recife	4620	4450	3995	5090K	5120K	4250	4115	4475
Reunion Island †	7437	7265	6800	7906K	7938K	7085	6934	7278
Rio de Janeiro	5690	5535	5080	6160K	6190K	5335	5190	5560
Salvador	5068	4835	4380	5478K	5510K	4635	4506	4860
Santos	5875	5710	5255	6345K	6375K	5510	5375	5735
Sao Vicente Island	3010	2838	2380	3480K	3515K	2636	2505	2862
Takoradi	4270	4180	3725	4740K	4775K	3980	3770	4115
Tema	4455	4280	3825	4925K	4955K	4040	3950	4295
Tramandai	6488	6235	5780	6898K	6930K	6035	5926	6260
Vitoria (Brazil)	5548	5285	4830	5938K	5970K	5085	4966	5310
Walvis Bay	5900	5860	5405	6370K	6400K	5660	5395	5740

^Special section on page 214 devoted to distances within the Plate and Parana rivers.

AREA D

AREA A	Klaipeda	Land's End	Leith	Leixoes	Lisbon	Liverpool	London	Lulea
Azores	2226	1121	1764	820	785	1415	1447	2690K
Bahia Blanca	7347	6242	6865	5753	5590	6520	6550	7640K
Beira †	8042	6926	7580	6386	6295	7235	7265	8425K
Belem	4884	3779	4440	3348	3245	4095	4125	5340K
Buenos Aires (^)	7068	5963	6645	5470	5370	6300	6330	7505K
Cape Horn	8167	7062	7699	6568	6418	7329	7510	8596K
Cape Town	6898	5793	6465	5272	5195	6120	6150	7335K
Conakry	3750	2645	3276	2119	1973	2914	2977	4171K
Dakar	3317	2212	2845	1686	1575	2500	2530	3755K
Dar es Salaam †	7142	6042	6670	5492	5355	6325	6355	7537K
Diego Suarez †	7241	6141	6770	5591	5455	6425	6455	7636K
Douala	5285	4180	4840	3659	3524	4466	4541	5735K
Durban C	7679	6574	7305	6089	6035	6960	6990	8110K
East London C	7423	6318	7020	5836	5750	6675	6705	7855K
Lagos	4906	3801	4555	3276	3285	4210	4240	5355K
Las Palmas	2481	1377	2000	852	720	1650	1682	2905K
Lobito	5845	4740	5360	4219	4026	4986	5061	6245K
Luanda	5712	4607	5210	4086	3894	4836	4911	6095K
Madeira	2265	1160	1774	653	525	1425	1457	2690K
Maputo C	7933	6868	7605	6385	6335	7260	7290	8405K
Mauritius †	7736	6636	7270	6086	5955	6925	6955	8131K
Mogadiscio †	6440	5384	6018	4872	4695	5688	5719	6915K
Mombasa †	7060	5944	6570	5404	5255	6225	6255	7445K
Monrovia	3999	2894	3540	2368	2270	3195	3225	4455K
Montevideo	6971	5866	6525	5373	5250	6180	6210	7395K
Mozambique I †	7525	6425	7080	5875	5765	6735	6765	7920K
Port Elizabeth C	7301	6196	6885	5715	5615	6540	6570	7735K
Port Harcourt	5149	4044	4660	3525	3390	4315	4345	5605K
Porto Alegre	6828	5723	6365	5230	5090	6020	6050	7295K
Recife	4908	3795	4430	3308	3155	4085	4115	5335K
Reunion Island †	7758	6658	7258	6108	5945	6930	6959	8153K
Rio de Janeiro	5972	4867	5515	4372	4240	5170	5200	6405K
Salvador	5281	4176	4815	3688	3540	4470	4500	5725K
Santos	6159	5045	5690	4559	4415	5345	5375	6595K
Sao Vicente Island	3295	2190	2820	1685	1545	2470	2500	3730K
Takoradi	4596	3491	4160	2966	2890	3815	3845	4990K
Tema	4692	3587	4260	3062	2990	3915	3945	5170K
Tramandai	6678	5573	6215	5080	4940	5870	5900	7165K
Vitoria (Brazil)	5703	4598	5265	4103	3990	4920	4950	6185K
Walvis Bay	6280	5175	5840	4654	4570	5495	5525	6615K

^Special section on page 214 devoted to distances within the Plate and Parana rivers.

AREA D

AREA A	Milford Haven	Murmansk	Narvik	Newcastle	Oslo	Rostock (via Kiel Canal)	Rotterdam	St Petersburg (via Kiel Canal)
Azores	1219	2825	2345	1705	2045	1911	1519	2696
Bahia Blanca	6360	7845	7570	6655	6995	7032	6615	7545
Beira †	7039	6910	8360	7440	7780	7722	7335	8330
Belem	3891	5775	5055	4350	4695	4569	4190	5245
Buenos Aires (^)	6078	7395	6275	6520	6860	6753	6395	7410
Cape Horn	7181	8900	8380	7600	7945	7852	7444	8496
Cape Town	5911	7730	7105	6345	6690	6583	6220	7240
Conakry	2763	4511	4011	3184	3526	3435	3024	4075
Dakar	2330	4065	3685	2770	3110	3002	2600	3660
Dar es Salaam †	6152	8019	7469	6550	6892	6832	6425	7341
Diego Suarez †	6251	8118	7568	6649	6991	6931	6525	7540
Douala	4298	6045	5663	4748	5090	4970	4588	5639
Durban C	6692	8520	7900	7125	7465	7365	7060	8015
East London C	6436	8270	7645	6870	7210	7109	6775	7760
Lagos	3919	5680	5180	4370	4710	4591	4310	5260
Las Palmas	1486	3255	2850	1920	2265	2166	1754	2810
Lobito	4858	6555	6185	5255	5600	5530	5095	6150
Luanda	4725	6415	6033	5118	5460	5397	4958	6009
Madeira	1268	2975	2575	1700	2045	1950	1529	2595
Maputo C	6986	8815	8200	7597	7760	7659	7360	8310
Mauritius †	6746	8613	8063	7144	7486	7426	7025	8005
Mogadiscio †	5502	7395	6845	5925	6270	6125	5760	6815
Mombasa †	6060	7925	7375	6460	6800	6740	6325	7350
Monrovia	3012	4765	4384	3468	3810	3684	3295	4359
Montevideo	5981	7730	7231	6405	6750	6656	6275	7295
Mozambique I †	6535	8402	7852	6933	7275	7215	6835	7724
Port Elizabeth C	6314	8150	7525	6750	7090	6987	6640	7640
Port Harcourt	4162	5915	5533	4618	4960	4834	4415	5509
Porto Alegre	5840	7352	7042	6305	6650	6513	8115	7199
Recife	3909	5605	5075	4345	4690	4585	4180	5240
Reunion Island †	6768	8635	8085	7166	7508	7448	7006	8057
Rio de Janeiro	4974	6695	6165	5420	5760	5657	5256	6310
Salvador	4293	5782	5472	4735	5080	4966	4565	5629
Santos	5166	6875	6345	5606	5950	5844	5440	6495
Sao Vicente Island	2295	4025	3640	2740	3085	2980	2574	3630
Takoradi	3609	5380	4630	4000	4345	4281	3915	4890
Tema	3705	6330	6000	4185	4525	4377	4015	5075
Tramandai	5690	7202	6892	6155	6500	6363	5965	7049
Vitoria (Brazil)	4710	6242	5932	5195	5540	5388	5015	6089
Walvis Bay	5293	6985	6410	5630	5970	5965	5595	6520

^Special section on page 214 devoted to distances within the Plate and Parana rivers.

AREA D

AREA A	Skaw	Southampton	Stockholm (via Kiel Canal)	Sunderland	Szczecin (via Kiel Canal)	Teesport	Trondheim	Vaasä (via Kiel Canal)
Azores	1965	1290	2320K	1656	2040	1646	2067	2507
Bahia Blanca	7077	6395	7270K	6760	6990	6750	7274	7610
Beira †	7767	7110	8055K	7475	7775	7465	8032	8325
Belem	4614	3970	4965K	4335	4685	4325	4720	5185
Buenos Aires (^)	6798	6175	7135K	6540	6855	6530	6992	7390
Cape Horn	7897	7223	8214K	7588	7938	7585	8096	8416
Cape Town	6628	5995	6960K	6360	6680	6350	6895	7160
Conakry	3480	2795	3799K	3161	3518	3141	3741	3996
Dakar	3047	2375	3385K	2740	3100	2730	3291	3580
Dar es Salaam †	6877	6200	7165K	6565	6884	6555	7142	7415
Diego Suarez †	6976	6300	7264K	6665	6983	6655	7241	7515
Douala	5025	4359	5365K	4725	5082	4700	5280	5560
Durban C	7410	6835	7740K	7200	7455	7190	7662	7935
East London C	7154	6550	7485K	6915	7200	6905	7409	7680
Lagos	4636	4085	4985K	4450	4700	4440	4898	5180
Las Palmas	2210	1525	2535K	1890	2255	1881	2456	2742
Lobito	5575	4870	5870K	5245	5590	5220	5838	6070
Luanda	5442	4729	5733K	5095	5452	5075	5705	5930
Madeira	1995	1300	2315K	1665	2035	1656	2218	2517
Maputo C	7704	7135	8035K	7500	7750	7490	7958	8230
Mauritius †	7471	6800	7759K	7165	7478	7155	7736	8015
Mogadiscio †	6219	5540	6540K	5905	6260	5885	6466	6740
Mombasa †	6785	6100	7075K	6465	6790	6455	7050	7315
Monrovia	3729	3070	4083K	3435	3802	3425	3990	4280
Montevideo	6701	6055	7020	6420	6740	6140	6895	7270
Mozambique I †	7260	6610	7548K	6975	7267	6965	7525	7825
Port Elizabeth C	7032	6415	7360K	6780	7080	6770	7288	7560
Port Harcourt	4879	4190	5233K	4555	4952	4545	5142	5430
Porto Alegre	6558	5895	6923K	6260	6642	6250	6756	7110
Recife	4630	3960	4960K	4325	4680	4315	4827	5175
Reunion Island †	7493	6777	7781K	7143	7500	7123	7758	7978
Rio de Janeiro	5702	5045	6035K	5410	5750	5400	5894	6260
Salvador	5011	4345	5353K	4710	5072	4700	5208	5560
Santos	5889	5220	6220K	5585	5940	5575	6085	6435
Sao Vicente Island	2984	2340	3385K	2710	2805	2701	3224	3562
Takoradi	4326	3690	4615K	4055	4335	4045	4588	4815
Tema	4422	3790	4800K	4155	4515	4145	4684	4995
Tramandai	6408	5745	6773K	6110	6492	6100	6606	6960
Vitoria (Brazil)	5433	4795	5813K	5160	5532	5150	5625	6010
Walvis Bay	6010	5370	6245K	5735	5960	5725	6273	6440

All distances on this page via the Suez Canal.

AREA E

AREA A	Aberdeen	Amsterdam	Antwerp	Archangel	Avonmouth	Belfast	Bergen	Bilbao
Abadan	6892	6642	6627	8502	6432	6567	7072	6145
Aden	4955	4705	4690	6565	4495	4630	5135	4205
Aqaba	3955	3705	3690	5565	3495	3630	4135	3205
Bahrain	6687	6437	6422	8297	6227	6362	6867	5935
Bandar Abbas	6408	6158	6143	8018	5948	6083	6588	5658
Basrah	6945	6695	6670	8550	6480	6615	7125	6190
Bassein	8240	8000	7975	9816	7746	7881	8386	7456
Bhavnagar	6692	6442	6427	8302	6232	6367	6972	5942
Bushehr	4747	6475	6480	8352	6282	6407	6927	5992
Calcutta	8305	8075	8000	9870	7800	7935	8440	7510
Chennai	7600	7400	7365	9220	7155	7285	7795	6860
Chittagong	8395	8065	8030	9917	7947	7982	8487	7557
Cochin	7805	6555	6540	8415	6345	6480	6985	6055
Colombo	7055	6825	6790	8660	6590	6725	7235	6300
Djibouti	4953	4705	4690	6565	4493	4628	5133	4203
Dubai	6486	6236	6221	8096	6026	6161	6666	5736
Fujairah	6320	6070	6055	7930	5860	5995	6500	5570
Jedda	4300	4020	4005	5885	3815	3950	4655	3525
Karachi	6430	6200	6265	8035	5965	6100	6605	5675
Kuwait	6872	6622	6607	8582	6412	6547	7152	6122
Malacca	8459	8209	8194	10065	7999	8134	8639	7709
Mangalore	6700	6450	6435	8310	6240	6375	6880	5950
Massawa	4547	4315	4280	6165	4095	4230	4730	3805
Mina al Ahmadi	6852	6602	6587	8462	6392	6527	7032	6102
Mongla	8265	8035	8000	9883	7813	7948	8453	7523
Mormugao	6655	6425	6390	8275	6205	6340	6845	5915
Moulmein	8325	8085	8060	9919	7849	7984	9489	7559
Mumbai	6625	6395	6360	8220	6155	6270	6780	5815
Musay'td	6657	6407	6392	8267	6197	6332	6837	5907
Penang	8330	8020	8065	9900	7835	7965	8475	7540
Port Blair	7921	7671	7675	9531	7461	7596	8101	7171
Port Kelang	8370	8120	8095	9995	7910	8045	8550	7620
Port Okha	6453	6203	6188	8063	5993	6128	6633	5703
Port Sudan	4350	4100	4090	5950	3885	4020	4525	3595
Quseir	3905	3655	3640	5515	3445	3580	4085	3155
Singapore	8620	8340	8355	1195	8125	8260	8765	7835
Sittwe	8245	8005	8030	9850	7780	7915	8420	7490
Suez	3647	3414	3380	5255	3190	3320	3825	2895
Trincomalee	7335	7085	7070	8945	6875	7010	7515	6585
Veraval	6512	6262	6241	8122	6052	6187	6692	5762
Vishakhapatnam	7880	7600	7605	9479	7409	7544	8065	7125
Yangon	8315	8085	8050	9870	7800	7935	8440	7510

All distances on this page via the Suez Canal.

AREA E / AREA A	Bordeaux	Bremen	Brest	Cherbourg	Copenhagen (via Kiel Canal)	Cork	Dublin	Dunkirk
Abadan	6287	6890	6247	6424	7097	6400	6477	6530
Aden	4350	4945	4310	4487	5160	4465	4540	4590
Aqaba	3350	3945	3310	3487	4160	3465	3540	3590
Bahrain	6082	6677	6042	6219	6892	6197	6272	6322
Bandar Abbas	5803	6398	5763	5940	6613	5918	5993	6043
Basrah	6335	6930	6295	6454	7145	6455	6525	6580
Bassein	7601	8220	7161	7738	8411	7690	7791	7875
Bhavnagar	6087	6682	6047	6224	6897	6202	6277	6327
Bushehr	6142	6737	6102	6279	6952	6255	6332	6380
Calcutta	7650	8285	7615	7791	8465	7755	7845	7889
Chennai	7005	7610	6970	7137	7815	7080	7200	7265
Chittagong	7702	8275	7662	7839	8512	7845	7892	7930
Cochin	6200	6795	6160	6337	7010	6315	6390	6440
Colombo	6445	7035	6405	6581	7255	6505	6640	6690
Djibouti	4348	4943	4308	4485	5158	4463	4538	4588
Dubai	5881	6476	5841	6018	6691	5996	6071	6121
Fujairah	5715	6310	5675	5852	6525	5830	5905	5955
Jedda	3670	4300	3630	3807	4480	3770	3860	3955
Karachi	5820	6410	5780	5957	6630	5880	6015	6065
Kuwait	6267	6862	6227	6404	7077	6382	6457	6507
Malacca	7854	8449	7814	7991	8664	7969	8044	8094
Mangalore	6095	6690	6055	6232	6905	6210	6285	6335
Massawa	3950	4545	3910	4087	4760	4065	4140	4190
Mina al Ahmadi	6247	6842	6207	6384	7057	6362	6437	6487
Mongla	7668	8245	7628	7805	8478	7810	7888	7900
Mormugao	6060	6635	6020	6174	6840	6165	6250	6290
Moulmein	7704	8305	7664	7841	8514	7775	7894	7960
Mumbai	6005	6605	5970	6144	6815	6075	6200	6260
Musay'td	6052	6647	6012	6189	6860	6167	6242	6292
Penang	7685	8310	7650	7823	8495	7780	7880	7965
Port Blair	7316	7911	7276	7453	8126	7431	7506	7556
Port Kelang	7765	8360	7725	7917	8575	7885	7955	7900
Port Okha	5848	6443	5808	5985	6658	5963	6038	6088
Port Sudan	3740	4375	3700	3877	4550	3850	3930	4025
Quseir	3300	3890	3260	3437	4110	3415	3490	3440
Singapore	7980	8600	7940	8114	8790	8100	8170	8255
Sittwe	7635	8235	7595	7772	8445	7745	7825	7880
Suez	3045	3625	3005	3187	3850	3165	3235	3290
Trincomalee	6730	7325	6690	6867	7540	6845	6920	6970
Veraval	5907	6502	5867	6044	6717	6022	6097	6147
Vishakhapatnam	7264	7965	7225	7401	8080	7379	7454	7505
Yangon	7655	8295	7615	7796	8465	7765	7845	7950

All distances on this page via the Suez Canal.

AREA E / AREA A	Emden	Esbjerg	Finisterre	Flushing	Gdansk (via Kiel Canal)	Gibraltar	Gijon	Glasgow
Abadan	6767	7013	5831	6572	7238	5240	5988	6647
Aden	4830	5076	3894	4635	5295	3310	4051	4705
Aqaba	3830	4076	2894	3635	4295	2310	3051	3705
Bahrain	6582	6808	5626	6367	7027	5042	5783	6442
Bandar Abbas	6283	6529	5347	6088	6748	4763	5504	6163
Basrah	6800	7043	5861	6600	7285	5285	6018	6700
Bassein	8081	8327	7145	7886	8546	6570	7302	7970
Bhavnagar	6567	6813	5631	6372	7032	5047	5788	6447
Bushehr	6622	6868	5686	6427	7087	5102	5843	6502
Calcutta	8135	6380	7198	7940	8600	6609	7355	8000
Chennai	7480	7726	6544	7290	7945	5980	6701	7380
Chittagong	8182	8428	7246	7987	8647	6662	7403	8065
Cochin	6680	6926	5744	6485	7145	5160	5901	6560
Colombo	6930	7170	5988	6730	7395	5404	6145	6805
Djibouti	4828	5074	3892	4633	5293	3308	4049	4703
Dubai	6361	6607	5425	6166	6826	4841	5582	6241
Fujairah	6195	6441	5259	6000	6660	4675	5416	6075
Jedda	4150	4396	3214	3955	4615	2635	3371	4030
Karachi	6305	6546	5364	6105	6770	4785	5521	6180
Kuwait	6747	6993	5811	6552	7212	5227	5968	6627
Malacca	8334	8580	7398	8139	8799	6814	7555	8214
Mangalore	6575	6821	5639	6480	7040	5055	5796	6455
Massawa	4430	4676	3494	4235	4895	2900	3651	4305
Mina al Ahmadi	6727	6974	5791	6532	6192	5207	5948	6607
Mongla	8148	8394	7212	7953	8613	6628	7369	8025
Mormugao	6520	6753	5581	6340	6982	4997	5738	6405
Moulmein	8184	8430	7248	7989	8649	6680	7401	8075
Mumbai	6490	6733	5551	6290	6955	4980	5708	6375
Musay'td	6532	6778	5596	6335	6997	5012	5751	6412
Penang	8170	8412	7230	7970	8635	6646	7387	8040
Port Blair	7796	8042	6860	7601	8261	6276	7017	7676
Port Kelang	8245	8506	7324	8060	8720	6750	7480	8135
Port Okha	6328	6574	5392	6133	6793	4808	5549	6208
Port Sudan	4220	4466	3284	4025	4685	2710	3440	4105
Quseir	3780	4026	2844	3585	4245	2260	3001	3660
Singapore	8460	8703	7521	8265	8925	6935	7678	8330
Sittwe	8115	8361	7179	7920	8580	6600	7336	8000
Suez	3525	3776	2594	3335	3990	2009	2751	3399
Trincomalee	7210	7456	6274	7015	7675	5690	6431	7090
Veraval	6383	6633	5451	6192	6852	4866	5608	6267
Vishakhapatnam	7744	7980	6708	7549	8209	6224	5696	7620
Yangon	8135	8385	7203	7940	8600	6609	7360	8005

All distances on this page via the Suez Canal.

AREA E	AREA A	Gothenburg	Hamburg	Havre	Helsinki (via Kiel Canal)	Hernosand (via Kiel Canal)	Hull	Ipswich	Kiel (via Canal)
Abadan		7052	6900	6425	7522	7557	6700	6552	6897
Aden		5115	4952	4495	5585	5620	4760	4615	4960
Aqaba		4115	3950	3495	4585	4620	3760	3615	3960
Bahrain		6847	6682	6222	7317	7352	6492	6347	6692
Bandar Abbas		6568	6403	5943	6038	7073	6213	6068	6413
Basrah		7085	6930	6470	7570	7605	6750	6600	6945
Bassein		8366	8205	7750	8836	8871	8005	7866	8200
Bhavnagar		6852	6687	6227	7322	7357	6497	6352	6697
Bushehr		6907	6742	6282	7377	7412	6550	6407	6752
Calcutta		8420	8300	7845	8890	8925	8100	7920	8325
Chennai		7775	7600	7170	8245	8275	7425	7270	7615
Chittagong		8467	8300	7835	8937	8972	8109	7967	8315
Cochin		6965	6800	6340	7435	7470	6610	6465	6810
Colombo		7215	7050	6595	7680	7715	6850	6710	7075
Djibouti		5113	4950	4493	5583	5618	4758	4613	4958
Dubai		6646	6481	6021	6116	7151	6291	6146	6491
Fujairah		6480	6315	5855	5950	6985	6125	5980	6325
Jedda		4335	4300	3805	4905	4940	4080	3935	4300
Karachi		6590	6425	5970	7055	7090	6225	6085	6450
Kuwait		7032	6867	6407	7402	7537	6677	6532	6877
Malacca		8619	8454	7194	9089	9124	8264	8119	8464
Mangalore		6860	6694	6235	7330	7365	6505	6360	6705
Massawa		4715	4540	4080	5185	5220	4340	4215	4565
Mina al Ahmadi		7012	6847	6387	7482	7517	6657	6512	6857
Mongla		8433	8268	7805	8903	8938	8080	7933	8285
Mormugao		6825	6650	6195	7295	7330	6450	6325	6675
Moulmein		8469	8300	7845	8939	8974	8120	7969	8305
Mumbai		6775	6620	6165	7245	7275	6420	6270	6645
Musay'td		6817	6652	6192	7287	7322	6462	6317	6662
Penang		8455	8325	7870	8925	8955	8125	7950	8300
Port Blair		8081	7916	7456	8551	8586	7726	7581	7926
Port Kelang		8530	8360	7900	9000	9030	8180	8030	8370
Port Okha		6613	6448	5988	7083	7118	6258	6113	6458
Port Sudan		4505	4350	3890	4975	5005	4150	4005	4375
Quseir		4065	3900	3440	4535	4570	3710	3565	3910
Singapore		8745	8615	8160	9215	9250	8415	8245	8645
Sittwe		8400	8240	7775	8870	8905	8040	7900	8245
Suez		3810	3640	3180	4280	4310	3440	3305	3665
Trincomalee		7495	7330	6870	7965	8000	7140	6995	7240
Veraval		6672	6407	6047	7142	7177	6317	6172	6517
Vishakhapatnam		8030	7864	7405	8500	8530	7674	7529	7880
Yangon		8420	8310	7855	8890	8925	8110	7920	8335

All distances on this page via the Suez Canal.

AREA E

AREA A	Klaipeda (via Kiel Canal)	Land's End	Leith	Leixoes	Lisbon	Liverpool	London	Lulea (via Kiel Canal)
Abadan	7297	6241	6870	5727	5555	6520	6550	7772
Aden	5360	4304	4938	3792	3615	4608	4639	5835
Aqaba	4360	3304	3938	2792	2615	3608	3639	4835
Bahrain	7092	6036	6670	5524	5350	6340	6371	7567
Bandar Abbas	6813	5757	6391	5245	5071	6061	6092	7286
Basrah	7327	6371	6925	5759	5605	6569	6625	7820
Bassein	8611	7555	8215	7043	6900	7870	7900	9086
Bhavnagar	7097	6041	6675	5529	5355	6345	6376	7572
Bushehr	7152	6096	6730	5584	5385	6385	6431	7627
Calcutta	8664	7608	8280	7096	6925	7905	7955	9140
Chennai	8010	6964	7605	6442	6290	7260	7290	8490
Chittagong	8712	7656	8290	7144	6955	7965	8000	9187
Cochin	7210	6154	6788	5642	5468	6458	6489	7685
Colombo	7454	6398	7030	5886	5715	6685	6715	7930
Djibouti	5358	4302	4928	3790	3615	4605	4635	5833
Dubai	6891	5835	6469	5323	5149	6139	6170	7364
Fujairah	6725	5669	6303	5157	4983	5973	6004	7198
Jedda	4680	3624	4255	3112	2935	3950	3960	5155
Karachi	6830	5774	6405	5262	5090	6060	6090	7305
Kuwait	7277	6221	6855	5709	5535	6525	6556	7752
Malacca	8864	7804	8442	7296	7122	8112	8143	9339
Mangalore	7105	6049	6683	5537	5363	6353	6384	7580
Massawa	4960	3904	4538	3392	3218	4205	4235	5435
Mina al Ahmadi	7257	6201	6835	5689	5515	6505	6536	7732
Mongla	8678	7622	8240	7010	6925	7925	7955	9154
Mormugao	7047	5991	6630	5479	5315	6285	6315	7540
Moulmein	8714	7658	8300	7146	6985	7955	7985	9189
Mumbai	7107	5961	6600	5449	5285	6255	6296	7490
Musay'td	7062	6006	6640	5494	5320	6310	6341	7537
Penang	8696	7640	8305	7128	6990	7960	7990	9170
Port Blair	8326	7270	7904	6758	6684	7574	7605	8801
Part Kelang	8790	7734	8368	7222	7048	8038	8069	9265
Port Okha	6858	5802	6436	5290	5116	6106	6137	7333
Port Sudan	4750	3694	4330	3182	3020	3985	4015	5220
Quseir	4310	3254	3888	2742	2568	3558	3589	4785
Singapore	8987	7931	8595	7419	7240	8250	8280	9465
Sittwe	8643	7589	8270	7077	6905	7925	7955	9120
Suez	4060	3004	3638	2492	2318	3275	3335	4525
Trincomalee	7740	6684	7318	6172	5998	6988	7019	8215
Veraval	6917	5861	6495	5349	5175	6165	6196	7392
Vishakhapatnam	8274	7218	7860	6706	6532	7522	7553	8750
Yangon	8669	7613	8240	7101	6975	7945	7975	9140

All distances on this page via the Suez Canal.

AREA **E**

AREA A	Milford Haven	Murmansk	Narvik	Newcastle	Oslo	Rostock (via Kiel Canal)	Rotterdam	St Petersburg (via Kiel Canal)
Abadan	6359	8252	7702	6782	7127	6982	6620	7674
Aden	4422	6315	5765	4845	5190	5045	4680	5735
Aqaba	3422	5315	4765	3845	4190	4045	3680	4735
Bahrain	6154	8047	7497	6577	6922	6777	6412	7469
Bandar Abbas	5875	7768	7218	6298	6643	6498	6133	7190
Basrah	6389	8300	7730	6809	7170	7012	6649	7725
Bassein	7673	9566	9016	8096	8441	8296	7930	8988
Bhavnagar	6159	8052	7502	6582	6927	6782	6417	7574
Bushehr	6212	8107	7557	6637	6982	6837	6480	7529
Calcutta	7726	9620	9070	8150	8495	8349	8000	9040
Chennai	7072	8970	8420	7505	7845	7695	7360	8395
Chittagong	7774	9667	9117	8197	8542	8397	8035	9089
Cochin	6272	8165	7615	6695	7040	6895	6530	7587
Colombo	6516	8410	7860	6940	7285	7139	6785	7835
Djibouti	4420	6313	5763	4843	5188	5043	4680	5733
Dubai	5953	7846	7296	6376	6721	6576	6211	7268
Fujairah	5787	7680	7130	6210	6555	6410	6045	7102
Jedda	3742	5635	5085	4165	4510	4365	4000	5057
Karachi	5892	7785	7235	6320	6660	6723	6160	7210
Kuwait	6339	8232	7682	6762	7107	6962	6597	7654
Malacca	7926	9819	9269	8349	8694	8549	8184	9241
Mangalore	6267	8060	7510	6590	6935	6790	6425	7482
Massawa	4022	5915	5365	4445	4790	4645	4275	5337
Mina al Ahmadi	6319	8212	7662	6742	7087	6942	6577	7634
Mongla	7740	9634	9084	8164	8509	8363	8005	9055
Mormugao	6019	8000	7445	6530	6870	6732	6385	7445
Moulmein	7776	9669	9119	8200	8544	8399	8035	9091
Mumbai	6079	7970	7420	6505	6845	6702	6337	7395
Musay'td	6124	8017	7467	6545	6892	6747	6382	7439
Penang	7758	9650	9100	8185	8525	8381	8009	9075
Port Blair	7388	9281	8731	7811	8156	8011	7946	8703
Port Kelang	7852	9739	9189	8269	8620	8475	8100	9167
Port Okha	5920	7813	7263	6340	6688	6543	6178	7235
Port Sudan	3812	5705	5155	4235	4575	4435	4080	5125
Quseir	3372	5265	4715	3795	4135	3995	3630	4687
Singapore	8049	9945	9395	8475	8820	8672	8308	9364
Sittwe	7707	9600	9050	8130	8475	8330	8000	9022
Suez	3122	5005	4455	3540	3880	3745	3375	4430
Trincomalee	6802	8695	8145	7225	7570	7425	7060	8117
Veraval	5979	7872	7322	6402	6747	6602	6237	7294
Vishakhapatnam	7336	9230	8700	7759	8100	7960	7600	8651
Yangon	7731	9620	9070	8150	8495	8354	8000	9040

All distances on this page via the Suez Canal.

AREA E

AREA A	Skaw	Southampton	Stockholm (via Kiel Canal)	Sunderland	Szczecin (via Kiel Canal)	Teesport	Trondheim	Vaasä (via Kiel Canal)
Abadan	7076	6400	7395	6765	7117	6755	7323	7597
Aden	5139	4460	5460	4825	5180	4805	5386	5660
Aqaba	4140	3460	4460	3825	4180	3805	4385	4660
Bahrain	6871	6192	7190	6557	6912	6537	7118	7392
Bandar Abbas	6592	5913	6915	6278	6633	6258	6839	7113
Basrah	7106	6405	7440	6800	7165	6772	7353	7627
Bassein	8390	7705	8711	8076	8431	8060	8637	8910
Bhavnagar	6876	6197	7200	6562	6915	6542	7123	7397
Bushehr	6931	6260	7250	6609	6972	6597	7178	7452
Calcutta	8443	7764	8765	8130	8485	8110	8690	8964
Chennai	7789	7105	8120	7500	7835	7455	8036	8310
Chittagong	8491	7809	8810	8165	8532	8155	8738	9012
Cochin	6989	6310	7310	6675	7030	6655	7236	7510
Colombo	7233	6560	7555	6925	7275	6910	7480	7754
Djibouti	5137	4458	5458	4823	5178	4805	5384	5658
Dubai	6670	5991	6993	6356	6711	6336	6917	7191
Fujairah	6504	5825	6827	6190	6545	6170	6571	7025
Jedda	4359	3780	4780	4155	4500	4125	4706	4980
Karachi	6609	5935	6930	6300	6650	6290	6856	7130
Kuwait	7056	6377	7377	6742	7097	6722	7303	7577
Malacca	8643	7964	8964	8330	8684	8309	8890	9164
Mangalore	6884	6205	7205	6575	6925	6550	7131	7405
Massawa	4739	4065	5060	4420	4780	4405	4986	5260
Mina al Ahmadi	7036	6357	7357	6722	7077	6702	7283	7557
Mongla	8457	7778	8780	8143	8498	8124	8704	8978
Mormugao	6826	6150	7145	6520	6869	6500	7073	7347
Moulmein	8493	7820	8814	8185	8534	8155	8740	9014
Mumbai	6696	6130	7120	6485	6840	6480	7043	7315
Musay'td	6841	6162	7162	6527	6882	6507	7088	7362
Penang	8475	7805	8800	8200	8515	8140	8722	8996
Port Blair	8105	7425	8426	7791	8145	7771	8352	8626
Port Kelang	8569	7890	8490	8255	8510	8235	8816	9090
Port Okha	6637	5958	6958	6323	6678	6303	6884	6158
Port Sudan	4529	3855	4850	4220	4570	4200	4776	5050
Quseir	4089	3410	4410	3775	4130	3755	4336	4610
Singapore	8766	8085	9090	8450	8810	8430	9003	9287
Sittwe	8424	7750	8745	8105	8465	8100	8671	8945
Suez	3839	3165	4155	3520	3880	3500	4086	4360
Trincomalee	7519	6840	7840	7205	7560	7185	7766	8040
Veraval	6696	6017	7017	6382	6737	6362	6943	7217
Vishakhapatnam	8053	7380	8385	7735	8100	7719	8300	8574
Yangon	8448	7769	8765	8135	8485	8109	8695	8969

All distances on this page via the Suez Canal.

AREA F / AREA A	Aberdeen	Amsterdam	Antwerp	Archangel	Avonmouth	Belfast	Bergen	Bilbao
Balikpapan	9615	9365	9340	11220	9155	9285	9795	8860
Bangkok	9430	9200	9165	11035	8970	9290	9800	8865
Basuo (Hainan Is)	9920	9640	9655	11495	9425	9560	10065	9135
Cam-Pha	10070	9840	9805	11655	9585	9720	10225	9295
Cebu	10020	9790	9755	11550	9480	9615	10120	9190
Dalian	11200	10950	10925	12805	10740	10870	11380	10445
Haiphong	9970	9740	9705	11555	9485	9620	10125	9195
Ho Chi Minh City	9245	9015	8980	10840	8775	8910	9415	8485
Hong Kong	10055	9825	9790	11645	9580	9715	10220	9290
Hungnam	11415	11185	11150	12950	10885	11020	11525	10595
Inchon	11180	10900	10915	12750	10680	10815	11320	10390
Kampong Saom	9130	8900	8865	10735	8670	8990	9500	8565
Kaohsiung (Taiwan)	10245	9965	9977	11820	9750	9886	10390	9460
Keelung (Taiwan)	10395	10140	10120	12000	9930	10065	10570	9640
Kobe	11250	11120	11085	12855	10790	10925	11430	10500
Makassar	9610	9380	9345	11220	9155	9285	9795	8860
Manila	10005	9775	9740	11525	9455	9590	10095	9165
Masinloc	9990	9710	9725	11565	9495	9630	10135	9205
Menado	10110	9830	9845	11685	9615	9750	10255	9325
Moji	11133	10945	10910	12745	10675	10810	11315	10385
Muroran	11858	11578	11593	13433	11363	11498	12003	11073
Nagasaki	11065	10835	10800	12610	10540	10675	11180	10250
Nagoya	11440	11190	11165	13045	10980	11115	11620	10690
Nampo	11241	10961	10976	12817	10746	10881	11386	10456
Osaka	11260	11005	10985	12865	10795	10930	11435	10505
Otaru	11896	11616	11631	13471	11401	11536	12041	11111
Palembang	8920	8640	8655	10495	8425	8560	9065	8135
Pusan	11123	10843	10858	12698	10628	10763	11268	10338
Qingdao	11055	10805	10780	12660	10590	10725	11230	10300
Qinhuangdao	11325	11075	11049	12932	10865	11000	11505	10574
Sabang	8020	7740	7755	9595	7525	7660	8165	7235
Shanghai	10860	10630	10595	12405	10335	10470	10975	10045
Shimonoseki	11147	10867	10882	12722	10652	10787	11292	10362
Singapore	8620	8340	8355	10195	8125	8260	8765	7835
Surabaya	9235	9000	8960	10833	8766	8900	9406	8475
Tanjung Priok	8855	8625	8590	10460	8395	8525	9035	8100
Tokyo	11593	11363	11328	13103	11038	11173	11678	10748
Toyama	11585	11395	11360	13195	11125	11260	11765	10835
Vladivostok	11660	11430	11395	13195	11130	11265	11770	10840
Yokohama	11575	11345	11310	13085	11020	11155	11660	10730

All distances on this page via the Suez Canal.

AREA F

AREA A	Bordeaux	Bremen	Brest	Cherbourg	Copenhagen (via Kiel Canal)	Cork	Dublin	Dunkirk
Balikpapan	9010	9600	8970	9112	9815	9125	9200	9250
Bangkok	9015	9610	8975	9117	9820	9080	9200	9265
Basuo (Hainan Is)	9280	9900	9240	9414	10090	9400	9470	9555
Cam-Pha	9440	10050	9400	9545	10250	9520	9630	9705
Cebu	9335	10000	9295	9440	10145	9470	9525	9655
Dalian	10595	11185	10555	10597	11400	10710	10785	10835
Haiphong	9340	9950	9300	9445	10150	9420	9530	9605
Ho Chi Minh City	8630	9225	8590	8734	9440	8695	8820	8880
Hong Kong	9435	10035	9395	9539	10245	9505	9625	9690
Hungnam	10740	11395	10700	10844	11550	10860	10930	10980
Inchon	10535	11160	10495	10669	11345	10650	10725	10815
Kampong Saom	8715	9310	8675	8817	9520	8780	8900	8965
Kaohsiung (Taiwan)	9605	10225	9565	9739	10415	9725	9895	9880
Keelung (Taiwan)	9785	10380	9745	9890	10595	9905	9975	10030
Kobe	10645	11230	10605	10748	11455	10800	10835	10885
Makassar	9010	9590	8970	9112	9815	9060	9200	9245
Manila	9310	9905	9270	9415	10120	9455	9500	9580
Masinloc	9350	9970	9310	9484	10160	9470	9540	9625
Menado	9470	10090	9430	9604	10280	9590	9660	9745
Moji	10530	11155	10490	10636	11340	10625	10725	10810
Muroran	11218	11838	11178	11352	12028	11338	11403	11493
Nagasaki	10395	10945	10355	10500	11205	10515	10585	10700
Nagoya	10835	11430	10795	10939	11645	10955	11025	11075
Nampo	10601	11221	10561	10735	11411	10721	10791	10876
Osaka	10650	11245	10610	10756	11460	10770	10845	10895
Otaru	11276	11875	11215	11390	12066	11376	11445	11531
Palembang	8280	8900	8240	8414	9090	8400	8470	8555
Pusan	10483	11103	10440	10617	11293	10603	10673	10758
Qingdao	10445	11040	10405	10451	11255	10565	10640	10690
Qinhuangdao	10720	11305	10680	10824	11529	10835	10911	10960
Sabang	7380	8000	7340	7514	8190	7500	7570	7655
Shanghai	10190	10840	10150	10295	11000	10310	10380	10435
Shimonoseki	10507	11127	10467	10641	11317	10627	10697	10782
Singapore	7980	8600	7940	8114	8790	8100	8170	8255
Surabaya	8621	9205	8581	8725	9430	8735	8812	8863
Tanjung Priok	8250	8835	8210	8352	9055	8305	8440	8490
Tokyo	10893	11573	10853	10997	11703	11043	11083	11133
Toyama	10980	11605	10940	11086	11790	11075	11175	11260
Vladivostok	10985	11640	10945	11089	11795	11110	11175	11225
Yokohama	10875	11555	10835	10979	11685	11025	11065	11115

All distances on this page via the Suez Canal.

AREA F	AREA A Emden	Esbjerg	Finisterre	Flushing	Gdansk (via Kiel Canal)	Gibraltar	Gijon	Glasgow
Balikpapan	9490	9589	8532	9290	9955	7995	8689	9375
Bangkok	9495	9379	8308	9300	9960	7785	8465	9180
Basuo (Hainan Is)	9760	9869	8739	9565	10225	8275	8996	9670
Cam-Pha	9920	10019	8899	9725	10385	8425	9056	9820
Cebu	9815	9969	8832	9620	10280	8375	8989	9770
Dalian	11075	11174	10096	10875	11540	9580	10253	10960
Haiphong	9820	9919	8799	9625	10285	8325	8956	9720
Ho Chi Minh City	9110	9190	8123	8915	9575	7600	8280	8995
Hong Kong	9915	10004	8937	9720	10380	8410	9094	9805
Hungnam	11220	11364	10237	11025	11685	9770	10394	11165
Inchon	11015	11129	10029	10820	11480	9535	10186	10930
Kampong Saom	9195	9079	8008	9000	9660	7485	8165	8880
Kaohsiung (Taiwan)	10085	10194	9098	9890	10550	8600	9255	9995
Keelung (Taiwan)	10265	10369	9289	10070	10730	8775	9446	10155
Kobe	11125	11300	10168	10925	11590	9705	10325	11100
Makassar	9490	9560	8579	9290	9955	7965	8736	9360
Manila	9790	9955	8818	9595	10255	8360	8975	9755
Masinloc	9830	9995	8858	9635	10295	8400	9005	9799
Menado	9950	10059	8970	9755	10415	8465	9127	9860
Moji	11015	11124	10017	10815	11480	9530	10174	10925
Muroran	11698	11807	10715	11503	12163	10213	10872	11608
Nagasaki	10875	11015	9894	10680	11340	9420	10051	10815
Nagoya	11315	11414	10267	11120	11780	9820	10424	11205
Nampo	11080	11191	10106	10886	11546	9597	10263	10990
Osaka	11135	11235	10172	10935	11600	9640	10329	11020
Otaru	11736	11846	10753	11541	12200	10251	10910	11646
Palembang	8760	8869	7739	8565	9225	7275	7896	8670
Pusan	10963	11074	9980	10768	11428	9480	10137	10873
Qingdao	10930	11029	9940	10730	11395	9435	10097	10815
Qinhuangdao	11201	11303	10202	11004	11666	9709	10359	11088
Sabang	7860	7969	6885	7665	8325	6375	7042	7770
Shanghai	10670	10809	9669	10475	11135	9215	9826	10610
Shimonoseki	10987	11096	10016	10792	11452	9502	10173	10897
Singapore	8460	8569	7477	8265	8925	6975	7634	8370
Surabaya	9202	9202	8117	8905	9567	7608	8274	8989
Tanjung Priok	8730	8804	7737	8530	9195	7210	7894	8605
Tokyo	11373	11540	10381	11178	11838	9948	10538	11343
Toyama	11465	11574	10457	11265	11930	9980	10614	11375
Vladivostok	11465	11610	10484	11270	11930	10015	10641	11410
Yokohama	11355	11522	10369	11160	11820	9930	10526	11325

All distances on this page via the Suez Canal.

AREA F

AREA A	Gothenburg	Hamburg	Havre	Helsinki (via Kiel Canal)	Hernosand (via Kiel Canal)	Hull	Ipswich	Kiel (via Canal)
Balikpapan	9775	9600	9140	10245	10275	9420	9270	9615
Bangkok	9780	9425	8970	10250	10280	9225	9275	9620
Basuo (Hainan Is)	10045	9915	9460	10515	10550	9715	9545	9890
Cam-Pha	10205	10065	9610	10675	10705	9865	9705	10050
Cebu	10100	10008	9560	10570	10605	9815	9600	9945
Dalian	11360	11185	19725	11830	11860	11007	10855	11200
Haiphong	10105	9965	9510	10575	10605	9765	9605	9950
Ho Chi Minh City	9395	9240	8785	9865	9895	9040	8895	9235
Hong Kong	10200	10050	9595	10670	10700	9850	9700	10040
Hungnam	11505	11410	10955	11975	12005	11210	11005	11350
Inchon	11300	11175	10720	11770	11805	10975	10800	11145
Kampong Saom	9480	9125	8670	9950	9980	8925	8975	9320
Kaohsiung (Taiwan)	10370	10240	9785	10840	10875	10040	9870	10215
Keelung (Taiwan)	10550	10380	9920	11020	11055	10200	10050	10395
Kobe	11410	11345	10890	11880	11910	11415	10905	11250
Makassar	9775	9605	9150	10245	10275	9405	9270	9615
Manila	10075	10000	9545	10545	10580	9725	9575	9920
Masinloc	10115	10040	9585	10585	10620	9765	9615	9960
Menado	10235	10105	9650	10705	10740	9905	9735	10080
Moji	11300	11170	10715	11765	11800	10970	10795	11140
Muroran	11983	11853	11398	12450	12488	11653	11485	11828
Nagasaki	11160	11060	10605	11630	11660	10860	10660	11005
Nagoya	11600	11430	11970	12070	12100	11250	11100	11440
Nampo	11366	11236	10781	11836	11871	11035	10866	11210
Osaka	11420	11245	10785	11885	11920	11065	10915	11230
Otaru	12021	11890	11435	12491	12526	11690	11520	11866
Palembang	9045	8915	8460	9515	9550	8715	8545	8890
Pusan	11248	11120	10663	11718	11753	10918	10750	11090
Qingdao	11215	11040	10580	11680	11715	10860	10710	11055
Qinhuangdao	11486	11309	10845	11955	11987	11130	10983	11327
Sabang	8145	8015	7560	8615	8650	7815	7645	7990
Shanghai	10955	10855	10400	11425	11460	10655	10455	10800
Shimonoseki	11272	11142	10687	11742	11777	10942	10772	11117
Singapore	8745	8615	8160	9215	9250	8415	8245	8590
Surabaya	9387	9215	8755	9856	9888	9035	8884	9228
Tanjung Priok	9015	8850	8395	9485	9515	8650	8510	8855
Tokyo	11658	11588	11133	12128	12163	11388	11158	11498
Toyama	11750	11620	11165	12215	12250	11420	11245	11590
Vladivostok	11750	11655	11200	12220	12250	11455	11250	11595
Yokohama	11640	11570	11115	12110	12145	11370	11140	11480

All distances on this page via the Suez Canal.

AREA F	AREA A Klaipeda (via Kiel Canal)	Land's End	Leith	Leixoes	Lisbon	Liverpool	London	Lulea (via Kiel Canal)
Balikpapan	10095	8995	9595	8449	8275	9265	9295	10490
Bangkok	9885	8785	9605	8454	8280	9260	9290	10495
Basuo (Hainan Is)	10375	9275	9895	8722	8550	9550	9580	10765
Cam-Pha	10525	9425	10045	8882	8705	9700	9730	10925
Cebu	10475	9375	9995	8777	8605	9650	9680	10820
Dalian	11680	10580	11180	10034	9860	10850	10880	12075
Haiphong	10425	9325	9945	8782	8605	9600	9630	10825
Ho Chi Minh City	9700	8600	9220	8091	7895	8875	8905	10110
Hong Kong	10510	9410	10080	8876	8700	9685	9715	10915
Hungnam	11870	10770	11390	10181	10005	11045	11075	12210
Inchon	11635	10535	11145	9977	9805	10810	10840	12020
Kampong Saom	9585	8485	9305	8154	7980	8760	8990	10195
Kaohsiung (Taiwan)	10700	9600	10220	9047	8875	9875	9905	11090
Keelung (Taiwan)	10875	9775	10375	9217	9055	10045	10075	11270
Kobe	11805	10705	11325	10085	9910	10980	11010	12125
Makassar	10065	8965	9585	8449	8275	9240	9270	10490
Manila	10460	9360	9980	8752	8575	9635	9665	10795
Masinloc	10500	9400	10020	8792	8615	9675	9705	10835
Menado	10565	9465	10085	8912	8740	9740	9770	10955
Moji	11630	10530	11150	9973	9800	10805	10835	12015
Muroran	12313	11213	11833	10660	10488	11488	11518	12703
Nagasaki	11520	10420	11040	9837	9665	10695	10725	11880
Nagoya	11920	10820	11420	10276	10100	11090	11125	12315
Nampo	11697	10597	11216	10043	9871	10871	10901	12086
Osaka	11740	10640	11240	10093	9920	10910	10940	12135
Otaru	12351	11251	11871	10698	10526	11526	11556	12741
Palembang	9375	8275	8895	7722	7550	8550	8580	9765
Pusan	11580	10480	11098	9925	9753	10753	10783	11968
Qingdao	11535	10435	11035	9888	9715	10705	10735	11930
Qinhuangdao	11809	10709	11309	10161	9987	10980	11005	12202
Sabang	8475	7375	7995	6822	6650	7650	7680	8865
Shanghai	11315	10215	10835	9632	9460	10490	10520	11670
Shimonoseki	11602	10502	11122	9952	9777	10777	10807	11992
Singapore	9075	7975	8595	7422	7250	8250	8280	9465
Surabaya	9708	8608	9208	8062	7888	8878	8909	10103
Tanjung Priok	9310	8210	8830	7689	7515	8485	8515	9730
Tokyo	12048	10948	11468	10334	10158	11223	11253	12373
Toyama	12080	10980	11500	10423	10250	11255	11285	12465
Vladivostok	12115	11015	11635	10526	10250	11290	11320	12465
Yokohama	12030	10930	11450	10316	10140	11205	11235	12355

All distances on this page via the Suez Canal.

AREA F

AREA A	Milford Haven	Murmansk	Narvik	Newcastle	Oslo	Rostock (via Kiel Canal)	Rotterdam	St Petersburg (via Kiel Canal)
Balikpapan	9105	10970	10420	9505	9845	9705	9345	10395
Bangkok	9130	10975	10425	9510	9850	9710	9160	10400
Basuo (Hainan Is)	9385	11245	10695	9775	10120	9980	9650	10865
Cam-Pha	9535	11405	10855	9935	10280	10140	9800	10825
Cebu	9485	11300	10750	9830	10175	10035	9750	10720
Dalian	10690	12555	12005	11090	11430	11290	10930	11980
Haiphong	9435	11305	10755	9835	10180	10040	9700	10725
Ho Chi Minh City	8710	10595	10045	9125	9465	9325	8975	10015
Hong Kong	9520	11400	10850	9930	10270	10130	9785	10820
Hungnam	10880	12705	12155	11235	11575	11440	11145	12325
Inchon	10645	12500	11950	11030	11375	11235	10910	12120
Kampong Saom	8595	10675	10125	9210	9550	9410	8860	10100
Kaohsiung (Taiwan)	9710	11570	11020	10100	10445	11305	9975	11190
Keelung (Taiwan)	9885	11750	11200	10280	10625	10485	10120	11170
Kobe	10815	12605	12060	11140	11480	11340	11080	12030
Makassar	9075	10970	10420	9505	9845	9705	9340	10395
Manila	9470	11275	10725	9805	10150	10010	9735	10895
Masinloc	9570	11315	10765	9845	10190	10050	9775	10935
Menado	9575	11435	10885	9965	10300	10170	9840	11055
Moji	10640	12495	11945	11025	11370	11230	10905	12120
Muroran	11323	13183	12633	11713	12058	11918	11588	12803
Nagasaki	10530	12360	11810	10890	11235	11095	10795	11980
Nagoya	10930	12800	12250	11330	11670	11530	11170	12920
Nampo	10707	12566	12015	11095	11441	11300	10970	12186
Osaka	10750	12615	12065	11150	11490	11320	10985	12240
Otaru	11361	13220	12671	11750	12096	11956	11626	12841
Palembang	8385	10245	9695	8775	9120	8980	8650	9865
Pusan	10590	12448	11898	10978	11323	11180	10853	11768
Qingdao	10545	12410	11860	10940	11285	11145	10780	12035
Qinhuangdao	10819	12684	12134	11215	11557	11417	11055	12106
Sabang	7485	9345	8795	7875	8220	8080	7750	8965
Shanghai	10325	12155	11605	10686	11028	10890	10590	11780
Shimonoseki	10612	12272	11922	11000	11347	11207	10877	12182
Singapore	8085	9945	9395	8475	8820	8680	8350	9565
Surabaya	8718	10585	10035	9116	9458	9318	8956	10007
Tanjung Priok	8320	10210	9660	8745	9085	8945	8585	9635
Tokyo	11058	12858	12308	11388	11728	11588	11223	12478
Toyama	11090	12945	12395	11475	11820	11680	11355	12570
Vladivostok	11125	12950	12400	11480	11820	11685	11390	12570
Yokohama	11040	12840	12290	11370	11710	11570	11205	12460

All distances on this page via the Suez Canal.

AREA F

AREA A	Skaw	Southampton	Stockholm	Sunderland	Szczecin	Teesport	Trondheim	Vaasä (via Kiel Canal)
Balikpapan	9825	9115	10120	9490	9840	9465	10071	10315
Bangkok	9615	9125	10125	9500	9845	9490	9861	10320
Basuo (Hainan Is)	10105	9425	10390	9765	10110	9735	10350	10590
Cam-Pha	10255	9575	10550	9925	10270	9895	10500	10750
Cebu	10205	9525	10445	9820	10165	9790	10450	10645
Dalian	11410	10700	11700	11080	11420	11050	11655	11900
Haiphong	10155	9475	10450	9825	10170	9795	10400	10650
Ho Chi Minh City	9430	8750	9740	9115	9460	9085	9675	9935
Hong Kong	10240	9560	10545	9920	10265	9890	10485	10740
Hungnam	11600	10820	11850	11225	11570	11195	11845	12050
Inchon	11365	10685	11645	11020	11365	10990	11610	11845
Kampong Saom	9315	8825	9825	9200	9545	9170	9560	10020
Kaohsiung (Taiwan)	10430	9750	10715	10080	10435	10060	10675	10915
Keelung (Taiwan)	10605	9890	10895	10270	10615	10240	10850	11095
Kobe	11535	10755	11755	11130	11470	11100	11780	11950
Makassar	9795	9115	10120	9495	9835	9470	10040	10315
Manila	10190	9410	10420	9795	10140	9765	10435	10620
Masinloc	10230	9450	10460	9835	10180	9805	10475	10660
Menado	10295	9615	10580	9955	10300	9800	10540	10780
Moji	11360	10680	11640	11015	11360	10975	11605	11840
Muroran	12043	11363	12328	11703	12048	11673	12288	12528
Nagasaki	11250	10570	11505	10880	11225	10850	11495	11705
Nagoya	11650	10940	11945	11320	11665	11395	11895	12140
Nampo	11427	10745	11710	11085	11430	11055	11672	11910
Osaka	11470	10760	11760	11140	11480	11140	11715	11930
Otaru	12080	11400	12366	11740	12086	11710	12326	12566
Palembang	9105	8425	9390	8765	9110	8735	9350	9590
Pusan	11310	10628	11593	10968	11313	10938	11555	11790
Qingdao	11265	10555	11555	10930	11275	10900	11510	11755
Qinhuangdao	11539	10826	11830	11200	11549	11175	11764	12027
Sabang	8205	7525	8490	7865	8210	7835	8450	8690
Shanghai	11045	10365	11300	10676	11020	10646	11290	11500
Shimonoseki	11332	10652	11617	11015	11337	10960	11577	11817
Singapore	8805	8125	9090	8465	8810	8435	9050	9290
Surabaya	9438	8727	9731	9106	9450	9076	9683	9928
Tanjung Priok	9040	8360	9360	8735	9075	8705	9285	9555
Tokyo	11778	11000	12005	11378	11723	11348	12023	12198
Toyama	11810	11130	12090	11465	11810	11435	12055	12290
Vladivostok	11845	11065	12095	11470	11815	11440	12090	12295
Yokohama	11760	10980	11985	11360	11705	11335	12005	12180

AREA G

AREA A	Aberdeen	Amsterdam	Antwerp	Archangel	Avonmouth	Belfast	Bergen	Bilbao
Adelaide †	11055	10825	10790	12865	10620	10755	11260	10330
Albany †	10080	9850	9815	11690	9260	9755	10260	9330
Apia *	10403	10568	10544	11579	10261	10327	10584	10210
Auckland *	11200	11330	11345	12375	11065	11380	11380	11005
Banaba *	11450	11618	11593	12628	11321	11377	11634	11265
Bluff *	11403	11568	11543	12578	11271	11327	11584	11210
Brisbane †	12330†	12100†	11965	13535*	11895†	12030†	12535†	11605†
Cairns †	11497	11247	11223	13103	11036	11170	11676	10745
Cape Leeuwin †	9897	9647	9623	11303	9436	9570	10076	9145
Darwin †	10308	10058	10034	11914	9847	9981	10487	9556
Esperance †	10338	10088	10064	11944	9877	10011	10517	9586
Fremantle †	9855	9625	9590	11485	9415	9550	10055	9125
Geelong †	11410	11160	11140	13020	10950	11085	11590	10660
Geraldton †	9727	9477	9453	11333	9266	9400	9906	8975
Honolulu *	9370	9530	9515	10550	9240	9185	9555	9180
Hobart †	11530	11300	11265	13150	11095	11230	11735	10805
Launceston †	11525	11275	11250	13130	11065	11200	11705	10775
Lyttelton *	11260	11425	11400	12440	11130	10075	11445	11070
Mackay †	11837	11587	11563	13443	11376	11510	12016	11085
Madang †	11384	11634	11610	13490	11423	11557	12063	11132
Makatea *	9135	9335	9300	10305	9000	8945	9310	8940
Melbourne †	11355	11125	11090	13020	10950	11100	11605	10675
Napier *	11088	11253	11229	12264	10956	11012	11269	10895
Nauru Island *	11650	11818	11793	12828	11521	11577	11834	11465
Nelson *	11341	11538	11495	12520	11210	11155	11525	11150
Newcastle (NSW) †	11890†	11660†	11625†	13515*	11490†	11625†	12130†	11200†
New Plymouth *	11326	11523	11480	12505	11195	11140	11510	11135
Noumea *	11670	11815	11880	12845	11535	11480	11850	11475
Otago Harbour *	11440 *	11605*	11580*	12615*	11305*	11255*	11620*	11700†
Papeete *	9185	9385	9350	10355	9050	8995	9360	8990
Portland (Victoria) †	11210	10960	10940	12820	10750	10885	11390	10460
Port Hedland †	9755	9525	9490	11385	9315	9450	9955	9025
Port Kembla †	11850	11570	11535	13455	11390	11525	12030	11100
Port Lincoln †	11005	10775	10740	12815	10570	10705	11210	10280
Port Moresby †	11326	11076	10052	11832	9865	9999	10505	9574
Port Pirie †	11155	10925	10890	12965	10720	10855	11360	10430
Rockhampton †	12017	11768	11745	13623	11556	11690	12196	11265
Suva *	11013	11178	11154	12189	10881	10821	11194	10820
Sydney †	11880	11600	11565	13485	11420	11555	12060	11130
Wellington *	11192	11380	11345	12370	11060	11005	11375	11000

AREA G

	AREA A							
	Bordeaux	Bremen	Brest	Cherbourg	Copenhagen	Cork	Dublin	Dunkirk
Adelaide †	10475	11035	10435	10565	11285K	10595	10665	10690
Albany †	9475	10060	9435	9590	10285K	9580	9670	9715
Apia *	10360	10786	10179	10211	10888	10089	10239	10442
Auckland *	11155	11580	10975	11060	11685	10885	11035	11235
Banaba *	11410	11836	11229	11261	11938	11139	11289	11492
Bluff *	11360	11786	11179	11211	11888	11089	11239	11442
Brisbane †	11750	12310	11710	11840	12560	11880	11940	11965
Cairns †	10891	11484	10851	10995	11700K	11009	11082	11133
Cape Leeuwin †	9290	9885	9251	9395	10100K	9409	9482	9533
Darwin †	9701	10296	9662	9806	10511K	9820	9893	9944
Esperance †	9731	10336	9692	9836	10541K	9850	9923	9974
Fremantle †	9270	9835	9230	9365	10080K	9321	9465	9490
Geelong †	10805	11400	10721	10911	11615K	11470	11000	11050
Geraldton †	9120	9715	9081	9225	9930K	9239	9312	9363
Honolulu *	9330	9755	9150	9180	9855	9060	9205	9410
Hobart †	10950	11540	10910	11040	11760K	11680	11140	11165
Launceston †	10920	11510	10880	10025	11730K	11040	11110	11160
Lyttelton *	11220	11645	11040	11070	11745	10950	11100	11300
Mackay †	11231	11824	11191	11335	12040K	11349	11422	11473
Madang †	11278	11871	11238	11382	12087K	11396	11469	11520
Makatea *	9085	9510	8905	9228	9615	8815	8965	9225
Melbourne †	10805	11435	10780	10865	11630K	11085	11010	10990
Napier *	11045	11471	10864	10896	11573	10774	10924	11127
Nauru Island *	11610	12036	11429	11461	12138	11339	11489	11692
Nelson *	11300	11740	11120	11160	11825	11035	11180	11395
Newcastle (NSW) †	11345	11890	11305	11400	12155K	11440	11535	11525
New Plymouth *	11285	11725	11105	11145	11810	11020	11165	11380
Noumea *	11625	12025	11445	11485	12155	11350	11505	11780
Otago Harbour *	11375	11820	11215	11240	11925	11125	11275	11480
Papeete *	9135	9560	8955	9040	9665	8865	9015	9275
Portland (Victoria) †	10605	11200	10484	10711	11415K	11270	10800	10850
Port Hedland †	9170	9735	9130	9265	9980K	9805	9365	9390
Port Kembla †	11245	11830	11205	11310	12055K	11350	11435	11455
Port Lincoln †	10425	10985	10385	10515	11235K	10545	10615	10640
Port Moresby †	9719	10314	9680	9824	10529K	9838	9911	10959
Port Pirie †	10575	11135	10535	10665	11385K	10695	10765	10790
Rockhampton †	11411	12010	11371	11510	12220K	11530	11602	11665
Suva *	10970	11393	10789	10821	11498	10699	10849	11052
Sydney †	11275	11860	11235	11340	12085K	11380	11465	11485
Wellington *	11150	11590	10970	11010	11675	10885	11030	11245

AREA G

AREA A	Emden	Esbjerg	Finisterre	Flushing	Gdansk (via Kiel Canal)	Gibraltar	Gijon	Glasgow
Adelaide †	10995	11076	9980	10760	11420	9410	10205	10805
Albany †	9960	10081	8985	9760	10425	8435	9205	9830
Apia *	10691	10740	9931	10494	11156	10169	10100	10253
Auckland *	11490	10540	10725	11290	11950	10865	10895	11255
Banaba *	11741*	11791*	10935*	11544*	12206*	11026†	11155*	11303*
Bluff *	11691*	11741	10930*	11494*	12156*	10778†	11100*	11253*
Brisbane †	12230	12356	11255	12035	12695	10785	11580	12080
Cairns †	11372	11494	10398	11175	11837	9878	10620	11259
Cape Leeuwin †	9772	9894	8798	9575	10237	8280	9019	9659
Darwin †	10183	10305	9209	9986	10648	8689	9431	10070
Esperance †	10223	10335	9239	10016	10678	8719	9461	10100
Fremantle †	9755	9876	8780	9555	10220	8260	9000	9605
Geelong †	11290	11410	10315	11090	11755	9795	10535	11175
Geraldton †	9602	9724	8628	9405	10067	8108	8850	9489
Honolulu *	9660	9710	8900	9465	10125	9040	9070	9220
Hobart †	11430	11551	10455	11230	11895	9885	10680	11280
Launceston †	11400	11521	10430	11205	11865	9905	10650	11290
Lyttelton *	11550	11600	10790	11355	12015	10925	10960	11110
Mackay †	11712	11834	10738	11515	12177	10218	10960	11599
Madang †	11759	11881	10785	11562	12224	10265	11007	11646
Makatea *	9420	9470	8650	9220	9885	8770	8830	8985
Melbourne †	11300	11426	10330	11105	11765	9810	10550	11185
Napier *	11376	11426	10616	11179	11841	10766	10785	10938
Nauru Island *	11941*	11991*	11137*	11744*	12406*	10866†	11355*	11503*
Nelson *	11630	11680	10870	11435	12095	11040	11040	11215
Newcastle (NSW) †	11825	11951	10855	11630	12290	10345	11075	11740
New Plymouth *	11615	11665	10855	11420	12080	11025	11025	11200
Noumea *	11955	12005	11195	11760	12420	11325	11365	11540
Otago Harbour *	11810*	11860*	10965*	11530*	12190*	10830†	9575†	11430*
Papeete *	9470	9520	8700	9270	9935	8820	8880	9035
Portland (Victoria) †	11090	11210	10115	10890	11555	9595	10335	10975
Port Hedland †	9655	9776	8680	9455	10120	8160	8900	9505
Port Kembla †	11725	11826	10750	11530	12190	10255	10975	11650
Port Lincoln †	10945	10960	9930	10710	11370	9360	10155	10755
Port Moresby †	10201	10323	10263	10004	10666	9707	9449	10088
Port Pirie †	11095	11176	10080	10860	11520	9510	10205	10905
Rockhampton †	11892	12014	10918	11695	12357	10285	10140	11780
Suva *	11301	11351	10540	11104	11766	10679	10710	10863
Sydney †	11755	11876	10780	11560	12220	10285	11005	11680
Wellington *	11480	11530	10720	11285	11945	10890	10890	11065

AREA G

AREA A	Gothenburg	Hamburg	Havre	Helsinki	Hernosand	Hull	Ipswich	Kiel (via Canal)
Adelaide †	11240	11050	10595	11700K	11740K	10850	10740	11080
Albany †	10245	10075	9620	10710K	10740K	9875	9740	10085
Apia *	10780	10806	10351	11428	11454	10620	10481	10817
Auckland *	11575	11655	11200	12225	12250	11455	11275	11615
Banaba *	11830	11856	11401	12478	12504	11670	11531	11867
Bluff *	11780	11806	11351	12428	12454	11620	11481	11817
Brisbane †	12515	12225	11870	12985K	13015K	12165	12015	12360
Cairns †	11657	11484	11025	12126K	12158K	11315	11154	11498
Cape Leeuwin †	10057	9880	9425	10526K	10558K	9715	9554	9898
Darwin †	10468	10291	9836	10937K	10969K	10126	9965	10309
Esperance †	10498	10321	9866	10967K	10999K	10156	9995	10339
Fremantle †	10040	9850	9395	10505K	10540K	9650	9535	9880
Geelong †	11573	11401	10941	12042K	12074K	11220	11070	11414
Geraldton †	9887	9710	9255	10356K	10388K	9545	9384	9728
Honolulu *	9750	9775	9320	10400	10420	9590	10880	9785
Hobart †	11715	11525	11070	12185K	12215K	11325	11210	11555
Launceston †	11685	11515	11055	12155K	12185K	11335	11185	11525
Lyttelton *	11640	11665	11210	12287	12313	11479	11340	11676
Mackay †	11997	11824	11365	12466K	12498K	11655	11494	11838
Madang †	12044	11871	11412	12513K	12545K	11702	11541	11885
Makatea *	9505	9585	9150	10215	10180	9385	9210	9545
Melbourne †	11585	11350	10895	12055K	12090K	11250	11085	11430
Napier *	11465	11491	11036	12113	12139	11305	11166	11502
Nauru Island *	12030	12056	11601	12678	12704	11870	11731	12067
Nelson *	11720	11755	11300	12365	12395	11555	11420	11750
Newcastle (NSW) †	12110	11885	11430	12580K	12615K	11785	11610	11955
New Plymouth *	11705	11740	11285	12350	12380	11540	11405	11735
Noumea *	12045	12040	11625	12695	12720	11940	11745	12085
Otaga Harbour *	11815	11880	11380	12465	12590	11685	11515	11855
Papeete *	9555	9635	9180	10265	10230	9435	9260	9595
Portland (Victoria) †	11373	11201	10741	11842K	11874K	11020	10870	11214
Port Hedland †	9940	9750	9295	10405K	10440K	9550	9435	9780
Port Kembla †	12010	11835	11340	12480K	12510K	11595	11510	11830
Port Lincoln †	11190	11000	10545	11650K	11690K	10800	10690	10030
Port Moresby †	10486	10309	9854	10955K	10987K	10144	9983	10327
Port Pirie †	11340	11150	10695	11800K	11840K	10950	10840	10180
Rockhampton †	12177	11995	11540	12646K	12678K	11835	11674	12018
Suva *	11390	11416	10961	12038	12064	11230	11091	11427
Sydney †	12040	11865	11370	12510K	12540K	11625	11540	11880
Wellington *	11570	11605	11150	12215	12245	11405	11270	11600

AREA G

AREA A	Klaipeda	Land's End	Leith	Leixoes	Lisbon	Liverpool	London	Lulea
Adelaide †	11530K	10420	11030	9865	9740	10685	10715	11955K
Albany †	10535K	9420	10055	8865	8745	9710	9760	10960K
Apia *	11220	10116	10481	9936	9911	10311	10499	11679
Auckland *	11220	10920	11835	10730	10705	11135	11290	12475
Banaba *	12270	11176	11531	10986	10917	11361	11549	12729
Bluff *	12220	11026	11481	10936	10910	11311	11499	12679
Brisbane †	12805K	11695	12305	11140	11015	12060	12060	13230†
Cairns †	11947K	10836	11478	10283	10158	11148	11179	12373K
Cape Leeuwin †	10347K	9236	9880	8683	8558	9548	9575	10773K
Darwin †	10758K	9647	10291	9094	8969	9959	9986	11184K
Esperance †	10788K	9677	10321	9124	8999	9989	10016	11214K
Fremantle †	10330K	9215	9830	8665	8540	9485	9515	10755K
Geelong †	11865K	10750	11395	10200	10075	11065	11095	12290K
Geraldton †	10177K	9066	9710	8513	8388	9378	9405	10603K
Honolulu *	10189	9095	9450	8905	8880	9280	9470	10650
Hobart †	12005K	10895	11505	10340	10215	11160	11190	12430K
Launceston †	11975K	10865	11480	10315	10190	11135	11165	12400K
Lyttelton *	12079	10985	11340	10795	10770	11170	11358	12540
Mackay †	12287K	11176	11818	10623	10498	11488	11519	12713K
Madang †	12334K	11223	11865	10670	10545	11535	11566	12760K
Makatea *	9949	8855	9215	8655	8630	9035	9250	10405
Melbourne †	11875K	10750	11430	10215	10090	10985	11015	12305K
Napier *	11905	10811	11366	10621	10596	10996	11184	12364
Nauru Island *	12470	11376	11731	11186	11117	11561	11749	12929
Nelson *	12159	11065	11435	10875	10850	11335	11420	12620
Newcastle (NSW) †	12400K	11290	11865	10740	10615	11620	11650	12830K
New Plymouth *	12144	11050	11420	10860	10835	11320	11405	12605
Noumea *	12484	11390	11745	11200	11175	11575	11765	12945
Otago Harbour *	12254	11160	11515	10970	10945	11345	11535	12715
Papeete *	9999	8805	9265	8705	8680	9085	9300	10455
Portland (Victoria) †	11665K	10550	11195	10000	9875	10865	10895	12090K
Port Hedland †	10230K	9115	9730	8565	8440	9385	9415	10655K
Port Kembla †	12300K	11190	11725	10635	10510	11530	11560	12725K
Port Lincoln †	12480K	10370	10980	10815	9690	10635	10665	11905K
Port Moresby †	10776K	10673	10309	9112	8987	9977	10004	11202K
Port Pirie †	11630K	10520	11130	9965	9840	10785	10815	12055K
Rockhampton †	11467K	10356	11995	10803	10678	11668	11699	12893K
Suva *	11830	10736	11091	10546	10521	10921	11109	12289
Sydney †	12330K	11220	11805	10665	10540	11560	11590	12755K
Wellington *	12009	10915	11285	10725	10700	11185	11270	12470

AREA G

AREA A	Milford Haven	Murmansk	Narvik	Newcastle	Oslo	Rostock (via Kiel Canal)	Rotterdam	St Petersburg
Adelaide †	10522	12440	11890	10970	11310	11165	10785	11860K
Albany †	9522	11440	10890	9970	10310	10170	9810	10865K
Apia *	10188	11384	10985	10553	10812	10902	10545	11579
Auckland *	10992	12180	11780	11350	11610	11700	11340	12375
Banaba *	11192	12434	12035	11603	11862	11952	11594	12629
Bluff *	11098	12384	11985	11553	11812	11902	11545	12579
Brisbane †	11795†	13340*	12940*	12245†	12585†	12545†	12080	13135K
Cairns †	10936	12805	12305	11386	11728	11583	11226	12277K
Cape Leeuwin †	9336	11255	10705	9786	10128	9983	9626	10677K
Darwin †	9747	11666	11116	10197	10539	11394	10037	11088K
Esperance †	9777	11696	11146	10227	10596	10424	10067	11118K
Fremantle †	9315	11235	10685	9765	10110	9965	9585	10660K
Geelong †	10850	12770	12220	11300	11645	11544	11140	12195K
Geraldton †	9166	11115	10535	9616	9958	9891	9456	10507K
Honolulu *	9167	10455	9955	9520	9870	9870	9515	10550
Hobart †	10995	12915	12365	11445	11785	11640	11260	12335K
Launceston †	10965	12885	12335	11415	11755	11610	11255	12310K
Lyttelton *	11057	12245	11845	11410	11670	11761	11405	12438
Mackay †	11276	13145	12645	11726	12068	11923	11566	12617K
Madang †	11323	13192	12692	11773	12115	11970	11613	12664K
Makatea *	8927	10110	9710	9280	9540	9630	9320	10305
Melbourne †	10850	12785	12235	11315	11660	11515	11085	12205K
Napier *	10883	12069	11670	11238	11497	11587	11230	12264
Nauru Island *	11392	12634	12235	11803	12062	12152	11794	12829
Nelson *	11448	12325	11925	11490	11750	11835	11490	12520
Newcastle (NSW) †	11390	13310	12760	11840	12185	12040	11620	12730K
New Plymouth *	11122	12310	11910	11475	11735	11820	11475	12505
Noumea *	11462	12650	12350	11820	12080	12170	11805	12845
Otago Harbour *	11232	12420	12020	11590	11850	11940	11580	12615
Papeete *	8877	10160	9760	9330	9590	9680	9370	10355
Portland (Victoria) †	10650	12570	12020	11100	11445	12299	10940	11995K
Port Hedland †	9215	11135	10585	9665	10010	9865	9967	10560K
Port Kembla †	11290	13210	12660	11740	12080	11915	11530	12630K
Port Lincoln †	10470	12390	11840	10920	11260	11115	10735	11810K
Port Moresby †	9765	11684	12119	10215	10557	10412	10055	11106K
Port Pirie †	10620	12540	11990	11070	11410	11265	10885	11960K
Rockhampton †	10465	13325	12825	11906	12248	12103	11760	12797K
Suva *	10808	11994	11595	11163	11422	11512	11155	12189
Sydney †	11320	13240	12690	11770	12110	11970	11560	12660K
Wellington *	10987	12175	11775	11340	11600	11685	11340	12370

AREA G

AREA A	Skaw	Southampton	Stockholm	Sunderland	Szczecin (via Kiel Canal)	Teesport	Trondheim	Vaasä
Adelaide †	11173	10560	11585K	10925	11300	10915	11526	11780K
Albany †	10173	9585	10585K	9950	10305	9940	10526	10780K
Apia *	10751	10311	11305	10551	11039	10540	10746	11501
Auckland *	11545	11105	12100	11330	11835	11320	11542	12295
Banaba *	11800	11361	12355	11601	12089	11591	11796	12550
Bluff *	11750	11311	12305	11551	12039	11541	11746	12500
Brisbane †	11415	11835	12860K	12200	12580	12090†	12801	13060K
Cairns †	11585	10997	12000K	11363	11720	11353	11942	12198K
Cape Leeuwin †	9985	9397	10400K	9736	10120	9753	12342	10598K
Darwin †	10398	9808	10811K	10174	10531	10164	12753	11009K
Esperance †	10428	9838	10841K	10204	10561	10194	10783	11039K
Fremantle †	9970	9360	10380K	9725	10100	9715	10321	10580K
Geelong †	11503	10915	11915K	11280	11635	11270	11856	12114K
Geraldton †	9817	9220	10230K	9593	9950	9583	10172	10428K
Honolulu *	9720	9280	10275	9520	10010	9510	9717	10470
Hobart †	11645	11055	12060K	11400	11780	11390	12001	12255K
Launceston †	11615	11025	12030K	11390	11750	11380	11971	12225K
Lyttelton *	11610	11170	12165	11410	11900	11400	11607	12360
Mackay †	11927	11337	12340K	11703	12060	11693	12282	12538K
Madang †	11974	11384	12387K	11750	12107	11740	12329	12585K
Makatea *	9475	9095	10050	9260	9765	9250	9472	10225
Melbourne †	11515	10960	11930K	11225	11650	11215	11871	12130K
Napier *	11435	10996	11990	11236	11724	11226	11431	12185
Nauru Island *	12000	11561	12555	11801	12289	11791	11996	12750
Nelson *	11690	11265	12245	11505	11975	11620	11687	12440
Newcastle (NSW) †	12040	11395	12455K	11760	12175	11750	12396	12655K
New Plymouth *	11675	11250	12230	11490	11960	11605	11672	12425
Noumea *	12015	11550	12570	11815	12305	11805	12012	12765
Otago Harbour *	11785	11345	12340	11890	12075	11880	11782	12535
Papeete *	9525	9145	10080	9310	9815	9300	9522	10275
Portland (Victoria) †	11303	10715	11715K	11080	11435	11070	11656	11914K
Port Hedland †	9870	9738	10741K	9679	10461	9669	10221	10580K
Port Kembla †	11940	11305	12355K	11670	12075	11660	12296	12530K
Port Lincoln †	11120	10510	11535K	10875	11250	10865	11476	11730K
Port Moresby †	11416	9826	10829K	10192	10549	10182	10771	11027K
Port Pirie †	11240	10660	11685K	11025	10400	11015	11626	10880K
Rockhampton †	12107	11525	12520K	11880	12240	11890	12462	12718K
Suva *	11360	10921	11915	11161	11649	11151	11356	12110
Sydney †	11970	11335	12385K	11700	12105	11690	12326	12580K
Wellington *	11540	11115	12095	11355	11825	11345	11537	12290

AREA H

AREA A	Aberdeen	Amsterdam	Antwerp	Archangel	Avonmouth	Belfast	Bergen	Bilbao
Antofagasta *	6838	7008	6973	8000	6695	6633	7005	6635
Arica *	6642	6812	6777	7785	6475	6437	6790	6415
Astoria *	8460	8730	8695	9645	8340	8355	8650	8275
Balboa *	4680	4880	4845	5865	4555	4505	4870	4495
Buenaventura *	5040	5205	5180	6215	4910	4655	5220	4845
Cabo Blanco (Peru) *	5492	5692	5657	6677	5367	5317	5682	5307
Caldera *	7370	7210	7175	8195	6885	6835	7200	6825
Callao *	6047	6212	6182	7210	5900	5842	6215	5840
Cape Horn	7708	7460	7445	9262	7225	7341	7878	6941
Chimbote *	5840	6040	6005	6025	5715	5665	6030	5655
Coos Bay *	8285	8450	8425	9460	8155	8100	8470	8095
Corinto *	5308	5578	5543	6546	5236	5403	5551	5176
Eureka *	8140	8380	8345	9320	8010	8005	8325	7950
Guayaquil *	5552	5722	5687	6685	5380	5347	5695	5320
Guaymas *	7092	7262	7227	8234	6924	6887	7239	6864
Honolulu *	9375	9545	9510	10550	9240	9170	9555	9180
Iquique *	6670	6880	6845	7850	6540	6485	6855	6480
Los Angeles *	7607	7787	7753	8770	7470	7412	7780	7405
Manzanillo (Mex) *	6400	6630	6595	7580	6270	6255	6585	6210
Mazatlan (Mex) *	6680	6950	6815	7870	6560	6575	6875	6500
Nanaimo *	8780	8850	8915	9900	8595	8575	8905	8535
New Westminster *	8745	8965	8930	9960	8605	8550	8920	8545
Portland (Oreg) *	8557	8787	8752	9730	8425	8312	8735	8365
Port Alberni *	8674	8874	8839	9859	8549	8499	8864	8489
Port Isabel *	7322	7492	7457	8464	7154	7117	7469	7094
Port Moody *	8791	8861	8926	9904	8599	8586	8909	8539
Prince Rupert *	8983	9183	9148	10168	8858	8808	9173	8798
Puerto Montt M	8644	8386	8381	10203	8165	8277	8814	7877
Punta Arenas (Ch) M	7684	7426	7421	9243	7208	7317	7854	6917
Puntarenas (CR) *	5150	5350	5315	6335	5025	4975	5340	4965
Salina Cruz *	5870	6040	6005	7025	5715	5665	6030	5655
San Francisco *	7987	8057	8122	9105	7800	7782	8115	7740
San Jose (Guat) *	5568	5768	5733	6754	5444	5393	5759	5384
Seattle *	8710	8875	8850	9890	8575	8525	8890	8515
Tacoma *	8740	8900	8880	9915	8605	8555	8920	8545
Talcahuano *	7910	7680	7645	8469	7359	7305	7674	7299
Tocopilla *	6728	6898	6863	7930	6625	6523	6935	6560
Valparaiso *	7318	7488	7453	8480	7170	7117	7485	7110
Vancouver (BC) *	8787	8857	8922	9900	8595	8582	8905	8535
Victoria (Vanc Is) *	8665	8885	8850	9880	8525	8470	8840	8465

AREA
H

AREA A	Bordeaux	Bremen	Brest	Cherbourg	Copenhagen	Cork	Dublin	Dunkirk
Antofagasta *	6873	7218	6605	6636	7310	6623	6665	6873
Arica *	6677	7022	6385	6440	7095	6637	6445	6677
Astoria *	8595	8940	8245	8358	8955	8345	8305	8505
Balbao *	4745	5090	4465	4508	5175	4495	4525	4745
Buenaventura *	4995	5420	4815	4843	5525	4925	4875	5070
Cabo Blanco (Peru) *	5557	5902	5277	5320	5987	5307	5337	5557
Caldera *	7075	7420	6795	6838	7505	6825	6855	7075
Callao *	6082	6427	5810	5845	6520	5832	5870	6082
Cape Horn	7080	7670	7000	7173	7874K	7128	7250	7325
Chimbote *	5905	6250	5625	5668	6335	5655	5685	5905
Coos Bay *	8245	8670	8060	8093	8770	7970	8110	8325
Corinto *	5443	5788	5146	5206	5856	5193	5206	5443
Eureka *	8245	8590	7920	8008	8630	7995	7980	8245
Guayaquil *	5587	5932	5290	5350	6000	5337	5350	5587
Guaymas *	7127	7472	6834	6890	7544	6877	6894	7127
Honolulu *	9410	9755	9150	9173	9855	9160	9210	9410
Iquique *	6745	7090	6450	6508	7160	6495	6510	6745
Los Angeles *	7652	7997	7375	7415	8085	7352	7435	7652
Manzanillo (Mex) *	6495	6840	6180	6258	6890	6245	6240	6495
Mazatlan (Mex) *	6815	7160	6470	6578	7180	6565	6530	6815
Nanaimo *	8815	9160	8505	8578	9210	8565	8560	8815
New Westminster *	8830	9175	8515	8593	8425	8580	8575	8830
Portland (Oreg) *	8652	8997	8335	8415	9040	8352	8390	8652
Port Alberni *	8739	9084	8459	8502	9169	8489	8519	8739
Port Isabel *	7357	7702	7064	7120	7774	7107	7124	7357
Port Moody *	8826	9171	8504	8589	8244	8576	8564	8826
Prince Rupert *	9048	9393	8768	8811	9478	8798	8828	9048
Puerto Montt M	8016	8606	7936	8109	8815K	8065	8185	8265
Punta Arenas (Ch) M	7056	7646	6976	7149	7850K	7104	7226	7300
Puntarenas (CR) *	5215	5560	4935	4978	5645	4965	4995	5215
Salina Cruz *	5905	6250	5625	5668	6335	5655	5685	5905
San Francisco *	8022	8367	7705	7785	8415	7722	7770	8022
San Jose (Guat) *	5633	5978	5354	5396	6064	5383	5414	5633
Seattle *	8665	9090	8485	8513	9195	8395	8545	8745
Tacoma *	8695	9120	8515	8543	9225	8425	8575	8780
Talcahuano *	7545	7890	7269	7308	7979	7295	7329	7545
Tocopilla *	6763	7108	6530	6526	7240	6513	6590	6763
Valparaiso *	7353	7698	7080	7116	7790	7103	7140	7353
Vancouver (BC) *	8822	9167	8500	8585	9211	8572	8560	8822
Victoria (Vanc Is) *	8750	9095	8435	8513	8345	8500	8495	8750

AREA H

AREA A	Emden	Esbjerg	Finisterre	Flushing	Gdansk (via Kiel Canal)	Gibraltar	Gijon	Glasgow
Antofagasta *	7115	7160	6233	6920	7580	6518	6513	6833
Arica *	6895	6945	6137	6700	7360	6322	6317	6737
Astoria *	8760	8805	8055	8560	9225	8240	8240	8655
Balbao *	4975	5025	4205	4780	5440	4390	4385	4806
Buenaventura *	5325	5375	4290	5130	5790	4705	4739	4890
Cabo Blanco (Peru) *	5787	5837	5017	5592	6252	5202	5197	5617
Caldera *	7305	7355	6535	7110	7770	6720	6715	7135
Callao *	6320	6370	5542	6125	6785	5727	5722	6142
Cape Horn	7588	7676	6625	7388	8253	6387	6818	7440
Chimbote *	6135	6185	5365	5940	6600	5550	5545	5965
Coos Bay *	8575	8620	7535	8375	9040	7950	7929	8135
Corinto *	5656	5706	4903	5461	6121	5088	5083	5503
Eureka *	8435	8480	7705	8235	8900	7890	7885	8305
Guayaquil *	5800	5850	5047	5605	6265	5232	5227	5647
Guaymas *	7344	7394	6587	7149	7809	6772	6767	7187
Honolulu *	9660	9705	8870	9465	10125	9055	9015	9470
Iquique *	6960	7010	6205	6765	7425	6390	6385	6805
Los Angeles *	7885	7935	7112	7650	8355	7297	7332	7712
Manzanillo (Mex) *	6695	6740	5955	6495	7160	6140	6135	6555
Mazatlan (Mex) *	6980	7030	6275	6785	7445	6460	6455	6875
Nanaimo *	9015	9060	8275	8820	9480	8430	8455	8875
New Westminster *	9025	8275	8290	8830	9490	8445	8470	8890
Portland (Oreg) *	8845	8890	8112	8650	9310	8297	8292	8712
Port Alberni *	8969	9019	8199	8774	9434	8384	8379	8799
Port Isabel *	7574	7624	6817	7379	8039	7002	6997	7417
Port Moody *	9019	8094	8286	8819	9484	8471	8466	8886
Prince Rupert *	9278	9328	8508	9083	9743	8693	8688	9108
Puerto Montt M	8525	8613	7761	8320	9189	7320	7754	8376
Punta Arenas (Ch) M	7564	7652	6601	7364	8229	6362	6794	7416
Puntarenas (CR) *	5445	5495	4675	5250	5910	4860	4855	5275
Salina Cruz *	6135	6185	5365	5940	6600	5550	5545	5965
San Francisco *	8220	8265	7482	8025	8685	7667	7662	8082
San Jose (Guat) *	5864	5914	5093	5669	6329	5278	5273	5693
Seattle *	8995	9045	7955	8800	9460	8375	8351	8555
Tacoma *	9025	9075	7990	8830	9495	8405	8382	8590
Talcahuano *	7779	7829	7005	7584	8244	7190	7185	7605
Tocopilla *	7045	7090	6223	6845	7510	6408	6403	6823
Valparaiso *	7590	7640	6813	7395	8055	6998	6993	7413
Vancouver (BC) *	9015	9065	8282	8815	9480	8467	8462	8882
Victoria (Vanc Is) *	8945	8995	8210	8750	9410	8365	8390	8810

AREA H

AREA A	Gothenburg	Hamburg	Havre	Helsinki	Hermosand	Hull	Ipswich	Kiel (via Canal)
Antofagasta *	7205	7233	6778	7850	7870	7033	6905	7240
Arica *	6985	7037	6582	7635	7670	6837	6665	7020
Astoria *	8845	8955	8500	9495	9520	8755	8590	8885
Balbao *	5065	5105	4650	5715	5740	4905	4765	5100
Buenaventura *	5415	5440	4985	6065	6090	5255	5110	5455
Cabo Blanco (Peru) *	5877	5917	5462	6527	6552	5717	5577	5912
Caldera *	7395	7435	6980	8045	8070	7235	7095	7430
Callao *	6410	6442	5987	7060	7085	6242	6110	6445
Cape Horn	7881	7685	7230	7968	8599	7485	7381	7710
Chimbote *	6225	6265	5810	6875	6900	6065	5925	6260
Coos Bay *	8665	8690	8235	9310	9335	8505	8365	8700
Corinto *	5746	5803	5348	6396	6421	5603	5446	5781
Eureka *	8520	8605	8150	9170	9195	8455	8225	8560
Guayaquil *	5890	5947	5492	6545	6575	5747	5590	5925
Guaymas *	7434	7487	7032	8084	8109	7287	7134	7469
Honolulu *	9750	9770	9315	10395	10425	9570	9450	9785
Iquique *	7050	7105	6650	7700	7725	6905	6750	7090
Los Angeles *	7975	8012	7557	8625	8651	7812	7680	8015
Manzanillo (Mex) *	6780	6855	6400	7430	7455	6655	6485	6820
Mazatlan (Mex) *	7070	7175	6720	7720	7745	6905	6770	7105
Nanaimo *	9105	9175	8720	9750	9780	8975	8805	9140
New Westminster *	9115	9190	8735	9765	9790	8990	8820	9155
Portland (Oreg) *	8935	9012	8557	9580	9605	8812	8635	8970
Port Alberni *	9059	9099	8644	9709	9734	8899	8759	9094
Port Isabel *	7664	7717	7262	8314	8339	7517	7364	7699
Port Moody *	9104	9186	8731	9754	9779	8986	8809	9144
Prince Rupert *	9368	9408	8953	10018	10043	9208	9068	9403
Puerto Montt M	8817	8691	8166	8904	9535	8421	8317	8646
Punta Arenas (Ch) M	7857	7661	7206	7944	8575	7461	7357	7686
Puntarenas (CR) *	5535	5575	5120	6185	6210	5375	5235	5570
Salina Cruz *	6225	6265	5810	6875	6900	6065	5925	6260
San Francisco *	8310	8382	7927	8955	8985	8182	8010	8345
San Jose (Guat) *	5954	5993	5538	6604	6629	5793	5654	5989
Seattle *	9085	9110	8655	9735	9765	8925	8785	9125
Tacoma *	9115	9145	8685	9765	9795	8955	8815	9155
Talcahuano *	7869	7905	7450	8509	8544	7705	7569	7904
Tocopilla *	7135	7123	6668	7780	7805	6923	6835	7170
Valparaiso *	7680	7713	7258	8330	8355	7513	7380	7715
Vancouver (BC) *	9100	9182	8727	9750	9775	8982	8805	9140
Victoria (Vanc Is) *	9035	9110	8655	9685	9710	8910	8740	9075

AREA H

AREA A	Klaipeda	Land's End	Leith	Leixoes	Lisbon	Liverpool	London	Lulea
Antofagasta *	7633	6560	7213	6365	6378	6813	6898	8105
Arica *	7437	6340	7017	6169	6182	6617	6702	7885
Astoria *	9355	8200	8940	8092	8105	8540	8625	9745
Balbao *	5505	4420	5085	4237	4250	4685	4770	5964
Buenaventura *	5840	4770	5439	4591	4604	5039	5124	6315
Cabo Blanco (Peru) *	6317	5232	5897	5049	5062	5497	5582	6776
Caldera *	7835	6750	7415	6567	6580	7015	7100	8294
Callao *	6842	5765	6422	5574	5587	6022	6107	7310
Cape Horn	8308	7047	7665	6568	6418	7320	7350	8781
Chimbote *	6665	5580	6245	5397	5410	5845	5930	7124
Coos Bay *	9090	8015	8364	7781	7794	8194	8382	9560
Corinto *	6203	5101	5783	4935	4948	5383	5468	6645
Eureka *	9005	7875	8585	7737	7750	8185	8270	9420
Guayaquil *	6347	5245	5927	5079	5092	5527	5612	6800
Guaymas *	7887	6789	7467	6619	6632	7067	7152	8333
Honolulu *	10190	9105	9750	8867	8880	9350	9435	10650
Iquique *	7505	6405	7085	6237	6250	6685	6770	7950
Los Angeles *	8412	7330	7992	7184	7197	7592	7677	8875
Manzanillo (Mex) *	7255	6135	6835	5987	6000	6435	6520	7680
Mazatlan (Mex) *	7575	6425	7155	6307	6320	6755	6840	7970
Nanaimo *	9575	8460	9145	8307	8320	8755	8837	10000
New Westminster *	9590	8470	9160	8322	8335	8770	8852	10015
Portland (Oreg) *	9412	8290	8992	8144	8157	8592	8677	9830
Port Alberni *	9499	8414	9079	8231	8244	8679	8764	9959
Port Isabel *	8117	7019	7697	6849	6862	7297	7382	8563
Port Moody *	9586	8459	9156	8318	8331	8764	8851	10004
Prince Rupert *	9808	8723	9388	8540	8553	8988	9073	10267
Puerto Montt M	9244	7983	8601	7504	7350	8255	8286	9717
Punta Arenas (Ch) M	8284	7023	7641	6544	6394	7296	7326	8757
Puntarenas (CR) *	5975	4890	5555	4707	4720	5155	5240	6434
Salina Cruz *	6665	5580	6245	5297	5410	5845	5930	7124
San Francisco *	8782	7660	8362	7484	7527	7962	8047	9210
San Jose (Guat) *	6393	5309	5973	5125	5138	5573	5658	6853
Seattle *	9510	8440	8786	8203	8216	8616	8804	9985
Tacoma *	9545	8470	8817	8234	8247	8647	8835	10015
Talcahuano *	8305	7224	7885	7037	7050	7485	7570	8770
Tocopilla *	7523	6485	7103	6255	6268	6703	6788	8005
Valparaiso *	8113	7035	7693	6845	6858	7293	7378	8580
Vancouver (BC) *	9582	8455	9152	8314	8327	8762	8847	10000
Victoria (Vanc Is) *	9510	8390	9080	8242	8255	8690	8772	9935

AREA H

AREA A	Milford Haven	Murmansk	Narvik	Newcastle	Oslo	Rostock	Rotterdam	St Petersburg
Antofagasta *	6612	7810	7410	6975	7325	7440	6968	8008
Arica *	6393	7190	7190	6760	7015	7220	6772	7812
Astoria *	8253	9450	9050	8620	8880	9085	8790	9730
Balbao *	4473	5670	5270	4840	5100	5300	4840	5880
Buenaventura *	4823	6020	5620	5190	5450	5655	5180	6205
Cabo Blanco (Peru) *	5285	6482	6082	5652	5912	6112	5652	6692
Caldera *	6803	8000	7600	7170	7430	7630	7170	8210
Callao *	5818	7015	6615	6185	6440	6645	6177	7212
Cape Horn	7181	8896	8383	7600	7945	8100	7415	8682
Chimbote *	5633	6830	6430	6000	6260	6460	6000	7040
Coos Bay *	8073	9265	8870	8435	8695	8900	8430	9450
Corinto *	5154	6351	5951	5521	5781	5981	5538	6578
Eureka *	7928	9125	8725	8295	8555	8760	8340	9380
Guayaquil *	5298	6495	6095	5672	5930	6125	5682	6722
Guaymas *	6842	8039	7639	7209	7469	7669	7222	8262
Honolulu *	9158	10450	9955	9520	9780	9985	9505	10545
Iquique *	6458	7655	7255	6825	7085	7290	6840	7880
Los Angeles *	7383	8580	8180	7750	8010	8215	7747	8787
Manzanillo (Mex) *	6188	7385	6985	6555	6815	7020	6590	7630
Mazatlan (Mex) *	6478	7675	7275	6845	7100	7305	6910	7950
Nanaimo *	8513	9710	9310	8875	9135	9340	8910	9850
New Westminster *	8523	9729	9320	8890	9150	9355	8925	9965
Portland (Oreg) *	8343	9535	9140	8705	8965	9170	8747	9787
Port Alberni *	8467	9664	9264	8834	9094	9294	8834	9874
Port Isabel *	7072	8269	7869	7439	7699	7899	7482	8492
Port Moody *	8517	9714	9314	8879	9139	9344	8921	9861
Prince Rupert *	8776	9973	9573	9143	9403	9603	9143	10183
Puerto Montt M	8117	9830	9310	8536	8880	9036	8350	9618
Punta Arenas (Ch) M	7157	8872	8359	7576	7921	8076	7391	8658
Puntarenas (CR) *	4943	6140	5740	5310	5570	5770	5310	6350
Salina Cruz *	5633	6830	6429	6050	6260	6460	6000	7040
San Francisco *	7718	8915	8515	8080	8340	8545	8117	9057
San Jose (Guat) *	5362	6559	6159	5729	5989	6189	5728	6768
Seattle *	8493	9690	9290	8860	9115	9325	8850	9875
Tacoma *	8523	9720	9320	8890	9150	9355	8880	9900
Talcahuano *	7277	8475	8075	7640	7900	8104	7640	8680
Tocopilla *	6538	7735	7335	6905	7165	7370	6858	7898
Valparaiso *	7088	8285	7885	7455	7710	7915	7448	8488
Vancouver (BC) *	8513	9710	9310	8875	9135	9340	8917	9857
Victoria (Vanc Is) *	8443	9640	9240	8810	9070	9275	8845	9885

AREA H	AREA A							
	Skaw	Southampton	Stockholm	Sunderland	Szczecin (via Kiel Canal)	Teesport	Trondheim	Vaasä
Antofagasta *	7176	6743	7730	6975	7465	7098	7108	7920
Arica *	6956	6547	7510	6756	7245	6902	6912	7720
Astoria *	8816	8465	9370	8615	9105	8825	8830	9570
Balbao *	5036	4615	5590	4835	5325	4970	4980	5790
Buenaventura *	5384	4945	5940	5185	5675	5324	5385	6140
Cabo Blanco (Peru) *	5848	5427	6402	5647	6137	5782	5792	6602
Caldera *	7366	6945	7920	7165	7655	7300	7310	8120
Callao *	6381	5952	6935	6180	6670	6307	6317	7135
Cape Horn	7897	7220	8413	7588	7932	7585	8086	8649
Chimbote *	6196	5772	6750	5995	6485	6130	6140	6950
Coos Bay *	8626	8195	9185	8435	8920	8570	8629	9385
Corinto *	5734	5313	6271	5516	6003	5668	5678	6417
Eureka *	8536	8115	9045	8295	8780	8470	8480	9245
Guayaquil *	5878	5457	6425	5670	6150	5812	5822	6625
Guaymas *	7418	6997	7959	7204	7697	7352	7362	8159
Honolulu *	9701	9280	10275	9520	10010	9635	9645	10475
Iquique *	7036	6615	7575	6820	7310	6970	6980	7775
Los Angeles *	7943	7522	8502	7750	8235	7872	7887	8701
Manzanillo (Mex) *	6786	6365	7305	6555	7040	6720	6730	7505
Mazatlan (Mex) *	7106	6685	7595	6840	7330	7040	7050	7495
Nanaimo *	9106	8685	9630	8875	9365	9040	9050	9830
New Westminster *	9076	8700	9641	8885	9380	9055	9065	9840
Portland (Oreg) *	8906	8522	9460	8705	9190	8877	8887	9655
Port Alberni *	9030	8609	9584	8829	9319	8964	8976	9754
Port Isabel *	7635	7227	8189	7434	7921	7582	7592	8389
Port Moody *	9075	8696	9634	8879	9364	9051	9061	9829
Prince Rupert *	9339	8918	9893	9138	9628	9273	9283	10093
Puerto Montt M	8775	8156	9349	8525	8868	8520	9022	9585
Punta Arenas (Ch) M	7815	7196	8389	7564	7908	7561	8062	8625
Puntarenas (CR) *	5506	5085	6060	5305	5795	5442	5450	6260
Salina Cruz *	6196	5775	6750	5995	6482	6130	6140	6950
San Francisco *	8281	7892	8835	8080	8570	8247	8257	9035
San Jose (Guat) *	5925	5503	6479	5724	6211	5855	5868	6679
Seattle *	9056	8615	9610	8855	9345	9000	9036	9815
Tacoma *	9081	8645	9640	8885	9375	9021	9056	9845
Talcahuano *	7840	7415	8395	7640	8130	7770	7780	8594
Tocopilla *	7106	6665	7655	6905	7390	6988	7091	7855
Valparaiso *	7651	7223	8205	7450	7940	7578	7588	8405
Vancouver (BC) *	9071	8692	9630	8875	9360	9047	9075	9825
Victoria (Vanc Is) *	9006	8620	9561	8805	9295	8975	8985	9760

AREA A

AREA A	Aalborg	Aalesund	Aberdeen	Antwerp	Archangel	Avonmouth	Bayonne	Bergen
Aarhus	119	575	543	528K	1914	1034K	1196K	432
Amsterdam	479K	637	380	148	1980	655	815	502
Antwerp	586K	790	450	–	2040	631	791	602
Archangel	1855	1447	1745	2040	–	2282	2719	1443
Avonmouth	1089K	1020	754	631	2282	–	581	935
Bilbao	1250K	1375	1061	787	2714	604	60	1240
Bordeaux	1237	1336	1026	745	2646	556	205	1194
Bremen	352K	603	460	333	1881	873	1052	481
Brest	975K	1014	770	491	2313	308	318	944
Copenhagen	132	598	566	600K	1937	1106K	1268K	455
Dublin	945	822	542	677	2084	220	627	752
Dunkirk	574K	674	418	102	2016	529	701	585
Gdynia	419	922K	841K	737K	2315	1243K	1405K	833
Gibraltar	1808K	1947	1619	1345	3225	1158	978	1798
Glasgow	902	597	499	854	2032	373	804	700
Gothenburg	92	490	458	616K	1829	1063	1225	356
Hamburg	279K	601	473	382	1917	893	1053	486
Havre	707	823	522	244	2104	438	593	702
Helsinki	681	1138	1106	1026K	2477	1532K	1694K	995
Hull	530	594	270	265	1926	707	873	474
La Pallice	1162	1261	951	670	2571	478	130	1119
Lisbon	1570K	1695	1381	1107	2968	893	630	1560
Liverpool	1000	848	597	698	2075	282	693	778
London	622	738	436	193	2061	586	747	613
Lulea	957	1389	1357	1273K	2728	1779K	1941K	1246
Malmo	157	603	571	603K	1942	1109K	1271K	460
Newcastle	513	535	145	351	1804	789	954	403
Oslo	227	523	488	657	1836	1082	1445	378
Plymouth	824	949	638	366	2243	278	473	819
Reykjavik	1200	850	805	1249	1883	1103	1369	873
Rotterdam	511K	673	391	121	1950	632	794	533
St Petersburg	868	1289	1257	1177K	2628	1683K	1845K	1146
Southampton	746	845	535	255	2155	345	536	703
Stockholm	559	1015	983	901K	2354	1407K	1569K	872
Szczecin	360	805K	724K	620K	2197	1126K	1288K	715

AREA A

AREA A	Christiansand	Cork	Dundee	Emden	Flushing	Ghent	Gibraltar	Glasgow
Aarhus	217	1007K	528	324K	480K	509K	1750K	961
Amsterdam	360	628	374	166	100	124	1369	865
Antwerp	451	604	442	276	51	55	1345	854
Archangel	1565	2555	1773	1878	1993	2023	3225	2032
Avonmouth	1010	230	818	778	581	610	1158	373
Bilbao	1142	577	1044	936	739	768	867	827
Bordeaux	1102	547	1053	895	705	734	1011	775
Bremen	326	846	471	162	319	353	1606	926
Brest	851	281	753	645	448	477	973	531
Copenhagen	240	1079K	605	399K	552K	581K	1822K	984
Dublin	798	185	606	824	627	656	1204	178
Dunkirk	475	502	402	264	55	85	1255	752
Gdynia	618	1216K	840K	536K	689K	718K	1959K	1288
Gibraltar	1699	1131	1592	1494	1297	1326	–	1381
Glasgow	755	338	563	868	804	833	1381	–
Gothenburg	132	1036	497	415K	517	546	1779	876
Hamburg	326	866	485	185	335	365	1607	939
Havre	600	411	505	396	197	227	1147	661
Helsinki	780	1505K	1145	825K	978K	1007K	2248K	1524
Hull	407	680	240	279	218	248	1427	744
La Pallice	1027	472	978	820	630	425	957	700
Lisbon	1462	833	1364	1256	1059	1088	280	1116
Liverpool	824	255	661	890	693	722	1270	215
London	514	559	420	318	146	176	1301	809
Lulea	1031	1752K	1396	1072K	1225K	1474K	2495K	1775
Malmo	245	1082K	610	402K	555K	584K	1825K	989
Newcastle	376	762	122	329	304	334	1508	649
Oslo	163	1077	536	449	607	637	1870	896
Plymouth	717	251	621	513	319	349	1036	501
Reykjavik	1025	979	864	1170	1199	1230	1930	854
Rotterdam	413	605	383	199	74	104	1348	855
St Petersburg	931	1656K	1296	976K	1129K	1158K	2399K	1675
Southampton	610	340	510	405	200	232	1119	564
Stockholm	657	1380K	1022	700K	853K	882K	2123K	1401
Szczecin	500	1099K	723K	419K	572K	601K	1842K	171K

AREA A

AREA A	Gothenburg	Grangemouth	Hernosand	Ipswich	Kiel	Kotka	Larvik	Leith
Aarhus	118	606	696	513K	130	703	205	599
Amsterdam	464	384	951K	149	291	973K	448	372
Antwerp	616K	394	1058K	148	398	1080K	534	453
Archangel	1829	1806	2053	1956	2037	2525	1647	1788
Avonmouth	1063	839	1564	568	904	1586K	1055	832
Bilbao	1221	1057	1722K	718	1062	1744K	1219	1042
Bordeaux	1178	1019	1902	684	1014	1899	1268	1000
Bremen	382K	508	824K	366	164	846K	409	475
Brest	930	766	1447K	427	787	1469K	928	751
Copenhagen	134	629	580	585	202	830	220	622
Dublin	919	627	1593	614	950	1615	883	620
Dunkirk	553	414	1046K	90	386	1068K	572	399
Gdynia	383	891K	509	722K	339	532	470	838K
Gibraltar	1779	1615	2280K	1276	1640	2302K	1777	1600
Glasgow	876	584	1550	791	949	1572	840	577
Gothenburg	–	521	724	539	218	725	94	514
Hamburg	402	501	751K	370	91	773K	399	486
Havre	681	518	1182K	172	522	1204K	670	503
Helsinki	657	1169	356	1011K	628	72	897	1127K
Hull	504	252	1024K	166	396	1078K	485	237
La Pallice	1103	944	1827	609	939	1824	1193	924
Lisbon	1541	1377	2042K	1038	1382	2064K	1539	1362
Liverpool	974	682	1648	680	1016	1670	938	675
London	596	432	1099K	83	439	1121K	608	417
Lulea	866	1420	222	1258K	875	599	1019	1413
Malmo	141	634	590	588K	205	587	233	627
Newcastle	487	131	1099K	264	439	1121K	468	116
Oslo	163	558	877	610	355	876	68	538
Plymouth	798	634	1299K	284	639	1321K	806	619
Reykjavik	1152	902	1867	1164	1252	1864	1115	888
Rotterdam	489	396	983K	131	323	1005K	494	381
St Petersburg	847	1320	507	1162K	779	108	919	1313
Southampton	695	528	1410	193	522	1400	690	508
Stockholm	512	1046	257	886K	503	279	645	1039
Szczecin	390	774K	548	605K	222	621	488	721K

AREA A

AREA A	Liverpool	London	Manchester	Murmansk	Narvik	Oporto	Oskarshamn	Oslo
Aarhus	1084	569K	1124	1540	1045	1340K	386	265
Amsterdam	767	208	807	1517	1090	959	648K	522
Antwerp	698	193	738	1629	1211	935	755K	630
Archangel	2075	2061	2115	473	986	2816	2179	1711
Avonmouth	282	586	322	1969	1379	745	1261K	1163
Bilbao	716	743	756	2213	1778	436	1419K	1292
Bordeaux	672	702	712	2277	1790	580	1590	1248
Bremen	985	409	1025	1492	1092	1196	521K	460
Brest	410	452	450	1959	1574	540	1144K	1001
Copenhagen	1082	641	1122	1563	1068	1412K	217	272
Dublin	121	632	161	1771	1181	791	1269	951
Dunkirk	641	112	681	1646	1165	845	743K	617
Gdynia	1460	970K	1500	1941	1446	1549K	218	528
Gibraltar	1270	1301	1310	2977	2427	454	1977K	1850
Glasgow	215	809	255	1719	1129	968	1226	908
Gothenburg	974	596	1014	1455	960	1369	422	159
Hamburg	1005	425	1045	1581	1081	1197	448K	461
Havre	550	205	590	1797	1304	737	879K	752
Helsinki	1622	1067K	1662	2103	1608	1838K	333	948
Hull	819	239	859	1566	1066	1017	753K	559
La Pallice	597	627	637	2202	1715	526	1515	1173
Lisbon	1005	1063	1045	2664	2164	176	1739K	1612
Liverpool	–	698	40	1797	1207	857	1324	1006
London	698	–	738	1715	1215	891	796K	668
Lulea	1873	1314K	1703	2354	1859	2085K	561	1063
Malmo	1087	644K	1127	1568	1073	1415K	291	280
Newcastle	747	325	787	1500	970	1098	796K	528
Oslo	969	666	1009	1450	976	1439	566	–
Plymouth	390	321	430	1928	1408	617	996K	869
Reykjavik	927	1231	967	1517	1096	1500	1555	1179
Rotterdam	744	184	784	1628	1139	938	680K	554
St Petersburg	1773	1218K	1813	2254	1759	1989K	508	963
Southampton	461	211	501	1786	1299	714	1099	757
Stockholm	1499	942K	1539	1980	1485	1713K	194	819
Szczecin	1242K	661K	1282K	1823	1328	1432K	298	541

AREA A

AREA A	Reykjavik	Riga	Rotterdam	Santander	Stockholm	Sunderland	Swansea	Turku
Aarhus	1235	570	453K	1169K	507	564	965K	580
Amsterdam	1462	846K	67	788	794K	268	547	867K
Antwerp	1250	953K	121	764	901K	318	525	974K
Archangel	1883	2403	1950	2689	2354	1833	2241	2429
Avonmouth	1100	1459K	632	569	1407K	770	62	1480K
Bilbao	1475	1617K	790	36	1565K	927	567	1638K
Bordeaux	1755	1763	743	235	1716	890	828	1789
Bremen	1236	719K	290	1025	667K	418	836	740K
Brest	1181	1342K	457	343	1290K	636	283	1363K
Copenhagen	1259	696	525K	1241K	409	587	1037K	467
Dublin	896	1493	678	615	1444	690	169	1519
Dunkirk	1215	941K	104	674	889K	286	492	962K
Gdynia	1521	309	662K	1378K	325	776K	1174K	384
Gibraltar	1933	2175K	1348	835	2123K	1485	1121	2196K
Glasgow	855	1450	855	792	1401	647	345	1476
Gothenburg	1152	586	489	1198	512	479	985	599
Hamburg	1234	646K	307	1026	594K	407	856	667K
Havre	1305	1077K	250	566	1025K	392	401	1098K
Helsinki	1809	315	951K	1667K	239	1065K	1495K	108
Hull	1050	951K	211	846	899K	128	670	972K
La Pallice	1680	1688	668	200	1641	815	753	1714
Lisbon	2235	1937K	1110	557	1885K	1247	856	1958K
Liverpool	927	1548	744	681	1499	882	236	1592K
London	1231	944K	184	720	942K	312	549	1015K
Lulea	2047	629	1198K	1914K	443	1312K	1742K	350
Malmo	1266	456	528K	1244K	422	592	1040K	483
Newcastle	935	994K	285	927	942K	15	752	1015K
Oslo	1179	744	555	1253	694	521	1046	763
Plymouth	1150	1194K	367	446	1142K	500	241	1215K
Reykjavik	–	1728	1182	1452	1681	936	1056	1755
Rotterdam	1182	878K	–	767	826K	286	595	899K
St Petersburg	1950	504	1102K	1818K	386	1214K	1614K	268
Southampton	1265	1272	252	528	1225	400	309	1298
Stockholm	1681	217	826K	1553K	–	940K	1370K	162
Szczecin	1638	495	545K	1272K	408	659K	1089K	503

Area B

Distances between principal ports in the Mediterranean Sea, the Black Sea and the Adriatic.

and

Area C The East Coast of North America and Canada (including the Great Lakes and St Lawrence Seaway), the US Gulf and Central America (including the Gulf of Mexico and the Caribbean Sea).

Area D The East Coast of South America, the Atlantic Islands, and West and East Africa.

Area E The Red Sea, The Gulf, the Indian Ocean and the Bay of Bengal.

Area F Malaysia, Indonesia, South East Asia, the China Sea and Japan.

Area G Australasia, New Guinea and the Pacific Islands.

Area H The West Coast of North and South America.

Area B Other ports in the Mediterranean Sea, the Black Sea and the Adriatic.

AREA B
Reed's Marine Distance Tables
MEDITERRANEAN

AREA B
Reed's Marine Distance Tables
MEDITERRANEAN

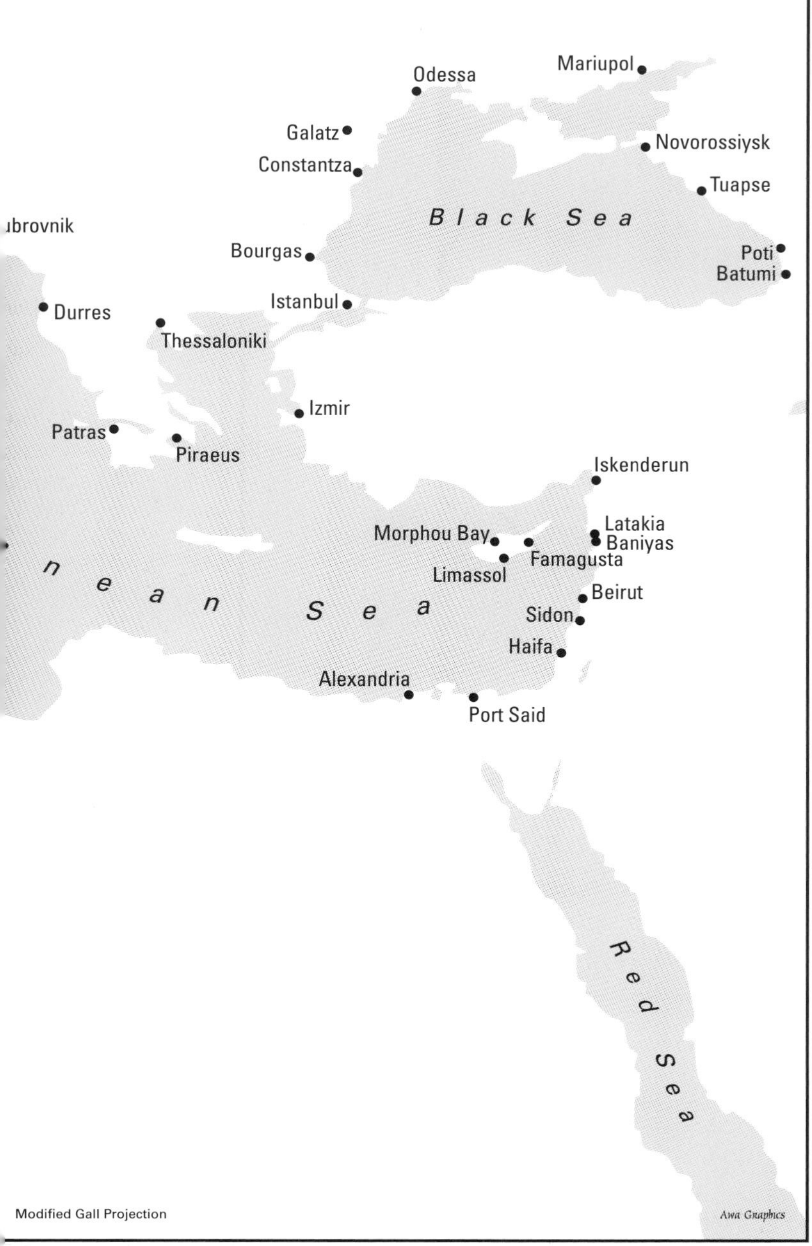

^Special section on page 209 devoted to the St Lawrence Seaway and the Great Lakes.

AREA C / AREA B	Alexandria	Algiers	Ancona	Barcelona	Beirut	Bourgas	Brindisi	Cagliari
Baie Comeau	4600	3210	4340	3330	4825	4725	4080	3510
Baltimore	5235	3845	4975	3965	5460	5360	4715	4145
Boston	4735	3345	4475	3465	4960	4860	4215	3645
Cartagena (Col)	5915	4525	5655	4645	6145	6040	5395	4825
Charleston	5360	3970	5100	4090	5585	5485	4840	4270
Churchill	5480	4096	5201	4373	5698	5580	4936	4404
Cienfuegos	6090	4700	5830	4820	6315	6215	5570	5000
Cristobal	6130	4740	5870	4860	6355	6255	5610	5040
Curacao	5550	4165	5295	4285	5780	5670	5035	4465
Duluth-Superior (^)	6120	4730	5860	4850	6345	6245	5600	5030
Freeport (Bahamas)	5463	4079	5184	4156	5681	5563	4919	4387
Galveston	6600	5210	6340	5330	6825	6725	6080	5510
Georgetown (G)	5174	3790	4895	3867	5392	5274	4630	4098
Halifax	4415	3025	4155	3145	4640	4540	3895	3325
Havana	5910	4520	5650	4640	6135	6035	5390	4820
Jacksonville	5540	4150	5280	4270	5765	5665	5020	4450
Key West	5850	4460	5590	4580	6075	5975	5330	4760
Kingston (Jamaica)	5765	4375	5505	4495	5995	5890	5245	4675
La Guiara	5465	4075	5205	4195	5695	5590	4945	4375
Maracaibo	5735	4351	5456	4428	5953	5835	5191	4659
Mobile	6360	4970	6100	5090	6585	6485	5840	5270
Montreal	4950	3560	4690	3680	5175	5075	4430	3860
New Orleans	6410	5020	6150	5140	6635	6535	5890	5320
New York	4935	3545	4675	3665	5160	5060	4415	3845
Norfolk (Va)	5105	3720	4845	3835	5335	5220	4590	4050
Nuevitas	5615	4230	5355	4345	5845	5730	5100	4560
Philadelphia	5085	3695	4825	3810	5310	5210	4565	3995
Port Au Prince	5665	4275	5405	4395	5890	5790	5145	4575
Portland (Maine)	4715	3325	4455	3445	4940	4840	4195	3625
Port of Spain	5250	3860	4990	3980	5475	5375	4730	4160
Puerto Limon	6280	4890	6020	5010	6515	6405	5760	5190
St John (NB)	4645	3255	4480	3375	4870	4770	4125	3555
St John's (NF)	3990	2600	3730	2720	4215	4115	3470	2900
San Juan (PR)	5156	3772	4877	3849	5374	5256	4612	4080
Santiago de Cuba	5690	4300	5530	4420	5915	5815	5170	4600
Santo Domingo	5390	4000	5130	4120	5715	5515	4870	4300
Tampa	6040	4650	5780	4770	6265	6165	5520	4950
Tampico	6740	5350	6480	5470	6965	6865	6120	5650
Veracruz	6700	5310	6440	5430	6925	6825	6180	5610
Wilmington (NC)	5356	3972	5077	4049	5574	5456	4812	4280

^Special section on page 209 devoted to the St Lawrence Seaway and the Great Lakes.

AREA C

AREA B	Casablanca	Constantza	Dubrovnik	Durres	Genoa	Gibraltar	Haifa	Iskenderun
Baie Comeau	2806	4775	4260	4180	3655	2810	4825	4885
Baltimore	3427	5410	4985	4815	4290	3445	5460	5520
Boston	3008	4910	4395	4315	3790	2945	4960	5020
Cartagena (Col)	4018	6090	5575	5490	4970	4125	6140	6200
Charleston	3512	5535	5020	4940	4415	3570	5585	5645
Churchill	3907	5693	5044	4957	4534	3657	5685	5676
Cienfuegos	3984	6265	5750	5670	5145	4300	6315	6375
Cristobal	4194	6305	5790	5710	5185	4340	6355	6415
Curacao	3572	5730	5215	5135	4610	3765	5780	5840
Duluth-Superior (^)	4326	6295	5780	5700	5175	4330	6345	6405
Freeport (Bahamas)	3636	5676	5027	4940	4517	3640	5668	5659
Galveston	4596	6775	6260	6180	5665	4810	6825	6885
Georgetown (G)	3247	5387	4738	4651	4228	3351	5379	5370
Halifax	2658	4590	4075	3995	3470	2625	4640	4700
Havana	3873	6085	5570	5490	4965	4120	6135	6195
Jacksonville	3696	5715	5200	5120	4595	3750	5765	5825
Key West	3828	6025	5510	5430	4905	4060	6075	6135
Kingston (Jamaica)	3788	5940	5425	5345	4820	3975	5990	6050
La Guiara	3531	5640	5125	5045	4520	3675	5690	5750
Maracaibo	3765	5948	5297	5212	4789	3912	5940	5931
Mobile	4359	6535	6020	5940	5415	4570	6585	6645
Montreal	3156	5197	4625	4540	4037	3160	5190	5250
New Orleans	4412	6585	6070	5990	5465	4620	6635	6695
New York	3160	5110	4595	4515	3990	3145	5160	5220
Norfolk (Va)	3329	5260	4755	4675	4150	3305	5320	5380
Nuevitas	3600	5852	5280	5195	4692	3815	5845	5905
Philadelphia	3320	5260	4745	4665	4140	3295	5310	5370
Port Au Prince	3649	5840	5325	5245	4720	3875	5890	5950
Portland (Maine)	2963	4890	4375	4295	3770	2925	4940	5000
Port of Spain	3294	5425	4910	4830	4305	3460	5475	5535
Puerto Limon	4345	6455	5945	5860	5335	4490	6505	6565
St John (NB)	2923	4820	4305	4225	3700	2855	4870	4930
St John's (NF)	2203	4165	3650	3570	3045	2200	4215	4275
San Juan (PR)	3249	5369	4720	4633	4210	3333	5361	5352
Santiago de Cuba	3655	5865	5350	5270	4745	3900	5915	5975
Santo Domingo	3437	5565	5050	4970	4445	3600	5615	5675
Tampa	4120	6215	5700	5620	5095	4250	6265	6325
Tampico	4720	6915	6400	6320	5795	4950	6965	7025
Veracruz	4680	6875	6360	6280	5755	4910	6925	6985
Wilmington (NC)	3424	5569	4920	4833	4410	3533	5561	5552

^Special section on page 209 devoted to the St Lawrence Seaway and the Great Lakes.

AREA C

AREA B	Istanbul	Izmir	Mariupol	Marseilles	Messina	Morphou Bay	Naples	Novorossiysk
Baie Comeau	4585	4425	5125	3490	3810	5355	3770	5030
Baltimore	5220	5060	5760	4125	4445	4855	4405	5665
Boston	4720	4560	5260	3625	3945	4720	3905	5165
Cartagena (Col)	5900	5740	6440	4805	5125	6035	5085	6345
Charleston	5345	5185	5885	4250	4570	5480	4530	5790
Churchill	5500	5341	6014	4369	4703	5567	4639	5943
Cienfuegos	6075	5915	6615	4980	5300	6210	4260	6520
Cristobal	6115	5955	6650	5020	5340	6250	5300	6560
Curacao	5540	5380	6080	4445	4765	5675	4725	5985
Duluth-Superior (^)	6105	5945	6645	5010	5330	6240	5290	6550
Freeport (Bahamas)	5483	5324	5997	4352	4686	5550	4622	5926
Galveston	6585	6425	7125	5490	5810	6720	5770	7030
Georgetown (G)	5194	5035	5708	4063	4397	5261	4333	5637
Halifax	4400	4240	4940	3305	3625	4535	3585	4845
Havana	5895	5735	6435	4800	5120	6030	5080	6340
Jacksonville	5525	5365	6065	4430	4750	5660	4710	5970
Key West	5835	5675	6375	4740	5060	5970	5020	6280
Kingston (Jamaica)	5750	5590	6290	4655	4975	5885	4935	6195
La Guiara	5450	5290	5990	4355	4675	5585	4635	5895
Maracaibo	5755	5596	6269	4624	4958	5822	4894	6198
Mobile	6345	6185	6885	5250	5570	6480	5530	6790
Montreal	4935	4775	5475	3840	4160	5070	4120	5380
New Orleans	6395	6235	6935	5300	5620	6530	5580	8840
New York	4920	4760	5460	3825	4145	5055	4105	5365
Norfolk (Va)	5080	4920	5620	3985	4305	5216	4265	5525
Nuevitas	5156	5497	6175	4525	4859	5723	4795	6099
Philadelphia	5070	4910	5610	3975	4295	5205	4255	5515
Port Au Prince	5650	5490	6190	4555	4875	5785	4835	6095
Portland (Maine)	4700	4540	5240	3605	3925	4835	3885	5145
Port of Spain	5235	5075	5775	4140	4460	5370	4420	5680
Puerto Limon	6265	6105	6805	5170	5490	6400	5450	6710
St John (NB)	4630	4470	5170	3535	3855	4765	3815	5075
St John's (NF)	3975	3815	4515	2880	3200	4110	3160	4420
San Juan (PR)	5176	5017	5690	4045	4379	5243	4315	5619
Santiago de Cuba	5675	5515	6215	4580	4900	5810	4860	6120
Santo Domingo	5375	5215	5915	4280	4600	5510	4560	5820
Tampa	6025	5865	6565	4930	5250	6160	5210	6470
Tampico	6725	6565	7265	5630	5950	6860	5910	7170
Veracruz	6685	6525	7225	5590	5910	6820	5870	7130
Wilmington (NC)	5376	5217	5890	3245	4579	5443	4515	5819

^Special section on page 209 devoted to the St Lawrence Seaway and the Great Lakes.

AREA C

AREA B	Odessa	Palmero	Piraeus	Port Said	Poti	Rijeka	Sfax	Siracusa
Baie Comeau	4930	3700	4310	4710	5180	4450	3750	3900
Baltimore	5565	4335	4945	5345	5815	5085	4385	4535
Boston	5065	3835	4445	4845	5315	4585	3885	4035
Cartagena (Col)	6245	5015	5625	6025	6495	5765	5065	5215
Charleston	5690	4460	5070	5470	5940	5210	4510	4660
Churchill	5843	4592	5179	5599	6057	5432	4737	4887
Cienfuegos	6420	5190	5800	6200	6670	5940	5240	5390
Cristobal	6460	5230	5840	6240	6710	5980	5280	5430
Curacao	5885	4655	5265	5665	6135	5405	4705	4855
Duluth-Superior (^)	6450	5220	5830	6230	6700	5970	5270	5420
Freeport (Bahamas)	5826	4575	5162	5582	6040	5305	4720	4870
Galveston	6930	5700	6310	6710	7180	6450	5750	5900
Georgetown (G)	5537	4286	4873	5293	5751	5016	4431	4581
Halifax	4745	3515	4125	4525	4995	4265	3565	3715
Havana	6240	5010	5620	6020	6490	5760	5060	5210
Jacksonville	5870	4640	5250	5650	6120	5390	4690	4840
Key West	6180	4950	5560	5960	6430	5700	5000	5150
Kingston (Jamaica)	6095	4865	5475	5875	6345	5615	4915	5065
La Guiara	5795	4565	5175	5575	6045	5315	4615	4765
Maracaibo	6098	4847	5434	5854	6312	5577	4992	5142
Mobile	6690	5460	6070	6470	6940	6210	5510	5660
Montreal	5280	4050	4660	5060	5530	4800	4100	4250
New Orleans	6740	5510	6120	6520	6990	6260	5560	5710
New York	5265	4035	4645	5045	5515	4785	4075	4235
Norfolk (Va)	5425	4195	4805	5205	5675	4945	4245	4395
Nuevitas	5999	4748	5335	5755	6213	5478	4893	5043
Philadelphia	5415	4185	4795	5195	5665	4935	4235	4385
Port Au Prince	5995	4765	5375	5775	6245	5515	4815	4965
Portland (Maine)	5045	3815	4425	4825	5295	4565	3865	4015
Port of Spain	5580	4350	4960	5360	5830	5100	4400	4550
Puerto Limon	6610	5380	5990	6390	6860	6130	5430	5580
St John (NB)	4975	3745	4355	4755	5225	4495	3795	3945
St John's (NF)	4320	3090	3700	4100	4570	3840	3140	3290
San Juan (PR)	5519	4268	4855	5275	5733	4998	4413	4563
Santiago de Cuba	6020	4790	5400	5800	6270	5540	4840	4900
Santo Domingo	5720	4490	5100	5500	5970	5240	4540	4690
Tampa	6370	5140	5750	6150	6620	5890	5190	5340
Tampico	7070	5840	6450	6850	7320	6590	5890	6040
Veracruz	7030	5800	6410	6810	7280	6550	5850	6000
Wilmington (NC)	5719	4468	5055	5475	5933	5198	4613	4763

^Special section on page 209 devoted to the St Lawrence Seaway and the Great Lakes.

AREA C

AREA C / AREA B	Tarabulus (Libya)	Taranto	Thessaloniki	Trieste	Tunis	Valencia	Valletta	Venice
Baie Comeau	3900	4040	4520	4485	3575	3190	3780	4475
Baltimore	4535	4675	5155	5120	4210	3825	4415	5110
Boston	4035	4175	4655	4620	3710	3325	3915	4610
Cartagena (Col)	5215	5355	5835	5800	4890	4505	5095	5790
Charleston	4660	4800	5280	5245	4335	3950	4540	5235
Churchill	4795	5027	5370	5367	4476	4070	4664	5374
Cienfuegos	5390	5530	6010	5975	5065	4680	5270	5965
Cristobal	5430	5570	6050	6015	5105	4720	5310	6005
Curacao	4855	4995	5475	5440	4530	4145	4735	5430
Duluth-Superior (^)	5420	5560	6040	6005	5095	4710	5300	5995
Freeport (Bahamas)	4778	4870	5353	5351	4459	4053	4647	5357
Galveston	5900	6040	6520	6485	5575	5190	5780	6475
Georgetown (G)	4489	4581	5064	5061	4170	3794	4358	5068
Halifax	3715	3855	4335	4300	3390	3005	3595	4290
Havana	5210	5350	5830	5795	4885	4500	5090	5785
Jacksonville	4840	4980	5460	5425	4515	4130	4720	5415
Key West	5150	5290	5770	5735	4825	4440	5030	5725
Kingston (Jamaica)	5065	5205	5885	5650	4740	4355	4945	5640
La Guiara	4765	4905	5385	5350	4440	4055	4645	5340
Maracaibo	5050	5142	5625	5622	4731	4325	4919	5629
Mobile	5660	5800	6280	6245	5335	4950	5540	6235
Montreal	4250	4390	4870	4835	3925	3540	4130	4825
New Orleans	5710	5850	6330	6295	5285	5000	5590	6285
New York	4235	4375	4855	4820	3910	3525	4115	4810
Norfolk (Va)	4395	4535	5015	4980	4070	3685	4275	4970
Nuevitas	4951	5043	5526	5523	4632	4226	4820	5530
Philadelphia	4385	4525	5005	4970	4060	3675	4265	4960
Port Au Prince	4965	5105	5585	5550	4640	4255	4845	5540
Portland (Maine)	4015	4155	4635	4600	3690	3305	3895	4590
Port of Spain	4550	4690	5170	5135	4225	3840	4430	5125
Puerto Limon	5580	5720	6200	6165	5255	4870	5460	6155
St John (NB)	3945	4085	4565	4530	3620	3235	3825	4520
St John's (NF)	3290	3430	3910	3875	2965	2580	3170	3865
San Juan (PR)	4471	4563	5046	5043	4152	3746	4340	5050
Santiago de Cuba	4990	5130	5610	5575	4665	4280	4870	5565
Santo Domingo	4690	4830	5310	5275	4365	3980	4570	5265
Tampa	5340	5480	5960	5925	5015	4630	5220	5915
Tampico	6040	6180	6660	6625	5715	5330	5920	6615
Veracruz	6000	6140	6620	6585	5675	5290	5880	6575
Wilmington (NC)	4671	4763	5246	5243	4352	3946	4540	5250

^Special section on page 214 devoted to distances within the Plate, Parana and Uruguay rivers.

AREA D

AREA B	Alexandria	Algiers	Ancona	Barcelona	Beirut	Bourgas	Brindisi	Cagliari
Azores	2787	1403	2509	1635	3005	2913	2269	1737
Bahia Blanca	7290	5906	7009	5985	7510	7508	6864	6332
Beira †	4146	5490	5183	5590	4220	4902	4918	5240
Belem	5114	3730	4834	3800	5330	5228	4584	4052
Buenos Aires (^)	7115	5731	6834	5810	7335	7288	6635	6110
Cape Horn	8209	6825	7930	6903	8428	8300	7666	7134
Cape Town	5517†	5574	6629	5600	5590†	6273†	6289	5937
Conakry	3759	2375	3480	2432	3957	3839	3195	2663
Dakar	3310	1926	3029	2005	3530	3439	2849	2317
Dar es Salaam †	3303	4648	4340	4747	3377	4059	4075	4397
Diego Suarez †	3396	4740	4433	4840	3470	4152	4168	4490
Douala	5291	3907	5012	3983	5508	5490	4746	4214
Durban	4723†	6067†	5760†	6375	4795†	5479†	5495†	5817†
East London	4986†	6047C	6024†	6125	5060†	5742†	5758†	6060†
Lagos	4923	3539	4644	3615	5140	5203	4559	4025
Las Palmas	2504	1120	2224	1195	2720	2638	1994	1462
Lobito	5818	4434	5539	4510	6035	5918	5275	4742
Luanda	5721	4337	5442	4353	5878	5760	5125	4584
Madeira	2414	1030	2134	1105	2630	2533	1889	1357
Maputo †	4504	5848	5540	5950	4580	5260	5276	5598
Mauritius †	4293	5237	4930	5337	3967	4649	4665	4987
Mogadiscio †	2619	3980	3660	4040	2720	3425	3460	3715
Mombasa †	3164	4508	4201	4610	3240	3920	3936	4258
Monrovia	4023	2639	3744	2781	4306	4188	3544	3012
Montevideo	7015	5631	6734	5710	7235	7168	6525	5990
Mozambique I †	3678	5022	4715	5122	3752	4434	4450	4772
Port Elizabeth	5115†	6459†	6152†	6003	5190†	5871†	5887†	6209
Port Harcourt	5163	3779	4884	3901	5426	5308	4664	4132
Porto Alegre	6874	5490	6595	5601	7125	7008	6365	5835
Recife	4948	3564	4669	3640	5165	5073	4429	3897
Reunion Island	3872†	5216	4909	5316	3946	4628†	4644†	4966†
Rio de Janeiro	6013	4629	5734	4705	6230	6158	5514	4982
Salvador	5358	3974	5060	4051	5575	5458	4814	4282
Santos	6201	4817	5922	4895	6420	6330	5689	5157
Sao Vicente Island	3383	1999	3104	2070	3600	3463	2820	2287
Takoradi	4656	3272	4379	3350	4875	4810	4165	3632
Tema	4723	3339	4444	3415	4940	4908	4264	3732
Tramandai	6724	5340	6445	5451	6976	6860	6203	5680
Vitoria (Brazil)	5747	4363	5468	4501	6026	5908	5264	4730
Walvis Bay	6183	4799	5904	4875	6400	6490	4834	5312

^Special section on page 214 devoted to distances within the Plate, Parana and Uruguay rivers.

AREA D

AREA B	Casablanca	Constantza	Dubrovnik	Durres	Genoa	Gibraltar	Haifa	Iskenderun
Azores	915	3000	2375	2290	1840	990	2990	2981
Bahia Blanca	5410	7505	6972	6887	6345	5585	7495	7486
Beira	6375C	4990†	6538†	6453†	5420†	5960†	4160†	4336†
Belem	3110	5325	4692	4607	4170	3305	5320	5311
Buenos Aires (^)	5135	7330	6750	6665	6170	5365	7320	7311
Cape Horn	6215	8422	7775	7690	7264	6387	8415	8406
Cape Town	4890	6360†	6383†	6298†	5960	5190	5530†	5736†
Conakry	1750	3972	3303	3218	2793	1916	3944	3935
Dakar	1335	3525	2957	2872	2365	1570	3515	3506
Dar es Salaam †	5216	4146	6073	5985	4476	5050	3315	3523
Diego Suarez †	5316	4239	6173	6085	4669	5150	3510	3616
Douala	3301	5504	4854	4769	4344	3467	5495	5486
Durban	5685C	5565†	5588†	5503†	5993†	6030C	4735†	4941†
East London	5430C	5830†	6768†	6683†	6260†	5745C	5000†	5216†
Lagos	2935	5135	4667	4582	3975	3280	5130	5121
Las Palmas	510	2715	2102	2017	1560	715	2710	2701
Lobito	3830	6030	5382	5297	4870	3995	6025	6016
Luanda	3671	5934	5224	5139	4715	3837	5865	5856
Madeira	475	2625	1997	1912	1470	610	2630	2621
Maputo	5980C	5345†	5373†	5288†	5775†	6330C	4520†	4725†
Mauritius †	5815	4736	4760	4675	5166	5650	3907	4113
Mogadiscio †	4556	3480	3510	3425	3930	4390	2625	2860
Mombasa †	5115	4005	4033	3948	4335	4950	3180	3386
Monrovia	2099	4236	3652	3567	3142	2265	4293	4284
Montevideo	5005	7230	6632	6547	6070	5245	7220	7211
Mozambique I †	5626	4521	4545	4460	4951	5460	3692	3893
Port Elizabeth	5310C	5960†	5983†	5898†	6365	5610C	5130†	5335†
Port Harcourt	3219	5376	4772	4687	4262	3385	5413	5404
Porto Alegre	4855	7087	6472	6387	5962	5085	7113	7104
Recife	2940	5160	4537	4452	4000	3150	5155	5146
Reunion Island †	5824	4715	4739	4654	5145	5658	3886	4092
Rio de Janeiro	4005	6225	5622	5537	5065	4235	6220	6211
Salvador	3346	5552	4922	4837	4410	3535	5563	5554
Santos	4190	6415	5797	5712	5255	4410	6405	6396
Sao Vicente Island	1385	3595	2927	2842	2417	1540	5325	5316
Takoradi	2605	4870	4273	4188	3710	2885	4860	4851
Tema	2820	4935	4372	4287	3775	2985	4930	4921
Tramandai	4705	6937	6320	6235	5812	4935	6965	6956
Vitoria (Brazil)	3796	5960	5372	5287	4862	3985	6013	6004
Walvis Bay	4260	6395	5950	5865	5235	4565	6390	6381

^Special section on page 214 devoted to distances within the Plate, Parana and Uruguay rivers.

AREA D

AREA B	Istanbul	Izmir	Mariupol	Marseilles	Messina	Morphou Bay	Naples	Novorossiysk
Azores	2805	2674	3345	1675	2036	2900	1945	3259
Bahia Blanca	7310	7269	7850	6180	6631	7495	6450	7764
Beira †	4795	4622	5335	5515	4932	3265	5105	5249
Belem	5135	4989	5675	4005	4350	5215	4275	5589
Buenos Aires (^)	7135	7050	7675	6005	6410	7275	6275	7589
Cape Horn	8230	8071	8770	7100	7433	8297	7386	8684
Cape Town	6165†	5992†	6705†	5795	6236	5635†	6065	6620†
Conakry	3759	3600	4299	2628	2962	3826	2915	4203
Dakar	3330	3254	3870	2200	2616	3480	2470	3784
Dar es Salaam †	3953	3780	4493	4671	4089	4322	4267	4407
Diego Suarez †	4046	3872	4586	4764	4182	3513	4260	4500
Douala	5310	5151	5850	4179	3513	5377	4466	5764
Durban	5375	5197	5915	6090	5507	4840	5685	5828
East London	5635	5462	6175	6355	5772	5105	5945	6090
Lagos	4945	4964	5485	3810	4325	5190	4080	5400
Las Palmas	2525	2399	3065	1395	1761	2625	1665	2979
Lobito	5840	5680	6380	4705	5040	5905	4975	6295
Luanda	5680	5521	6220	4549	4883	5747	4836	6134
Madeira	2435	2294	2975	1300	1656	2520	1575	2888
Maputo †	5155	4982	5695	5870	5292	4625	5465	5620
Mauritius †	4543	4369	5083	5261	4679	4012	4857	4997
Mogadiscio †	3295	3110	3835	4000	3400	2740	3580	3730
Mombasa †	3815	3645	4355	4530	3952	3285	4125	4270
Monrovia	4108	3950	4648	2977	3311	4175	3264	4662
Montevideo	7035	6929	7575	5905	6291	7155	6175	7489
Mozambique I †	4328	4154	4868	5046	4464	3797	4642	4782
Port Elizabeth	5765†	5590†	6305†	6200	5902†	5235†	6470C	6220†
Port Harcourt	5228	5069	5763	4097	4431	5295	4384	5682
Porto Alegre	6930	6770	7470	5797	6131	6995	6084	7384
Recife	4970	4834	5510	3835	4206	5060	4105	5425
Reunion Island †	4522	4348	5062	5240	4658	3991	4836	4976
Rio de Janeiro	6035	5920	6575	4900	5281	6145	5170	6489
Salvador	5378	5219	5918	4245	4585	5445	4534	5832
Santos	6220	6095	6760	5090	5456	6320	5360	6674
Sao Vicente Island	3335	3224	3945	2270	2586	3450	2540	3859
Takoradi	4675	4569	5215	3545	3931	4795	3815	5130
Tema	4745	4669	5285	3610	4031	4895	3880	5199
Tramandai	6780	6620	7320	5647	5981	6845	5934	7234
Vitoria (Brazil)	5828	5670	6568	4697	5030	5900	4984	6282
Walvis Bay	6205	6249	6745	5070	5611	6475	5342	6659

^Special section on page 214 devoted to distances within the Plate, Parana and Uruguay rivers.

AREA D

AREA B	Odessa	Palermo	Piraeus	Port Said	Poti	Rijeka	Sfax	Siracusa
Azores	3150	1925	2485	2905	3388	2630	2070	2090
Bahia Blanca	7655	6520	6990	7410	7893	7130	6665	6685
Beira †	5140	5049	4580	3990	5378	5260	5165	4890
Belem	4575	4240	4815	5235	5720	4955	4385	4405
Buenos Aires (^)	7480	6310	6815	7235	7718	6955	6445	6465
Cape Horn	8573	7322	7909	8322	8813	8052	7467	7487
Cape Town	6510†	6125†	5950†	5360†	6750†	6630†	6270	6290
Conakry	4102	2851	3438	3851	4342	3581	2996	3016
Dakar	3675	2505	3010	3430	3915	3150	2650	2670
Dar es Salaam †	4296	4206	3744	3147	4536	4416	4322	4047
Diego Suarez †	4389	4299	3837	3240	4629	4509	4415	4140
Douala	5653	4402	4989	5402	5893	5132	4547	4567
Durban †	5715	5624	5160	4565	5958	5835	5740	5465
East London †	5980	5889	5420	4830	6220	6100	6005	5730
Lagos	5285	4215	4620	5040	5528	4765	4360	4380
Las Palmas	2865	1650	2200	2625	3108	2345	1795	1815
Lobito	6180	4930	5525	5935	6423	5660	5075	5095
Luanda	6023	4772	5359	5772	6263	5500	4917	4937
Madeira	2775	1545	2115	2535	3018	2255	1690	1710
Maputo †	5445	5409	4940	4350	5738	5615	5525	5250
Mauritius †	4886	4796	4334	3737	5125	5006	4912	4637
Mogadiscio †	3640	3530	3070	2480	3890	3725	3655	3380
Mombasa †	4155	4069	3600	3010	4397	4275	4185	3910
Monrovia	4451	3200	3787	4200	4691	3930	3345	3365
Montevideo	7380	6180	6715	7135	7618	6855	6325	6345
Mozambique I †	4671	4581	4119	3522	4910	4791	4697	4422
Port Elizabeth †	6110†	6019	5950	4960	6350	6230	6135	5860
Port Harcourt	5770	4320	4907	5320	5811	5050	4465	4485
Porto Alegre	7273	6020	6607	7020	7513	7750	6165	6185
Recife	5310	4085	4645	5065	5553	4790	4230	4195
Reunion Island †	4865	4775	4313	3716	5105	4985	4891	4616
Rio de Janeiro	6375	5170	5710	6130	6618	5855	5315	5335
Salvador	5721	4470	5057	5470	5961	5200	4615	4635
Santos	6565	5345	5900	6320	6803	6045	5490	5510
Sao Vicente Island	3745	2478	3080	3465	3988	3225	2620	2640
Takoradi	5020	3820	4355	4775	5258	4500	3965	3985
Tema	5085	3920	4420	4840	5328	4565	4065	4085
Tramandai	7123	5870	6457	6870	7363	6600	6015	6035
Vitoria (Brazil)	6171	4920	5507	5920	6411	5650	5065	5085
Walvis Bay	6545	5500	5880	6050	6788	6025	5645	5665

^Special section on page 214 devoted to distances within the Plate, Parana and Uruguay rivers.

AREA D

AREA B	Tarabulus (Libya)	Taranto	Thessaloniki	Trieste	Tunis	Valencia	Valletta	Venice
Azores	2128	3220	2695	2675	1785	1375	1970	2680
Bahia Blanca	6723	6815	7195	7175	6285	5880	6475	7185
Beira †	4984	4930	4740	5295	5145	5685	4940	5305
Belem	4443	4635	5020	5000	4110	3705	4300	5010
Buenos Aires (^)	6503	6695	7020	7000	6110	5705	6300	7010
Cape Horn	7525	7717	8100	7960	7206	6800	7394	8104
Cape Town	6328	6520	6110†	6665†	5900	5495	6090	6675†
Conakry	3053	3246	3629	3626	2735	2329	2923	3633
Dakar	2708	2900	3215	3195	2305	1900	2445	3205
Dar es Salaam †	4141	4087	3887	4453	4302	4813	4086	4460
Diego Suarez †	4234	4180	3980	4546	4395	4911	4179	4553
Douala	4505	4797	5180	5177	4286	3880	4474	5184
Durban †	5559	5505	5315	5875	5720	6260	5515	5880
East London †	5824	5770	5580	6135	5985	6525	5780	6145
Lagos	4418	4610	4830	4810	3920	3515	4105	4815
Las Palmas	1853	2045	2410	2390	1500	1095	1690	2400
Lobito	5133	5325	5725	5705	4815	4410	5000	5710
Luanda	4975	5167	5550	5525	4656	4250	4844	5554
Madeira	1748	1940	2320	2300	1410	1005	1600	2310
Maputo †	5344	5290	5100	5655	5505	6045	5300	5660
Mauritius †	4731	4677	4477	5043	4592	5408	4676	5050
Mogadiscio †	3480	3436	3230	3760	3670	4175	3430	3755
Mombasa †	4004	3950	3760	4310	4165	4705	3960	4325
Monrovia	3403	3595	3978	3975	3084	2678	3272	3982
Montevideo	6383	6775	6920	6900	6010	5605	6200	6910
Mozambique I †	4516	4462	4262	4828	4677	5193	4461	4835
Port Elizabeth	5954†	5900	5710†	6265†	6115†	5900C	6495C	6270†
Port Harcourt	4523	4715	5098	5095	4204	3798	4392	5102
Porto Alegre	6223	6415	6798	6795	5904	5498	6092	6802
Recife	4288	4480	4855	4835	3945	3540	4130	4840
Reunion Island †	4710	4656	4456	5022	4871	5387	4655	5029
Rio de Janeiro	5373	5565	5920	5900	5010	4605	5200	5910
Salvador	4673	4865	5248	5245	4354	3948	4542	5252
Santos	5548	5740	6110	6090	5195	4790	5385	6095
Sao Vicente Island	2678	2870	3290	3270	2380	1975	2548	3275
Takoradi	4023	4215	4565	4545	3650	3246	3840	4550
Tema	4123	4215	4630	4610	3720	3315	3905	4615
Tramandai	6073	6265	6648	6645	5754	5348	5942	6652
Vitoria (Brazil)	5123	5315	5698	5695	4804	4398	4992	5702
Walvis Bay	5705	5895	6090	6070	5180	4775	5365	6075

All distances on this page via the Suez Canal.

AREA E	AREA B	Alexandria	Algiers	Ancona	Barcelona	Beirut	Bourgas	Brindisi	Cagliari
Abadan		3470	4819	4498	4905	3535	4217	4252	4555
Aden		1539	2900	2580	2960	1640	2345	2380	2635
Aqaba		546	1894	1573	1980	610	1292	1329	1630
Bahrain		3297	4646	4325	4732	3362	4044	4081	4382
Bandar Abbas		2993	4342	4021	4428	3058	3740	3777	4078
Basrah		3535	4885	4564	4971	3601	4283	4320	4621
Bassein		4824	6185	5865	6245	4945	5630	5680	5885
Bhavnagar		3277	4626	4305	4712	3342	4029	4066	4362
Bushehr		3189	4550	4230	4610	3310	3995	4030	4405
Calcutta		4889	6250	5930	6310	5010	5695	5730	5885
Chennai		4214	5575	5255	5635	4335	5020	5057	5310
Chittagong		4979	6340	6020	6400	5100	5785	5920	5975
Cochin		3290	4639	4318	4725	3355	4037	4074	4375
Colombo		3639	5000	4680	5060	3760	4445	4480	4635
Djibouti		1537	2898	2578	2958	1605	2343	2378	2533
Dubai		3071	4420	4099	4506	3136	3818	3855	4156
Fujairah		2905	4254	3933	4340	2970	3652	3689	3990
Jedda		888	2263	1943	2323	952	1638	1675	1968
Karachi		3014	4375	4055	4435	3135	3820	3855	4010
Kuwait		3457	4806	4485	4892	3522	4204	4241	4542
Malacca		5071	5420	6099	6506	5136	5818	5855	6156
Mangalore		3285	4634	4313	4720	3350	4032	4069	4370
Massawa		1222	2583	2263	2643	1271	1958	1995	2290
Mina al Ahmadi		3437	4786	4465	4872	3502	4184	4221	4522
Mongla		4858	6207	5886	6293	4923	5605	5642	5943
Mormugao		3239	4600	4280	4660	3360	4045	4080	4235
Moulmein		4909	6270	5950	6330	5030	5715	5752	5905
Mumbai		3209	4570	4250	4630	3330	4015	4052	4305
Musay'td		3242	4591	4270	4677	3307	3989	4022	4327
Penang		4914	6275	5955	6335	5035	5720	5757	5910
Port Blair		4505	5855	5534	5941	4571	5253	5290	5591
Port Kelang		4980	6329	6008	6415	5045	5727	5764	6065
Port Okha		3038	4387	4066	4473	3103	3785	3822	4123
Port Sudan		954	2298	1978	2358	1018	1700	1737	2038
Quseir		492	1853	1533	1913	560	1238	1275	1574
Singapore		5204	6565	6245	6625	5325	6010	6047	6200
Sittwe		4880	6240	5920	6300	5000	5685	5722	5875
Suez		253	1588	1268	1648	318	1000	1038	1338
Trincomalee		3920	5269	4948	5355	3985	4667	4704	5005
Veraval		3096	4445	4124	4531	3161	3843	3880	4181
Vishakhapatnam		4454	5803	5482	5889	4519	5201	5238	5539
Yangon		4899	6260	5940	6320	5020	5705	5742	5895

All distances on this page via the Suez Canal.

AREA E

AREA B	Casablanca	Constantza	Dubrovnik	Durres	Genoa	Gibraltar	Haifa	Iskenderun
Abadan	5406	4304	4328	4250	4734	5240	3476	3681
Aden	3476	2400	2430	2345	2850	3310	1545	1780
Aqaba	2476	1379	1403	1325	1809	2310	551	756
Bahrain	5208	4131	4155	4077	4561	5042	3303	3508
Bandar Abbas	4929	3827	3851	3773	4257	4763	2999	3204
Basrah	5451	4370	4391	4316	4800	5285	3541	3747
Bassein	6736	5634	5715	5630	6135	6570	4830	5065
Bhavnagar	5213	4111	4135	4057	4541	5047	3283	3488
Bushehr	5268	4166	4080	3995	4500	5102	3195	3430
Calcutta	6775	5700	5780	5695	6200	6609	4895	5130
Chennai	6146	5080	5105	5020	5525	5980	4220	4455
Chittagong	6828	5726	5870	5785	6290	6662	4985	5220
Cochin	5326	4124	4148	4070	4554	5160	3296	3501
Colombo	5570	4500	4530	4445	4950	5404	3645	3880
Djibouti	3474	2374	2428	2343	2848	3308	1543	1778
Dubai	5007	3905	3929	3851	4335	4841	3077	3282
Fujairah	4841	3739	3763	3685	4169	4675	2911	3116
Jedda	2801	1723	1793	1708	2213	2635	893	1103
Karachi	4951	3880	3905	3820	4325	4785	3020	3255
Kuwait	5393	4291	4315	4237	4721	5227	3463	3668
Malacca	6980	5905	5929	5851	6335	6814	5077	5282
Mangalore	5221	4119	4143	4065	4549	5055	3291	3496
Massawa	3066	2040	2113	2028	2533	2900	1228	1415
Mina al Ahmadi	5373	4271	4295	4217	4701	5207	3443	3648
Mongla	6794	5692	5716	5638	6122	6628	4864	5069
Mormugao	5163	4080	4130	4045	4550	4997	3245	3480
Moulmein	6846	5750	5800	5715	6220	6680	4915	5150
Mumbai	5146	4050	4100	4015	4520	4980	3215	3450
Musay'td	5178	4076	4100	4022	4506	5012	3248	3453
Penang	6812	5735	5805	5720	6225	6646	4920	5155
Port Blair	6442	5340	5364	5386	5770	6276	4511	4717
Port Kelang	6916	5814	5838	5760	6244	6750	4986	5191
Port Okha	4974	3872	3896	3818	4302	4808	3044	3249
Port Sudan	2876	1800	1828	1743	2248	2710	960	1170
Quseir	2426	1323	1383	1298	1803	2260	498	703
Singapore	7101	6020	6095	6010	6515	6935	5210	5445
Sittwe	6766	5664	5770	5685	6190	6600	4885	5040
Suez	2175	1088	1118	1033	1538	2009	258	468
Trincomalee	5856	4754	4778	4700	5184	5690	3926	4131
Veraval	5032	3930	3954	3876	4360	4866	3102	3307
Vishakhapatnam	6390	5288	5312	5234	5718	6224	4460	4665
Yangon	6775	5714	5790	5705	6210	6609	4905	5140

All distances on this page via the Suez Canal.

AREA E

AREA B	Istanbul	Izmir	Mariupol	Marseilles	Messina	Morphou Bay	Naples	Novorossiysk
Abadan	4111	3937	4651	4855	4247	3565	4425	4565
Aden	2215	2030	2755	2920	2320	1660	2500	2650
Aqaba	1186	1012	1726	1904	1322	640	1500	1640
Bahrain	3938	3764	4478	4656	4074	3392	4254	4392
Bandar Abbas	3634	3460	4174	4352	3770	3088	3948	4088
Basrah	4178	4004	5717	4895	4313	3631	4491	4631
Bassein	5500	5315	6040	6205	5605	4895	5785	5895
Bhavnagar	3918	3744	4458	4636	4059	3372	4232	4372
Bushehr	3965	3680	4405	4570	3970	3427	4150	4415
Calcutta	5505	5380	6105	6270	5670	4960	5850	5960
Chennai	4890	4705	5430	5595	4995	4315	5175	5325
Chittagong	5530	5470	6195	6360	5760	4987	5940	6000
Cochin	4291	4117	4471	4649	4067	3385	4245	4385
Colombo	4315	4130	4855	5020	4420	3745	4600	4750
Djibouti	2213	2028	2753	2918	2318	1634	2498	2648
Dubai	3712	3538	4252	4430	3848	3166	4026	4166
Fujairah	3546	3372	4086	4264	3682	3000	3860	4000
Jedda	1528	1393	2068	2283	1683	982	1860	1983
Karachi	3680	3505	4230	4395	3795	3125	3975	4125
Kuwait	4098	3924	4638	4816	4234	3552	4412	4552
Malacca	5712	5538	6252	6430	5848	5166	6026	6166
Mangalore	3926	3752	4466	4644	4062	3380	4240	4380
Massawa	1848	1673	2387	2565	1990	1301	2163	2303
Mina al Ahmadi	4078	3904	4618	4796	4214	3532	4392	4532
Mongla	5499	5325	6039	6330	5635	4953	5813	5953
Mormugao	3915	3730	4455	4620	4020	3338	4200	4350
Moulmein	5585	5400	6125	6290	5690	5005	5870	6020
Mumbai	3885	3700	4425	4590	3990	3310	4170	4320
Musay'td	3883	3709	4423	4601	4019	3337	4197	4337
Penang	5590	5405	6130	6295	5695	4993	5875	6025
Port Blair	5147	4973	5687	5865	5283	4601	5461	5601
Port Kelang	5621	5447	6161	6339	5757	5075	5935	6075
Port Okha	3679	3505	4219	4397	3815	3133	3993	4133
Port Sudan	1600	1428	2133	2313	1728	1048	1898	2048
Quseir	1128	953	1670	1848	1270	585	1450	1600
Singapore	5880	5695	6420	6585	5985	5280	6165	6315
Sittwe	5555	5370	6095	6260	5660	4925	5840	5990
Suez	900	728	1440	1608	1030	348	1208	1338
Trincomalee	4561	4387	5101	5279	4697	4015	4875	5015
Veraval	3737	3562	4277	4455	3873	3191	4051	4191
Vishakhapatnam	5095	4921	5635	5813	5231	4549	5409	5549
Yangon	5575	5390	6115	6280	5680	4875	5860	6010

All distances on this page via the Suez Canal.

AREA E

AREA B	Odessa	Palermo	Piraeus	Port Said	Poti	Rijeka	Sfax	Siracusa
Abadan	4464	4364	3902	3305	4694	4574	4358	4205
Aden	2560	2450	1990	1400	2810	2645	2575	2300
Aqaba	1539	1439	977	380	1769	1649	1433	1280
Bahrain	4291	4191	3729	3132	4521	4401	4185	4032
Bandar Abbas	3987	3887	3425	2828	4217	4097	3881	3728
Basrah	4531	4430	3968	3371	4760	4640	4424	4271
Bassein	5800	5735	5275	4635	6095	5930	5860	5585
Bhavnagar	4271	4171	3709	3112	4501	4381	4165	4012
Bushehr	4314	4100	3640	3167	4460	4295	4225	3950
Calcutta	5859	5800	5340	4700	6160	5995	5925	5650
Chennai	5224	5125	4665	4055	5485	5320	5250	4975
Chittagong	5899	5890	5430	4727	6250	6085	6015	5740
Cochin	4284	4184	3722	3125	4514	4394	4178	4025
Colombo	4649	4550	4090	3485	4910	4745	4675	4400
Djibouti	2547	2448	1988	1374	2808	2643	2573	2298
Dubai	4065	3965	3503	2906	4295	4175	3959	3806
Fujairah	3899	3799	3337	2740	4129	4009	3793	3640
Jedda	1882	1781	1320	722	2108	2000	1758	1663
Karachi	4024	3925	3465	2865	4285	4120	4050	3775
Kuwait	4451	4351	3889	3292	4681	4561	4345	4192
Malacca	6065	5965	5503	4906	6295	6175	5959	5806
Mangalore	4279	4179	3717	3120	4509	4389	4173	4020
Massawa	2202	2133	1678	1041	2430	2338	2100	1980
Mina al Ahmadi	4431	4331	3869	3272	4661	4541	4325	4172
Mongla	5852	5752	5290	4693	6082	5962	5746	5593
Mormugao	4249	4150	3690	3078	4510	4345	4275	4000
Moulmein	5930	5825	5360	4745	6180	6015	5945	5670
Mumbai	4230	4120	3660	3050	4480	4315	4245	3970
Musay'td	4236	4136	3674	3077	4466	4346	4130	3977
Penang	5819	5825	5365	4733	6185	6020	5950	5675
Port Blair	5500	5400	4938	4341	5730	5610	5394	5241
Port Kelang	5974	5874	5412	4815	6204	6084	5868	5715
Port Okha	4032	3932	3470	2873	4262	4142	3926	3773
Port Sudan	1947	1848	1388	788	2177	2058	1873	1698
Quseir	1499	1384	923	325	1713	1598	1358	1253
Singapore	6214	6115	5655	5020	6475	6310	6240	5965
Sittwe	5900	5790	5330	4665	6150	5985	5915	5640
Suez	1239	1148	688	88	1480	1358	1142	988
Trincomalee	4914	4814	4352	3755	5144	5024	4808	4655
Veraval	4090	3990	3528	2931	4320	4200	3984	3831
Vishakhapatnam	5448	5348	4886	4289	5678	5558	5342	5189
Yangon	5909	5810	5350	4715	6170	5905	5935	5660

All distances on this page via the Suez Canal.

AREA E	AREA B	Tarabulus (Libya)	Taranto	Thessaloniki	Trieste	Tunis	Valencia	Valletta	Venice
Abadan		4299	4261	4045	4611	4460	4976	4244	4618
Aden		2400	2356	2150	2680	2590	3095	2350	2675
Aqaba		1374	1336	1120	1686	1535	2051	1319	1693
Bahrain		4126	4088	3872	4438	4287	4803	4071	4445
Bandar Abbas		3822	3784	3568	4134	3983	4499	3767	4141
Basrah		4365	4327	4110	4677	4526	5042	4310	4684
Bassein		5685	5641	5435	5965	5875	6380	5635	5960
Bhavnagar		4106	4068	3852	4418	4267	4783	4051	4425
Bushehr		4050	4006	3800	4330	4240	4745	4000	4325
Calcutta		5750	5706	5500	6030	5940	6445	5700	6025
Chennai		5075	5031	4825	5355	5265	5770	5025	5350
Chittagong		5840	5796	5590	6120	6030	6535	5790	6115
Cochin		4119	4081	3865	4431	4280	4796	4064	4438
Colombo		4500	4456	4250	4780	4690	5195	4450	4775
Djibouti		2398	2354	2148	2678	2588	3093	2348	2673
Dubai		3900	3862	3646	4212	4061	4577	3845	4219
Fujairah		3734	3696	3480	4046	3895	4411	3679	4053
Jedda		1763	1719	1462	2040	1880	2400	1703	2038
Karachi		3875	3831	3625	4155	4065	4570	3825	4150
Kuwait		4286	4248	4032	4598	4447	4963	4231	4605
Malacca		5900	5862	5646	6212	6061	6577	5845	6219
Mangalore		4114	4076	3860	4428	4275	4791	5059	4433
Massawa		2080	2036	1783	2450	2200	2720	2020	2360
Mina al Ahmadi		4266	4228	4012	4578	4427	4943	4211	4585
Mongla		5687	5649	5433	5999	5848	6364	5632	6006
Mormugao		4100	4056	3850	4380	4290	4795	4050	4375
Moulmein		5770	5726	5520	6050	5960	6465	5720	6045
Mumbai		4070	4026	3820	4350	4260	4765	4020	4345
Musay'td		4071	4033	3817	4383	4232	4748	4016	4390
Penang		5775	5731	5525	6055	5965	6470	5725	6050
Port Blair		5335	5297	5181	5647	5496	5011	5280	4653
Port Kelang		5807	5771	5555	6121	5970	6486	5754	6128
Port Okha		3867	3829	3613	4179	4028	4544	3812	4186
Port Sudan		1790	1754	1530	2098	1943	2480	1740	2123
Quseir		1350	1309	1063	1633	1500	2000	1300	1628
Singapore		6065	6021	5815	6345	6255	6760	6015	6340
Sittwe		5740	5696	5490	6020	5930	6435	5690	6015
Suez		1080	1044	830	1395	1248	1788	1030	1400
Trincomalee		4749	4711	4495	5061	4910	5426	4694	5068
Veraval		3925	3887	3671	4237	4086	4602	3870	4244
Vishakhapatnam		5283	5245	5029	5595	5444	5960	5228	5602
Yangon		5760	5716	5510	6040	5950	6455	5710	6035

All distances on this page via the Suez Canal.

AREA F

AREA B	Alexandria	Algiers	Ancona	Barcelona	Beirut	Bourgas	Brindisi	Cagliari
Balikpapan	6209	7553	7253	7653	6283	6872	7009	7310
Bangkok	6020	7375	7055	7435	6135	6820	6775	7010
Basuo (Hainan Is)	7990	7850	7533	7940	6570	7552	7289	7590
Cam-Pha	6655	8000	7683	8090	6720	7402	7439	7740
Cebu	6610	7965	7645	8025	6725	7410	7365	7600
Dalian	7794	9138	8831	9238	7868	8550	8587	8888
Haiphong	6560	7915	7595	7975	6675	7360	7315	7550
Ho Chi Minh City	5835	7190	6870	7250	5950	6635	6590	6825
Hong Kong	6645	8000	7680	8060	6760	7445	7400	7635
Hungnam	8000	9345	9028	9435	8065	8747	8784	9085
Inchon	7770	9125	8805	9185	7885	8570	8525	8760
Kampong Saom	5715	7060	6743	7150	5780	6462	6499	6800
Kaohsiung (Taiwan)	6830	8175	7858	8265	6895	7577	7614	7915
Keelung (Taiwan)	6987	8331	8024	8431	7061	7743	7780	8081
Kobe	7940	9295	8975	9355	8055	8740	8695	8930
Makassar	6200	7555	7235	7615	6315	7000	6955	7190
Manila	6595	7950	7630	8010	6710	7395	7350	7585
Masinloc	6615	7975	7658	8065	6695	7377	7414	7715
Menado	6680	8040	7823	8130	6760	7442	7479	7780
Moji	7765	9120	8800	9180	7880	8565	8520	8755
Muroran	8443	9788	9471	9878	8508	9190	9227	9528
Nagasaki	7600	8940	8640	9039	7670	8455	8410	8645
Nagoya	8039	9380	9079	9480	8110	8792	8829	9130
Nampo	7818	9178	8855	9262	7892	8574	8611	8912
Osaka	7857	9197	8890	9298	7927	8609	8646	8947
Otaru	8476	9826	9509	9916	8546	9228	9265	9566
Palembang	6990	6850	6533	6940	5570	6252	6289	6590
Pusan	7710	9055	8738	9145	7775	8457	8494	8795
Qingdao	7648	8992	8685	9092	7722	8404	8441	8742
Qinhuangdao	7921	9265	8958	9365	7995	8677	8714	9015
Sabang	4605	5950	5633	6040	4670	5352	5389	5690
Shanghai	7450	8805	8485	8865	7565	8250	8205	8440
Shimonoseki	7732	9077	8760	9167	7797	8479	8516	8817
Singapore	5210	6565	6245	6625	5325	6010	5965	6200
Surabaya	5865	7220	6900	7280	5980	6665	6620	6855
Tanjung Priok	5445	6800	6480	6860	5560	6245	6200	6435
Tokyo	8183	9538	9218	9598	8298	8983	8938	9173
Toyama	8210	9555	9238	9645	8275	8957	8994	9295
Vladivostok	8250	9605	9285	9665	8365	9050	9005	9240
Yokohama	8165	9520	9200	9580	8280	8965	8920	9155

All distances on this page via the Suez Canal.

AREA F

AREA B	Casablanca	Constantza	Dubrovnik	Durres	Genoa	Gibraltar	Haifa	Iskenderun
Balikpapan	8161	7052	7083	6998	7482	7995	6223	6436
Bangkok	7945	6885	6905	6820	7325	7785	6020	6255
Basuo (Hainan Is)	8448	7339	7363	7285	7769	8275	6511	6716
Cam-Pha	8598	7489	7513	7435	7919	8425	6661	6866
Cebu	8535	7475	7495	7410	7915	8375	6610	6845
Dalian	9746	8637	8661	8583	9067	9580	7808	8014
Haiphong	8485	7425	7445	7360	7865	8325	6560	6795
Ho Chi Minh City	7760	6700	6720	6635	7140	7600	5835	6070
Hong Kong	8570	7510	7530	7445	7950	8410	6645	6880
Hungnam	9943	8834	8858	8780	9264	9770	8006	8211
Inchon	9695	8635	8655	8570	9075	9535	7770	8005
Kampong Saom	7658	6549	6573	6495	6979	7485	5721	5926
Kaohsiung (Taiwan)	8773	7664	7688	7610	8094	8600	6836	7041
Keelung (Taiwan)	8939	7830	7854	7776	8260	8775	7001	7207
Kobe	9865	8805	8825	8740	9245	9705	7940	8175
Makassar	8125	7065	7085	7000	7505	7965	6200	6435
Manila	8520	7355	7380	7300	7785	8360	6530	6732
Masinloc	8573	7464	7489	7410	7894	8400	6629	6831
Menado	8638	7529	7553	7475	7959	8465	6701	6906
Moji	9690	8630	8650	8565	9070	9530	7765	8000
Muroran	10386	9277	9301	9223	9707	10213	8449	8654
Nagasaki	9550	8440	8540	8455	8900	9400	7605	7890
Nagoya	9988	8879	8903	8825	9339	9822	8050	8256
Nampo	9770	8661	8685	8607	9081	9597	7833	8038
Osaka	9805	8696	8720	8642	9126	9640	7867	8073
Otaru	10424	9315	9339	9261	9745	10251	8487	8692
Palembang	7448	6339	6363	6285	6769	7275	5511	5716
Pusan	9653	8544	8568	8490	8974	9480	7716	7921
Qingdao	9600	8491	8516	8437	8921	9435	7662	7868
Qinhuangdao	9873	8764	8788	8710	9194	9709	7935	8141
Sabang	6548	5439	5463	5385	5869	6375	4611	4816
Shanghai	9375	8315	8335	8250	8755	9215	7450	7685
Shimonoseki	9675	8566	8590	8512	8996	9502	7738	7943
Singapore	7135	6075	6095	6010	6515	6975	5210	5445
Surabaya	7790	6730	6750	6665	7170	7630	5865	6100
Tanjung Priok	7370	6310	6330	6245	6750	7210	5445	5680
Tokyo	10108	9048	9068	8983	9488	9948	8183	8418
Toyama	10158	9044	9075	8990	9474	9980	8190	8425
Vladivostok	10175	9115	9135	9050	9555	10015	8250	8485
Yokohama	10090	9309	9050	8965	9470	9930	8165	8400

All distances on this page via the Suez Canal.

AREA F

AREA F / AREA B	Istanbul	Izmir	Mariupol	Marseilles	Messina	Morphou Bay	Naples	Novorossiysk
Balikpapan	6859	6692	7446	7577	7002	6300	7169	7320
Bangkok	6690	6505	7225	7395	6790	6115	6975	7125
Basuo (Hainan Is)	7146	6972	7733	7864	7282	6580	7460	7600
Cam-Pha	7296	7122	7883	8014	7432	6730	7610	7750
Cebu	7280	7095	7815	7985	7380	6705	7565	7715
Dalian	8444	8270	9031	9162	8580	6878	8754	8898
Haiphong	7230	7045	7765	7935	7330	6655	7515	7665
Ho Chi Minh City	6505	6320	7040	7210	6605	5930	6790	6940
Hong Kong	7315	7130	7850	8020	7415	6740	7600	7750
Hungnam	8641	8467	9228	9359	8777	8075	8955	9095
Inchon	8440	8255	8975	9145	8540	7865	8725	8875
Kampong Saom	6356	6182	6943	7074	6492	5790	6670	6810
Kaohsiung (Taiwan)	7471	7297	8058	8189	7607	6905	7785	7925
Keelung (Taiwan)	7637	7463	8224	8355	7773	7071	7947	8091
Kobe	8610	8425	9145	9315	8710	8035	8895	9045
Makassar	6870	6685	7405	7575	6970	6295	7155	7305
Manila	7162	6988	7800	7880	7298	6596	7476	7616
Masinloc	7271	7097	7858	7989	7407	6705	7585	7725
Menado	7336	7162	7923	8054	7472	6770	7650	7790
Moji	8435	8250	8970	9140	8535	7860	8720	8870
Muroran	9084	8910	9671	9802	9220	8518	9398	9538
Nagasaki	8247	8140	8860	9000	8425	7680	8560	8700
Nagoya	8686	8512	9279	9439	8822	8120	8999	9140
Nampo	8468	8294	9055	9186	8604	7902	8782	8922
Osaka	8483	8329	9090	9221	8639	7937	8639	8957
Otaru	9122	8948	9709	9840	9258	8556	9436	9576
Palembang	6146	5972	6733	6864	6282	5580	6460	6600
Pusan	8351	8177	8938	9069	8487	7785	8665	8805
Qingdao	8298	8124	8885	9016	8434	7732	8608	8752
Qinhuangdao	8571	8397	9158	9289	8707	7005	8881	9025
Sabang	5246	5072	5833	5964	5382	4680	5560	5700
Shanghai	8120	7935	8655	8825	8220	7545	8405	8555
Shimonoseki	8373	8199	8960	9091	8509	7807	8687	8827
Singapore	5880	5695	6415	6585	5980	5305	6185	6315
Surabaya	6135	6350	7070	7240	8220	5960	6820	6970
Tanjung Priok	6115	5930	6650	6820	6215	5540	6400	6550
Tokyo	8853	8668	9388	9558	8953	8278	9138	9288
Toyama	8860	8675	9518	9565	8960	8365	9245	9385
Vladivostok	8920	8735	9455	9625	9020	8345	9205	9355
Yokohama	8835	8650	9370	9540	8935	8260	9120	9270

All distances on this page via the Suez Canal.

AREA F

AREA B	Odessa	Palermo	Piraeus	Port Said	Poti	Rijeka	Sfax	Siracusa
Balikpapan	7202	7112	6674	6060	7449	7322	7160	6960
Bangkok	7035	6925	6465	5875	7285	7125	7050	6775
Basuo (Hainan Is)	7489	7399	6937	6340	7729	7609	7440	7242
Cam-Pha	7639	7549	7087	6490	7879	7759	7590	7392
Cebu	7625	7515	7055	6465	7875	7715	7640	7365
Dalian	8787	8697	8228	7638	9027	8907	8738	8540
Haiphong	7575	7465	7005	6415	7825	7665	7590	7315
Ho Chi Minh City	6850	6740	6280	5690	7100	6940	6865	6590
Hong Kong	7660	7550	7090	6500	7910	7750	7675	7400
Hungnam	8984	8894	8432	7835	9224	9104	8935	8737
Inchon	8785	8675	8215	7625	9035	8875	8800	8525
Kampong Saom	6699	6609	6147	5550	6939	6819	6650	6452
Kaohsiung (Taiwan)	7814	7724	7262	6665	8054	7934	7765	7567
Keelung (Taiwan)	7980	7890	7421	6831	8220	8100	7931	7733
Kobe	8955	8845	8385	7795	9205	9045	8970	8695
Makassar	7215	7105	6645	6055	7465	7305	7230	6955
Manila	7499	7500	6954	6356	7860	7625	7625	7350
Masinloc	7614	7524	7062	6465	7874	7734	7565	7367
Menado	7679	7589	7127	6530	7919	7799	7630	7432
Moji	8780	8670	8210	7620	9030	8870	8795	8520
Muroran	9427	9337	8875	8278	9667	9547	9378	9180
Nagasaki	8600	8509	8030	7440	8920	8709	8685	8410
Nagoya	9039	8940	8469	7880	9269	9148	8980	8782
Nampo	8811	8721	8259	7662	9051	8931	8762	8564
Osaka	8846	8756	8287	7697	9086	8966	8797	8599
Otaru	9465	9375	8913	8316	9705	9585	9416	9218
Palembang	6489	6399	5937	5340	6729	6609	6440	6242
Pusan	8684	8594	8142	7545	8934	8814	8645	8447
Qingdao	8645	8551	8082	7492	8881	8761	8592	8394
Qinhuangdao	8914	8824	8355	7765	9154	9034	8835	8667
Sabang	5589	5499	5037	4440	5829	5709	5540	5342
Shanghai	8465	8355	7895	7305	8715	8555	8480	8205
Shimonoseki	8716	8626	8164	7567	8956	8836	8667	8469
Singapore	6225	6115	5655	5065	6475	6315	6240	5965
Surabaya	6880	6770	6310	5720	7130	6970	6895	6620
Tanjung Priok	6460	6350	5890	5300	6710	6550	6475	6200
Tokyo	9198	9088	8628	8038	9448	9297	9213	8938
Toyama	9274	9184	8640	8125	9514	9394	9225	9027
Vladivostok	9265	9155	8695	8105	9515	9355	9280	9005
Yokohama	9180	9070	8610	8020	9430	9279	9195	8920

All distances on this page via the Suez Canal.

AREA F

AREA B	Tarabulus (Libya)	Taranto	Thessaloniki	Trieste	Tunis	Valencia	Valletta	Venice
Balikpapan	7054	7016	6800	7359	7208	7748	7003	7366
Bangkok	6875	6831	6625	7155	7065	7575	6825	7145
Basuo (Hainan Is)	7334	7296	7080	7646	7495	8011	7279	7653
Cam-Pha	7484	7446	7230	7796	7645	8161	7429	7803
Cebu	7465	7421	7215	7745	7655	8165	7415	7735
Dalian	8632	8594	8738	8944	8793	9333	8588	8951
Haiphong	7415	7371	7165	7695	7605	8115	7365	7685
Ho Chi Minh City	6690	6646	6440	6970	6880	7390	6640	6960
Hong Kong	7500	7456	7250	7780	7690	8200	7450	7770
Hungnam	8829	8791	8575	9141	8990	9506	8774	9148
Inchon	8625	8581	8375	8905	8815	9325	8575	8895
Kampong Saom	6544	6506	6290	6856	6705	7221	6489	6863
Kaohsiung (Taiwan)	7659	7621	7405	7971	7820	8336	7604	7978
Keelung (Taiwan)	7825	7787	7571	8137	7986	8526	7781	8144
Kobe	8795	8751	8545	9075	8965	9495	8745	9065
Makassar	7055	7011	6805	7335	7245	7755	7005	7325
Manila	7350	7312	7096	7662	7640	8030	7295	7669
Masinloc	7459	7421	7205	7771	7620	8136	7404	7778
Menado	7524	7486	7270	7836	7685	8201	7469	7843
Moji	8620	8576	8370	8900	8810	9320	8570	8890
Muroran	9272	9234	9018	9584	9433	9949	9217	9591
Nagasaki	8510	8396	8200	8748	8596	9136	8400	8760
Nagoya	8874	8836	8620	9187	9035	9575	8839	9199
Nampo	8656	8618	8402	8968	8827	9333	8601	8975
Osaka	8691	8653	8437	9003	8852	9392	8647	9010
Otaru	9310	9772	9056	9522	9471	9987	9255	9629
Palembang	6334	6296	6080	6646	6495	7011	6279	6653
Pusan	8539	8501	8285	8851	8700	9216	8484	8858
Qingdao	8486	8448	8232	8798	8647	9187	8442	8805
Qinhuangdao	8759	8721	8505	9071	8920	9460	8715	9078
Sabang	5434	5396	5180	5746	5595	6111	5379	5753
Shanghai	8305	8261	8055	8585	8495	9005	8255	8575
Shimonoseki	8561	8523	8307	8873	8732	9238	8506	8880
Singapore	6065	6021	5815	6345	6255	6765	6015	6335
Surabaya	6720	6676	7470	7000	6910	7420	6670	6990
Tanjung Priok	6300	6256	6050	6580	6490	7000	6250	6570
Tokyo	9038	8994	8788	9318	9228	9738	8988	9308
Toyama	9119	9081	8865	9431	9280	9796	9064	9438
Vladivostok	9105	9061	8855	9385	9295	9805	9055	9375
Yokohama	9020	8976	8770	9300	9210	9720	8970	9290

All distances via the Suez Canal except when marked *.

AREA G

AREA B	Alexandria	Algiers	Ancona	Barcelona	Beirut	Bourgas	Brindisi	Cagliari
Adelaide	7685	9020	8713	9120	7750	8432	8469	8770
Albany	6680	8020	7713	8120	6750	7432	7469	7770
Apia	10380	10458	11403	10536*	10443	11125	11162	10808*
Auckland	9545	10880	10573	10980	9610	10292	10329	10630
Banaba	9280	10629	10312	10719	9349	10031	10068	10369
Bluff	8994	10339	10022	10429	9059	9741	9778	10079
Brisbane	8960	10295	9988	10395	9025	9707	9744	10045
Cairns	8104	9449	9132	9539	8169	8851	8888	9189
Cape Leeuwin	6510	7855	7538	7945	6575	7257	7294	7595
Darwin	6960	8305	7988	8395	7025	7707	7744	8045
Esperance	6950	8295	7978	8385	7015	7697	7734	8035
Fremantle	6480	7820	7508	7920	6550	7227	7264	7565
Geelong	8010	9360	9043	9450	8080	8762	8799	9100
Geraldton	6340	7690	7373	7780	6410	7092	7129	7430
Hobart	8180	9495	9188	9595	8225	8907	8944	9245
Honolulu *	10860	9480	10582	9555	11080	10959	10315	9783
Launceston	8130	9465	9158	9565	8195	8877	8914	9215
Lyttleton	9250	10595	10288	11445	9325	10007	10044	10345
Mackay	8444	9789	9472	9879	8509	9191	9228	9529
Madang	7992	9337	9020	9427	8057	8739	8776	9077
Makatea *	10550	9204	10309	9301	10806	10688	10044	9512
Melbourne	8030	9365	9058	9465	8095	8777	8814	9115
Napier	9524	10869	10552	10959	9589	10271	10308	10609
Nauru Island	9125	10469	10152	10559	9189	9871	9908	10209
Nelson	9334	10679	10362	10769	9399	10081	10118	10419
Newcastle (NSW)	8555	9890	9583	9990	8620	9302	9339	9640
New Plymouth	9299	10644	10327	10734	9364	10046	10083	10384
Noumea	9250	10580	10273	10680	9310	9992	10029	10330
Otago Harbour	9058	10390	10083	10490	9120	9802	9839	10140
Papeete *	10638	9285	10390	9362	10887	10767	10123	9591
Portland (Victoria)	7819	9164	8847	9254	7884	8566	8603	8904
Port Hedland	6360	7710	7393	7800	6430	7112	7149	7450
Port Kembla	8437	9782	9465	9872	8502	9184	9221	9522
Port Lincoln	7615	8960	8643	9050	7680	8362	8399	8700
Port Moresby	7934	9279	8962	9369	7999	8681	8718	9019
Port Pirie	7765	9110	8793	9200	7830	8512	8549	8850
Rockhampton	8624	9969	9652	10059	8689	9371	9408	9709
Suva	9837	11120*	10865	11195*	9902	10584	10621	10922
Sydney	8485	9820	9513	9920	8550	9232	9269	9570
Wellington	9375	10710	10403	10810*	9440	10122	10159	10460

All distances via the Suez Canal except when marked *.

AREA G

AREA B	Casablanca	Constantza	Dubrovnik	Durres	Genoa	Gibraltar	Haifa	Iskenderun
Adelaide	9630	8520	8543	8465	8950	9460	7690	7896
Albany	8630	7520	7543	7465	7950	8465	6690	6896
Apia	9904*	11212	11236	11158	10938*	10061*	10384	10589
Auckland	10750*	10380	10403	10325	10810	10865*	9550	9756
Banaba	11054	10118	10142	10064	10548	11054	9290	9495
Bluff	10934	9828	9852	9774	10258	10764	9000	9205
Brisbane	10900	9795	9818	9740	10225	10740	8965	9171
Cairns	10140	8938	8962	8884	9368	9874	8110	8315
Cape Leeuwin	8453	7344	7368	7290	7774	8280	6516	6721
Darwin	8903	7794	7818	7740	8224	8730	6966	7171
Esperance	8886	7784	7808	7730	8214	8720	6956	7161
Fremantle	8425	7315	7338	7260	7745	8260	6490	6691
Geelong	9960	8850	8873	8795	9280	9795	8025	8226
Geraldton	8261	7179	7203	7125	7609	8115	6351	6556
Honolulu *	8920	10775	10423	10336	9915	9040	11065	11055
Hobart	10100	8995	9018	8940	9425	9935	8165	8371
Launceston	10075	8965	8988	8910	9395	9905	8136	8341
Lyttleton	10810*	10095	10118	10040	10525	10930*	9265	9471
Mackay	10380	9278	9302	9224	9708	10214	8450	8655
Madang	9928	8826	8850	8772	9256	9762	7998	8203
Makatea *	8608	10801	10152	10065	9642	8765	10793	10784
Melbourne	9975	8865	8888	8810	9295	9810	8035	8241
Napier	10771*	10358	10382	10304	10788	10769*	9530	9735
Nauru Island	11060	9958	9982	9904	10388	10894	9130	9335
Nelson	10970*	10168	10192	10114	10598	10968*	9340	9545
Newcastle (NSW)	10500	9390	9413	9335	9820	10335	7040	8766
New Plymouth	11027*	10133	10157	10079	10563	11025*	9305	9510
Noumea	11190	10080	10103	10025	10510	11335*	9250	9456
Otago Harbour	10990*	9890	9913	9835	10320	10830	9060	9266
Papeete *	8687	10880	10231	10318	9721	8844	10872	10863
Portland (Victoria)	9755	8653	8677	8599	8083	9589	7825	8030
Port Hedland	8301	7199	7223	7145	7629	8135	6371	6576
Port Kembla	10380	9271	9295	9217	9701	10207	8443	8648
Port Lincoln	9551	8449	8473	8395	8879	9385	7621	7826
Port Moresby	9870	8768	8792	8714	9198	9704	7940	8145
Port Pirie	9701	8599	8623	8545	9029	9535	7771	7976
Rockhampton	10560	9458	9482	9404	9888	10394	8630	8835
Suva	10519*	10671	10695	10617	11101	10676*	9843	10048
Sydney	10425	9320	9345	9265	9750	10260	8965	8696
Wellington	10740*	10210	10233	10155	10645	10860*	9380	9586

All distances via the Suez Canal except when marked *.

AREA G	AREA B	Istanbul	Izmir	Mariupol	Marseilles	Messina	Morphou Bay	Naples	Novorossiysk
Adelaide		8325	8152	8866	9045	8462	7780	8635	8780
Albany		7328	7152	7866	8045	7462	6780	7640	7780
Apia		11019	10845	11559	10772*	11107*	10473	11060*	11473
Auckland		10190	10012	10726	10905	10322	9640	10500	10640
Banaba		9925	9751	10465	10643	10061	9379	10239	10379
Bluff		9635	9461	10175	10353	9771	9089	9949	10089
Brisbane		9600	9427	10141	10320	9737	9055	9910	10055
Cairns		8745	8571	7691	9463	8881	8199	9059	9199
Cape Leeuwin		7151	6977	7691	7869	7287	6605	7465	7605
Darwin		7601	7427	8141	8319	7737	7055	7915	8055
Esperance		7591	7417	8131	8309	7727	7045	7905	8045
Fremantle		7125	6947	7661	7840	7527	6575	7435	7575
Geelong		8660	8482	9196	9375	8792	8110	8970	9110
Geraldton		6986	7812	7526	7704	7122	6440	7300	7440
Hobart		8800	8627	11393	9520	8937	8255	9110	9255
Honolulu *		10880	10720	9341	9750	10082	10946	10020	11261
Launceston		8770	8597	9311	9490	8907	8225	9080	9225
Lyttleton		9900	9727	10441	10620	10037	9355	10210	10355
Mackay		9085	8911	9625	9803	9221	8539	9399	9539
Madang		8633	8459	9173	9351	8769	8087	8947	9087
Makatea *		10584	10449	11122	9477	9811	10675	9764	11062
Melbourne		8670	8497	9211	9390	8807	8125	8980	9125
Napier		10165	9991	10705	10883	10301	9619	10479	10619
Nauru Island		9765	9591	10305	10483	9901	9219	10079	10219
Nelson		9975	9801	10515	10693	10111	9429	10289	10429
Newcastle (NSW)		9200	9022	9736	9915	9332	8650	9505	9650
New Plymouth		9940	9766	10480	10658	10076	9394	10254	10394
Noumea		9890	9712	10426	10605	10022	9340	10200	10340
Otago Harbour		9695	9522	10236	10415	9832	9150	10005	10150
Papeete		10663*	10528	11201	9555*	9890*	10754*	9843*	11069
Portland (Victoria)		8469	8286	9000	9178	8596	7914	8774	8914
Port Hedland		7006	6832	7546	7724	7142	6460	7320	7460
Port Kembla		9078	8904	9618	9796	9214	8532	9392	9532
Port Lincoln		8256	8085	8796	8974	8392	7710	8570	8710
Port Moresby		8575	8401	9115	9293	8711	8029	8889	9029
Port Pirie		8406	8232	8946	8124	8542	7860	8720	8860
Rockhampton		9265	9091	7805	9983	9401	8719	9575	9719
Suva		10578	10304	11018	11196	10614	9932	10792	10932
Sydney		9125	8952	9666	9845	9262	8580	9435	9580
Wellington		10015	9842	10556	10734	10152	9470	10330	10470

All distances via the Suez Canal except when marked *.

AREA G

AREA B	Odessa	Palermo	Piraeus	Port Said	Poti	Rijeka	Sfax	Siracusa
Adelaide	8670	8579	8110	7520	8895	8790	8640	8420
Albany	7670	7579	7110	6520	7895	7790	7640	7420
Apia	11363	10996*	10810	10213	11588	11482	11141*	11113
Auckland	10530	10439	9970	9380	10755	10650	10500	10280
Banaba	10268	10178	9716	9119	10508	10388	10234	10019
Bluff	9979	9888	9426	8829	10204	10098	9949	9729
Brisbane	9945	9854	9385	8795	10170	10065	9915	9695
Cairns	9088	8998	8536	7939	9328	9208	9054	8839
Cape Leeuwin	7495	7404	6942	6345	7720	7614	7465	7245
Darwin	7845	7854	7392	6795	8170	8064	7915	7695
Esperance	7934	7844	7382	6785	9174	8054	7900	7685
Fremantle	7470	7374	6905	6315	7695	7585	7435	7215
Geelong	9000	8909	8440	7850	9225	9120	8970	8750
Geraldton	7329	7239	6777	6180	7569	7449	7295	7080
Honolulu	9145	9971*	10560*	10906*	11450*	10705*	10116*	10136*
Hobart	11225	9054	8585	7995	9370	9265	9115	8895
Launceston	9115	9024	8555	7965	9340	9235	9085	8865
Lyttleton	10245	10154	9685	9095	10470	10365	10215	9995
Mackay	9428	9338	8876	8279	9668	9548	9394	9179
Madang	8976	8886	8424	7827	9216	9096	8942	8727
Makatea *	10951	9700	10287	10700	11165	10430	9845	9865
Melbourne	9015	8924	8455	7865	9240	9135	8985	8765
Napier	10508	10418	9956	9359	10748	10628	10474	10259
Nauru Island	10108	10018	9556	8959	10348	10228	10074	9859
Nelson	10318	10228	9766	9169	10558	10538	10284	10069
Newcastle (NSW)	9540	9449	8980	8390	9765	9660	9510	9290
New Plymouth	10283	10193	9731	9134	10523	10403	10249	10034
Noumea	10230	10139	9670	9080	10455	10350	10200	9980
Otago Harbour	10040	9949	9480	8890	10265	10160	10010	9790
Papeete	10959	9779*	10366*	10788*	11184	10509*	9924*	9944*
Portland (Victoria)	8803	8713	8251	7654	8043	8923	8769	8554
Port Hedland	7349	7259	6797	6200	7589	7469	7315	7100
Port Kembla	9422	9331	8869	8272	9647	9541	9392	9172
Port Lincoln	8599	8509	8047	7450	8839	8719	8565	8350
Port Moresby	8918	8828	8366	7769	9158	9038	8884	8669
Port Pirie	8749	8659	8197	7600	8989	8869	8715	8500
Rockhampton	9608	9518	9056	8459	9848	9728	9574	9359
Suva	10822	10731	10269	9672	11047	10941	10792	10572
Sydney	9470	9379	8910	8320	9695	9590	9440	9220
Wellington	11360	10269	9800	9210	11585	10480	10330	10110

All distances via the Suez Canal except when marked *.

AREA G

AREA B	Tarabulus (Libya)	Taranto	Thessaloniki	Trieste	Tunis	Valencia	Valletta	Venice
Adelaide	8514	8460	8270	8825	8675	9214	8470	8832
Albany	7514	7460	7270	7830	7680	8220	7470	7835
Apia	11200	11153	10953	11519	10880*	10474*	11068*	11526
Auckland	10374	10320	10135	10690	10540	11080	10335	10695
Banaba	10113	10059	9859	10425	10274	10790	10058	10432
Bluff	9823	9769	9565	10135	9984	10480	9768	10142
Brisbane	9789	9735	9545	10100	9950	10490	9745	10110
Cairns	8933	8879	8679	7651	9094	9610	8878	7658
Cape Leeuwin	7339	7285	7085	7651	7500	8016	7284	7658
Darwin	7789	7735	7535	8101	7950	8466	7734	8108
Esperance	7779	7725	7525	8091	7940	8456	7724	8098
Fremantle	7309	7255	7070	7625	7470	8010	7265	7630
Geelong	8844	8790	8600	9160	9005	9545	8800	9165
Geraldton	7174	7120	6820	7486	7335	7851	7119	7493
Honolulu *	10174	10266	10770	10750	9860	9450	10045	10755
Hobart	8989	8935	8745	9300	9150	9690	8945	9305
Launceston	8959	8905	8715	9270	9120	9660	8915	9280
Lyttleton	10089	10035	9845	10402	10250	10790	10045	10410
Mackay	9273	9219	9019	9585	9434	9950	9218	9592
Madang	8821	8767	8567	9133	8982	9498	8766	9140
Makatea *	9903	9995	10478	10475	9584	9178	9772	10482
Melbourne	8859	8805	8615	9170	9020	9560	8615	9180
Napier	10353	10299	10099	10665	10514	11030	10298	10672
Nauru Island	9953	9899	9699	10265	10114	10630	9898	10272
Nelson	10163	10109	9808	10475	10324	10840	10108	10482
Newcastle (NSW)	9384	9330	9140	9700	9545	10085	9340	9705
New Plymouth	10129	10074	9874	10440	10289	10805	10073	10447
Noumea	10074	10020	9830	10390	10240	10780	10035	10395
Otago Harbour	9884	9830	9640	10195	10045	10585	9840	10200
Papeete *	9982	10074*	10577	10554	9663	9257	9851	10561
Portland (Victoria)	8648	8594	8394	8960	8809	9325	8593	8967
Port Hedland	7194	7140	6940	7506	7355	7871	7139	7513
Port Kembla	9266	9212	9012	9578	9427	9943	9211	9585
Port Lincoln	8444	8390	8190	8756	8605	9121	8389	8763
Port Moresby	8763	8709	8509	9075	8924	9440	8708	9083
Port Pirie	8594	8540	8340	8906	8755	9271	8539	8913
Rockhampton	9453	9399	9199	9765	9614	10130	9398	9772
Suva	10666	10612	10412	10978	10827	11089*	10611	10985
Sydney	9314	9260	9070	9625	9475	10015	9270	9635
Wellington	9204	10150	9960	10515	10365	10905	10160	10525

All distances via the Panama Canal except where otherwise indicated.

AREA H

AREA B	Alexandria	Algiers	Ancona	Barcelona	Beirut	Bourgas	Brindisi	Cagliari
Antofagasta	8315	6930	8039	7010	8535	8414	7774	7242
Arica	8100	6715	7819	6790	8315	8198	7554	7022
Astoria	9960	8575	9679	8650	10177	10058	9415	8882
Balbao	6175	4795	5899	4870	6395	6278	5634	5102
Buenaventura	6530	5145	6250	5220	6745	6628	5984	5452
Cabo Blanco	6929	5545	6650	5632	7147	7029	6385	5853
Caldera	8476	7092	8197	7179	8694	8576	7932	7400
Callao	7520	6140	7244	6215	7740	7623	6979	6447
Cape Horn (direct)	8073	6689	7794	6776	8291	8173	7529	6997
Chimbote	7332	5948	7053	6035	7550	7432	6788	6256
Coos Bay	9775	8390	9494	8470	9995	9873	9229	8697
Corinto	6858	5474	6579	5561	7076	6958	6314	5782
Eureka	9635	8250	9354	8330	9850	9733	9089	8557
Guayaquil	7000	5615	6724	5695	7220	7103	6459	5927
Guaymas	8544	7160	8265	7427	8762	8644	7980	7468
Honolulu	10860	9480	10582	9555	11080	10959	10315	9783
Iquique	8165	6780	7884	6855	8380	8263	7619	7087
Los Angeles	9090	7705	8809	7780	9310	9188	8545	8012
Manzanillo (Mex)	7895	6545	7614	6585	8110	7993	7350	6817
Mazatlan	8180	6800	7903	6875	8400	8282	7638	7106
Nanaimo	10215	8830	9939	8910	10435	10318	9674	9142
New Westminster	10223	8839	9948	8926	10443	10323	9679	9147
Portland (Oreg)	10045	8660	9764	8740	10265	10143	9499	8967
Port Alberni	10168	8784	9889	8871	10386	10268	9624	9092
Port Isabel	8823	7439	8544	7526	9041	8923	8279	7747
Port Moody	10224	8839	9943	8919	10444	10322	9678	9146
Prince Rupert	10477	9093	10198	9180	10695	10577	9933	9401
Puerto Montt M	9135	7751	8856	7838	9353	9235	8591	8059
Puntarenas (CR)	6645	5261	6366	5348	6863	6745	6101	5569
Punta Arenas (Ch) M	8175	6791	7896	6878	8398	8275	7631	7097
Salina Cruz	7344	5960	7065	6047	7562	7444	6800	6268
San Francisco	9420	8040	9144	8115	9640	9523	8879	8347
San Jose	7060	5676	6781	5763	7278	7160	6516	5984
Seattle	10195	8815	9919	8890	10415	10298	9654	9122
Tacoma	10230	8845	9949	8920	10445	10328	9684	9152
Talcahuano	8979	7595	8700	7682	9197	9079	8435	7903
Tocopilla	8245	6860	7964	6935	8460	8343	7699	7167
Valparaiso	8790	7410	8514	7485	9010	8893	8249	7717
Vancouver (BC)	10215	8830	9934	8910	10435	10313	9669	9137
Victoria (Vanc Is)	10150	8765	9869	8840	10365	10248	9604	9072

All distances via the Panama Canal except where otherwise indicated.

AREA H

AREA B	Casablanca	Constantza	Dubrovnik	Durres	Genoa	Gibraltar	Haifa	Iskenderun
Antofagasta	6375	8530	7882	7795	7370	6495	8520	8511
Arica	6160	8310	7662	7575	7150	6275	8300	8291
Astoria	8020	10170	9522	9435	9015	8125	10165	10156
Balbao	4240	6390	5742	5655	5230	4390	6380	6371
Buenaventura	4590	6740	6090	6003	5580	4705	6735	6726
Cabo Blanco	4091	7142	6493	6406	5983	5106	7134	7125
Caldera	6538	8689	8040	7953	7530	6653	8681	8672
Callao	5585	7735	7087	7000	6575	5700	7725	7716
Cape Horn (direct)	6135	8286	7637	7550	7127	6387	8278	8269
Chimbote	5394	7545	6896	6809	6386	5509	7537	7528
Coos Bay	7835	9690	9337	9250	8830	7950	9980	9971
Corinto	4920	7071	6422	6335	5912	5035	7063	7054
Eureka	7695	9545	9197	9110	8690	7810	9840	9831
Guayaquil	5060	6915	6567	6480	6055	5180	7205	7196
Guaymas	6606	8757	8108	8021	7598	6721	8749	8740
Honolulu	8920	10775	10423	10336	9915	9040	11065	11055
Iquique	6225	8075	7727	7640	7215	6340	8370	8361
Los Angeles	7150	9000	8652	8565	8145	7265	9295	9286
Manzanillo (Mex)	5955	7805	7457	7370	6950	6070	8100	8091
Mazatlan	6245	8095	7746	7659	7236	6359	8390	8381
Nanaimo	8280	10130	9782	9695	9270	8395	10420	10411
New Westminster	8285	10436	9787	9700	9277	8400	10428	10419
Portland (Oreg)	8105	9960	9607	9520	9100	8220	10250	10241
Port Alberni	8230	10381	9732	9645	9222	8345	10371	10362
Port Isabel	6885	9036	8387	8300	7877	7000	9028	9019
Port Moody	8284	10139	9786	9699	9279	8399	10429	10420
Prince Rupert	8539	10690	10041	9954	9531	8654	10682	10673
Puerto Montt M	7162	9348	8699	8612	8189	7312	9340	9331
Puntarenas (CR)	4707	6858	6209	6122	5699	4822	6850	6841
Punta Arenas (Ch) M	6202	8388	7739	7652	7229	6352	8380	8371
Salina Cruz	5406	7557	6908	6821	6398	5521	7549	7540
San Francisco	7480	9335	8987	8900	8475	7667	9625	9616
San Jose	5122	7273	6624	6537	6114	5237	7265	7256
Seattle	8260	10110	9762	9675	9250	8375	10400	10391
Tacoma	8290	10140	9792	9705	9280	8405	10435	10426
Talcahuano	7041	9192	8543	8456	8033	7156	9184	9175
Tocopilla	6305	8155	7807	7720	7300	6420	8500	8491
Valparaiso	6855	8705	8357	8270	7845	6970	8995	8986
Vancouver (BC)	8275	10130	9777	9690	9270	8390	10420	10411
Victoria (Vanc Is)	8210	10060	9712	9625	9202	8325	10355	10346

All distances via the Panama Canal except where otherwise indicated.

AREA H

AREA B	Istanbul	Izmir	Mariupol	Marseilles	Messina	Morphou Bay	Naples	Novorossiysk
Antofagasta	8335	8179	8852	7205	7540	8405	7475	8792
Arica	8115	7959	8632	6985	7311	8185	7255	8572
Astoria	9980	9819	10492	8850	9181	10045	9120	10432
Balbao	6200	6040	6712	5065	5400	6265	5335	6652
Buenaventura	6550	6389	7060	5415	5751	6615	5685	7000
Cabo Blanco	6925	6690	7463	5818	6152	7016	6105	7403
Caldera	8472	8337	9010	7365	7699	8563	7652	8950
Callao	7540	7384	8057	6410	6746	7610	6680	7997
Cape Horn (direct)	8230	7934	8607	6962	7296	8160	7249	8547
Chimbote	7328	7193	7866	6221	6555	7419	6508	7806
Coos Bay	9795	9634	10307	8665	8996	9860	8935	10247
Corinto	6854	6719	7392	5747	6081	6945	6034	7332
Eureka	9655	9495	10167	8525	8856	9720	8795	10107
Guayaquil	7020	6864	7537	5890	6226	7090	6160	7477
Guaymas	8540	8405	9078	7433	7767	8631	7720	9018
Honolulu	10880	10720	11393	9750	10082	10946	10020	11261
Iquique	8185	8025	8697	7050	7386	8250	7320	8637
Los Angeles	9110	8950	9622	7980	8311	9175	8248	9562
Manzanillo (Mex)	7915	7754	8425	6785	7116	7980	7055	8365
Mazatlan	8200	8043	8716	7070	7505	8269	7341	8656
Nanaimo	10235	10079	10752	9105	9441	10305	9375	10692
New Westminster	10219	10084	10757	9112	9446	10310	9399	10697
Portland (Oreg)	10065	9904	10577	8935	9266	10130	9205	10517
Port Alberni	10264	10029	10702	9057	9391	10255	9344	10642
Port Isabel	8819	8684	9357	7712	8046	8910	7999	9297
Port Moody	10244	10083	10756	9114	9444	10309	9384	10696
Prince Rupert	10473	10338	11011	9366	9700	10564	9653	10591
Puerto Montt M	9131	8996	9669	8024	8358	9222	8311	9609
Puntarenas (CR)	6641	6506	7179	5534	5868	6732	5821	7119
Punta Arenas (Ch) M	8171	8036	8710	7064	7398	8262	7351	8649
Salina Cruz	7340	7205	7878	6233	6567	7431	6520	7818
San Francisco	9419	9284	9957	8312	8646	9510	8599	9897
San Jose	7056	6921	7594	5949	6283	7147	6236	7534
Seattle	10215	10059	10732	9085	9420	10285	9355	10672
Tacoma	10250	10089	10762	9115	9450	10315	9385	10702
Talcahuano	8975	8840	9513	7868	8202	9066	8155	9453
Tocopilla	8265	8104	8777	7135	7466	8330	7405	8717
Valparaiso	8810	8654	9327	7680	8016	8880	7950	9267
Vancouver (BC)	10235	10074	10747	9105	9435	10300	9375	10687
Victoria (Vanc Is)	10165	10009	10682	10035	9371	10235	9305	10622

All distances via the Panama Canal except where otherwise indicated.

AREA H

AREA B	Odessa	Palermo	Piraeus	Port Said	Poti	Rijeka	Sfax	Siracusa
Antofagasta	8680	7430	8015	8435	8895	8160	7575	7595
Arica	8460	7210	7795	8215	8675	7940	7355	7375
Astoria	10320	9070	9660	10080	10535	9800	9215	9235
Balbao	6540	5290	5875	6295	6755	6020	5435	5455
Buenaventura	6890	5640	6225	6645	7103	6370	5785	5805
Cabo Blanco	7291	6041	6628	7041	7506	6771	6186	6206
Caldera	8842	7588	8175	8588	9053	8318	7733	7753
Callao	7885	6635	7720	7640	8100	7365	6780	6800
Cape Horn (direct)	8435	7185	7772	8322	8650	7915	7330	7350
Chimbote	7694	6444	7031	7444	7909	7174	6589	6609
Coos Bay	10140	8885	9475	9895	10350	9615	9030	9050
Corinto	7220	5970	6557	6970	7435	6700	6115	6135
Eureka	10005	8745	9335	9755	10210	9475	8890	8910
Guayaquil	7365	6115	6700	7120	7580	6845	6260	6280
Guaymas	8906	7656	8243	8656	9121	8386	7801	7821
Honolulu	11225	9971	10560	10906	11450	10705	10116	10136
Iquique	8525	7275	7862	8280	8740	8005	7420	7440
Los Angeles	9450	8200	8790	9210	9665	8930	8345	8365
Manzanillo (Mex)	8253	7005	7595	8015	8468	7735	7150	7170
Mazatlan	8545	7294	7880	8300	8759	8025	7439	7459
Nanaimo	10580	9330	9915	10335	10795	10060	9475	9495
New Westminster	10585	9335	9922	10340	10800	10065	9480	9500
Portland (Oreg)	10405	9155	9745	10165	10620	9885	9300	9320
Port Alberni	10530	9280	9867	10280	10745	10010	9425	9445
Port Isabel	9185	7935	8522	8935	9400	8665	8080	8100
Port Moody	10584	9334	9924	10344	10799	10064	9479	9499
Prince Rupert	10839	9589	10176	10589	11054	10319	9734	9754
Puerto Montt M	9497	8247	8834	9247	9712	8977	8392	8412
Puntarenas (CR)	7007	5757	6344	6757	7222	6487	5902	5922
Punta Arenas (Ch) M	8537	7287	7874	8287	8753	8017	7432	7452
Salina Cruz	7706	6456	7043	7456	7921	7186	6601	6621
San Francisco	9785	8535	9120	9540	10000	9265	8680	8700
San Jose	7422	6172	6759	7172	7637	6902	6317	6337
Seattle	10560	9310	9895	10315	10775	10040	9455	9475
Tacoma	10590	9340	9925	10345	10805	10070	9485	9505
Talcahuano	9341	8091	8678	9091	9556	8821	8236	8256
Tocopilla	8605	7355	7945	8365	8820	8085	7500	7520
Valparaiso	9155	7905	8490	8910	9370	8635	8050	8070
Vancouver (BC)	10575	9325	9915	10335	10790	10055	9470	9490
Victoria (Vanc Is)	10510	9260	9845	10265	10725	9990	9405	9425

All distances via the Panama Canal except where otherwise indicated.

AREA H

AREA B	Tarabulus (Libya)	Taranto	Thessaloniki	Trieste	Tunis	Valencia	Valletta	Venice
Antofagasta	7633	7725	8208	8205	7310	6905	7500	8210
Arica	7413	7505	7988	7985	7095	6685	7280	7990
Astoria	9273	9365	9848	9845	8955	8550	9145	9855
Balbao	5493	5585	6068	6065	5175	4765	5360	6070
Buenaventura	5843	5935	6418	6415	5525	5120	5710	6420
Cabo Blanco	6244	6336	6819	6816	5925	5519	6113	6823
Caldera	7791	7883	8366	8363	7472	7066	7660	8370
Callao	6838	6930	7413	7410	6520	6110	6705	7415
Cape Horn (direct)	7388	7480	7963	7960	7069	6663	7394	7967
Chimbote	6647	6739	7222	7219	6328	5922	6512	7226
Coos Bay	9088	9180	9663	9660	8770	8365	8960	9670
Corinto	6173	6265	6748	6745	5854	5448	6038	6752
Eureka	8948	9040	9523	9520	8630	8225	8820	9530
Guayaquil	6318	6410	6893	6890	5995	5590	6185	6895
Guaymas	7859	7951	8434	8431	7540	7134	7724	8438
Honolulu	10174	10266	10770	10750	9860	9450	10045	10755
Iquique	7478	7570	8053	8050	7160	6755	7345	8055
Los Angeles	8403	8495	8978	8975	8085	7680	8275	8985
Manzanillo (Mex)	7208	7300	7783	7780	6890	6485	7080	7790
Mazatlan	7497	7589	8072	8070	7180	6770	7365	8075
Nanaimo	9533	9625	10108	10105	9210	8808	9400	10110
New Westminster	9538	9630	10113	10110	9219	8813	9405	10117
Portland (Oreg)	9358	9450	9933	9930	9040	8635	9230	9940
Port Alberni	9483	9575	10058	10055	9164	8758	9348	10062
Port Isabel	8138	8230	8713	8710	7819	7413	8003	8717
Port Moody	9537	9629	10112	10109	9219	8814	9409	10124
Prince Rupert	9792	9884	10367	10364	9473	9067	9657	10371
Puerto Montt M	8450	8542	9025	9022	8131	7725	8315	9029
Puntarenas (CR)	5960	6052	6535	6532	5641	5235	5825	6539
Punta Arenas (Ch) M	7490	7582	8065	8062	7171	6765	7355	8069
Salina Cruz	6659	6751	7234	7231	6340	5934	6524	7238
San Francisco	8738	8830	9313	9310	8415	8010	8605	9315
San Jose	6375	6467	6950	6947	6056	5650	6240	6954
Seattle	9513	9605	10085	10084	9195	8785	9380	10090
Tacoma	9543	9635	10118	10115	9225	8820	9410	10120
Talcahuano	8294	8386	8869	8866	7975	7569	8159	8873
Tocopilla	7558	7650	8133	8130	7240	6835	9430	8140
Valparaiso	8108	8200	8683	8680	7790	7380	7975	8685
Vancouver (BC)	9528	9620	10103	10100	9210	8805	9400	10115
Victoria (Vanc Is)	9464	9555	10038	10035	9145	8740	9330	10040

AREA B

AREA B	Algiers	Annaba	Batumi	Beirut	Bourgas	Brindisi	Civitavecchia	Durres
Alexandria	1388	1164	1308	340	848	825	1126	856
Algiers	–	241	1970	1594	1516	874	525	905
Ancona	1139	921	1637	1266	1183	270	824	295
Baniyas	1607	1383	1391	85	931	1009	1322	1040
Barcelona	279	377	2055	1673	1595	934	439	965
Beirut	1594	1370	1396	–	942	1000	1314	1031
Cartagena	203	427	2163	1787	1703	1063	651	1094
Casablanca	599	826	2573	2191	2119	1469	1069	1500
Catania	644	420	1390	1048	930	277	348	308
Constantza	1580	1357	588	1006	126	982	1295	1013
Genoa	528	450	1871	1500	1411	745	190	776
Gibraltar	412	639	2386	2004	1926	1282	882	1313
Iskenderun	1612	1388	1396	172	942	1014	1327	1044
Istanbul	1384	1161	586	810	126	786	1099	817
La Spezia	533	450	1835	1464	1375	709	154	740
Latakia	1592	1368	1376	100	916	994	1307	1025
Limassol	1477	1253	1278	132	818	885	1196	916
Mariupol	1947	1724	440	1373	492	1349	1662	1380
Marseilles	410	410	1964	1595	1510	838	312	869
Oran	202	437	2166	1790	1706	1070	700	1101
Patras	916	692	1192	821	732	239	606	270
Piraeus	1070	845	938	645	480	475	785	506
Port Said	1503	1280	1372	228	912	928	1233	959
Poti	1987	1764	31	1413	629	1389	1702	1420
Split	1080	862	1577	1207	1117	193	765	203
Trieste	1240	1022	1738	1367	1284	372	925	408
Tuapse	1875	1652	185	1301	518	1277	1590	1308
Tunis	384	161	1628	1252	1174	555	323	586
Valletta	575	352	1402	1029	942	365	455	407
Venice	1256	1038	1755	1383	1295	387	941	418

AREA B

AREA B	Famagusta	Galatz	Haifa	Marseilles	Melilla	Messina	Naples	Novorossiysk
Alexandria	332	1042	292	1405	1689	826	1001	1178
Algiers	1544	1704	1589	410	304	615	579	1840
Ancona	1216	1371	1262	1103	1440	524	700	1507
Baniyas	96	1125	154	1601	1908	1022	1197	1261
Barcelona	1629	1789	1674	185	442	675	555	1925
Beirut	107	1130	72	1595	1895	1014	1189	1266
Cartagena	1737	1897	1782	458	166	802	753	2033
Casablanca	2141	2207	2187	877	324	1210	1166	2443
Catania	984	1124	1014	627	945	48	223	1260
Constantza	955	143	1012	1574	1881	995	1170	402
Genoa	1449	1605	1496	201	787	486	334	1741
Gibraltar	1954	2120	2000	690	137	1023	979	2256
Iskenderun	140	1130	240	1606	1913	1027	1202	1266
Istanbul	759	320	816	1378	1685	799	974	456
La Spezia	1413	1569	1460	228	803	450	298	1705
Latakia	92	1110	169	1586	1893	1007	1182	1246
Limassol	72	1012	144	1475	1778	896	1071	1148
Mariupol	1322	533	1379	1941	2248	1362	1537	205
Marseilles	1542	1698	1589	–	618	579	457	1834
Oran	1740	1900	1785	534	120	810	772	2036
Patras	770	926	817	885	1217	306	481	1062
Piraeus	590	670	640	1063	1370	485	660	806
Port Said	255	1106	169	1512	1804	933	1108	1242
Poti	1362	626	1419	1981	2288	1402	1577	227
Split	1156	1311	1202	1044	1381	465	640	1447
Trieste	1317	1472	1363	1204	1541	625	800	1608
Tuapse	1250	488	1307	1869	2176	1290	1465	63
Tunis	1202	1362	1247	472	685	296	309	1498
Valletta	994	1136	1032	650	878	153	331	1272
Venice	1333	1489	1379	1220	1558	641	816	1625

AREA B

AREA B	Odessa	Rijeka	Savona-Vado	Sfax	Sidon	Tarragona	Torrevieja	Valencia	Valletta
Alexandria	1064	1151	1317	988	318	1507	1560	1554	820
Algiers	1726	1200	511	595	1586	270	192	226	575
Ancona	1393	110	1015	838	1258	1232	1304	1287	630
Baniyas	1147	1335	1513	1255	110	1726	1779	1773	1053
Barcelona	1811	1260	338	691	1665	52	202	164	673
Beirut	1152	1327	1505	1235	27	1713	1766	1760	1029
Cartagena	1919	1387	601	788	1779	249	43	155	771
Casablanca	2329	1795	1019	1192	2183	668	462	574	1138
Catania	1146	603	539	317	1038	763	817	810	114
Constantza	173	1308	1486	1245	998	1699	1752	1746	1007
Genoa	1627	1071	22	652	1492	399	576	510	586
Gibraltar	2142	1608	832	1005	1996	481	275	387	1008
Iskenderun	1152	1340	1518	1260	196	1731	1784	1778	1059
Istanbul	342	1112	1290	1049	802	1503	1556	1550	811
La Spezia	1591	1035	67	626	1456	426	603	537	556
Latakia	1132	1320	1498	1240	119	1711	1764	1758	1055
Limassol	1034	1210	1387	1116	132	1596	1649	1643	914
Mariupol	450	1675	1853	1612	1365	2066	2119	2114	1356
Marseilles	1720	1164	187	674	1587	232	423	345	650
Oran	1922	1396	670	791	1782	333	136	239	778
Patras	948	564	797	586	813	1014	1085	1069	373
Piraeus	692	798	975	734	633	1188	1241	1235	539
Port Said	1122	1254	1424	1115	204	1622	1675	1669	925
Poti	550	1715	1893	1652	1405	2106	2159	2153	1431
Split	1333	165	956	778	1199	1173	1244	1228	589
Trieste	1494	110	1116	939	1359	1333	1402	1388	727
Tuapse	415	1603	1781	1540	1293	1994	2047	2041	1315
Tunis	1384	881	472	252	1244	519	560	543	238
Valletta	1158	691	604	233	1052	698	750	749	–
Venice	1511	129	1132	955	1375	1349	1421	1404	746

Area C

Distances between principal ports on the East Coast of North America and Canada (including the Great Lakes and St Lawrence Seaway), the US Gulf and Central America (including the Gulf of Mexico and the Caribbean Sea).

and

Area D The East Coast of South America, the Atlantic Islands, and East and West Africa.

Area E The Red Sea, The Gulf, the Indian Ocean and the Bay of Bengal.

Area F Malaysia, Indonesia, South East Asia, the China Sea and Japan.

Area G Australasia, New Guinea and the Pacific Islands (via the Panama Canal).

Area H The West Coast of North and South America.

Area C Other ports on the East Coast of North America and Canada, the US Gulf and Central America (including the Caribbean Sea).

AREA C

Reed's Marine Distance Tables

WEST ATLANTIC, HUDSON BAY TO CARIBBEAN

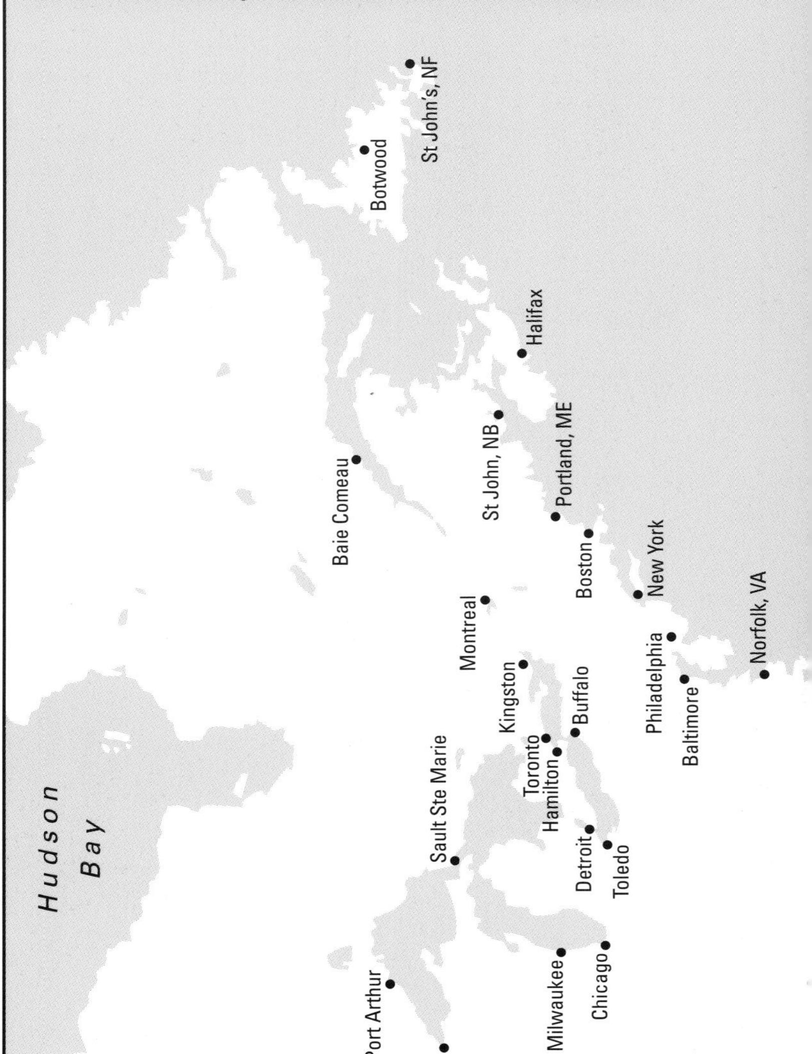

Modified Gall Projec

AREA C

Reed's Marine Distance Tables

WEST ATLANTIC, HUDSON BAY TO CARIBBEAN

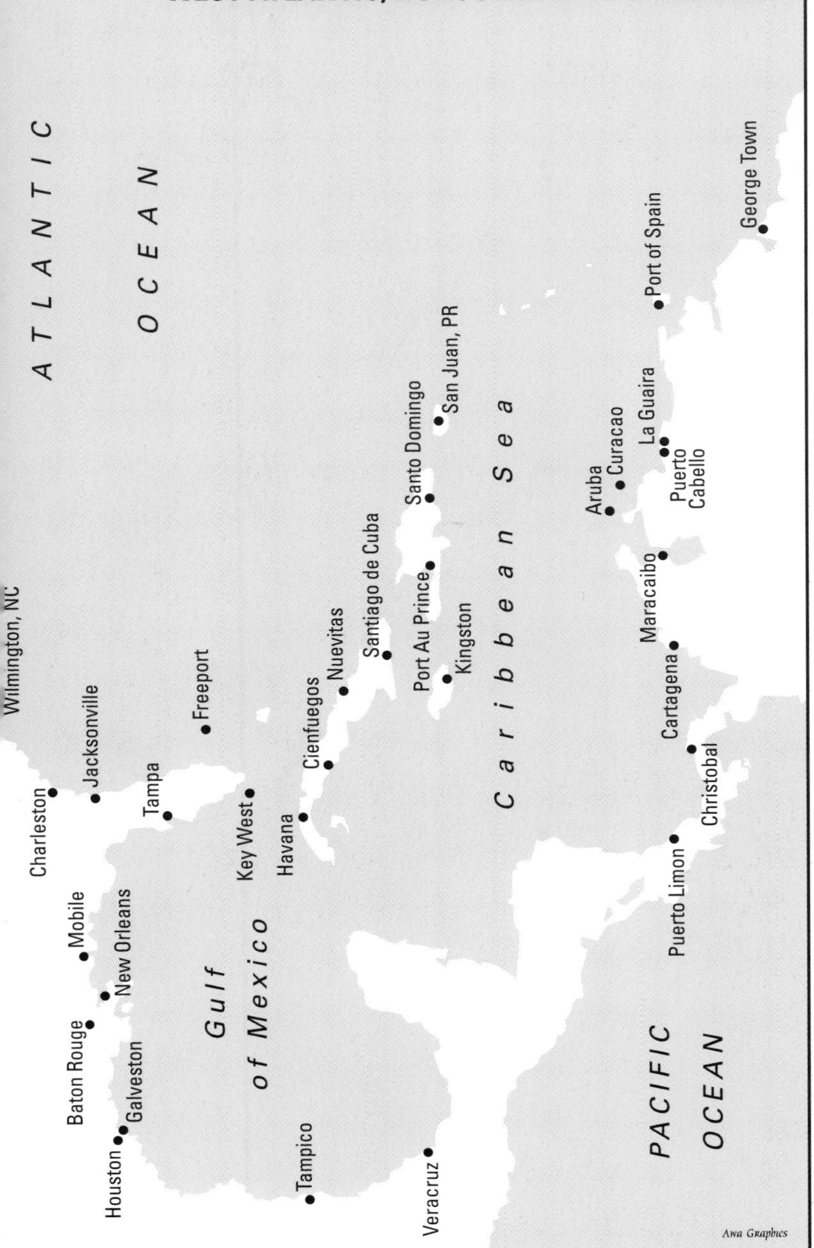

^Special section on page 214 devoted to distances within the Plate, Parana and Uruguay rivers.

AREA D

AREA C	Baie Comeau	Baltimore	Boston	Cartagena (Colombia)	Charleston	Churchill	Cienfuegos	Cristobal
Azores (St Michaels)	1955	2590	2090	3170	2685	2852	3073	3400
Bahia Blanca	6296	6195	6100	5259	6065	7789	5768	5734
Beira C	8260	8390	8176	7727	8292	9447	8081	7935
Belem	3358	2953	2970	2172	2786	4755	2527	2309
Buenos Aires (^)	6124	5979	5880	5154	5845	7397	5526	5390
Cape Horn	7188	6007	6914	6207	6868	8608	6595	6442
Cape Town	6770	6900	6707	6207	6830	7971	6580	6465
Conakry	3603	3801	3606	3724	3904	4769	4005	3951
Dakar	3210	3526	3221	3431	3557	4399	3540	3694
Dar es Salaam	8026†	8600†	8170†	8564C	8725†	8700†	9244†	8772C
Diego Suarez	8074†	8648†	8218†	8567C	8773†	8800†	9292†	8825C
Douala	5149	5422	5134	5169	5423	6353	5460	5404
Durban	7567C	7740C	7483C	7034	7599	8755C	7388	7242C
East London C	7314	7455	7230	6781	7346	8499	7135	6989
Lagos	4867	5063	4774	4801	5065	5982	5174	5050
Las Palmas	2730	3265	2765	3557	3360	3729	3685	3750
Lobito	5643	5958	5693	5577	5925	6400	6059	5805
Luanda	5575	5850	5563	5522	5853	6332	5863	5757
Madeira	2490	3025	2525	3542	3235	3463	3574	3735
Maputo C	7863	8040	7779	7330	7895	9049	7684	7538C
Mauritius	9005C	9135C	8942C	8442C	9065C	9293†	8815C	8700C
Mogadiscio †	7236	7891	7449	8505	8015	8063	8527	8731
Mombasa	7846†	8420†	7990†	8744C	8545†	8561†	9064†	8952C
Monrovia	3911	4225	3908	3936	4207	5077	4308	4266
Montevideo	6010	5855	5760	4836	5725	7380	5547	5336
Mozambique I	8740C	8870C	8656C	8207C	8772C	9082†	8561C	8415C
Porto Alegre	5850	5669	5580	4870	5530	7270	5259	5104
Port Elizabeth C	7193	7311	7109	6660	7225	8377	7014	6868
Port Harcourt	5019	5293	5005	5040	5294	6223	5331	5276
Recife	3951	3772	3669	2869	3649	5939	3414	3217
Reunion Island	8880C	9015C	8817C	8317C	8940C	9315†	8680C	8575C
Rio de Janeiro	5023	4845	4750	4139	4715	6412	4490	4289
Salvador	4342	4163	4060	3266	4040	5726	3770	3696
Sao Vicente Island	2850	3150	2845	2993	3100	4097	3233	3225
Santos	5180	5020	4925	4162	4890	6599	4675	4565
Takoradi	4447	4761	4444	4472	4743	5664	4844	4802
Tema	4650	4945	4606	4400	4870	5762	4870	4899
Tramandai	5723	5545	5450	4839	5415	7120	5190	4989
Vitoria (Brazil)	4773	4595	4500	3889	4465	6162	4240	4039
Walvis Bay	6142	6325	6131	5802	6356	7354	6324	6017

^Special section on page 214 devoted to distances within the Plate, Parana and Uruguay rivers.

AREA D

AREA C	Curacao	Duluth-Superior	Freeport (Bahamas)	Galveston	Georgetown (Guyana)	Halifax	Havana	Jacksonville
Azores (St Michaels)	2782	3475	2719	3925	2565	1770	3057	2865
Bahia Blanca	4918	7916	5829	6669	4237	6010	5945	6127
Beira C	7191	9780	7981	8771	6480	8000	8220	8316
Belem	1623	4878	2429	3363	896	3025	2654	2690
Buenos Aires (^)	4639	7944	5525	6421	3954	5790	5725	5808
Cape Horn	5752	8708	6554	7476	5033	6809	6734	6880
Cape Town	5811	8290	6681	7472	4996	6510	6724	6854
Conakry	3276	5123	3748	4820	2650	3349	4083	4000
Dakar	3050	4730	3336	4452	2450	2956	3716	3650
Dar es Salaam	8028C	9546†	8770†	9860†	7317C	7785†	9154†	8877†
Diego Suarez	8171C	9594†	8818†	9908†	7456C	7833†	9202†	8925†
Douala	4717	6670	5262	6280	4074	4881	5538	5505
Durban	6498	9087	7288	8077	5787	7350	7527	7623
East London C	6245	8834	7035	7825	5534	7065	7274	7370
Lagos	4359	6387	4793	5940	3642	4426	5083	4932
Las Palmas	3098	4250	3372	4365	2740	2445	3738	3480
Lobito	5119	7163	5856	6793	4413	5294	6044	6024
Luanda	5069	7100	5684	6681	4386	5336	5941	5934
Madeira	3118	4010	3166	4240	2771	2205	3564	3255
Maputo C	6794	9383	7584	8374	6083	7650	7823	7919
Mauritius	8046	10525	9611	9707	7231	8745	8959	9089
Mogadiscio †	8117	8756	8106	9131	7783	7120	8435	8164
Mombasa	8208C	9366†	8590†	9680†	7497C	7605†	8974†	8697†
Monrovia	3404	5431	4057	5063	2832	3590	4402	4196
Montevideo	4430	7530	5380	6306	3840	5670	5610	5727
Mozambique I	7671	10260	8461	9251	6960	8480	8700	8796
Porto Alegre	4414	7370	5218	6140	3695	5471	5399	5542
Port Elizabeth C	6124	8713	6914	7704	5413	6930	7153	7249
Port Harcourt	4588	6539	5133	6151	3949	4752	5409	5376
Recife	2463	5471	3348	4248	1781	3558	3513	3668
Reunion Island	7921	10400	9486	9582	7106	8620	8834	8964
Rio de Janeiro	3535	6543	4420	5320	2853	4660	4595	4740
Salvador	2853	5862	3776	4639	2172	3949	3939	4127
Sao Vicente Island	2514	4370	2886	4080	2037	2670	3284	3200
Santos	3714	6700	4599	5507	3066	4835	4770	4940
Takoradi	4040	5967	4593	5599	3368	4120	4938	4732
Tema	4130	6170	4623	5724	3180	4465	4929	4959
Tramandai	4735	7243	5120	6020	3553	5360	5295	5440
Vitoria (Brazil)	3285	6293	4170	5070	2603	4410	4345	4490
Walvis Bay	5354	7662	6131	7091	4580	5935	6367	6384

^Special section on page 214 devoted to distances within the Plate, Parana and Uruguay rivers.

AREA D

AREA C	Key West	Kingston (Jamaica)	La Guaira	Maracaibo	Mobile	Montreal	New Orleans	New York
Azores (St Michaels)	3175	2877	2765	2952	3685	2305	3635	2290
Bahia Blanca	6250	5367	4807	5117	6432	6746	6485	6130
Beira C	6199	7705	7061	7376	8633	8610	8651	8290
Belem	2604	2160	1622	1838	3126	3708	3179	3015
Buenos Aires (^)	5663	5224	4576	4914	6184	6474	6237	5910
Cape Horn	6728	6294	5633	5958	7249	7538	7321	6939
Cape Town	6718	6278	5597	6003	7237	7120	7290	6800
Conakry	4051	3728	3175	3473	4583	3953	4636	3707
Dakar	3709	3436	2911	3214	4215	3560	4268	3335
Dar es Salaam	9079†	8542C	7998C	8213C	9623†	8396†	9676†	8331†
Diego Suarez	9172†	8638C	7957C	8363C	9671†	8424†	9724†	8379†
Douala	5532	5192	4601	4929	6053	5500	6125	5240
Durban C	7506	7012	6368	6683	7939	7917	7957	7640
East London C	7253	6759	6115	6430	7687	7664	7705	7355
Lagos	5051	4800	3997	4463	5696	5217	5749	4883
Las Palmas	3615	3450	3086	3379	4185	3080	4275	2965
Lobito	6048	5640	4993	5314	6556	5993	6609	5725
Luanda	5933	5579	4948	5276	6455	5929	6526	5671
Madeira	3450	3349	3075	3368	4000	2840	4050	2725
Maputo C	7802	7308	6664	6979	8238	8213	8254	7840
Mauritius C	8953	8513	7832	8238	9472	9355	9525	9035
Mogadiscio †	8374	8319	8062	8291	8903	7586	8976	7612
Mombasa	8899†	8722C	8078C	8393C	9443†	8196†	9496†	8151†
Monrovia	4370	3971	3484	3782	4826	4261	4879	4089
Montevideo	5600	4967	4632	4645	6046	6360	6122	5750
Mozambique I C	8679	8185	7541	7856	9113	9091	9131	8770
Porto Alegre	5392	4956	4311	4622	5911	6200	5985	5604
Port Elizabeth C	7132	6638	5994	6309	7566	7543	7584	7200
Port Harcourt	5403	5063	4461	4800	5924	5369	5996	5111
Recife	3539	3000	2270	2678	4011	4301	4064	3698
Reunion Island C	8828	8388	7707	8113	9347	9230	9400	8910
Rio de Janeiro	4600	4193	3461	3750	5083	5373	5136	4780
Salvador	3942	3374	2742	3052	4402	4692	4455	4089
Sao Vicente Island	3250	3019	2491	2729	3800	3200	3890	2800
Santos	4795	4293	3641	3929	5245	5530	5298	4955
Takoradi	4906	4507	4020	4318	5362	4797	5415	4625
Tema	4943	4587	4057	4307	5487	5000	5603	4745
Tramandai	5300	4893	4161	4450	5783	6073	5836	5480
Vitoria (Brazil)	4350	3943	3211	3500	4833	5123	4886	4530
Walvis Bay	6367	5730	5232	5569	6854	6492	6907	6225

^Special section on page 214 devoted to distances within the Plate, Parana and Uruguay rivers.

AREA D

AREA C	Norfolk (Virginia)	Nuevitas	Philadelphia	Port Au Prince	Portland (Maine)	Port of Spain	Puerto Limon	St John (New Brunswick)
Azores (St Michaels)	2450	2728	2440	2773	2070	2557	3391	2000
Bahia Blanca	6101	5611	6180	5399	6135	4444	5784	6115
Beira C	8256	7837	8365	7813	8215	6847	8023	8137
Belem	2838	2171	2950	2192	2997	1212	2478	2998
Buenos Aires (^)	5824	5368	5960	5258	5915	4279	5407	5853
Cape Horn	6884	6425	6985	6314	6945	5332	6603	7940
Cape Town	6790	6395	6875	6311	6725	5307	6586	6667
Conakry	3771	3786	3812	3501	3613	2871	4111	3514
Dakar	3408	3412	3441	3333	3239	2628	3851	3140
Dar es Salaam †	8479	8943	8474	8650	8134	7684	8063	8036
Diego Suarez †	8527†	8991†	8522†	8670C	8182†	7667C	8858C	8084C
Douala	5299	5228	5339	5118	5123	4300	5565	5077
Durban C	7563	7144	7715	7120	7565	6154	7341	7444
East London C	7310	6891	7430	6867	7280	5901	7085	7191
Lagos	4941	4776	4985	4130	4789	3910	5194	4704
Las Palmas	3125	3435	3115	3342	2745	2746	3956	2600
Lobito	5771	5719	5836	5852	5631	4697	5988	5532
Luanda	5727	5635	5770	5521	5555	4647	5918	5506
Madeira	2885	3142	2875	3247	2505	2819	3880	2485
Maputo C	7859	7440	8015	7416	7865	6450	7635	7740
Mauritius C	9025	8630	9110	8546	8960	7542	8836	8902
Mogadiscio †	7768	8223	7753	8188	7413	7827	8864	7339
Mombasa †	8299	8763	8294	8830	7954	7864	9012	7856
Monrovia	4084	4087	4169	3940	3875	3092	4305	3838
Montevideo	5710	5243	5840	5222	5795	4150	5310	5739
Mozambique I C	8763	8317	8845	8293	8695	7321	8386	8617
Porto Alegre	5546	5087	5648	4976	5610	4090	5267	5605
Port Elizabeth C	7189	6770	7295	6746	7145	5780	6963	7070
Port Harcourt	5170	5099	5210	4989	4994	4430	5436	4948
Recife	3651	3169	3745	3030	3700	2106	3336	3498
Reunion Island	8900	8505	8985	8421	8835	7417	8589	8777
Rio de Janeiro	4723	4308	4830	4221	4785	3240	4410	4752
Salvador	4042	3619	4136	3406	4091	2379	3721	4050
Sao Vicente Island	3000	2969	3050	2915	2845	2225	3402	2750
Santos	4910	4554	5005	4314	4960	3368	4595	4935
Takoradi	4620	4623	4708	4476	4410	3632	4884	4374
Tema	5155	4618	4845	4487	4640	3428	4980	4629
Tramandai	5423	5008	5530	4921	5485	3940	5117	5452
Vitoria (Brazil)	4473	4058	4580	3971	4535	2990	4141	4502
Walvis Bay	6275	6052	6300	5711	6150	4878	6201	5964

^Special section on page 214 devoted to distances within the Plate, Parana and Uruguay rivers.

AREA D

AREA C	St John's (Newfoundland)	San Juan (Puerto Rico)	Santiago de Cuba	Santo Domingo	Tampa	Tampico	Veracruz	Wilmington (N Carolina)
Azores (St Michaels)	1325	2412	2751	2620	3365	3965	3831	2504
Bahia Blanca	5927	5027	5388	4977	6193	6793	6753	6088
Beira C	7689	7262	7819	7227	8470	8791	8729	8288
Belem	2968	1668	2175	1866	2887	3387	3325	2753
Buenos Aires (^)	5666	4755	5215	4881	5945	6437	6378	5805
Cape Horn	6749	5832	6308	5950	6991	7515	7451	6858
Cape Town	6205	5767	6311	5934	6998	7492	7430	6804
Conakry	3026	3116	3462	3348	4344	4944	4904	3793
Dakar	2646	2812	3350	3036	3976	4576	4536	3406
Dar es Salaam	7313†	8099C	8656C	8064C	9384†	9984†	9926†	8663†
Diego Suarez	7461†	8127C	8671C	8294C	9432†	10032†	9874†	8711†
Douala	4590	4585	5146	4794	5795	6390	6325	5366
Durban C	6996	6569	7126	6534	7777	8097	8035	7595
East London C	6743	6316	6873	6281	7524	7878	7783	7342
Lagos	4592	3590	4205	4447	5457	6057	6017	4863
Las Palmas	2030	2863	3320	3004	3945	4545	4505	3311
Lobito	5056	5038	5619	5255	6317	6917	6877	5919
Luanda	5019	4983	5549	5187	6196	6792	6728	5793
Madeira	1850	2773	3225	2977	3750	4342	4302	3193
Maputo C	7292	6865	7422	6830	8073	8394	8332	7891
Mauritius C	7440	8002	8546	8169	9233	9727	9665	9039
Mogadiscio †	6605	7764	8213	7976	8646	9263	9233	7954
Mombasa	7133†	8279C	8836C	8244C	9204†	9804†	9746C	8483†
Monrovia	3338	3360	3918	3581	4587	5187	5147	4123
Montevideo	5551	4640	5100	4766	5830	6322	6263	5690
Mozambique I C	7169	7742	8299	7707	8950	9271	9209	8768
Porto Alegre	5413	4463	4972	4379	5653	6179	6113	5520
Port Elizabeth C	6622	6195	6752	6160	7412	7724	7662	7221
Port Harcourt	4461	4455	5017	4664	5666	6261	6196	5237
Recife	3491	2609	2995	2757	3772	4266	4204	3600
Reunion Island C	7315	7877	8421	8044	9108	9602	9540	8914
Rio de Janeiro	4563	3613	4200	3829	4844	5338	5276	4704
Salvador	3862	2962	3395	2964	4163	4763	4723	4023
Sao Vicente Island	2300	2354	2893	2572	3550	4150	4115	3057
Santos	4744	3832	4293	4014	5031	5513	5451	4877
Takoradi	3874	3896	4454	4117	5123	5723	5683	4659
Tema	4087	4004	4539	4135	5248	5804	5742	4817
Tramandai	5263	4313	4900	4529	5544	6038	5976	5404
Vitoria (Brazil)	4313	3363	3950	3579	4594	5088	5026	4454
Walvis Bay	5567	5107	5692	5538	6615	7215	7175	6270

All distances on this page via the Suez Canal.

AREA E

AREA C	Baie Comeau	Baltimore	Boston	Cartagena (Colombia)	Charleston	Churchill	Cienfuegos	Cristobal
Abadan	8164	8738	8308	9369	8863	8897	9382	9578
Aden	6234	6808	6378	7439	6933	6964	7452	7648
Aqaba	5133	5788	5346	6402	5912	5957	6424	6628
Bahrain	7967	8522	8080	9136	8646	8691	9158	9362
Bandar Abbas	7588	8143	7800	8857	8337	8412	8879	9083
Basrah	8228	8794	8369	6425	8919	8926	9438	9634
Bassein	9519	10093	9663	10724	10218	10208	10737	10933
Bhavnagar	7763	8418	7976	9028	8542	8587	9054	9258
Bushehr	8004	8578	8148	9209	8703	8751	9222	9418
Calcutta	9539	10113	9683	10744	10238	10261	10757	10953
Chennai	8891	9465	9035	10096	9590	9607	8923	10305
Chittagong	9674	10248	9818	10879	10373	10309	10892	11088
Cochin	8030	8604	8174	9235	8729	8807	9248	9444
Colombo	8330	8904	8474	9535	9029	9051	9548	9744
Djibouti	6114	6688	6258	7319	6813	6947	7332	7528
Dubai	7666	8221	7878	8935	8415	8490	8957	9161
Fujairah	7500	8055	7712	8769	8249	8324	8791	8995
Jedda	5554	6128	5698	6759	6253	6293	6772	6968
Karachi	7705	8279	7849	8910	8404	8429	8923	9119
Kuwait	8053	8708	8266	9322	8832	8876	9344	9548
Malacca	9756	10430	9900	10961	10455	10461	10974	10872
Mangalore	6052	8568	8138	9199	8693	8696	9212	9408
Massawa	5834	6408	5978	7039	6533	6630	7052	7248
Mina al Ahmadi	8033	8688	8246	9302	8812	8856	9324	9528
Mongla	9644	10218	9788	10849	10343	10275	10862	11058
Mormugao	6002	8518	8088	9149	8643	8646	9162	9358
Moulmein	9604	10178	9748	10809	10303	10312	10822	11018
Mumbai	7891	8465	8035	9096	8590	8616	9109	9305
Musay'td	7833	8488	8046	9102	8612	8661	9124	9328
Penang	9571	10145	9715	10776	10270	10393	10789	10915
Port Blair	9099	9754	9312	10368	9878	9930	10390	10594
Port Kelang	9648	10222	9792	10853	10347	10387	10866	10764
Port Okha	7633	8288	7846	8902	8412	8457	8924	9128
Port Sudan	5623	6197	5767	6828	6322	6351	6841	7037
Quseir	5184	5758	5328	6389	5883	5912	6402	6598
Singapore	9864	10438	10008	10829	10563	10584	11082	10548
Sittwe	9574	10148	9718	10779	10273	10242	10792	10988
Suez	4926	5500	5070	6131	5623	5657	6144	6340
Trincomalee	8514	9088	8658	9719	10113	9337	9732	9928
Veraval	7623	8278	7836	8892	8402	8447	8914	9118
Vishakhapatnam	7264	9780	9350	10411	9905	9871	10424	10620
Yangon	9539	10113	9683	10744	10238	10266	10757	10953

All distances on this page via the Suez Canal.

AREA E	AREA C	Curacao	Duluth-Superior	Freeport (Bahamas)	Galveston	Georgetown (Guyana)	Halifax	Havana	Jacksonville
Abadan		8953	9684	8908	9998	8619	7923	9292	9015
Aden		7023	7754	6978	8068	6689	5993	7362	7085
Aqaba		6014	6653	6003	7026	5680	5017	6332	6061
Bahrain		8748	9387	8737	9862	8414	7751	9066	9795
Bandar Abbas		8469	9108	8458	9483	8135	7472	8787	8516
Basrah		9009	9748	8964	10054	8675	7979	9348	9071
Bassein		10308	11039	10263	11353	9974	9278	10647	10370
Bhavnagar		8644	9283	8633	9658	8310	7647	8962	8691
Bushehr		8793	9124	8748	9838	8459	7763	9132	8860
Calcutta		10328	11059	10283	11373	9994	9298	10667	10390
Chennai		9680	10411	9635	10725	9346	8650	10019	9742
Chittagong		10463	11194	11418	11508	10129	9433	10802	10525
Cochin		8819	9550	8774	9864	8485	7789	9158	8881
Colombo		9119	9850	9074	10164	8785	8089	9458	9181
Djibouti		6903	7634	6858	7948	6560	5873	7242	6965
Dubai		8547	9186	8536	9561	8213	7550	8865	8594
Fujairah		8381	9020	8370	9395	8047	7384	8699	8428
Jedda		6343	7074	6298	7388	6009	5313	6682	6405
Karachi		8494	9225	8449	9539	8160	7464	8833	8556
Kuwait		8934	9573	8923	9948	8600	7937	9252	8981
Malacca		10545	11276	10500	11591	10211	9515	10884	10607
Mangalore		8783	7572	8710	9828	8449	7753	9122	8845
Massawa		6623	7354	6578	7668	8289	5593	6962	6685
Mina al Ahmadi		8914	9553	8903	9928	8580	7917	9232	8961
Mongla		10433	11164	11388	11478	10099	9403	10772	10495
Mormugao		8733	7522	8660	9778	8399	7703	9072	8795
Moulmein		10393	11124	10348	11438	10059	9363	10732	10455
Mumbai		8680	9411	8635	9725	8346	7650	9019	8742
Musay'td		8714	8353	8703	9728	8380	7717	9032	8761
Penang		10360	11091	10315	11405	10026	9330	10699	10422
Port Blair		9980	10619	9969	10994	9646	8983	10298	10027
Port Kelang		10437	11168	10392	11483	10103	9407	10776	10499
Port Okha		8514	9153	8503	9528	8180	7517	8832	8561
Port Sudan		6412	7143	6367	7457	6078	5382	6751	6474
Quseir		5973	6704	5928	7018	5639	4943	6312	6035
Singapore		10653	11384	10608	11698	10319	9623	10992	10715
Sittwe		10363	11094	10318	11408	10029	9333	10702	10425
Suez		5715	6446	5670	6760	5381	4685	6054	6777
Trincomalee		9303	10034	9258	10348	8969	8273	9642	9365
Veraval		8504	9143	8493	9518	8170	7507	8822	8551
Vishakhapatnam		9995	8784	9950	11040	9661	8965	10334	10057
Yangon		10328	11059	10283	11373	9994	9298	10667	10390

All distances on this page via the Suez Canal.

AREA E

AREA C	Key West	Kingston (Jamaica)	La Guaira	Maracaibo	Mobile	Montreal	New Orleans	New York
Abadan	9217	9186	8902	9180	9761	8514	9814	8469
Aden	7287	7256	6972	7250	7831	6584	7884	6539
Aqaba	6271	6216	5956	6188	6800	5483	6873	5509
Bahrain	9005	8950	8690	8922	9534	8217	9607	8243
Bandar Abbas	8726	8671	8411	8643	9255	7938	9328	7964
Basrah	9273	9242	8928	9236	9817	8578	9870	8525
Bassein	10572	10541	10257	10535	11116	9869	11169	9824
Bhavnagar	8901	8846	8600	8818	9430	8113	9503	8139
Bushehr	9062	9031	8747	9025	9606	8359	9654	8309
Calcutta	10592	10561	10277	10555	11136	9889	11189	9844
Chennai	9944	9913	9629	9907	10488	9241	10541	9196
Chittagong	10727	10696	10412	10690	11271	10024	11324	9979
Cochin	9083	9052	8768	9046	9627	8380	9680	9335
Colombo	9383	9352	9068	9346	9927	8680	9980	8635
Djibouti	7167	7136	6852	7130	7711	6464	7764	7419
Dubai	8804	8749	8489	8721	9333	8016	9406	8042
Fujairah	8638	8583	8323	8555	9167	7850	9240	7876
Jedda	6607	6576	6292	6570	7151	5904	7204	5859
Karachi	8785	8727	8443	8721	9302	8055	9355	8010
Kuwait	9191	9136	8875	9108	9720	8403	9793	8429
Malacca	10809	10778	10494	10772	11353	10106	11406	10061
Mangalore	9047	9016	8732	9010	9591	6402	9596	8721
Massawa	6887	6856	6572	6850	7431	6184	7484	6139
Mina al Ahmadi	9171	9116	8855	9088	9700	8383	9773	8409
Mongla	10697	10666	10382	10660	11241	9994	11294	9949
Mormugao	8997	8966	8682	8960	9541	6352	9546	8221
Moulmein	10657	10626	10342	10620	11201	9954	11254	9909
Mumbai	8944	8913	8629	8907	9488	8241	9541	8196
Musay'td	8971	8916	8660	8888	9500	8183	9573	8209
Penang	10624	10593	10309	10587	11168	9921	11221	9876
Port Blair	10237	10182	9922	10154	10766	9449	10839	9475
Port Kelang	10701	10670	10386	10664	11245	9998	11298	9953
Port Okha	8771	8716	8470	8688	9300	7983	9373	8009
Port Sudan	6676	6645	6361	6639	7220	5973	7273	5928
Quseir	6237	6206	5922	6200	6781	5534	6834	5489
Singapore	10917	10886	10602	10880	11461	10214	11514	10169
Sittwe	10627	10596	10312	10590	11171	9924	11224	9879
Suez	5979	5948	5664	5942	6523	5276	6576	5231
Trincomalee	9567	9536	9252	9530	10111	8864	10164	8819
Veraval	8761	8706	8460	8678	9290	7973	9372	7999
Vishakhapatnam	10259	10228	9860	10222	10803	7614	10856	9511
Yangon	10592	10561	10277	10555	11136	9889	11189	9844

All distances on this page via the Suez Canal.

AREA E

AREA C	Norfolk (Virginia)	Nuevitas	Philadelphia	Port Au Prince	Portland (Maine)	Port of Spain	Puerto Limon	St John (New Brunswick)
Abadan	8617	9081	8612	9025	8272	8671	9699	8174
Aden	6687	7151	6682	7095	6342	6741	7767	6244
Aqaba	5665	6120	5650	6085	5309	5715	6761	5236
Bahrain	8400	8854	8384	8819	8043	8449	9495	7970
Bandar Abbas	8129	8575	8105	8540	7764	8170	9216	7691
Basrah	8673	9137	8668	9081	8328	8727	9729	8230
Bassein	9972	10436	9967	10380	9627	10026	11011	9529
Bhavnagar	8295	8750	8280	8715	7939	8345	9391	7866
Bushehr	8462	8921	8452	8865	8112	8511	9554	8014
Calcutta	9992	10456	9987	10400	9647	10046	11064	9549
Chennai	9344	9808	9339	9752	8999	9398	10410	8901
Chittagong	10127	10591	10122	10535	9782	10181	11112	9684
Cochin	8483	8947	9478	9891	8138	8537	9610	8040
Colombo	8783	9247	8778	9191	8438	8837	9854	8340
Djibouti	6567	7031	6562	6975	6222	6621	7763	6124
Dubai	8207	8653	8183	8618	7842	8248	9294	7769
Fujairah	8041	8487	8017	8452	7676	8082	9128	7603
Jedda	6007	6471	6002	6415	5662	6061	7096	5564
Karachi	8158	8622	8153	8566	7813	8212	9232	7715
Kuwait	8585	9040	8570	9005	8229	8634	9681	8156
Malacca	10209	10673	10204	10617	9864	10263	11264	9766
Mangalore	8419	8883	8414	8827	8074	8473	9499	7976
Massawa	6287	6751	6282	6695	5942	6341	7435	5844
Mina al Ahmadi	8565	9020	8550	8985	8209	8614	9661	8136
Mongla	10097	10561	10092	10505	9752	10151	11078	9654
Mormugao	8369	8833	8364	8777	8024	8423	9449	7926
Moulmein	10057	10521	10052	10465	9712	10111	11115	9614
Mumbai	8344	8808	8339	8752	7999	8398	9416	7901
Musay'td	8365	8820	8350	8785	8009	8419	9461	7936
Penang	10024	10488	10019	10432	9679	10078	11096	9581
Port Blair	9631	10080	9616	10051	9275	9681	10727	9202
Port Kelang	10101	10565	10096	10509	9756	10155	11190	9658
Port Okha	8165	8620	8150	8585	7809	8215	9261	7736
Port Sudan	6076	6540	6071	6484	5731	6130	7154	5633
Quseir	5637	6101	5632	6045	5292	5691	6715	5194
Singapore	10317	10781	10312	10725	9972	10371	11387	9874
Sittwe	10027	10491	10022	10435	9682	10081	8309	9584
Suez	5379	5843	5374	5787	5034	5433	6460	4936
Trincomalee	8967	9431	8962	9375	8622	9021	10140	8524
Veraval	8155	8610	8140	8575	7799	8205	9251	7726
Vishakhapatnam	9859	10123	9654	10067	9314	9629	10674	9216
Yangon	9992	10456	9987	10400	9647	10046	11069	9549

All distances on this page via the Suez Canal.

AREA E

AREA C	St John's (Newfoundland)	San Juan (Puerto Rico)	Santiago de Cuba	Santo Domingo	Tampa	Tampico	Veracruz	Wilmington (N Carolina)
Abadan	7451	8601	9060	8823	9522	10122	10082	8801
Aden	5521	6671	7130	6893	7592	8192	8152	6871
Aqaba	4502	5658	6110	5870	6543	7810	7122	5851
Bahrain	7236	8392	8844	8604	9277	9894	9856	8575
Bandar Abbas	6957	8113	8565	8325	8998	9615	9517	8306
Basrah	7507	8657	9116	8879	9578	10178	10138	8857
Bassein	8806	9956	10415	10178	10877	11477	11437	10156
Bhavnagar	7132	8299	8740	8521	9173	9790	9752	8481
Bushehr	7291	8441	8900	8663	9362	9962	9922	8641
Calcutta	8826	9976	10435	10198	10897	11497	11457	10176
Chennai	8179	9328	9787	9550	10249	10849	10809	9528
Chittagong	8961	10111	10570	10333	11032	11632	11592	10311
Cochin	7217	8467	8926	8689	9388	9988	9948	8667
Colombo	7617	8767	9226	8989	9688	10288	10248	8967
Djibouti	5401	6551	7010	6773	7472	8072	8032	6751
Dubai	7035	8191	8643	8403	9076	9693	9595	8384
Fujairah	6869	8025	9477	8237	8910	9527	9429	8218
Jedda	4841	5991	6450	6213	6912	7512	7472	6191
Karachi	8992	8142	8601	8364	9063	9663	9623	8342
Kuwait	7422	8577	9030	8789	9463	10080	10042	8771
Malacca	9043	10193	10652	10415	11084	11714	11674	10393
Mangalore	7253	8403	8862	8653	9304	9904	9864	8603
Massawa	5121	6271	6730	6493	7192	7792	7752	6471
Mina al Ahmadi	7402	8557	9010	8769	9443	10060	10022	8751
Mongla	8931	10081	10540	10303	11002	11602	11562	10281
Mormugao	7203	8353	8812	8603	9254	9854	9814	8553
Moulmein	8891	10041	10500	10273	10962	11562	11522	10241
Mumbai	7178	8328	8787	8550	9249	9849	9809	8528
Musay'td	7202	8362	8810	8574	9243	9860	9822	8551
Penang	8858	10008	10487	10230	10929	11529	11489	10208
Port Blair	8468	9624	10076	9836	10509	11126	11086	9817
Port Kelang	8935	10085	10544	10307	10976	11606	11566	10285
Port Okha	7002	8169	8610	8391	9043	9660	9622	8351
Port Sudan	4910	6060	6519	6282	6981	7581	7541	6260
Quseir	4471	5621	6080	5843	6542	7142	7102	5821
Singapore	9151	10301	10760	10523	11222	11622	11582	10501
Sittwe	8861	10011	10470	10233	10932	11532	11492	10211
Suez	4213	5363	5822	5585	6284	6884	6844	5563
Trincomalee	7801	8951	9410	9173	9872	10472	10511	9151
Veraval	6992	8159	8600	8381	9033	9650	9612	8341
Vishakhapatnam	8493	9572	10102	9785	10564	11164	11124	9843
Yangon	8826	9976	10435	10198	10897	11497	11457	10176

AREA F	AREA C Baie Comeau	Baltimore	Boston	Cartagena (Colombia)	Charleston	Churchill	Cienfuegos	Cristobal
Balikpapan	10891†	11163*	11035†	9543*	11590†	11652†	10034*	9262*
Bangkok	10896†	11280†	11040†	11048*	11595†	11857†	11537*	19765*
Basuo (Hainan Is)	11150†	11575*	11294†	9955*	11238*	11911†	10446*	9750*
Cam-Pha	11324†	11583*	11468†	9963*	11246*	12085†	10454*	8682*
Cebu	11219†	11157*	11363†	9537*	10820*	11980†	10028*	9526*
Dalian	11581*	10586*	10842*	8966*	10249*	13127*	9457*	8685*
Haiphong	11224†	11613*	11368†	9993*	11276*	11985†	10484*	9712*
Ho Chi Minh City	10513†	11087†	10657†	10342*	11625*	11274†	10833*	10061*
Hong Kong	11318†	11140*	11395*	9519*	10810*	12079†	10010*	9238*
Hungnam	10384*	9381*	9637*	8761*	9044*	11982*	8252*	7540*
Inchon	12132*	11129*	11385*	9509*	10792*	13184†	10000*	9228*
Kampong Saom	10590†	10980†	10740†	10745*	11295†	11351†	11235*	10465*
Kaohsiung (Taiwan)	11381†	10897*	11129*	9269*	10553*	12142†	9768*	8993*
Keelung (Taiwan)	11669†	10668*	10924*	9048*	10331*	12430†	9539*	8767*
Kobe	10908*	9905*	10161*	8285*	9568*	12446*	8776*	8004*
Makassar	10854†	11428†	10998†	9839*	11553†	11619†	10798*	10036*
Manila	11194*	11291*	11338†	9671*	10954*	11955†	10162*	9390*
Masinloc	11235*	11330*	11378†	9715*	10995*	11622†	10205*	9430*
Menado	11321†	11297*	11465†	9677*	10960*	12082†	10168*	9396*
Moji	11157*	10154*	10410*	8534*	9817*	12695*	9025*	8253*
Muroran	11017*	10014*	10270*	8394*	9677*	12555*	8885*	7483*
Nagasaki	11148*	10145*	10401*	8525*	9808*	12686*	9016*	8244*
Nagoya	10664*	9961*	9917*	8041*	9324*	12202*	8536*	7760*
Nampo	11531*	10536*	10792*	8916*	10199*	13077*	9407*	8625*
Osaka	10916*	9913*	10169*	8293*	9576*	12454*	8784*	8012*
Otaru	11152*	10149*	10405*	8529*	9812*	12690*	9020*	8248*
Palembang	10046†	10620†	10190†	11317*	10745†	11250*	11264†	11036*
Pusan	11257*	10254*	10510*	8634*	9917*	12795*	9125*	8353*
Qingdao	11523*	10520*	10776*	8900*	10183*	13061*	9391*	8619
Qinhuangdao	11840*	10837*	11093*	9217*	10500*	13362†	9703*	8936*
Sabang	9263†	9837†	9408†	10472†	9963†	10028†	10480†	10681†
Shanghai	11597*	10594*	10850*	8966*	10260*	12835†	9467*	8690*
Shimonoseki	11182*	10179*	10435*	8559*	9842*	12720*	9050*	8278*
Singapore	9864†	10438†	10008†	10829*	10563†	10629†	11082†	10548*
Surabaya	10504†	11088†	10648†	10594*	11311†	11265†	11085*	10313*
Tanjung Priok	10131†	10715†	10275†	10967*	10830†	10892†	11349†	10686*
Tokyo	10647*	9644*	9900*	8024*	9307*	12185*	9515*	7743*
Toyama	11335*	10334*	10590*	8715*	9995*	12875*	9185*	8433*
Vladivostok	10689*	9686*	9942*	8066*	9349*	12227*	8557*	7785*
Yokohama	10629*	9626*	9882*	8006*	9289*	12167*	8497*	7725*

AREA F

AREA C	Curacao	Duluth-Superior	Freeport (Bahamas)	Galveston	Georgetown (Guyana)	Halifax	Havana	Jacksonville
Balikpapan	9939*	12411†	10440*	10755*	10777*	10650†	10265*	10778*
Bangkok	11442*	12416†	11640†	12258*	11351†	10655†	11768*	11747†
Basuo (Hainan Is)	10427*	12670†	10928*	11243*	11265*	10909†	10753*	11190*
Cam-Pha	10359*	12844†	10860*	11175*	11197*	11083†	10685*	11198*
Cebu	9933*	12739†	10434*	10749*	10776*	10978†	10259*	10772*
Dalian	9362*	13101*	9863*	10178*	10200*	10980*	9688*	10201*
Haiphong	10389*	12744†	10890*	11205*	11227*	10983†	10715*	11228*
Ho Chi Minh City	10738*	12033†	11239*	11554*	10968†	10272†	11064*	11364†
Hong Kong	9927*	12838†	10416*	10731*	10753*	11077†	10240*	10754*
Hungnam	8217*	11964*	8718*	9033*	9055*	9835*	8543*	9056*
Inchon	9905*	13652*	10406*	10721*	10743*	11523*	10231*	10744*
Kampong Saom	11140*	12115†	11340†	11955*	11050†	10355†	11465*	11447†
Kaohsiung (Taiwan)	9684*	12901†	10158*	10478*	10468*	11291*	9983*	10498*
Keelung (Taiwan)	9444*	13189†	9945*	10260*	10282*	11062*	9770*	10283*
Kobe	8681*	12428*	9182*	9497*	9519*	10299*	9007*	9520*
Makassar	10703*	12374†	11204*	11519*	11309†	10613†	11029†	11542†
Manila	10067*	12714†	10568*	10883*	10905*	10953†	10393*	10906*
Masinloc	10107*	12755†	10609*	10925*	10945*	10995†	10435*	10945*
Menado	10073*	12841†	10574*	10989*	10911*	11080†	10399*	10909*
Moji	8930*	12677*	9431*	9746*	9768*	10548*	9256*	9769*
Muroran	8790*	12537*	9291*	9606*	9628*	10408*	9116*	9629*
Nagasaki	8921*	12668*	9422*	8737*	9759*	10539*	9247*	9760*
Nagoya	8437*	12184*	8938*	9253*	9275*	10055*	8763*	9276*
Nampo	9312*	13051*	9813*	10128*	10150*	10930*	9638*	10151*
Osaka	8689*	12436*	9190*	9505*	9527*	10307*	9015*	9528*
Otaru	8925*	12672*	9426*	9741*	9763*	10543*	9251*	9764*
Palembang	10835†	11566†	10790†	11880†	10501†	9805†	11174†	10897†
Pusan	9030*	12777*	9531*	9846*	9876*	19648*	9356*	9869*
Qingdao	9296*	13043*	9797*	10112*	10134*	10914*	9622*	10135*
Qinhuangdao	9613*	13360*	10114*	10429*	10451*	11231*	9939*	10452*
Sabang	10052†	10783†	10007†	11097†	9718†	9022†	10391†	10114†
Shanghai	9377*	13117*	9811*	10186*	10208*	10988*	9693*	10209*
Shimonoseki	8955*	12702*	9456*	9771*	9793*	10573*	9281*	9794*
Singapore	10653†	11384†	10608†	11698†	10319†	9623†	10992†	10715†
Surabaya	10990*	12024†	11248†	11806*	10551C	10263†	11316*	11355†
Tanjung Priok	10889C	11651†	10875†	11965†	10178C	9890†	11259†	10982†
Tokyo	8420*	12167*	8921*	9236*	9258*	10038*	8746*	9259*
Toyama	9110*	12857*	9611*	9926*	9948*	10728*	9436*	9949*
Vladivostok	8462*	12209*	8963*	9678*	9300*	10080*	8788*	9301*
Yokohama	8402*	12149*	8903*	9218*	9240*	10020*	8788*	9241*

AREA F

AREA C	Key West	Kingston (Jamaica)	La Guaira	Maracaibo	Mobile	Montreal	New Orleans	New York
Balikpapan	10327*	9813*	10103*	9862*	10632*	11241†	10652*	11196†
Bangkok	11830*	11316*	11606*	11356*	12140*	11246†	12155*	11201†
Basuo (Hainan Is)	10739*	10225*	10515*	10274*	11044*	11500†	11064*	11455†
Cam-Pha	10747*	10233*	10523*	10282*	11052*	11674†	11072*	11629†
Cebu	10321*	9807*	10097*	9856*	10626*	11569†	10646*	11230*
Dalian	9750*	9236*	9526*	9285*	10055*	11931*	10075*	10659*
Haiphong	10777*	10263*	10553*	10312*	11082*	11574†	11102*	11529†
Ho Chi Minh City	11126*	10612*	10902*	10661*	11431*	10863†	11451*	10818†
Hong Kong	10306*	9789*	10079*	9838*	10608*	11668*	10630*	11230*
Hungnam	8605*	8091*	8381*	8140*	8910*	10794*	8930*	9514*
Inchon	10293*	9779*	10069*	9828*	10598*	12482*	10618*	11202*
Kampong Saom	11530*	11015*	11305*	11055*	11840*	10946†	9115*	9699*
Kaohsiung (Taiwan)	10047*	9548*	9910*	9669*	10356*	11731†	10383*	10967*
Keelung (Taiwan)	9832*	9318*	9608*	9367*	10137*	12019†	10157*	10741*
Kobe	9069*	8555*	8845*	8604*	9374*	11258*	9394*	9978*
Makassar	11091*	10577*	10867*	10626*	11396*	11204†	11416*	11159†
Manila	10455*	9941*	10231*	9990*	10760*	11544†	10780*	11364*
Masinloc	10495*	9980*	10270*	10030*	10800*	11585†	10820*	11405*
Menado	10460*	9950*	10240*	10000*	10766*	11671†	10786*	11370*
Moji	9318*	8804*	9094*	8853*	9623*	11507*	9643*	10227*
Muroran	9178*	8664*	8954*	8713*	9483*	10600*	9503*	10087*
Nagasaki	9309*	8795*	9085*	8844*	9614*	11498*	9634*	10218*
Nagoya	8825*	8311*	8601*	8360*	9130*	11014*	9150*	9734*
Nampo	9700*	9186*	9476*	9235*	10005*	11881*	10025*	10609*
Osaka	9077*	8563*	8853*	8612*	9382*	11266*	9402*	9986*
Otaru	9313*	8799*	9089*	8848*	9618*	11502*	9638*	10222*
Palembang	11099†	11068†	10784†	11062†	11643†	10396†	10696†	10351†
Pusan	9418*	8904*	9194*	8953*	9723*	11607*	9743*	10327*
Qindao	9684*	9170*	9460*	9219*	9989*	11873*	10009*	10593*
Qinhuangdao	10001*	9487*	9777*	9536*	10306*	12190*	10326*	10910*
Sabang	10316†	10285†	10001†	10279†	10860†	9613†	9913†	9568†
Shanghai	9758*	9244*	9534*	9293*	10070*	11947*	10080*	10669*
Shimonoseki	9343*	8829*	9119*	8878*	9648*	11532*	9668*	10242*
Singapore	10917†	10886†	10602†	10880†	11461†	10214†	10514†	10619†
Surabaya	11378*	10864*	11154*	10913*	11683*	10854†	11703*	10809†
Tokyo	8808*	8294*	8588*	8343*	9113*	10997*	9133*	9717*
Toyama	9498*	8984*	9274*	9033*	9803*	11687*	9823*	10407*
Tanjung Priok	11184†	11153†	10759C	11147†	11728†	10481†	11781†	10436†
Vladivostok	8850*	8336*	8626*	8385*	9155*	11039*	9175*	9759*
Yokohama	8790*	8276*	8570*	8325*	9095*	10979*	9115*	9699*

AREA F

AREA C	Norfolk (Virginia)	Nuevitas	Philadelphia	Port Au Prince	Portland (Maine)	Port of Spain	Puerto Limon	St John (New Brunswick)
Balikpapan	11041*	10196*	11208*	10036*	10999†	10421*	9452*	10901†
Bangkok	11349†	11699*	11344†	11539*	11004†	11403†	10955*	10906†
Basuo (Hainan Is)	11453*	10608*	11620*	10444*	11258†	10833*	9864*	11160†
Cam-Pha	11461*	10616*	11628*	10452*	10432†	10841*	8872*	11334†
Cebu	11035*	10190*	11202*	10030*	11327†	10415	9446*	11229†
Dalian	10464*	9619*	10631*	9459*	10883*	9844*	8875*	11003*
Haiphong	11491*	10646*	11658*	10482*	11332†	10871*	9902*	11234†
Ho Chi Minh City	10966†	10995*	10961†	10835*	10621†	11020†	10251†	10523†
Hong Kong	11017*	10172*	11184*	10012*	11436*	10397*	9428*	11328†
Hungnam	9319*	8474*	9486*	8314*	9738*	8699*	7730*	9858*
Inchon	11007*	10162*	11174*	10002*	11426*	10387*	9418*	11546*
Kampong Saom	11050†	11399*	11045†	11239*	10704†	11103†	10655*	10606†
Kaohsiung (Taiwan)	10774*	9927*	10939*	9767*	11191*	10152*	9183*	11311*
Keelung (Taiwan)	10546*	9701*	10713*	9541*	10965*	9926*	8957*	11085*
Kobe	9783*	8978*	9950*	8778*	10202*	9163*	8194*	10322*
Makassar	11805*	10960*	11302†	10800*	10962†	11185*	10226*	10873†
Manila	11169*	10324*	11336*	10164*	11302†	10549*	9580*	11204†
Masinloc	11210*	10365*	11377*	10205*	11345†	10590*	9620*	11245†
Menado	11175*	10330*	11342*	10170*	11429†	10555*	9586*	11331†
Moji	10032*	9187*	10190*	9027*	10451*	9412*	8443*	10571*
Muroran	9892*	9047*	10059*	8887*	10311*	9272*	8303*	10431*
Nagasaki	10023*	9178*	10199*	9018*	10442*	9403*	8434*	10562*
Nagoya	9535*	8894*	9706*	8534*	9958*	8919*	7950*	10078*
Nampo	10414*	9579*	10581*	9409*	10833*	9794*	8825*	10953*
Osaka	9791*	8946*	9958*	8786*	10210*	9171*	8202*	10330*
Otaru	10027*	9182*	10194*	9012*	10446*	9407*	8438*	10566*
Palembang	10499†	10963†	10494†	10907†	10154†	10553†	11226*	10056†
Pusan	10132*	9287*	10290*	9127*	10551*	9372*	8543*	10671*
Qingdao	10398*	9553*	10565*	9393*	10817*	9778*	8809*	10937*
Qinhuangdao	10715*	9875*	10882*	9710*	11134*	10095*	9126*	11254*
Sabang	9716†	10180†	9711†	10124†	9371†	9770†	10690†	9273†
Shanghai	10472*	9625*	10639*	9467*	10891*	9857*	8880*	11011*
Shimonoseki	10057*	9212*	10215*	9052*	10476*	9437*	8468*	10596*
Singapore	10317†	10781†	10312†	10725†	9972†	10371†	10738*	9874†
Surabaya	10957†	11247*	10952†	11087*	10612†	11011†	10503*	10514†
Tanjung Priok	10584†	11048†	10579†	10992†	10239†	10638†	10876*	10141†
Tokyo	9522*	8673*	9689*	8517*	9941*	9205*	7933*	10061*
Toyama	10212*	9367*	10379*	9207*	10631*	9592*	8623*	10751*
Vladivostok	9564*	8719*	9731*	8559*	9983*	8944*	8975*	10103*
Yokohama	9504*	8659*	9671*	8499*	9923*	9187*	7915*	10043*

AREA F

AREA C	St John's (Newfoundland)	San Juan (Puerto Rico)	Santiago de Cuba	Santo Domingo	Tampa	Tampico	Veracruz	Wilmington (N Carolina)
Balikpapan	10178†	10255*	9945*	10064*	10480*	10747*	10682*	10875*
Bangkok	10183†	11758*	11448*	11567*	11983*	12250*	12185*	11533†
Basuo (Hainan Is)	10437†	10667*	10357*	10476*	10892*	11159*	11098*	10287*
Cam-Pha	10611†	10675*	10365*	10484*	10900*	11167*	11106*	10295*
Cebu	10506†	10249*	9939*	10058*	10474*	10741*	10676*	10869*
Dalian	11377*	9678*	9368*	9487*	9903*	10170*	10105*	10298*
Haiphong	10511†	10705*	10395*	10514*	10930*	11197*	11136*	10325*
Ho Chi Minh City	9800†	11054*	10744*	10863*	11279*	11546*	11481*	11150†
Hong Kong	10605†	10231*	9921*	10040*	10456*	10723*	10658*	10851*
Hungnam	10232*	8533*	8223*	8342*	8758*	9025*	8960*	9093*
Inchon	11920*	10221*	9911*	10030*	10446*	10713*	10648*	10841*
Kampong Saom	9883†	11458*	11148*	11267*	11683*	11950*	11885*	11230†
Kaohsiung (Taiwan)	11182†	9986*	9676*	9795*	10211*	10478*	10413*	10602*
Keelung (Taiwan)	10956†	9760*	9450*	9569*	9985*	10252*	10187*	10380*
Kobe	10696*	8997*	8687*	8806*	9222*	9489*	9424*	9617*
Makassar	10141†	11019*	10709*	10828*	11244*	11411*	11446*	11491†
Manila	10481†	10383*	10073*	10192*	10608*	10875*	10810*	11003*
Masinloc	10521†	10425*	10115*	10232*	10650*	10915*	10850*	11045*
Menado	10680†	10389*	10079*	10198*	10614*	10881*	10816*	11009*
Moji	10945*	9246*	8936*	9055*	9471*	9738*	9673*	9866*
Muroran	10805*	9106*	8796*	8915*	9331*	9598*	9533*	9726*
Nagasaki	10936*	9237*	8927*	9046*	9462*	9729*	9964*	9857*
Nagoya	10452*	8753*	8443*	8562*	8978*	9245*	9180*	9373*
Nampo	10327*	9628*	9318*	9437*	9853*	10120*	10055*	10248*
Osaka	10704*	9005*	8695*	8814*	9230*	9497*	9432*	9625*
Otaru	10940*	9241*	8931*	9050*	9466*	9733*	9668*	9861*
Palembang	9333†	10483†	10942†	10705†	11404†	12004†	11964†	10683†
Pusan	11045*	9346*	9036*	9155*	9571*	9838*	9773*	9966*
Qingdao	11311*	9612*	9302*	9421*	9837*	10104*	10039*	10232*
Qinhuangdao	11628*	9929*	9619*	9738*	10154*	10421*	10356*	10549*
Sabang	8550†	9700†	10159†	9922†	10621†	11221†	11181†	9900†
Shanghai	11360†	9686*	9376*	9493*	9911*	10178*	10113*	10306*
Shimonoseki	10970*	9271*	8961*	9080*	9496†	9763†	9698†	9891*
Singapore	9151†	10301†	10760†	10523†	11222†	11822†	11782†	10501†
Surabaya	9791†	10941†	10996*	11115*	11531*	11798*	11733*	11141†
Tanjung Priok	9418†	10568†	11027†	10790†	11489†	12089†	12049†	10768†
Tokyo	10435*	8736*	8426*	8561*	8961*	9228*	9163*	9356*
Toyama	11125*	9426*	9116*	9235*	9651*	9918*	9853*	10045*
Vladivostok	10477*	8778*	8468*	8587*	9003*	9270*	9205*	9398*
Yokohama	10417*	8718*	8408*	8543*	8943*	9210*	9145*	9338*

All distances on this page via the Panama Canal except where otherwise indicated.

AREA C	Baie Comeau	Baltimore	Boston	Cartagena (Colombia)	Charleston	Churchill	Cienfuegos	Cristobal
Adelaide	11214	10204	10467	8600	9874	12742	9082	8300
Albany	11360†	11029	11285	9409	10692	12121†	9900	9128
Apia	8123	7120	7376	5500	6783	9767	5991	5325
Auckland	9459	8466	8712	6836	8119	10997	7327	6555
Banaba	9672	8669	8923	7049	8332	11166	7540	6769
Bluff	9749	8746	9002	7126	8409	11287	7619	6845
Brisbane	10620	9614	9873	7996	9280	12142	8487	7700
Cairns	11428	10425	10681	8805	10088	12972	9296	8530
Cape Leeuwin	11195†	11194	11450	9574	10857	11956†	10065	9293
Darwin	1510†	11087	11343	9467	10750	12400†	9958	9186
Esperance	11620†	10759	11015	9139	10422	12381†	9630	8858
Fremantle	11155†	11379	11299	9759	11042	11916†	10250	9478
Geelong	10875	9820	10128	8200	9483	12413	8743	7971
Geraldton	10975†	11199	11119	9579	10862	12513†	10070	9298
Hobart	10577	9574	9830	7954	9237	12115	8445	7673
Honolulu	7632	6629	6885	5009	6292	9170	5500	4728
Launceston	10759	9756	10012	8136	9419	12297	8626	7855
Lyttleton	9522	8519	8775	6899	8182	11060	7390	6618
Mackay	11160	10280	10412	8536	9830	12697	9030	8255
Madang	11222	10219	10475	8599	9882	12716	9090	8319
Makatea	7370	6360	6623	4747	6030	8908	5238	4466
Melbourne	10875	9820	10128	8200	9540	12442	8743	8000
Napier	9312	8354	8555	6676	7960	10842	7167	8400
Nauru Island	9777	8774	9028	7154	8437	11271	7645	6874
Nelson	9525	8585	8765	6895	8180	11062	7385	6620
Newcastle (NSW)	10601	9964	9854	7978	9260	12132	8467	7690
New Plymouth	9612	8674	8865	7986	8270	11152	7477	6710
Noumea	9929	9049	9182	7306	8600	11467	7800	7025
Otago Harbour	9699	8696	8952	7076	8359	11237	7569	6795
Papeete	7440	6437	6693	4817	6100	8978	5308	4536
Port Hedland	10897†	11532†	11082†	10481	11657†	11786†	10972	10201
Port Kembla	10646	10039	9899	8023	8135	12184	7342	7742
Portland (Victoria)	10914	9904	10167	8300	9574	12442	8782	8000
Port Lincoln	11359	10356	10602	8726	10009	12887	9217	8445
Port Moresby	11147	10144	10400	8524	9807	12641	9015	8244
Port Pirie	11459	10466	10712	8836	10119	12997	9327	8555
Rockhampton	10670	9790	9922	8046	9340	12210	8540	7765
Suva	9273	8270	8526	6650	7933	10811	7141	6369
Sydney	10621	10014	9874	7998	9280	12159	8489	7717
Wellington	9452	8514	8705	6826	8110	10992	7317	6550

All distances on this page via the Panama Canal except where otherwise indicated.

AREA G

AREA C	Curacao	Duluth-Superior	Freeport (Bahamas)	Galveston	Georgetown (Guyana)	Halifax	Havana	Jacksonville
Adelaide	8987	12734	9488	9808	9825	10605	9313	9826
Albany	9805	12880†	10306	10621	10643	11119†	10131	10644
Apia	5896	9643	6397	6712	6734	7514	6222	6735
Auckland	7237	10979	7733	8050	8070	8850	7558	8071
Banaba	7445	11192	7946	8261	8283	9063	7771	8284
Bluff	7522	11289	8023	8338	8360	9140	7848	8361
Brisbane	8393	12140	8894	9209	9231	10011	8719	9232
Cairns	9201	12948	9702	10017	10039	10819	9527	10040
Cape Leeuwin	9970	12715†	10471	10786	10808	10954†	10296	10809
Darwin	9863	13030†	10364	10679	10701	11325†	10189	10702
Esperance	9535	13140†	10036	10351	10373	11399†	9861	10374
Fremantle	10155	12675†	10656	10971	9781C	10914†	10481	10994
Geelong	8596	12395	9149	9464	9486	10266	8974	9487
Geraldton	9975	12495†	10476	10791	9961C	10734†	10301	10814
Hobart	8350	12097	8851	9166	9188	9968	8676	9189
Honolulu	5405	9152	5906	6221	6243	7023	5731	6244
Launceston	8532	12279	9033	9348	9418	10150	8858	9371
Lyttleton	7295	11042	7796	8111	8133	8913	7621	8134
Mackay	8932	12679	9433	9748	9770	10550	9258	9771
Madang	8945	12742	9496	9811	9833	10613	9321	9834
Makatea	5143	8890	5644	5959	5981	6761	5469	5982
Melbourne	8577	12395	9149	9464	9434	10266	8973	9487
Napier	7077	10822	7576	7891	7913	8693	7410	7914
Nauru Island	7639	11368	8140	8455	8477	9257	7965	8478
Nelson	7295	11040	7795	8110	8135	8915	7630	8135
Newcastle (NSW)	8377	12121	8875	9190	9212	9992	8700	9213
New Plymouth	7287	11132	7886	8200	8225	9003	7720	8224
Noumea	7702	11449	8203	8518	8540	9320	8028	8541
Otago Harbour	7472	11219	7973	8288	8310	9090	7798	8831
Papeete	5213	8960	5714	6029	6051	6831	5539	6052
Port Hedland	10877	12417†	11378	11693	11480†	10712†	11202	11716
Port Kembla	8422	12166	8920	9235	9257	10035	8745	9258
Portland (Victoria)	8687	12434	9188	9503	9525	10305	9013	9526
Port Lincoln	9127	12869	9623	9940	9960	10740	9448	9961
Port Moresby	8920	12667	9421	9736	9758	10538	9246	9759
Port Pirie	9237	12979	9733	10050	10070	10850	9558	10071
Rockhampton	8442	12189	8943	9258	9280	10060	8768	9281
Suva	7046	10793	7547	7862	7884	8664	7372	7884
Sydney	8397	12141	8895	9210	9232	10012	8720	9233
Wellington	7227	10972	7726	8041	8063	8843	7560	8064

All distances on this page via the Panama Canal except where otherwise indicated.

AREA G

AREA C	Key West	Kingston (Jamaica)	La Guaira	Maracaibo	Mobile	Montreal	New Orleans	New York
Adelaide	9880	8861	9150	8910	9680	11564	9700	10280
Albany	10193	9679	9969	9728	10498	11710†	10518	11102
Apia	6284	5770	6050	5819	6589	8473	6609	7193
Auckland	7620	7106	7396	7155	7925	9809	7945	8529
Banaba	7833	7319	7609	7368	8138	10022	8158	8742
Bluff	7910	7396	7686	7445	8215	10099	8235	8819
Brisbane	8780	8266	8556	8316	9086	10970	9106	9890
Cairns	9589	9075	9365	9124	9894	11778	9914	10498
Cape Leeuwin	10358	9844	10134	9893	10663	11545†	10673	11267
Darwin	10251	9737	10027	9780	10556	11860†	10576	11160
Esperance	9923	9407	9699	9458	10428	11970†	10248	10832
Fremantle	10543	10029	10319	10078	10848	11505†	10868	11452
Geelong	9036	8522	8812	8571	9341	11225	9361	9945
Geraldton	10363	9849	10139	9898	10668	11325†	10688	11272
Hobart	8738	8224	8514	8273	9043	10927	9063	9647
Honolulu	5800	5279	5569	5328	6098	7982	6118	6702
Launceston	8920	8406	8696	8455	9225	11109	9245	9829
Lyttleton	7683	7169	7459	7218	7988	9872	8008	8592
Mackay	9320	8810	9096	8855	9530	11509	9639	10229
Madang	9383	8869	9159	8918	9688	11572	9708	10292
Makatea	5531	5017	5307	5066	5836	7720	5875	6459
Melbourne	9036	8520	8810	8571	9341	11225	9360	9950
Napier	7466	6949	7239	6998	7770	9652	7788	8370
Nauru Island	7938	7424	7714	7473	8243	10127	8263	8847
Nelson	7685	7165	7455	7215	7990	9870	8010	8590
Newcastle (NSW)	8760	8248	8538	8297	9070	10951	9088	9680
New Plymouth	7776	7259	7549	7308	8080	9962	8098	8680
Noumea	8090	7480	7866	7825	8400	10279	8409	8999
Otago Harbour	7860	7346	7636	7395	8165	10049	8185	8769
Papeete	5601	5087	5377	5136	5906	7790	5926	6510
Port Hedland	11265	10751	11041	10800	11570	11247†	11590	11232†
Port Kembla	8805	8293	8583	8342	9112	10996	9133	9716
Portland (Victoria)	9080	8561	8850	8610	9380	11264	9400	9980
Port Lincoln	9510	8996	9286	9045	9815	11699	9649	10233
Port Moresby	9308	8794	9084	8843	9513	11497	9633	10217
Port Pirie	9620	9106	9396	9155	9925	11809	9945	10529
Rockhampton	8830	8320	8606	8365	9140	11019	9149	9739
Suva	7434	6920	7210	6969	7739	9623	7795	8343
Sydney	8780	8268	8558	8317	9087	10971	9108	9691
Wellington	7616	7099	7389	7148	7920	9802	7938	8520

All distances on this page via the Panama Canal except where otherwise indicated.

AREA G

AREA C	Norfolk (Virginia)	Nuevitas	Philadelphia	Port Au Prince	Portland (Maine)	Port of Spain	Puerto Limon	St John (New Brunswick)
Adelaide	10089	9244	10256	9084	10508	9469	9490	10628
Albany	10907	10062	11074	9902	11326	10287	9318	11370†
Apia	6998	6153	7165	5993	7417	6378	5315	7537
Auckland	8334	7489	8499	7329	8753	7714	6745	8873
Banaba	8547	7702	8714	7542	8966	7927	6958	9086
Bluff	8624	7779	9791	7619	9043	8004	7035	9163
Brisbane	9495	8650	9660	8490	9914	8875	7890	10034
Cairns	10303	9458	10470	9298	10722	9683	8720	10842
Cape Leeuwin	11072	10227	11239	10067	11491	10452	9483	11205†
Darwin	10965	10120	11132	9960	11384	10345	9376	11855†
Esperance	10637	9792	10804	9632	11056	10017	9048	11630†
Fremantle	11257	10412	11424	10252	11263	10148C	9668	11165†
Geelong	9750	8905	9917	8745	10169	9130	8161	10289
Geraldton	11077	10232	11244	10072	11083	10328C	9488	10985†
Hobart	9750	8607	9619	8447	9871	8832	7863	9991
Honolulu	6507	5662	6674	5502	6926	5887	4918	7046
Launceston	9634	8789	9801	9629	10053	9014	8045	10173
Lyttleton	8397	7552	8564	7392	8816	7777	6808	8936
Mackay	10034	9189	10200	9030	10453	9414	8445	10573
Madang	10097	9252	10264	9092	10516	9477	9508	10636
Makatea	6245	5419	6430	5259	6683	5644	4656	6784
Melbourne	9750	8905	9916	8745	10169	9130	8190	10289
Napier	8177	7332	8350	7170	8596	7557	6590	8716
Nauru Island	8652	7807	8819	7647	9071	8032	7063	9191
Nelson	8395	7550	8570	7390	8815	7775	6810	8935
Newcastle (NSW)	9476	8631	9643	8470	9895	8857	7880	10015
New Plymouth	8487	7642	8660	7480	8906	7867	6900	9046
Noumea	8804	7959	8970	7800	9223	8184	7215	9343
Otago Harbour	8574	7729	8741	7569	8993	7954	6985	9113
Papeete	6315	5470	6482	5310	6734	5695	4726	6854
Port Hedland	11392†	11134	11382†	10974	11012†	11359	10390	10942†
Port Kembla	9521	8676	9685	8515	9940	8902	7932	10060
Portland (Victoria)	9789	9544	9956	8784	10208	9169	8190	10328
Port Lincoln	10224	9379	10450	9380	10805	9767	8635	10763
Port Moresby	10022	9177	10189	9017	10441	9402	8433	10561
Port Pirie	10334	9489	10500	10329	10753	9714	8745	10873
Rockhampton	8944	8699	9710	8540	9963	8924	7955	10083
Suva	8148	7303	8315	7143	8567	7528	6559	8687
Sydney	9496	8651	9660	8490	9915	8877	7907	10035
Wellington	8327	7482	8500	7320	8740	7707	6740	8866

All distances on this page via the Panama Canal except where otherwise stated.

AREA G

AREA C	St John's (Newfoundland)	San Juan (Puerto Rico)	Santiago de Cuba	Santo Domingo	Tampa	Tampico	Veracruz	Wilmington (N Carolina)
Adelaide	11002	9303	8993	9112	9528	9795	9730	9923
Albany	10647†	10121	9811	9930	10346	10613	10548	10741
Apia	7911	6212	5902	6021	6437	6704	6639	6832
Auckland	9247	7548	7238	7358	7773	8040	7976	8168
Banaba	9460	7761	7451	7570	7986	8253	8188	8381
Bluff	9537	7838	7528	7647	8063	8330	8265	8458
Brisbane	10408	8709	8399	8520	8934	9200	9136	9329
Cairns	11216	9517	9207	9326	9742	10009	9944	10137
Cape Leeuwin	10482†	10286	9976	10095	10511	10778	10713	10906
Darwin	10925†	10179	9869	9988	10404	10671	10606	10799
Esperance	10907†	9851	9541	9660	10076	10343	10278	10471
Fremantle	10442†	10471	10161	10280	10699	10963	10898	11091
Geelong	10663	8964	8654	8773	9189	9456	9391	9584
Geraldton	10262†	10291	9981	10100	10519	10783	10718	10911
Hobart	10365	8666	8356	8475	8891	9158	9093	9286
Honolulu	7420	5721	5411	5530	5946	6213	6148	6341
Launceston	10547	8848	8538	8657	9073	9340	9275	9468
Lyttleton	9310	7611	7301	7420	7836	8103	8038	8231
Mackay	10947	9248	8938	9058	9473	9739	9675	9868
Madang	11010	9311	9001	9120	9536	9803	9738	9931
Makatea	7158	7948	5149	5268	5682	5994	5932	6079
Melbourne	10663	8964	8654	8793	9189	9457	9390	9584
Napier	9090	7391	7081	7198	7616	7883	7818	8011
Nauru Island	9565	7866	7556	7675	8091	8358	8293	8486
Nelson	9310	7610	7300	7410	7835	8105	8035	8230
Newcastle (NSW)	10389	8690	8380	8499	8915	9182	9116	9310
New Plymouth	9400	7701	7391	7508	7926	8193	8128	8821
Noumea	9717	8018	7708	7828	8243	8509	8445	8638
Otago Harbour	9487	7788	7478	7597	8013	8280	8215	8408
Papeete	7228	5529	5219	5338	5752	6064	6002	6149
Port Hedland	19287†	11193	10883	11002	11418	11685	11620	11662†
Port Kembla	10434	8735	8425	8544	8960	9227	9161	9355
Portland (Victoria)	10702	9003	8693	8812	9228	9495	9430	9623
Port Lincoln	11137	9438	9128	9248	9663	9930	9866	10058
Port Moresby	10935	9236	8926	9045	9461	9728	9663	9856
Port Pirie	11247	9548	9238	9358	9773	10040	9976	10168
Rockhampton	10457	8758	8448	8568	8983	9249	9185	9378
Suva	9061	7362	7052	7171	7587	7854	7789	7982
Sydney	10409	8710	8400	8519	8935	9202	9136	9330
Wellington	9240	7541	7231	7348	7766	8033	7968	8161

All distances on this page via the Panama Canal.

AREA H

AREA C	Baie Comeau	Baltimore	Boston	Cartagena (Colombia)	Charleston	Churchill	Cienfuegos	Colon
Antofagasta	5087	4142	4340	2444	3738	6620	2945	2178
Arica	4868	3946	4121	2248	3542	6424	2749	1982
Astoria	6730	5727	5983	4107	5390	8268	4593	3826
Balbao	2948	1945	2201	325	1608	4442	816	45
Buenaventura	4299	2296	2552	676	1959	4837	1167	395
Cabo Blanco	3698	2695	2951	1075	2358	5242	1566	800
Caldera	5278	4300	4531	2646	3940	6822	3147	2380
Callao	4293	3300	3546	1653	2947	5829	2161	1387
Cape Horn	6985	5985	6240	4350	5635	8527	4850	4085
Chimbote	4113	3120	3366	1473	2767	5649	1981	1207
Coos Bay	6546	5543	5799	3925	5206	8084	4414	3642
Corinto	3646	2643	2899	1024	2308	5190	1515	748
Eureka	6405	5402	5658	3782	5065	7943	4273	3501
Guayaquil	3772	2856	3023	1158	2452	5334	1659	892
Guaymas	5330	4326	4583	2698	3992	6874	3119	2432
Honolulu	7632	6079	6885	4981	6275	9157	5482	4715
Iquique	4937	4014	4187	2316	3610	6492	2817	2050
Los Angeles	5860	4857	5113	3237	4520	7398	3728	2956
Manzanillo (Mex)	4665	3764	3918	2066	3360	6242	2567	1800
Mazatlan	4953	4084	4206	2386	3680	6562	2887	2120
Nanaimo	6987	5984	6240	4364	5647	8525	4855	4083
New Westminster	6995	5992	6248	4372	5655	8533	4863	4091
Portland (Oreg)	6816	5813	6069	4193	5476	8354	4684	3912
Port Alberni	6942	5939	6195	4319	5602	8436	4810	4039
Port Isabel	5610	4606	4863	2978	4272	7154	3479	2712
Port Moody	6990	5987	6243	4367	5650	8528	4858	4086
Prince Rupert	7251	6248	6504	4628	5911	8745	5119	4348
Puerto Montt	5920	4920	5173	3288	4570	7464	3789	3022
Puntarenas (CR)	3413	2410	2666	790	2073	4957	1281	515
Punta Arenas (Ch)	6880	5880	6133	4248	5530	8424	4749	3982
Salina Cruz	4108	3104	3361	1486	2770	5652	1977	1210
San Francisco	6192	5291	5445	3593	4887	7769	4094	3327
San Jose	3836	2833	3089	1209	2498	5380	1705	938
Seattle	6968	5965	6221	4345	5628	4506	4836	4064
Tacoma	6999	5996	6252	4376	5659	8537	4867	4095
Talcahuano	5755	4814	5005	3116	4410	7292	3617	2850
Tocopilla	5015	4012	4268	2392	3675	6553	2883	2111
Valparaiso	5563	4622	4816	2924	4218	7100	3425	2658
Vancouver (BC)	6986	5983	6239	4363	5646	8524	4854	4082
Victoria (Vanc Is)	6919	5916	6172	4296	5579	8457	4787	4015

All distances on this page via the Panama Canal.

AREA H

AREA C	Curacao	Duluth-Superior	Freeport (Bahamas)	Galveston	Georgetown (Guyana)	Halifax	Havana	Jacksonville
Antofagasta	2855	6607	3361	3659	3698	4478	3191	3699
Arica	2659	6388	3142	3463	3479	4259	2995	3480
Astoria	4503	8250	5004	5319	5341	6121	4829	5342
Balbao	721	4468	1222	1537	1559	2339	1047	1560
Buenaventura	1072	5119	1572	1888	1910	2690	1398	1911
Cabo Blanco	1471	5218	1972	2287	2309	3089	1797	2310
Caldera	3057	6798	3552	3867	3889	4669	3380	3890
Callao	2064	5813	2567	2868	2904	3684	2400	2905
Cape Horn	4760	8505	5255	5563	5595	6370	5085	5592
Chimbote	1884	5633	2387	2688	2724	3504	2220	2725
Coos Bay	4319	8066	4820	5135	5157	5937	4645	5158
Corinto	1420	5166	1920	2239	2257	3037	1745	2258
Eureka	4178	7925	4679	4994	5016	5796	4504	5017
Guayaquil	1569	5292	2046	2373	2383	3163	1905	2384
Guaymas	3109	6850	3604	3913	3941	4721	3430	3942
Honolulu	5392	9152	5906	6196	6243	7023	5728	6244
Iquique	2727	6457	3208	3531	3545	4325	3063	3546
Los Angeles	3633	7280	4134	4449	4471	5251	3959	4472
Manzanillo (Mex)	2477	6185	2939	3281	3276	4056	2900	3277
Mazatlan	2797	6473	3227	3541	3564	4344	3033	3565
Nanaimo	4760	8507	5261	5576	5598	6378	5086	5599
New Westminster	4768	8515	5269	5584	5606	6386	5094	5607
Portland (Oreg)	4589	8336	5090	5405	5427	6207	4915	5428
Port Alberni	4715	8462	5216	5531	5553	6333	5041	5554
Port Isabel	3389	7130	3884	4193	4221	5001	3710	4222
Port Moody	4763	8511	5264	5579	5601	6381	5089	5602
Prince Rupert	5024	8771	5525	5840	5862	6642	5350	5863
Puerto Montt	3699	7440	4194	4503	4531	5311	4920	4532
Puntarenas (CR)	1186	4933	1687	2002	2024	2804	1512	2025
Punta Arenas (Ch)	4659	8400	5154	5463	5491	6271	4980	5492
Salina Cruz	1880	5628	2382	2697	2719	3499	2208	2720
San Francisco	4004	7712	4466	4788	4803	5583	4340	4804
San Jose	1610	5356	2110	2419	2447	3227	1935	2448
Seattle	4741	8488	5242	5557	5579	6359	5067	5580
Tacoma	4772	8519	5273	5588	5610	6390	5098	5611
Talcahuano	3527	7272	4026	4331	4363	5143	3863	4364
Tocopilla	2788	6535	3289	3604	3626	4406	3114	3627
Valparaiso	3335	7083	3837	4149	4174	4954	3671	4175
Vancouver (BC)	4759	8507	5260	5575	5597	6377	5085	5598
Victoria (Vanc Is)	4692	8439	5193	5508	5530	6310	5018	5531

All distances on this page via the Panama Canal.

AREA H	AREA C	Key West	Kingston (Jamaica)	La Guaira	Maracaibo	Mobile	Montreal	New Orleans	New York
Antofagasta		3264	2724	2904	2783	3549	5437	3558	4158
Arica		3068	2528	2708	2564	3333	5218	3362	3962
Astoria		4891	4377	4667	4426	5196	7080	5216	5800
Balbao		1109	595	885	644	1414	3162	1434	2018
Buenaventura		1460	946	1236	995	1765	3649	1785	2369
Cabo Blanco		1859	1345	1635	1394	2164	4048	2184	2768
Caldera		3440	2926	3206	2974	3744	5628	3760	4350
Callao		2473	1933	2113	1989	2758	4643	2767	3367
Cape Horn		5148	4630	4910	4675	5450	7330	5462	6060
Chimbote		2293	1753	1933	1809	2578	4463	2587	3187
Coos Bay		4707	4193	4483	4242	5012	6896	5032	5616
Corinto		1804	1294	1584	1342	2112	3996	2130	2720
Eureka		4566	4052	4342	4101	4871	6755	4891	5475
Guayaquil		1978	1438	1618	1468	2233	4122	2272	2872
Guaymas		3500	2978	3268	3026	3800	5680	3812	4400
Honolulu		5800	5261	5441	5328	6088	7982	6095	6695
Iquique		3106	2586	2776	2630	3400	5287	3430	4030
Los Angeles		4021	3507	3797	3556	4326	6210	4346	4930
Manzanillo (Mex)		2826	2308	2526	2361	3131	5015	3180	3780
Mazatlan		3116	2600	2846	2649	3420	5303	3500	4100
Nanaimo		5148	4634	4924	4683	5453	7337	5473	6057
New Westminster		5156	4642	4932	4691	5461	7345	5481	6065
Portland (Oreg)		4977	4463	4753	4512	5282	7166	5302	5886
Port Alberni		5103	4589	4879	4638	5408	7292	5428	6012
Port Isabel		3780	3258	3548	3306	4080	5960	4092	4680
Port Moody		5151	4637	4927	4686	5456	7340	5476	6062
Prince Rupert		5412	4898	5188	4947	5717	7601	5737	6321
Puerto Montt		4088	3568	3848	3616	4390	6270	4402	5000
Puntarenas (CR)		1574	1060	1350	1109	1879	3763	1899	2483
Punta Arenas (Ch)		5048	4528	4808	4576	5350	7230	5362	5960
Salina Cruz		2268	1756	2050	1804	2580	4458	2590	3180
San Francisco		4413	3873	4053	3888	4658	6542	4707	5307
San Jose		2000	1484	1800	1532	2309	4186	2318	2908
Seattle		5129	4615	4905	4664	5434	7318	5454	6038
Tacoma		5160	4646	4936	4695	5465	7349	5485	6069
Talcahuano		3936	3396	3576	3448	4220	6102	4230	4830
Tocopilla		3176	2662	2952	2711	3481	5365	3501	4085
Valparaiso		3744	3204	3384	3259	4029	5913	4038	4638
Vancouver (BC)		5147	4633	4923	4682	5452	7336	5472	6056
Victoria (Vanc Is)		5080	4566	4856	4615	5385	7269	5405	5989

All distances on this page via the Panama Canal.

AREA H

AREA C	Norfolk (Virginia)	Nuevitas	Philadelphia	Port Au Prince	Portland (Maine)	Port of Spain	Puerto Limon	St John (New Brunswick)
Antofagasta	3962	3117	4148	2948	4381	3315	2368	4501
Arica	3743	2898	3952	2752	4162	3119	2172	4282
Astoria	5605	4760	5772	4600	6024	4985	4016	6144
Balbao	1823	978	1990	818	2242	1203	234	2362
Buenaventura	2174	1329	2341	1169	2593	1554	585	2713
Cabo Blanco	2573	1728	2740	1568	2992	1953	990	3112
Caldera	4153	3308	4320	3150	4572	3533	2570	4692
Callao	3168	2323	3357	2157	3587	2524	1577	3707
Cape Horn	5855	5010	6020	4855	6280	5240	4275	6394
Chimbote	2988	2143	3177	1977	3407	2344	1397	3527
Coos Bay	5421	4576	5588	4416	5840	4801	3832	5960
Corinto	2521	1676	2688	1518	2940	1885	938	3060
Eureka	5280	4435	5447	4275	5699	4660	3691	5819
Guayaquil	2647	1802	2862	1662	3066	2029	1082	3186
Guaymas	4205	3360	4372	3200	4624	3589	2622	4744
Honolulu	6507	5662	6685	5485	6926	5887	4905	7046
Iquique	3809	2964	4020	2820	4228	3187	2240	4348
Los Angeles	4735	3890	4902	3730	5154	4115	3146	5274
Manzanillo (Mex)	3540	2695	3770	2570	3959	2937	1990	4079
Mazatlan	3828	2983	4090	2890	4247	3257	2310	4367
Nanaimo	5862	5017	6029	4857	6281	5242	4273	6401
New Westminster	5870	5025	6037	4865	6289	5250	4281	6409
Portland (Oreg)	5691	4846	5858	4686	6110	5071	4102	6230
Port Alberni	5817	4972	5984	4812	6236	5197	4228	6356
Port Isabel	4485	3640	4652	3480	4904	3869	2902	5024
Port Moody	5865	5020	6032	4860	6284	5245	4276	6404
Prince Rupert	6126	5281	6293	5121	6545	5506	4537	6665
Puerto Montt	4795	3950	4962	3792	5214	4180	3212	5334
Puntarenas (CR)	2288	1443	2455	1283	2707	1668	705	2827
Punta Arenas (Ch)	5755	4910	5922	4752	6174	5140	4172	6294
Salina Cruz	2983	2138	3150	1980	3402	2363	1400	3522
San Francisco	5067	4222	5297	4097	5486	4464	3517	5606
San Jose	2711	1866	2880	1708	3130	2095	1128	3250
Seattle	5843	4998	6010	4838	6262	5223	4254	6382
Tacoma	5874	5029	6041	4869	6293	5254	4285	6413
Talcahuano	4627	3782	4820	3620	5046	3987	3040	5166
Tocopilla	3890	3045	4057	2885	4309	3270	2301	4429
Valparaiso	4438	3593	4628	3428	4857	3795	2848	4977
Vancouver (BC)	5861	5016	6028	4856	6280	5241	4272	6400
Victoria (Vanc Is)	5794	4949	5961	4789	6213	5174	4205	6333

All distances on this page via the Panama Canal.

AREA H	AREA C	St John's (Newfoundland)	San Juan (Puerto Rico)	Santiago de Cuba	Santo Domingo	Tampa	Tampico	Veracruz	Wilmington (N Carolina)
Antofagasta		4875	3176	2866	2971	3401	3655	3594	3796
Arica		4656	2957	2647	2775	3182	3459	3398	3577
Astoria		6518	4819	4509	4628	5044	4311	5246	5439
Balbao		2736	1037	727	846	1262	1529	1464	1657
Buenaventura		3087	1388	1078	1197	1613	1880	1815	2008
Cabo Blanco		3486	1787	1477	1596	2012	2279	2214	2407
Caldera		5066	3367	3057	3176	3592	3859	3796	3987
Callao		4081	2382	2072	2180	2607	2864	2803	3002
Cape Horn		6768	5070	4760	4875	5295	5560	5500	5696
Chimbote		3901	2202	1892	2000	2427	2684	2623	2822
Coos Bay		6334	4635	4325	4444	4860	5127	5062	5255
Corinto		3434	1735	1425	1544	1960	2225	2164	2355
Eureka		6193	4494	4184	4303	4719	4986	4921	5114
Guayaquil		3560	1861	1551	1685	2086	2369	2308	2481
Guaymas		5118	3419	3109	3225	3644	3909	3848	4039
Honolulu		7420	5721	5411	5508	5946	6192	6131	6341
Iquique		4722	3023	2713	2843	3248	3527	3466	3643
Los Angeles		5648	3949	3639	3758	4174	4441	4376	4569
Manzanillo (Mex)		4453	2754	2444	2595	2979	3277	3216	3374
Mazatlan		4741	3042	2732	2913	3267	3597	3536	3662
Nanaimo		6775	5076	4766	4885	5301	5568	5503	5696
New Westminster		6783	5084	4774	4893	5309	5576	5511	5704
Portland (Oreg)		6604	4905	4595	4714	5130	5397	5332	5525
Port Alberni		6730	5031	4721	4840	5256	5523	5458	5651
Port Isabel		5398	3699	3389	3505	3924	4189	4128	4319
Port Moody		6778	5079	4769	4888	5304	5571	5506	5699
Prince Rupert		7039	5340	5030	5149	5565	5832	5767	5960
Puerto Montt		5708	5009	3699	3815	4234	4499	4438	4629
Puntarenas (CR)		3201	1502	1192	1311	1727	1994	1929	2122
Punta Arenas (Ch)		6668	4969	4659	4775	5194	5459	5398	5589
Salina Cruz		3896	2197	1887	2003	2422	2689	2620	2817
San Francisco		5980	4281	3971	4120	4506	4804	4743	4901
San Jose		3624	1925	1615	1734	2150	2415	2354	2545
Seattle		6756	5057	4747	4866	5282	5549	5484	5677
Tacoma		6787	5088	4778	4897	5313	5580	5515	5708
Talcahuano		5540	3841	3531	3643	4066	4327	4266	4461
Tocopilla		4803	3104	2794	2913	3329	3596	3531	3724
Valparaiso		5351	3652	3342	3451	3877	4135	4074	4272
Vancouver (BC)		6774	5075	4765	4884	5300	5567	5502	5695
Victoria (Vanc Is)		6707	5008	4698	4817	5233	5500	5435	5628

AREA C

AREA C	Aruba	Baie Comeau	Baton Rouge	Boston	Botwood	Cienfuegos	Cristobal	Halifax
Albany (NY)	1888	1326	1965	503	1457	1748	2097	718
Baie Comeau	2539	–	2887	994	958	2573	2875	643
Baltimore	1725	1505	1763	682	1633	1544	1904	899
Barranquilla	324	2715	1600	1973	2733	733	340	2131
Beaumont	1752	2909	546	2099	3008	1004	1506	2303
Brownsville	1751	2999	708	2189	3098	1003	1500	2393
Cape Race (NF)	2226	643	2671	811	315	2312	2615	463
Charleston	1393	1685	1314	870	1806	1094	1560	1077
Cristobal	632	2875	1536	2136	2930	775	–	2298
Galveston	1734	2909	523	2099	3008	986	1485	2303
Georgetown (G)	847	1793	2509	2268	2705	1629	1475	2295
Halifax	1984	643	2281	386	778	1991	2298	–
Havana	1087	2213	754	1408	2313	473	990	1608
Jacksonvillle	1345	1849	1204	1032	1970	987	1505	1240
Key West	1080	2143	749	1343	2254	536	1054	1549
Montreal	2854	315	3202	1309	1273	2888	3117	958
New Orleans	1630	2754	133	1944	2853	885	1403	2148
New York	1763	1201	1840	379	1332	1623	1972	593
Newport News	1599	1379	1637	556	1507	1327	1778	773
Norfolk (Va)	1602	1382	1640	559	1510	1330	1781	776
Portland (Maine)	1913	954	2120	102	1086	1873	2179	344
Quebec	2715	188	3063	1170	1134	2749	3051	819
St John (NB)	2004	905	2238	290	1037	1990	2296	295
Santa Marta	284	2690	1618	1948	2708	750	360	2106
Santo Domingo	373	2292	1655	1600	2267	715	800	1710
Savannah	1393	1763	1284	946	1882	1065	1563	1156
Tampa	1343	2422	627	1615	2524	697	1212	1819
Tampico	1741	3039	866	2235	3144	1000	1473	2438
Three Rivers	2746	219	3094	1201	1165	2780	3082	850
Veracruz	1677	3003	943	2196	3105	937	1410	2399

AREA C

AREA C	Houston	Jacksonville	Kingston	Maracaibo	Montreal	New Orleans	New York	Nuevitas
Albany (NY)	2030	916	1597	2027	1641	1832	125	1389
Baie Comeau	2952	1849	2375	2680	315	2754	1201	2200
Baltimore	1828	715	1404	1834	1820	1630	410	1187
Barranquilla	1610	1348	463	410	3030	1468	1808	777
Beaumont	143	1226	1274	1815	3224	413	1862	1080
Brownsville	305	1316	1273	1814	3314	575	1952	1156
Cape Race (NF)	2736	1649	2115	2367	958	2538	1017	1946
Charleston	1379	199	1060	1490	2000	1181	629	740
Cristobal	1528	1505	555	676	3190	1403	1972	941
Galveston	48	1226	1256	1797	3224	390	1862	1080
Georgetown (G)	2574	1974	1329	990	3108	2376	2216	1480
Halifax	2346	1240	1795	2125	958	2148	593	1615
Havana	813	531	743	1184	2528	621	1167	340
Jacksonville	1269	–	1012	1442	2164	1071	791	635
Key West	814	470	747	1177	2468	616	1106	332
Montreal	3267	2164	2690	2995	–	3069	1516	2514
New Orleans	433	1071	1155	1693	3069	–	1707	925
New York	1905	791	1472	1902	1516	1707	–	1264
Newport News	1702	589	1278	1708	1694	1504	284	1061
Norfolk (Va)	1705	592	1281	1711	1697	1507	287	1064
Portland (Maine)	2185	1073	1677	2054	1269	1987	419	1488
Quebec	3128	2025	2551	2856	139	2930	1377	2375
St John (NB)	2303	1195	1794	2145	1220	2105	537	1605
Santa Marta	1627	1323	438	375	3005	1485	1783	752
Santo Domingo	1666	1174	428	491	2607	1522	1491	627
Savannah	1349	148	1060	1490	2078	1151	705	713
Tampa	722	742	964	1440	2737	494	1378	595
Tampico	516	1361	1263	1850	3354	733	2000	1196
Three Rivers	3159	2056	2582	2887	108	2961	1408	2406
Veracruz	665	1321	1200	1740	3318	810	1958	1143

AREA C

AREA C	Philadelphia	Port Arthur (Texas)	Port of Spain	Puerto Cabello	Puerto Rico	St John's (Newfoundland)	Tampico	Wilmington (N Carolina)
Albany (NY)	360	1962	2057	1964	1524	1222	2124	684
Baie Comeau	1350	2884	2580	2791	2130	723	3039	1615
Baltimore	376	1760	1919	1800	1378	1400	1919	482
Barranquilla	1740	1561	830	475	692	2498	1561	1403
Beaumont	1833	25	2220	1917	1711	2773	548	1425
Brownsville	1923	311	2228	1916	1787	2863	258	1515
Cape Race (NF)	1176	2668	2211	2300	1804	78	2826	1418
Charleston	599	1311	1677	1548	1139	1571	1468	149
Cristobal	1946	1481	1140	788	992	2697	1473	1609
Galveston	1833	75	2211	1899	1711	2773	473	1425
Georgetown (G)	2224	2506	364	740	876	2471	2551	2008
Halifax	743	2278	2055	2060	1580	543	2438	1007
Havana	1140	749	1478	1240	969	2078	864	727
Jacksonvillle	763	1201	1663	1500	1121	1735	1361	306
Key West	1078	746	1472	1235	965	2017	905	668
Montreal	1665	3199	2895	2930	2445	1038	3354	1930
New Orleans	1678	388	2065	1795	1556	2618	733	1270
New York	235	1837	1932	1839	1399	1097	1999	559
Newport News	250	1634	1793	1675	1252	1274	1793	356
Norfolk (Va)	253	1637	1796	1678	1255	1277	1796	359
Portland (Maine)	570	2117	2042	1989	1533	853	2276	841
Quebec	1526	3060	2756	2791	2306	899	3215	1791
St John (NB)	688	2235	2110	2080	1615	802	2393	961
Santo Domingo	1481	1616	678	480	230	2032	1637	1205
Santa Marta	1757	1578	790	440	667	2473	1578	1420
Savannah	676	1281	1690	1548	1155	1647	1439	223
Tampa	1347	652	1735	1498	1226	2289	917	940
Tampico	1965	523	2220	1906	1818	2908	–	1557
Three Rivers	1557	3091	2787	2822	2332	930	3246	1822
Veracruz	1926	660	2158	1842	1754	2870	221	1519

Area D

Distances between principal ports on the East Coast of South America, the Atlantic Islands, and West and East Africa.

and

Area E The Red Sea, The Gulf, the Indian Ocean and the Bay of Bengal.

Area F Malaysia, Indonesia, South East Asia, the China Sea and Japan.

Area G Australasia, New Guinea and the Pacific Islands.

Area H The West Coast of North and South America.

Area D Other ports on the East Coast of South America, the Atlantic Islands, and West and East Africa.

AREA D
Reed's Marine Distance Tables
SOUTH ATLANTIC & EAST AFRICA
Azores
(Ponta Delgada)
Madeira
NORTH
ATLANTIC
OCEAN
Las Palmas
Nouadhibou
Dakar
São Vicente I
Banjul
Conakry
Pepe
Belem
Fortaleza
Recife
Salvador
Rio de Janeiro
Vitoria (Brazil)
Santos
Paranagua
Tubarao
Porto Alegre
Tramandai
SOU
ATLAN
OCE
Buenos Aires
Montevideo
Bahia Blanca
PACIFIC OCEAN
Cape Horn
© Adlard Coles Nautical 2004
Modified Gall Projection

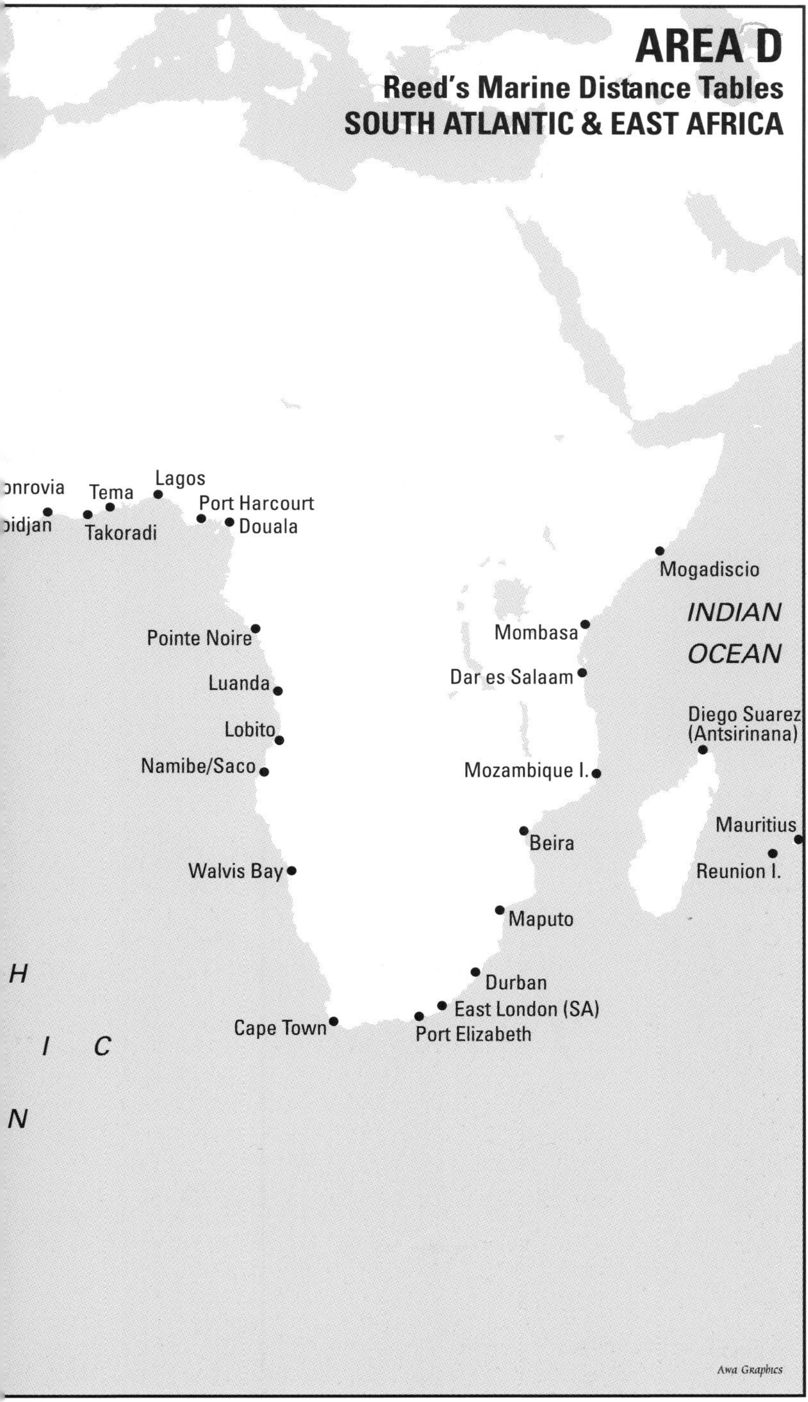
AREA D
Reed's Marine Distance Tables
SOUTH ATLANTIC & EAST AFRICA
Tema
Lagos
Port Harcourt
Takoradi
Douala
Mogadiscio
INDIAN
OCEAN
Pointe Noire
Mombasa
Luanda
Dar es Salaam
Lobito
Diego Suarez
(Antsirinana)
Namibe/Saco
Mozambique I.
Mauritius
Beira
Reunion I.
Walvis Bay
Maputo
Durban
East London (SA)
Cape Town
Port Elizabeth
Awa Graphics

AREA E

AREA D	Azores (via Suez Canal)	Bahia Blanca (via Cape of Good Hope (except where marked †)	Beira	Belem	Buenos Aires (via Cape of Good Hope (except where marked †)	Cape Horn (via Cape of Good Hope (except where marked †)	Cape Town	Conakry
Abadan	6250	9270	3829	8547†	9184	9680	5189	7177†
Aden	4302	7695†	2600	6629†	7635	8124	4000	5244†
Aqaba	3040	7870†	3839	5603†	7592†	9345	5199	4237†
Bahrain	6034	8730	3624	8333†	8644	9140	4984	6967†
Bandar Abbas	5723	8450	3345	8053†	8364	8860	4705	6687†
Basrah	6288	8959	3942	8615†	8899	9374	5229	7206†
Bassein	7585	9170	4220	9731C	9084	9580	5390	8487†
Bhavnagar	6007	8591	3340	8376†	8531	9980	4860	6927†
Bushehr	5920	8790	3684	8403†	8704	9200	5044	7037†
Calcutta	7607	9263	4200	9866C	9203	9644	5535	8675C
Chennai	6959	8609	3635	9286†	8549	8990	4885	8020C
Chittagong	7635	9311	4548	9914C	9251	9692	5537	8723C
Cochin	6120	8107	3043	6453†	8021	8517	4362	7087†
Colombo	6398	8128	3175	8725†	8068	8517	4395	7332†
Djibouti	4300	7697	2602	6630†	7637	8126	4002	5242†
Dubai	5801	8528	3423	8131	8442	8938	4783	6765
Fujairah	5635	8362	3257	7965	8276	8772	4617	6599
Jedda	3602	8398	3300	5939†	8335	8824	4700	4544†
Karachi	5773	8403	3225	8100†	8343	8826	4675	6709†
Kuwait	6045	8914	3809	8523†	8829	9325	5169	7157†
Malacca	7774	9230	4396	9791C	9144	9640	5490	8670C
Mangalore	6015	8121	3046	8724C	8061	8570	4391	6977†
Massawa	3902	8090	2991	6273†	8000	8500	4351	4907†
Mina al Ahmadi	6167	8890	3789	8503†	8804	9300	5149	7137†
Mongla	7621	9277	4214	9880C	9217	9658	5549	8689C
Mormugao	5984	8196	3121	8799C	8136	8645	4466	6927†
Moulmein	7640	9270	4305	9831	9184	9680	5475	8710C
Mumbai	5959	8361	3250	8286†	8301	9750	4630	6897†
Musay'td	5972	8690	3594	8303†	8604	9100	4955	6937†
Penang	7639	9026	4235	9659C	8996	9475	5325	8505C
Port Blair	7236	8810	3586	8873C	8795	9693	5075	8239C
Port Kelang	7716	9160	4320	9727C	9074	9570	5404	8607C
Port Okha	5768	8390	3284	8103†	8304	8800	4641	6737†
Port Sudan	3691	8194†	3247	6018†	8019†	8765	4576	4632†
Quseir	3252	7795†	3653	5528†	7517†	8611†	5013	4162†
Singapore	7932	9361	4515	9964C	9301	9760	5630	8790C
Sittwe	7640	9215	4175	9776C	9129	9625	5445	8512†
Suez	2994	7947†	3904	5321†	7322†	8386	5275	3937†
Trincomalee	6650	8310	3352	8871C	8224	9880	4565	7750C
Veraval	5826	8360	3250	8186†	8300	9750	4630	6797†
Vishakhapatnam	7274	8920	3882	9523C	8860	9250	5000	8280C
Yangon	7607	9263	4280	9866C	9203	9640	5540	8670C

AREA E

AREA D	Dakar (via Suez Canal)	Dar es Salaam	Diego Suarez	Douala (via Cape of Good Hope (except where marked †)	Durban	East London	Lagos (via Cape of Good Hope (except where marked †)	Las Palmas (via Suez Canal)
Abadan	6741	2988	3013	7890	4399	4650	8580	5940
Aden	4825	1740	1840	6324	3169	3435	6438†	4019
Aqaba	3801	2982	3081	5768†	4409	4660	5397†	3000
Bahrain	6531	2783	2808	7350	4195	4445	7540	5730
Bandar Abbas	6250	2504	2529	7070	3915	4166	7350	5450
Basrah	6681	3018	3043	7584	4429	4688	7786	6005
Bassein	8051	3700	3257	7790	4670	4891	7980	7250
Bhavnagar	6572	2560	2670	7190	4030	4303	7418	5766
Bushehr	6601	2843	2868	5410	4254	4505	7600	5800
Calcutta	8130	3490	3285	7854	4735	4990	8090	7324
Chennai	7482	2840	2635	7200	4088	4449	7436	6673
Chittagong	8178	3538	3333	7902	4783	5038	8138	7372
Cochin	6450	2427	2090	6727	3572	3823	6917	3850
Colombo	6921	2380	2175	6726	3615	3824	6955	6115
Djibouti	4823	1742	1842	6326	3202	3437	6440†	4021
Dubai	6328	2582	2607	7148	3993	4244	7428	5528
Fujairah	6162	2416	2441	6982	3827	4078	7262	5362
Jedda	4125	2440	2540	6104	3900	4135	5738	3319
Karachi	6296	2405	2515	7036	3895	4160	7230	5490
Kuwait	6720	2968	2993	7535	4379	4630	7725	5920
Malacca	8300	3920	3427	7850	4744	4953	8040	7500
Mangalore	6585	2364	2148	6780	3608	3864	6948	5776
Massawa	3470	2134	2233	6710	3561	3812	6067†	3670
Mina al Ahmadi	6700	2948	2973	7510	4359	4610	7700	5900
Mongla	8144	3504	3299	7868	4749	5004	8104	7338
Mormugao	6535	2439	2223	6855	3683	3939	7023	5726
Moulmein	8151	3808	3363	7890	4775	4990	8080	7350
Mumbai	6482	2330	2440	6960	3800	4073	7188	5676
Musay'td	6501	2755	2780	7310	4165	4410	7500	5700
Penang	8162	3780	3235	7685	4580	4794	7883	7349
Port Blair	7782	2745	2712	7485	4279	4532	7647	6976
Port Kelang	8239	3845	3353	7780	4683	4904	7970	7426
Port Okha	6300	2467	2390	7010	3850	4105	7200	5500
Port Sudan	4214	2395	2492	6163	3824	4087	5827	3401
Quseir	3725	2796	2895	5693	4223	4474	5322†	2925
Singapore	8455	3999	3555	7970	5191	5082	8188	7647
Sittwe	8086	3738	3293	7835	4725	4933	8025	7285
Suez	3517	3040	3140	5468	4481	4744	5130	2704
Trincomalee	7180	2833	2388	6930	3818	4020	7120	6380
Veraval	6382	2330	2440	6960	3800	4073	7188	5576
Vishakhapatnam	7707	3370	2920	7460	4378	4551	7747	6988
Yangon	8130	3750	3295	7850	4741	5007	8090	7317

AREA E

AREA D	Lobito (via Cape of Good Hope (except where marked †)	Luanda (via Cape of Good Hope (except where marked †)	Madeira (via Suez Canal)	Maputo	Mauritius	Mogadiscio	Mombasa	Monrovia
Abadan	6920	7116	6851	4181	3399	2352	2828	5440†
Aden	5373	5550	3929	2960	2340	1106	1620	5493†
Aqaba	6585	6781	2911	4191	3576	2346	2842	4486†
Bahrain	6380	6576	5641	3976	3194	2147	2643	7216†
Bandar Abbas	6100	6296	5361	3697	2915	1868	2364	6936†
Basrah	6637	6840	5915	4361	3429	2382	2879	7455†
Bassein	6820	7016	7161	4530	3140	3250	3646	8345C
Bhavnagar	6269	6416	5656	3750	2755	2145	2630	7745C
Bushehr	6440	6636	5711	4036	3254	2207	2703	7286†
Calcutta	6941	7080	7234	4500	3205	3305	3699	8409C
Chennai	6287	6426	6586	3895	2555	2651	3040	7444C
Chittagong	6989	7128	7282	4548	3253	3353	3747	8457C
Cochin	5757	5953	3761	3359	2143	1900	2354	5336†
Colombo	5806	5953	6025	3555	2095	2101	2519	5581†
Djibouti	5375	5552	3927	2962	2342	1109	1622	5491†
Dubai	6178	6374	5439	3775	2993	1946	2442	7014
Fujairah	6012	6208	5273	3609	2827	1780	2276	6484
Jedda	6073	6250	3229	3660	3040	1806	2320	4793†
Karachi	6081	6262	5400	3675	2785	1863	2365	6958†
Kuwait	6565	6761	5736	4161	3380	2332	2828	7406†
Malacca	6880	7076	7411	4639	3200	3488	3885	8986†
Mangalore	5799	6006	5689	3405	2270	1789	2265	7335C
Massawa	5740	5936	3581	3343	2730	1500	1995	5156†
Mina al Ahmadi	6540	6736	5811	4140	3360	2312	2808	7386†
Mongla	6955	7094	7248	4514	3219	3319	3713	8423C
Mormugao	5874	6081	5639	3480	2345	1864	2340	7410C
Moulmein	6920	7116	7261	4655	3225	3356	3752	8445C
Mumbai	6039	6186	5486	3520	2535	1915	2400	7515C
Musay'td	6340	6536	5611	3945	3165	2115	2615	7186†
Penang	6734	6911	7266	4485	3075	3321	3699	8265C
Port Blair	6425	6702	6886	3983	2825	2220	2569	7972C
Port Kelang	6802	7006	7343	4553	3130	3410	3812	8335C
Port Okha	6040	6236	5411	3633	2660	1875	2360	6986†
Port Sudan	6026	6201	3318	3605	2990	1760	2219	4881†
Quseir	6410	6606	2836	4005	3390	2160	2656	4411†
Singapore	7039	7196	7559	4800	3330	3611	3990	8525C
Sittwe	6865	7061	7196	4525	3195	3286	3682	8390C
Suez	6025†	5898†	2621	4264	3640	2406	2922	4186†
Trincomalee	5960	6156	6291	3660	2295	2381	2775	7485C
Veraval	6039	6186	5586	3520	2535	1915	2400	7515C
Vishakhapatnam	6598	6686	6901	4190	2830	2915	3305	8105C
Yangon	6941	7076	7234	4545	3215	3310	3720	8405C

AREA E

AREA D	Montevideo (via Cape of Good Hope (except where marked †)	Mozambique I	Porto Alegre (via Cape of Good Hope (except where marked †)	Port Elizabeth	Port Harcourt (via Cape of Good Hope (except where marked †)	Recife (via Cape of Good Hope (except where marked †)	Reunion Island	Rio de Janeiro (via Cape of Good Hope (except where marked †)
Abadan	9087	3356	9105	4780	7942	8371†	3450	8751
Aden	7523	2150	7539	3560	6376	6463†	2358	7197
Aqaba	7495†	3365	7351†	4790	5640†	5431†	3598	6493†
Bahrain	8637	3149	8565	4575	7402	8270	3245	8211
Bandar Abbas	8267	2872	8282	4296	7122	7990	2966	7931
Basrah	8787	3386	8799	4883	7636	8449	3480	8461
Bassein	8987	3776	9005	4990	7842	8710	3261	8651
Bhavnagar	8419	2980	8405	4430	7242	8164	2830	8093
Bushehr	8607	3211	8625	4635	7462	8330	3305	8271
Calcutta	9091	3785	9069	5105	7906	8836	3325	8765
Chennai	8437	3135	8415	4415	7252	8182	2670	8111
Chittagong	9139	3833	9117	5153	7954	8884	3373	8813
Cochin	7924	2598	7942	3953	6490†	6281†	2234	7587
Colombo	7956	2675	7942	3975	6789	7701	2203	7588
Dubai	8345	2950	8360	4374	7200	8068	3044	8009
Fujairah	8179	2784	8194	4208	7034	7902	2878	7843
Djibouti	7525	2152	7541	3562	6378	6461†	2360	7199
Jedda	8223	2850	8239	4260	5976†	5763†	3058	6829†
Karachi	8231	2825	8251	4255	7088	7976	2820	7905
Kuwait	8732	3336	8750	4760	7587	8455	3430	8396
Malacca	9047	3952	9065	5080	7902	8770	3316	8711
Mangalore	7949	2605	7995	4014	6832	7694	2357	7623
Massawa	7907	2515	7925	3940	6762	6101†	2750	7571
Mina al Ahmadi	8707	3316	8725	4740	7562	8430	3410	8371
Mongla	9105	3799	9083	5119	7920	8850	3339	8779
Mormugao	8024	2680	8070	4089	6907	7769	2432	7698
Moulmein	9087	3882	9105	5095	7940	8810	3354	8751
Mumbai	8189	2750	8175	4200	7012	7934	2600	7863
Musay'td	8507	3121	8525	4545	7362	8230	3215	8171
Penang	8884	3785	8900	4925	7737	8629	3150	8558
Port Blair	8683	3276	8898	4653	7320	8393	2944	8348
Port Kelang	8972	3878	8995	5009	7832	8700	3245	8646
Port Okha	8207	2812	8425	4232	7062	7930	2737	7871
Port Sudan	7919†	2776	8190	4199	6035†	5852†	3010	6917†
Quseir	7420†	3179	7276†	4604	5565†	5356†	3412	6418†
Singapore	9189	4075	9185	5209	8022	8934	3440	8863
Sittwe	9032	3812	9050	5065	7887	8755	3306	8696
Suez	7222†	3425	7051†	4873	5340†	5155†	3658	6220†
Trincomalee	8127	2905	8145	4156	6982	7850	2401	7791
Veraval	8190	2750	8175	4200	7010	7935	2600	7865
Vishakhapatnam	8748	3440	8675	4698	7512	8493	2935	8322
Yangon	9091	3795	9065	5065	7902	8836	3320	8765

AREA E

AREA D	Salvador (via Cape of Good Hope (except where marked †)	Santos (via Cape of Good Hope (except where marked †)	Sao Vicente Island (via Suez Canal)	Takoradi (via Cape of Good Hope (except where marked †)	Tema	Tramandai (via Cape of Good Hope (except where marked †)	Vitoria (Brazil) (via Cape of Good Hope (except where marked †)	Walvis Bay (via Cape of Good Hope (except where marked †)
Abadan	6614	8880	6798	8110	8105C	8955	8683	6220
Aden	6822	7369	4898	6171†	6238†	7389	7117	4652
Aqaba	5815†	6680†	3858	5087†	5176†	7201†	6224†	5884
Bahrain	8283	8342	6588	7570	7565C	8415	8143	5679
Bandar Abbas	8003	8062	6308	7290	7285C	8135	7863	5399
Basrah	8517	8633	6884	7808	7804C	8660	8377	5916
Bassein	8723	8782	8108	8010	8005C	8855	8583	6119
Bhavnagar	8123	8265	6645	7440	7436C	8255	7983	5548
Bushehr	8343	8402	6658	7630	7625C	8475	8203	5739
Calcutta	8787	8937	8203	8122	8108C	8919	8647	6220
Chennai	8133	8281	7555	7458	7454	8265	7993	5566
Chittagong	8834	8985	8251	8160	8156C	8967	8695	6268
Cochin	6665	7719	4708	5937	6026†	7792	7520	5056
Colombo	6910	7802	6994	6977	6937C	7792	7520	5085
Djibouti	6820	7371	4896	6169	6236†	7391	7119	4654
Dubai	8081	8140	6386	7368	7363	8213	7941	5477
Fujairah	7915	7974	6220	7202	7197	8047	7775	5311
Jedda	6122†	7016†	4198	5471†	5538†	7537†	7104†	5352
Karachi	7969	8077	6369	7252	7348	8101	7829	5360
Kuwait	8468	8527	6778	7755	7750C	8600	8328	5864
Malacca	8783	8842	8358	8070	8065C	8915	8643	6179
Mangalore	7713	7795	6630	6970	6966C	7845	7213	5108
Massawa	6485	7702	4528	5757	5846†	7775	6894	5039
Mina al Ahmadi	8443	8502	6758	7730	7725C	8575	8303	5839
Mongla	8800	8951	8217	8126	8122C	8933	8661	6234
Mormugao	7788	7870	6580	7045	7041C	7920	7648	5183
Moulmein	8823	8882	8208	8110	8105C	8955	8683	6219
Mumbai	7893	8035	6555	7210	7206C	8025	7753	5318
Musay'td	8243	8302	6558	7530	7525C	8375	8103	5639
Penang	8618	8730	8215	7905	7901C	8750	8478	6013
Port Blair	8408	8484	7855	7672	8650C	8748	8368	5780
Port Kelang	8713	8768	8312	8003	7995C	8845	8573	6101
Port Okha	7943	8002	6358	7230	7225C	8075	7803	5339
Port Sudan	6210†	7105†	4287	5560†	5627†	7596†	6619†	5304
Quseir	5740†	6605†	3783	5012†	5100†	7126†	6150†	5710
Singapore	8903	9035	8528	8210	8206C	9035	8763	6318
Sittwe	8768	8827	8143	8055	8050C	8900	8628	6164
Suez	5515†	6408†	3590	4863†	4870†	6901†	5924†	5962
Trincomalee	7863	7908†	7238	7152	7145C	7995	7723	5259
Veraval	7895	8035	6455	7210	7205C	8025	7755	5320
Vishakhapatnam	8393	8594	7870	7769	7765C	8525	8253	5787
Yangon	8783	8937	8203	8112	8108C	8915	8643	6220

AREA F

AREA F	AREA D Azores	Bahia Blanca	Beira	Belem	Buenos Aires	Cape Horn	Cape Town	Conakry (via Cape of Good Hope)
Balikpapan	8959†	9677C	5169	10280C	9617C	9024	5947	9152
Bangkok	8964†	10132C	5362	10735C	10072C	10304	6402	9607
Basuo (Hainan Is)	9114†	10237C	5729	10840C	10177C	10065	6510	9712
Cam-Pha	9392†	10690C	5965	11293C	10630C	10125	6960	10165
Cebu	9287†	10100C	5875	11078C	10415C	8893	6745	9952
Dalian	10544†	11959C	7132	10994*	11899C	10096	8229	11333
Haiphong	9292†	10590C	5865	11193C	10530C	10155	6860	10065
Ho Chi Minh City	8581†	9920C	5160	10523C	9860C	10045	6190	9395
Hong Kong	9386†	10647C	5950	10848C	10587C	9745	6909	10122
Hungnam	11371*	10899M	7279	10304*	11267M	9665	8222	11427
Inchon	10484†	11772C	7275	11387*	11712C	9961	8042	11324
Kampong Saom	8664†	9835C	5060	10435C	9770C	10004	6100	9305
Kaohsiung (Taiwan)	9557†	10653C	6145	11256C	10593C	9494	6926	10128
Keelung (Taiwan)	9737†	11012M	6325	11076*	10964C	9308	7294	10499
Kobe	10595†	10433M	7200	10313*	10801M	9450	8049	11248
Makassar	8922†	9644C	5094	10205C	9542C	8734	5875	9075
Manila	9262†	10267M	5860	11021C	10358C	9250	6700	9893
Masinloc	9302†	10307M	5890	11061C	10598C	9303	6740	9933
Menado	9422†	9605M	5767	10774C	10033M	8679	6428	9653
Moji	10483†	10486M	7070	10572*	10854M	9556	7880	11080
Muroran	11171†	10750M	7864	10430*	11122M	9496	8979	11741
Nagasaki	10347†	10573M	6960	10553*	10941M	9600	7894	11099
Nagoya	10786†	10316M	7374	10069*	10684M	9432	8304	11509
Nampo	10555†	11969C	7145	10944*	11910C	10046	8240	11343
Osaka	10603†	10441M	7191	10321*	10809M	9454	8051	11256
Otaru	11208†	10900M	7902	10580*	11268M	9646	9017	11855
Palembang	8114†	9237C	4729	9840C	9177C	9359	5510	8712
Pusan	10435†	10607M	7129	10685*	10977M	9663	8244	11006
Qingdao	10398†	10885M	6986	10928*	11253M	10031	7969	11180
Qinhuangdao	10671†	11991C	7259	11245*	11931C	10202	8261	11360
Sabang	7335†	8770C	3921	9331C	8684C	9180C	4980	8210
Shanghai	10142†	10831M	6735	11002*	11199M	9807	7649	10850
Shimonoseki	10473†	10476M	7660	10552*	10844M	9557	7870	11070
Singapore	7932†	9361C	4515	9694C	9301C	9557	5630	8836
Surabaya	8572†	9290C	4800	9893C	9230C	8984	5560	8765
Tanjung Priok	8199†	8917C	4409	9520C	8857C	9066	5190	8392
Tokyo	10844†	10297M	7438	10052*	10665M	9313	8338	11542
Toyama	10933†	10936M	7520	10750*	11304M	9812	8330	11530
Vladivostok	11161*	11144M	7524	10094*	11512M	9906	8467	11672
Yokohama	10826†	10279M	7420	10034*	10647M	9301	8320	11524

AREA F

AREA D	Dakar (via Suez Canal)	Dar es Salaam	Diego Suarez	Douala (via Cape of Good Hope)	Durban	East London	Lagos (via Cape of Good Hope)	Las Palmas (via Suez Canal)
Balikpapan	9482	4783	4177	8287	5253	5372	8504	8676
Bangkok	9487	5423	4817	8927	5735	5827	8959	8681
Basuo (Hainan Is)	9537	5363	4757	8867	5479	5932	9064	8829
Cam-Pha	9915	5982	5376	9486	5935	6385	9517	9109
Cebu	9810	5606	4600	9110	6009	6170	9302	9004
Dalian	11067	7049	6043	10553	7395	7654	10685	10261
Haiphong	9815	5882	5276	9386	6113	6285	9517	9009
Ho Chi Minh City	9104	5068	4462	8572	5477	5615	8747	8296
Hong Kong	9909	5825	7219	9329	6233	6342	9474	9103
Hungnam	11214	7136	6530	10640	7194	7647	10779	10406
Inchon	11027	6515	6305	10374	7333	7467	9599	12412
Kampong Saom	9185	9120	4515	8625	5070	5525	8660	8380
Kaohsiung (Taiwan)	9080	5779	5173	9283	6402	6348	9480	9541
Keelung (Taiwan)	10260	6174	5568	9678	6603	6719	9851	9454
Kobe	11118	7030	6424	10534	7465	7468	10600	10312
Makassar	9445	4728	4122	8232	5252	5297	8429	8680
Manila	9785	5602	4996	9106	6007	6113	9245	8977
Masinloc	9825	5642	5036	9146	5710	6153	9285	9017
Menado	9948	5328	4722	8833	5768	5972	9023	9140
Moji	11006	6875	6269	10379	7313	7300	10432	10198
Muroran	11693	7712	7106	11216	7508	7961	11093	10900
Nagasaki	10870	6755	6149	10259	7192	7319	10451	10062
Nagoya	11309	6895	6289	10399	7570	7729	10861	10501
Nampo	11077	7059	6053	10556	7211	7664	10695	10271
Osaka	11126	6925	6319	10429	7469	7476	10608	10318
Otaru	11731	7650	7044	11154	7547	8000	11131	10923
Palembang	8537	4363	3757	7867	4791	4932	8064	7829
Pusan	10958	6463	6253	10322	7284	7226	10358	10150
Qingdao	10921	6828	6222	10332	7244	7394	10526	10113
Qinhuangdao	11194	7157	6551	10661	7501	7754	10718	10388
Sabang	7858	3443	2959	7390	4273	4485	7580	7052
Shanghai	10665	6565	5959	10069	6968	7070	10202	9858
Shimonoseki	10996	6865	6259	10369	7312	7290	10422	10188
Singapore	8455	3940	3326	7858	5191	5080	8188	7647
Surabaya	9195	4426	3820	7930	4876	4985	8117	8304
Tanjung Priok	8722	4043	3437	7547	4498	4612	7744	7916
Tokyo	11367	7255	6649	10759	7679	7762	10894	10558
Toyama	11456	7325	6719	10829	7295	7750	10882	10648
Vladivostok	11459	7381	6775	10885	7784	7892	11024	10651
Yokohama	11349	7237	6631	10741	7667	7744	10876	10540

AREA F

AREA D	Lobita (via Cape of Good Hope)	Luanda (via Cape of Good Hope)	Madeira (via Suez Canal)	Maputo	Mauritius	Mogadiscio	Mombasa	Monrovia (via Cape of Good Hope)
Balikpapan	7355	7567	8586	5118	3052	4465	4741	8912
Bangkok	7810	8022	8591	5573	4392	4534	4829	9367
Basuo (Hainan Is)	7915	8130	8881	5678	4306	4967	5320	9475
Cam-Pha	8368	8580	8905	6120	4950	5553	5447	9925
Cebu	8153	8365	8914	5916	4575	5177	5342	9710
Dalian	9536	9849	10171	7400	6018	6620	6599	11194
Haiphong	8268	8480	8905	6020	4850	5453	5347	9825
Ho Chi Minh City	7598	7810	8208	5365	4038	4129	4636	9155
Hong Kong	8325	8529	9013	6230	4794	5396	5441	9874
Hungnam	9630	9842	10318	7393	6105	6707	6746	11187
Inchon	9450	9662	8114	7312	6043	6340	6855	11007
Kampong Saom	7510	7720	8290	5270	4090	4230	4525	9065
Kaohsiung (Taiwan)	8331	8546	9452	6094	4748	5461	5736	9891
Keelung (Taiwan)	8702	8914	9364	6465	5143	5745	5792	10259
Kobe	9451	9669	10222	7220	5999	6601	6650	11014
Makassar	7280	7495	8549	5043	3697	4410	4685	8840
Manila	8096	8320	8889	5859	4580	5173	5317	9665
Masinloc	8136	8360	8929	5899	4620	5213	5357	9705
Menado	7863	8059	9052	5698	4297	5010	5317	9385
Moji	9283	9500	10110	7048	5846	6446	6538	10845
Muroran	10038	10599	10797	7793	6726	7023	7349	11944
Nagasaki	9302	9514	9974	7064	5724	6326	6402	10859
Nagoya	9712	9924	10413	7475	5866	6466	6841	11269
Nampo	9546	9860	10181	7410	6028	6630	6609	11205
Osaka	9459	9671	10230	7222	5784	6396	6658	11016
Otaru	10067	10637	10894	7832	6763	7061	7313	11982
Palembang	6915	7130	7881	4678	3306	3967	4320	8475
Pusan	9209	9864	10062	6974	5991	6288	6464	11209
Qingdao	9377	9589	10025	7140	5797	6399	6453	10934
Qinhuangdao	9569	9881	10298	7432	6130	6728	6726	11226
Sabang	6420	6616	6962	4171	2731	3015	3388	7945
Shanghai	9053	9269	9765	6809	5534	6136	6197	10614
Shimonoseki	9273	9490	10100	7038	5836	6436	6528	10835
Singapore	7039	7250	7559	4769	3488	3785	3990	8595
Surabaya	6968	7180	8199	4730	3395	4105	4354	8525
Tanjung Priok	6595	6710	7726	4358	3012	3725	4000	8155
Tokyo	9745	9958	10473	7518	6224	6826	6899	11303
Toyama	9733	9950	10560	7498	6296	6896	6988	11295
Vladivostok	9875	10087	10563	7638	6350	6952	6991	11432
Yokohama	9727	9940	10455	7500	6206	6808	6881	11285

AREA F / AREA D	Montevideo	Mozambique I	Porto Alegre	Port Elizabeth	Port Harcourt (via Cape of Good Hope)	Recife	Reunion Island	Rio de Janeiro
Balikpapan	9505C	4706	9524C	5547	8405	9250C	3167	9179C
Bangkok	9960C	5346	9979C	6002	8855	9705C	4507	9634C
Basuo (Hainan Is)	10065C	5258	10082C	6109	8964	9810C	4421	9739C
Cam-Pha	10518C	5905	10537C	6560	9417	10263C	5065	10192C
Cebu	10303C	5529	10322C	6345	9200	10048C	4690	9977C
Dalian	11428M	6972	11813M	7289	10585	11431C	6133	11360C
Haiphong	10418C	5805	10437C	6460	9315	10163C	4965	10092C
Ho Chi Minh City	9748C	4991	9767C	5785	8647	9493C	4153	9422C
Hong Kong	10475C	5748	10494C	6516	9372	10220C	4909	10149C
Hungnam	11202M	7059	11587M	7822	10679	11212*	6220	11454C
Inchon	11220M	6855	11605M	7650	9500	11489C	6158	11274C
Kampong Saom	9660C	5045	9675C	5700	8560	9405C	4205	9330C
Kaohsiung (Taiwan)	10481C	5702	10500C	6525	9380	10559C	4863	10155C
Keelung (Taiwan)	10852C	6097	10771C	6894	9751	10597C	5258	10526C
Kobe	10736M	6953	11749C	7649	10500	11221*	6114	11275C
Makassar	9430C	4651	9449C	5474	8329	9629C	3812	9104C
Manila	10246C	5525	10265C	6300	9145	9991C	4695	9920C
Masinloc	10286C	5565	10305C	6340	9185	10031C	4735	9960C
Menado	10033M	5251	10048C	6078	8885	9753C	4411	9694C
Moji	10789M	6798	11174M	7478	10332	11470*	5961	11107C
Muroran	11044C	7678	11438M	8138	10993	11340*	6841	11768C
Nagasaki	10876M	6678	11261M	7494	10351	11470*	5839	11126C
Nagoya	10619M	6818	11004M	7904	10761	10977*	5981	11536C
Nampo	11438M	6982	11823M	7839	10595	11441C	6143	11370C
Osaka	10744M	6748	11129M	7651	10508	11229*	5909	11283C
Otaru	11564M	7716	11588M	8253	11031	11497*	6878	11882C
Palembang	9065C	4258	9082C	5109	7964	8810C	3421	8739C
Pusan	10912M	6943	11297M	7404	10258	11437C	6106	11033C
Qingdao	11188M	6751	11573M	7569	10426	11272C	5912	11201C
Qinhuangdao	11528M	7084	11913M	7929	10618	11464C	6245	11393C
Sabang	8587C	3481	8605C	4610	7442	8310C	2846	8251C
Shanghai	11134M	6488	11519M	7249	10102	10948C	5649	10877C
Shimonoseki	10779M	6788	11164M	7468	10322	11495*	5951	11097C
Singapore	9189C	4440	9208C	5209	8088	8934C	3603	8863C
Surabaya	9118C	4349	9137C	5160	8017	8863C	3510	8792C
Tanjung Priok	8745C	3966	8764C	4789	7644	8490C	3127	8419C
Tokyo	10600M	7178	10985M	7938	10794	10960*	6339	11535M
Toyama	11239M	7248	11624M	7952	10782	11660*	6411	11557C
Vladivostok	11447M	7304	11832M	8067	10924	11002*	6465	11699C
Yokohama	10582M	7160	10967M	7920	10776	10942*	6321	11517M

AREA F

AREA D	Salvador	St Vincent Island (via Suez Canal)	Santos	Takoradi (via Cape of Good Hope)	Tema (via Cape of Good Hope)	Tramandai	Vitoria (Brazil)	Walvis Bay (via Cape of Good Hope)
Balikpapan	9282C	9555	9451C	8521	8522	9374C	9102C	6634
Bangkok	9737C	9560	9806C	8981	8977	9829C	9557C	7089
Basuo (Hainan Is)	9842C	9700	9911C	9086	9082	9932C	9660C	7199
Cam-Pha	10295C	9988	10364C	9539	9535	10387C	10115C	7647
Cebu	10080C	9883	10149C	9324	9320	10172C	9900C	7432
Dalian	11564C	11140	11532C	10707	10703	11663M	11346C	8815
Haiphong	10195C	9888	10264C	9439	9435	10287C	10015C	7547
Ho Chi Minh City	9525C	9177	9594C	8769	8765	9617C	9345C	6877
Hong Kong	10252C	9985	10321C	9496	9492	10344C	10072C	7604
Hungnam	11686	11287	11626C	10801	10797	11437M	11425C	8809
Inchon	11526C	11083	11446C	10621	10817	11455M	11245C	8734
Kampong Saom	9435C	9260	9505C	8680	8677	9525C	9255C	6789
Kaohsiung (Taiwan)	10258C	10420	10327C	9502	9498	10350C	10078C	7615
Keelung (Taiwan)	10629C	10333	10698C	9873	9869	10621C	10349C	7981
Kobe	11378C	11191	11447C	10622	10618	11599C	11327C	8730
Makassar	9207C	9785	9276C	8451	8447	9299C	9027C	6564
Manila	10023C	9858	10092C	9267	9263	10115C	9843C	7375
Masinloc	10063C	9898	10132C	9307	9303	10155C	9883C	7415
Menado	9766C	10021	9825C	9053	9043	9898C	9626C	7162
Moji	11210C	11079	11279C	10454	10450	11024M	11083M	8562
Muroran	11816*	11766	11940C	11109	11555	11288M	11686C	9228
Nagasaki	11229C	10943	11298C	10473	10469	11111M	11052C	8581
Nagoya	11456*	11382	11708C	10883	10879	10854M	11192C	8991
Nampo	11574C	11150	11542C	10717	10715	11673M	11362C	8825
Osaka	11386C	11199	11455C	10630	10626	10979M	11122C	8738
Otaru	11958*	11854	12054C	11229	11593	11438M	11790C	9337
Palembang	8842C	8700	8911C	8086	8082	8932C	8660C	6199
Pusan	11333C	11031	11205C	10380	10809	11147M	11183C	8488
Qingdao	11304C	10994	11373	10548	10544	11423M	11125C	8656
Qinhuangdao	11596C	11267	11565C	10740	10736	11763M	11454C	8848
Sabang	8323	7931	8382C	7610	7605	8455C	8183C	5719
Shanghai	10980C	10783	11049C	10224	10220	11369M	10862C	8332
Shimonoseki	11200C	11069	11269C	10444	10440	11014M	11075C	8552
Singapore	8966C	8528	9035C	8210	8206	9058C	8786C	6318
Surabaya	9895C	9168	8964C	8139	8135	8987C	8715C	6247
Tanjung Priok	8522C	8795	8591C	7766	7762	8614C	8342C	5879
Tokyo	11439*	11440	11354M	10916	10912	10835M	11785M	9024
Toyama	11660C	11529	11729C	10904	10900	11474M	11533M	9012
Vladivostok	11481*	11532	11871	11046	11042	11682M	11678C	9154
Yokohama	11421*	11422	11336	10898	10894	10817M	11767M	9006

AREA G

AREA D	Azores	Bahia Blanca	Beira	Belem	Buenos Aires	Cape Horn	Cape Town	Conakry
Adelaide	10400†	7379M	5360	10619*	7737M	6297	5880	8951C
Albany	9428†	8117M	4385	9108C	8085M	7055	4805	9760C
Apia	9138*	6038M	9160	8076*	6705M	5245	9861	10060M
Auckland	9934*	5818M	6760	8864*	6186M	4800	7150C	9532M
Banaba	10186*	7653M	8081	9126*	8050M	5570	8772	10759*
Bluff	10137*	5803M	6731	9094M	6200M	4740	7087C	9487M
Brisbane	11090*	7067M	6715	10025*	7435M	6030	6945C	10250C
Cairns	11901*	7853M	6765	10836*	8250M	6790	7358C	10540C
Cape Leeuwin	9148†	8108M	4277	8978C	8215M	7182	4675C	7830C
Darwin	9694†	9183M	5544	10443C	9580M	8120	6137	9330C
Esperance	9684†	8023M	4657	9291C	8420M	6960	4983	8170C
Fremantle	9223†	8426C	4355	9028C	8398C	7362	4790C	7900C
Geelong	10758†	6987M	5780	10284M	7385M	5925	6096C	9290C
Geraldton	9079†	8460C	4334	9081C	8394C	7540	4767	7950C
Hobart	10798C	8435M	5580	10126C	8803M	5650	5790C	9415C
Honolulu	8107*	7374M	10350	7034*	7742M	6477	11080C	8681*
Launceston	11138C	6868M	5883	10466C	7236M	5739	6133C	9365C
Lyttleton	9997*	5735M	6728	8927*	6103M	4620	6828C	9367M
Mackay	11178†	7521M	7109	10460*	7918M	6458	7489C	10680C
Madang	10726†	8181M	7766	10587*	8850M	7456	8259C	11452
Makatea	7920*	5228M	9230	6765*	5637M	4332	8532M	9079M
Melbourne	10780†	6983M	5780	10284M	7375M	5920	6086C	9286C
Napier	9820*	5663M	7027	8750*	6060M	4600	7353C	9347M
Nauru Island	10341*	7743M	7921	9276*	8140M	6680	8622	10909*
Nelson	10019*	5774M	6808	8956*	6170M	4711	6965	9457M
Newcastle (NSW)	11300†	6404M	6290	9741M	6772M	5890	6545C	9610C
New Plymouth	10076*	5831M	6798	9008*	6227M	4768	6955	9514M
Noumea	10405*	6531M	7247	9334*	6899M	5660	7479C	10407M
Otago Harbour	10174*	5704M	6895	9004M	6100M	4650	6655C	9397M
Papeete	7920*	5237M	9200	6845*	5605M	4300	8500M	9047M
Portland (Victoria)	10580†	7053M	5580	10354M	7445M	5970	5886C	9086C
Port Hedland	9099†	9015C	4705	9576C	8929C	9425	5270C	8455C
Port Kembla	11051*	6366M	6190	10072*	6734M	5840	6430C	9499C
Port Lincoln	10349†	7297M	5377	10744M	7835M	6371	5675C	8830C
Port Moresby	10668†	8001M	6593	10515*	8428M	6957	7149C	10342C
Port Pirie	10499†	7398M	5500	10844M	7935M	6472	5898C	9053C
Rockhampton	11369*	7216M	6980	10050*	7633M	6270	7359C	10550C
Suva	9748*	6448M	7873	8678*	6816M	5402	8105C	10207M
Sydney	11096*	6397M	6235	10026*	6765M	5823	6470C	9535C
Wellington	9930*	5638M	6880	8857*	6006M	4607	7025C	9397M

AREA G

AREA D	Dakar	Dar es Salaam	Diego Suarez	Douala	Durban	East London	Lagos	Las Palmas
Adelaide	9364C	5640	4965	8131C	5150	5156	8346C	10145†
Albany	8350C	4647	3972	7140C	4280	4364	7332C	9145†
Apia	9450*	8907	8277	10587M	9223	9365	10456M	9564*
Auckland	9742M	7346	5294	9990C	6738	6803	9710C	10385*
Banaba	10500*	7828	7198	11150C	8144	8286	11340C	10614*
Bluff	9680M	6961	6286	9452C	6633	6682	9642C	10457M
Brisbane	10520C	6937	6262	9430C	6608	6657	9502C	11335C
Cairns	10940C	6616	5975	9720C	6779	6889	9910C	10540†
Cape Leeuwin	8220C	4517	3842	7010C	4150	4234	7202C	9015†
Darwin	9730C	5427	4773	8510C	5558	5678	8700C	9355†
Esperance	8570C	4857	4182	7350C	4529	4578	7540C	9393C
Fremantle	8365C	4500	3827	7080C	4250	4264	7267C	8940†
Geelong	9691C	5977	5302	8470C	5659	5696	8673C	10511C
Geraldton	8350C	4437	3763	7130C	4263	4336	7320C	8780†
Hobart	9368C	6095	5427	8595C	5230	5192	8350C	10188C
Honolulu	8422*	9943	9337	10136*	10394	10562	9778*	8555*
Launceston	9708C	6045	5377	8545C	5470	5395	8690C	10585†
Lyttleton	9659M	7077	6402	9185C	6183	6653	9385C	10445*
Mackay	11080C	6960	6319	9860C	7035	7084	10050C	10083†
Madang	11852C	7549	6895	10632C	7680	8000	9922C	11477†
Makatea	8150*	9477	8802	9606M	9098	8946	9325M	8283*
Melbourne	9688C	5973	5298	8465	5640	5694	8670C	10500C
Napier	9540M	7227	6552	9630C	6899	6948	9743M	10244*
Nauru Island	10650*	7668	7038	10990C	7984	8126	11180C	10764*
Nelson	9651M	7200	6527	9320C	6250	6753	9510C	10428M
Newcastle (NSW)	10116C	6437	5762	8990C	5965	5985	9190C	11011†
New Plymouth	9708M	7190	6517	9310C	6240	6743	9500C	10485M
Noumea	10455M	7427	6752	9845C	6903	6926	10036C	10852*
Otago Harbour	9590M	7100	6424	9590C	6600	5950	9780C	10352M
Papeete	8230*	9377	8702	9574M	8998	8846	9293M	8363*
Portland (Victoria)	9488C	5773	5098	8265C	5440	5494	8470C	10300C
Port Hedland	8835C	4658	3997	7635C	4702	4806	7825C	8819†
Port Kembla	10004C	6322	5647	8875C	5885	5885	8986C	10895†
Port Lincoln	9220C	5617	4942	8010C	5250	5334	8202C	10115†
Port Moresby	10742C	6439	5785	9522C	6570	6690	9712C	10367†
Port Pirie	9343	5840	5165	8133C	5373	5457	8325C	10338†
Rockhampton	10950C	6830	6189	9730C	6905	6954	9920C	10753†
Suva	10063*	8337	7696	10491C	7529	7377	10504M	10196*
Sydney	10044C	6362	5687	8915C	5895	5925	9026C	10935†
Wellington	9562M	7270	6597	9741C	6320	6823	9587C	10375*

AREA G

AREA D	Lobito	Luanda	Madeira	Maputo	Mauritius	Mogadiscio	Mombasa	Monrovia
Adelaide	7197C	7357C	10050†	5142	4352	5708	5690	8686C
Albany	6183C	6366C	9055†	4300	3350	4642	4669	7695C
Apia	10029M	10174M	9543*	9168	7800	8619	8900	9984M
Auckland	8561C	9216C	10290*	6730	6225	7494	7575	9456
Banaba	10180C	10376C	10550*	8089	6275	7582	7820	10955*
Bluff	8482C	8678C	10453*	6686	5649	6956	7029	9411M
Brisbane	8453C	8656C	11330†	6415	5600	6932	6784	9985C
Cairns	8750C	8946C	10450†	6758	5461	6351	6615	10275C
Cape Leeuwin	6053C	6236C	8925†	4202	3165	4472	4539	7565C
Darwin	7540C	7736C	9266†	5537	4239	5167	5434	9065C
Esperance	6380C	6576C	9241†	4582	3545	4852	4925	7805C
Fremantle	6118C	6306C	8850†	4300	3200	4481	4564	7635
Geelong	7494C	7696C	10385†	5690	4665	5972	6000	9025C
Geraldton	6160C	6356C	8691	4289	3149	4381	4993	7685C
Hobart	7201C	7636C	10450C	5320	4625	6097	6270	9050C
Honolulu	10533*	10489*	8470*	10299	8912	9625	9868	8876*
Launceston	7541C	7586C	10498†	5440	4575	6047	6231	9000C
Lyttleton	8236C	8411C	10360*	6365	5765	7072	7461	9291M
Mackay	8890C	9086C	10794†	7086	5805	6695	6959	10415C
Madang	9662C	9858C	11388†	7659	6361	7289	7556	11187C
Makatea	9056M	9510M	8198*	9146	8165	9472	9554	9003M
Melbourne	7491C	7690C	10400†	5680	4665	5968	5998	9020C
Napier	8660C	8856C	10181*	6952	5915	7222	7295	9271M
Nauru Island	10020C	10216C	10700*	7929	6564	7380	7660	11105*
Nelson	8350C	8546C	10379*	6575	5700	7695	7413	9382M
Newcastle (NSW)	7950C	8216C	10924†	6035	5193	6432	6531	9545C
New Plymouth	8340C	8536C	10436*	6565	5690	7685	7403	9439M
Noumea	8887C	9071C	10767*	7293	6115	7422	7469	10331M
Otago Harbour	8621C	8816C	10537*	5920	5700	7092	7200	9321M
Papeete	9024M	9481M	8278*	9046	8065	9372	9454	8971M
Portland (Victoria)	7291C	7490C	10299†	5480	4465	5768	5798	8820C
Port Hedland	6665C	6861C	8729†	4692	3431	4504	4691	8190C
Port Kembla	7837C	8033C	10810†	5935	5090	6317	6419	9430C
Port Lincoln	7053C	7236C	10025†	5202	4165	5472	5639	8565C
Port Moresby	8552C	8748C	10278†	6549	5251	6179	6446	10077C
Port Pirie	7176C	7359C	10248†	5325	4288	5595	5862	8688C
Rockhampton	8760C	8956C	10664†	6956	5675	6565	6829	10285C
Suva	9513C	9709C	10111*	7778	7182	8043	8144	10134M
Sydney	7877C	8073C	10850†	5975	5130	6357	6459	9470C
Wellington	8438C	8634C	10300*	6625	5900	7365	7483	9324M

AREA G

AREA D	Montevideo	Mozambique I	Porto Alegre	Port Elizabeth	Port Harcourt	Recife	Reunion Island	Rio de Janeiro
Adelaide	7672M	5496	8037M	5420	8183C	9622M	4393	8608M
Albany	8020M	4500	8355C	4360	7192C	8078C	3400	8007C
Apia	6608M	8820	6889M	9470	10534M	8451M	7911	7441M
Auckland	6120M	7352	6525M	6848	10006M	8071M	6252	7056M
Banaba	7953M	7440	8330M	8392	11302C	9865M	6862	8856M
Bluff	6103M	6814	6480M	6754	9504C	8015M	5714	7006M
Brisbane	7370M	6790	7770M	6235	9482C	10933*	5690	8305M
Cairns	8153M	6506	8530M	6985	9772C	10060M	5560	9056M
Cape Leeuwin	8150M	4330	8225C	4230	7062C	7928C	3270	8335C
Darwin	9483M	5322	9725C	5431	8562C	9430C	4338	9370C
Esperance	8293M	4710	8700M	4650	7402C	8270C	3610	8211C
Fremantle	8273C	4363	8295C	4370	7132C	8093C	3269	8000C
Geelong	7288M	5830	7665M	5770	8522C	8700M	4730	8191M
Geraldton	8327C	4299	8345C	4417	7182C	8053C	3227	7991C
Hobart	8738M	5955	7390M	5220	8562C	9096C	4855	7916M
Honolulu	7649M	9866	8217M	10728	10008*	7549*	9026	8612M
Launceston	7171M	5905	7479M	5362	8512C	9436C	4805	8005M
Lyttleton	6038M	6930	6300M	6512	9237C	7988M	5830	6973M
Mackay	7821M	6850	8198M	7156	9912C	9733M	5904	8724M
Madang	8756M	7444	9142M	7553	10684C	10050C	5392	9694M
Makatea	8788M	9330	6072M	8964	9873M	7607M	8330	6607M
Melbourne	7260M	5825	7660M	5759	8520C	8700M	4728	8187M
Napier	5963M	7080	6340M	7020	6982C	7875M	5980	6866M
Nauru Island	8043M	7582	8420M	8232	11142C	9955M	6672	8946M
Nelson	6074M	7055	6451M	6295	9372C	7986M	5820	6977M
Newcastle (NSW)	6707M	6290	7090M	5819	9042C	8657M	5190	7642M
New Plymouth	6131M	7045	6508M	6285	9362C	8043M	5810	7034M
Noumea	6834M	7280	7400M	7017	9897C	8784M	6180	7769M
Otago Harbour	6007M	6950	6390M	6005	9642C	7557M	5852	6922M
Papeete	5640M	9230	6040M	8864	9841M	7490M	8230	6575M
Portland (Victoria)	7330M	5625	7730M	5559	8320C	9270M	4528	8257M
Port Hedland	8832C	4530	8850C	4900	7687C	8555C	3520	8492C
Port Kembla	6669M	6175	7053M	5719	8855C	8524M	5150	7604M
Port Lincoln	7720M	5330	8120M	5230	8062C	8928C	4270	8647M
Port Moresby	8334M	6334	8720M	6443	9574C	10286M	5350	9272M
Port Pirie	8120M	5453	8610M	5353	8316C	9051C	4493	8747M
Rockhampton	7820M	6720	8225M	7026	9782C	9460M	5774	8477M
Suva	6751M	8198	7130M	7395	10706M	8701M	7252	7686M
Sydney	6700M	6215	7084M	5759	8895C	8650M	5190	7635M
Wellington	5940M	7193	6320M	6355	9793C	7891M	6093	6880M

AREA G

	AREA D Salvador	Santos	Sao Vicente Island	Takoradi	Tema	Tramandai	Vitoria (Brazil)	Walvis Bay
Adelaide	9243M	8426M	9712C	8368C	8634C	7887M	8791M	6476C
Albany	8073C	8179C	8698C	7354C	7350C	8205C	7933C	5462C
Apia	8123M	7308M	9000*	10202M	10216M	6739M	7669M	9676M
Auckland	7713M	6875M	9680M	9838M	9728M	6375M	7279M	7840C
Banaba	9536M	8739M	10050*	11370C	11365C	8180M	9084M	9479C
Bluff	7686M	6889M	9620M	9629M	9667C	6327M	7234M	7781C
Brisbane	8976M	8124M	10868C	9524C	9630C	7620M	8524M	7632C
Cairns	9736M	8930M	11280C	9940C	9935C	8380M	9284M	7909C
Cape Leeuwin	8405C	8467C	8568C	7188C	7183C	8075C	8265C	5332C
Darwin	9443C	9502C	10070C	8730C	8725C	9575C	9303C	6839C
Esperance	8283C	8342C	8910C	7570C	7565C	8415C	8143C	5679C
Fremantle	8013C	8094C	8623C	7309C	7295C	8200C	7873C	5407C
Geelong	8871M	7504M	9999C	8695C	8691C	7515M	8419M	6793C
Geraldton	8063C	8122C	8690C	7350C	7355C	8195C	7923C	5459C
Hobart	8596M	9197C	9716C	8372C	8368C	7240M	8144M	6480C
Honolulu	8292*	8431M	7984*	9530*	9627*	8067M	8709*	10551M
Launceston	8685M	9537C	10056C	8712C	8708C	7369M	8233M	6820C
Lyttleton	7566M	6792M	9874*	9407C	9403C	6210M	7114M	7515C
Mackay	9404M	8607M	11420C	10080C	10050C	8044M	8952M	8189C
Madang	10344M	9549M	11522*	10944C	10939C	8992M	9924M	8961C
Makatea	7257M	6462M	7782*	9074M	9155M	5922M	6837M	8696M
Melbourne	8868M	7504M	9986C	8685C	8688C	7508M	8417M	6780C
Napier	7546M	6749M	9480M	9489M	9571M	6190M	7094M	7959C
Nauru Island	9626M	8829M	10200*	11210C	11205C	8270M	9174M	9319C
Nelson	7657M	6860M	9591M	9540C	9535C	6301M	7205M	7649C
Newcastle (NSW)	8836M	10464C	10461M	9120C	9116C	7480M	8384M	7228C
New Plymouth	7714M	6917M	9648M	9530C	9525C	6358M	7262M	7639C
Noumea	8606M	7588M	10281*	10058C	10054C	7250M	8154M	8166C
Otago Harbour	7596M	6361M	10051*	9532M	9621M	6240M	7144M	7340C
Papeete	7246M	6294M	7862*	9257M	9123M	5890M	6794M	8664M
Portland (Victoria)	8938M	7574M	9786C	8485C	8488C	7578M	8487M	6580C
Port Hedland	8562C	8624C	9195C	7855C	7850C	8700C	8422C	5964C
Port Kembla	8254M	7459M	10350C	9004C	8999C	6903M	7834M	7116C
Port Lincoln	9297M	8502M	9568C	8288C	8283C	7970M	8877M	6332C
Port Moresby	9927M	9127M	11082C	9771C	9766C	8570M	9502M	7851C
Port Pirie	9397M	8602M	9691C	8411C	8406C	8460M	8977M	6455C
Rockhampton	9127M	8332M	11290C	9926C	9921C	7975M	8707M	8059C
Suva	8369M	7505M	9625*	10468M	11268*	6980M	7917M	8792C
Sydney	8318M	7454M	10390C	9048C	9044C	6934M	7866M	7156C
Wellington	7559M	6695M	9493M	9609C	9605C	6170M	7107M	7717C

AREA H

AREA D	Azores	Bahia Blanca	Beira	Belem	Buenos Aires	Cape Horn	Cape Town	Conakry
Antofagasta	5570*	3000M	7718M	4492*	3368M	2130	6627M	6134*
Arica	5342*	3305M	8023M	4273*	3673M	2405	6932M	5915*
Astoria	7205*	7731M	11576	6135*	8099M	6880	10291*	7777*
Balbao	3430*	5778*	7979*	2353*	5304M	4085	6509*	3995*
Buenaventura	3774*	6129*	8330*	7204*	4804M	3867	6860*	4346*
Cabo Blanco	4180*	6528*	8729*	3103*	4554M	3299	7259*	4745*
Caldera	5780*	2813M	7388M	4683*	3583M	1899	6295M	6325*
Callao	4767*	3675M	8393M	3698*	4043M	2825	7302M	5340*
Cape Horn	6200	1060	5725C	4340	1535	–	4256	4800
Chimbote	4587*	3855	8573M	3518*	4223M	2987	7482M	5160*
Coos Bay	7021*	9376*	11464	5951*	8071M	6690	10107*	7593*
Corinto	4148*	6476*	8677*	3051*	5574M	4330	7207*	4693*
Eureka	6880*	9235*	11436*	5810*	7642M	6535	9966*	7452*
Guayaquil	4250*	6602*	8803*	3177*	4679M	3449	7333*	4819*
Guaymas	5832*	8160*	10367*	4735*	7830*	5539	8891*	6377*
Honolulu	8107*	7374M	10350	7037*	7742M	6477	11080C	8679*
Iquique	5409*	3205M	7923M	4339*	3573M	2345	6832M	5981*
Los Angeles	6335*	8690*	10891*	5265*	7243M	6005	9421*	6907*
Manzanillo (Mex)	5140*	7495*	9696*	4070*	5946M	4931	8226*	5712*
Mazatlan	5428*	7783*	9984*	4358*	7434*	5206	8514*	6000*
Nanaimo	7462*	9817*	11592*	6392*	8350M	7113	10548*	8034*
New Westminster	7470*	9825*	11600	6400*	8357M	7121	10556*	8042*
Portland (Oreg)	7291*	9646*	11662	6221*	8185M	6967	10377*	7863*
Port Alberni	7424*	9772*	11503	6347*	8258M	7058	10503*	7989*
Port Isabel	6112*	8440*	10647*	5015*	8110*	5769	9171*	6657*
Port Moody	7465*	9820*	11595	6395*	8348M	7116	10551*	8037*
Prince Rupert	7726*	10081*	11856	6656*	8613M	7351	10812*	8298*
Puerto Montt	6422*	2030M	6695M	5407*	2395M	1315	5306M	5681
Puntarenas (CR)	3895*	6243*	8444*	2818*	5434M	4114	6970*	4460*
Punta Arenas (Ch)	6208	1020M	5735M	4350M	1435M	1415	4346M	4721
Salina Cruz	4610*	6938*	9139*	3413*	5916M	4582	7669*	5155*
San Francisco	6667*	9022*	11223*	5597*	7565M	6338	9753*	7239*
San Jose	4338*	6666*	8867*	3141*	5705M	4440	7395*	4383*
Seattle	7443*	9798*	10582	6373*	8339M	7098	10529	8015*
Tacoma	7474*	9829*	11604	8404*	8361M	7115	10560*	8046*
Talcahuano	6230*	2229M	8947M	5157*	2597M	1373	5856M	5931M
Tocopilla	5490*	7854*	7902M	4420*	3552M	2218	6811M	6062*
Valparaiso	6038*	2433M	7151M	4968*	2801M	1580	6060M	6135M
Vancouver (BC)	7461*	9816*	11591	6391*	8348M	7112	10547*	8033*
Victoria (Vanc Is)	7394*	9749*	11524	6324*	8281M	7035	10480*	7966*

AREA H

AREA D	Dakar	Dar es Salaam	Diego Suarez	Douala	Durban	East London	Lagos	Las Palmas
Antofagasta	5877*	8951M	8899M	7887*	7025M	6772M	7233*	6010*
Arica	5658*	9256M	9204M	7368*	7330M	7077M	7014*	5792*
Astoria	7520*	11375	10769*	11068*	10815*	10600*	8850*	7653*
Balboa	3738*	8833	8781	5448*	7286*	7033*	5094*	3870*
Buenaventura	4089*	9184*	9132*	5799*	7637*	7384*	5445*	4222*
Cabo Blanco	4488*	9583*	9531*	6198*	8036*	7783*	5844*	4620*
Caldera	6068*	8619M	8567M	7778*	6855M	6611M	7424*	6180*
Callao	5083*	9526M	9574M	6793*	7700M	7447M	6439*	5217*
Cape Horn	5005	6600	6520	5275	5035	4791	5075	5800
Chimbote	4903*	9806M	9754M	6613*	7880M	7627M	6259*	5037*
Coos Bay	7336*	11526	10920	9046*	10884*	10631*	8692	7469*
Corinto	3346*	9531*	9479*	6146*	7984*	7723*	5792*	4568*
Eureka	7195*	11571	10965	8905*	10743*	10490*	8551*	7328*
Guayaquil	4562*	9657*	9605*	6272*	8110*	7857*	5918*	4692*
Guaymas	6120*	11215*	11163*	7830*	9668*	9415*	7476*	6252*
Honolulu	8422*	9977	9371	10132*	10244	10092	9778*	8555*
Iquique	5724*	9156M	9105M	7434*	7230M	6977M	7080*	5858*
Los Angeles	6650*	11399	10793	8360*	10198*	9945*	8006*	6783*
Manzanillo (Mex)	5455*	10550*	10498*	7165*	9003*	8750*	6811*	5588*
Mazatlan	5743*	10838*	10786*	7453*	9291*	9036*	7099*	5870*
Nanaimo	7777*	11404	10798	9487*	11325*	11072*	9133*	7910*
New Westminster	7785*	11412	10806	9495*	11333*	11080*	9141*	7918*
Portland (Oreg)	7606*	11458	10852	9316*	11154*	10901*	8962*	7739*
Port Alberni	7732*	11313	10707	9442*	11280*	11027*	9088*	7864*
Port Isabel	6400*	11495*	11443*	8110*	9948*	9695*	7756*	7032*
Port Moody	7780*	11407	10801	9490*	11328*	11075*	9136*	7913*
Prince Rupert	8041*	11668	11062	9751*	11589*	11336*	9397*	8174*
Puerto Montt M	5903	7930	7460	6285	5900	5751	6035	6922*
Puntarenas (CR)	4203*	9294*	9242M	5913*	7751*	7498*	5559*	3325*
Punta Arenas (Ch) M	4943	6530	6500	5325	5000	4750	5025	5700
Salina Cruz	4898*	9993*	9941*	6608*	8446*	8193*	6254*	4999
San Francisco	6982*	11684	11078	8692*	10530	10277*	8338*	7209*
San Jose	4626*	9719*	9667*	5336*	8174*	7921*	5982	4658
Seattle	7758*	11394	10788	9468*	11306*	11053*	9114*	7891*
Tacoma	7789*	11416	10810	9499*	11337*	11084*	9145*	7922*
Talcahuano	6153M	8180M	8128M	6035M	6245M	6001M	6285M	6675*
Tocopilla	5805*	9135M	9083M	7515*	7209M	6956M	7161*	5938*
Valparaiso	6353*	8384M	8332M	6240M	6458M	6205M	6489M	6488*
Vancouver (BC)	7776*	11403	10797	9486*	11324*	11071*	9132*	7909*
Victoria (Vanc Is)	7709*	11336	10730	9419*	11257*	11004*	9065*	7842*

AREA H	AREA D Lobito	Luanda	Madeira	Maputo	Mauritius	Mogadiscio	Mombasa	Monrovia
Antofagasta	7154M	7304M	5923*	7321M	8877M	9482M	8735	6312
Arica	7456M	7606M	5707*	7626M	9182M	9787M	9040	6193*
Astoria	9631*	9583*	7624*	11364*	10345	11057	11043	7955*
Balbao	5849*	5801*	3785*	7582*	8759*	9364*	8996*	4173*
Buenaventura	6200*	6125*	4137*	7933*	9110*	9715*	9347*	4524*
Cabo Blanco	6599*	6551*	4535*	8332*	9509*	10114*	9746*	4923*
Caldera	6950M	7100M	6115*	7106M	8545M	9150M	8520M	6503*
Callao	7194*	7141*	5132*	7996M	9552M	10157M	9410M	5518*
Cape Horn	4699	4861	5900	5245	6456	7055	6662M	4643
Chimbote	7014*	6959*	4952*	7816	9732M	10337M	8700M	5338*
Coos Bay	9447*	9399*	7384*	11180*	10498	11205	10931	7771*
Corinto	6547*	6482*	4683*	8280*	9457*	10062*	9694*	4871*
Eureka	9306*	9258*	7243*	11039*	10543	11253	11225	7630*
Guayaquil	6673*	6638*	4610*	8406*	9583*	10188*	9820*	5097*
Guaymas	8231*	8170*	6167*	10864*	11141*	11746*	11721*	6555*
Honolulu	10533*	10489*	8470*	10299	8949	9659	9868	8857*
Iquique	7356M	7506M	5780*	7526M	9082M	9687M	8940M	6159*
Los Angeles	8761*	8713*	6698*	10494*	10471	11061	11908*	7085*
Manzanillo (Mex)	7566*	7518*	5505*	9299*	10476*	11081*	11021*	5890*
Mazatlan	7854*	7811*	5800*	9587*	10764*	11369*	11001*	6178*
Nanaimo	9888*	9840*	7825*	11621*	10376	11086	11059	8212*
New Westminster	9896*	9848*	7833*	11629	10384	11094	11067	8220*
Portland (Oreg)	9717*	9669*	7654*	11450*	10430	11140	11129	8041*
Port Alberni	9843*	9769*	7779*	11576*	10285	10995	10968	8167*
Port Isabel	8511*	8400*	6447*	11144*	10421*	12026*	12001*	6835*
Port Moody	9891*	9826*	7828*	11624*	10379	11089	11062	8215*
Prince Rupert	10152*	10104*	8089*	11885*	10640	11350	11323	8476*
Puerto Montt	6115M	6265M	6335M	6255M	7856M	8461M	7714	5503
Puntarenas (CR)	6314*	6272*	4250*	8050*	9220*	9825*	9461*	4638*
Punta Arenas (Ch) M	5155	5303	5875	5295	6496	7097	6745	4543
Salina Cruz	7009*	6971*	4945*	8742*	9919*	10524*	10156*	5333*
San Francisco	9093*	9046*	7030*	10826*	10656	11366	11340*	7417*
San Jose	6737*	6687*	4673*	8470*	9645*	2050*	9884*	4561*
Seattle	9869*	9821*	7806*	11602*	10366	11706	11049*	8193*
Tacoma	9900*	9852*	7837*	11633*	10388	11098	11071*	8224*
Talcahuano	6424M	6574M	6585*	6550M	8106M	8711M	7964	5753
Tocopilla	7222M	7372M	5853*	7505M	9061M	9666M	8919M	6240*
Valparaiso	6587M	6737M	6399*	6754M	8310M	8915M	8168	5957
Vancouver (BC)	9887*	9822*	7824*	11620*	10375	11085	11058	8211*
Victoria (Vanc Is)	9820*	9746*	7757*	11553*	10308	11018	10991	8144*

AREA H	AREA D Montevideo	Mozambique I	Porto Alegre	Port Elizabeth	Port Harcourt	Recife	Reunion Island	Rio de Janeiro
Antofagasta	3303M	8426M	3688M	6651M	7445*	5253M	8752M	4238M
Arica	3608M	8731M	3993M	6956M	7241*	5181*	9057M	4543M
Astoria	8034M	11298	8965*	10694*	9102*	7043*	10456	8115*
Balboa	5239M	8299*	5183*	6912*	5320*	3261*	8634*	4333*
Buenaventura	4739M	8659*	5534*	7263*	5674*	3612*	8985*	4684*
Cabo Blanco	3989M	9058*	5940*	7662*	6132*	4011*	9384*	5090*
Caldera	3088M	8094M	3473M	6436M	7622*	5038M	8420M	4023
Callao	3978M	9001M	4363M	7326M	6660*	4606*	9427	4913M
Cape Horn	1350	6000	1695	4580	5221	3300	6331	2245
Chimbote	4158M	9281M	4543M	7506M	6478*	4426*	9607M	5093M
Coos Bay	8006M	11449	8781*	10510*	9918*	6859*	10609	7931*
Corinto	5586M	9006*	5881*	7600*	6001*	3959*	9332*	5031*
Eureka	7577M	11494	8640*	10369*	8777*	6718*	10654	7790*
Guayaquil	4614M	9132*	6007*	7736*	6157*	4085	9458*	5157*
Guaymas	6581M	10690*	7600*	9329*	7689*	5643*	11016*	6750*
Honolulu	7649M	9900	8062M	10728	10008*	7945*	9060	8612M
Iquique	3508M	6631M	3893M	6856M	7300*	5247*	8957M	4443M
Los Angeles	7178M	11322	8095*	9824*	8232*	6173*	10582	7245*
Manzanillo (Mex)	5881M	10025*	6900*	8629*	7037*	4978*	10351*	6050*
Mazatlan	6180M	10313*	7188	8917*	7330*	5266*	10641*	6338*
Nanaimo	8283M	11327	9222*	10951*	9342*	7300*	10487	8372*
New Westminster	8291M	11335	9230*	10959*	9350*	7308*	10495	8380*
Portland (Oreg)	8120M	11381	9051*	10780*	9176*	7129*	10541	8201*
Port Alberni	8293M	11236	9177*	10906*	9288*	7255*	10396	8327*
Port Isabel	6881M	10970*	7880*	9609*	7919*	5923*	11296*	7030*
Port Moody	8387M	11330	9225*	10954*	9345*	7303*	10490	8375*
Prince Rupert	8547M	11591	9486*	11215*	9623*	7564*	10751	8636*
Puerto Montt M	2282	7405M	2682	5630	6222	4300	7731	3232
Puntarenas (CR)	5204M	8769*	5506*	7380*	5791*	3626*	9095*	4656*
Punta Arenas (Ch) M	1322	6045	1722	4670	5262	3340	6421	2272
Salina Cruz	5794M	9468*	6343*	8079*	6490*	4421*	9794*	5493*
San Francisco	7500M	11607	8427*	10156*	8566*	6505*	10767	7577*
San Jose	5585M	9194*	6071*	7805*	6209*	4149*	9520*	5221*
Seattle	8374M	11317	9212*	10932*	9325*	7281*	10477	8362*
Tacoma	8396M	11339	9234*	10963*	9345*	7312*	10499	8384*
Talcahuano M	2532	7655M	2917	5880	6521	4482	7981	3467
Tocopilla	3487M	8510M	3872M	6835M	7380*	5328*	8936M	4422M
Valparaiso M	2736	7859M	3121	6084	6725	4686	8185	3671M
Vancouver (BC)	8282M	11326	9221*	10950*	9341*	7299*	10486	8371*
Victoria (Vanc Is)	8316M	11259	9154*	10883*	9265*	7232*	10419	8304*

AREA H

AREA D	Salvador	Santos	Sao Vicente Island	Takoradi	Tema	Tramandai	Vitoria (Brazil)	Walvis Bay
Antofagasta	4912M	4057M	5439*	6985*	6886M	3538M	4508M	6177M
Arica	5226M	4362M	5220*	6766*	6863*	3843M	4813M	6482M
Astoria	7522*	8391*	7082*	8628*	8725*	8815*	7845*	9843*
Balboa	3725*	4609*	3295*	4846*	4943*	5033*	4063*	6061*
Buenaventura	4091*	4960*	3651*	5197*	5294*	5384*	4514*	6412*
Cabo Blanco	4345*	5303*	4045*	5596*	5693*	5790*	4820*	6811*
Caldera M	4768	3810	5605	6833	6671M	3323	4293	5990
Callao	5085*	4732M	4642*	6191*	6288*	4213M	5183M	6852M
Cape Horn	2990	2132	4880	4889	5000	1545	2512	4363
Chimbote	5838M	4880M	4462M	6011*	6468*	4393M	5363M	7032M
Coos Bay	7338*	8207*	6898*	8444*	8541*	8631*	7661*	9659*
Corinto	4286*	5244*	3973*	5544*	5641*	5731*	4761*	6759*
Eureka	7197*	8066*	6757*	8303*	8400*	8490*	7520*	9518*
Guayaquil	4564*	5368M	4127*	5760*	5767*	5857*	4887*	6885*
Guaymas	6005*	6963*	5657*	7228*	7325*	7450*	6480*	8443*
Honolulu	8424*	8431M	7984*	9530*	9627*	7912M	8882M	10551M
Iquique	5126M	4262M	5285*	6832*	6929*	3743M	4713M	6382M
Los Angeles	6652*	7521*	6212*	7758*	7855*	7945*	6975*	8973*
Manzanillo (Mex)	5457*	6326*	5020*	6563*	6660*	6750*	5780*	7778*
Mazatlan	5745*	6614*	5305*	6851*	6948*	7038*	6068*	8066*
Nanaimo	7779*	8648*	7339*	8885*	8982*	9072*	8102*	10100*
New Westminster	7787*	8656*	7347*	8893*	8990*	9080*	8110*	10108*
Portland (Oreg)	7608*	8477*	7168*	8714*	8811*	8901*	7931*	9929*
Port Alberni	7719*	8603*	7289*	8840*	8937*	9027*	8057*	10055*
Port Isabel	6285*	7243*	5937*	7508*	7605*	7730*	6760*	8723*
Port Moody	7782*	8651*	7342*	8888*	8985*	9075*	8105*	10103*
Prince Rupert	8043*	8912*	7603*	9149*	9246*	9336*	8366*	10364*
Puerto Montt M	3977	3019	5837	6000	5865M	2532	3502	7576
Puntarenas (CR)	3911*	4869*	3760*	5311*	5408*	5356*	4386*	6526*
Punta Arenas (Ch) M	3017	2159	4877	4900	4905M	1572	2520	4616
Salina Cruz	4748*	5706*	4435*	6006*	6104*	6193*	5223*	7221*
San Francisco	6984*	7853*	6550*	8090*	8187*	8277*	7307*	9305*
San Jose	4476*	5434*	4163*	5734*	5831*	5921*	4951*	6949*
Seattle	7760*	8638*	7320*	8866*	8963*	9062*	8092*	10081*
Tacoma	7791*	8660*	7351*	8897*	8994*	9084*	8114*	10112*
Talcahuano M	4150	3286	6085	6249	6115M	2767	3737	5406
Tocopilla	5105M	4241M	5367*	6913*	7010*	3722M	4692M	6361M
Valparaiso	4354M	3490M	5913*	6453M	6319M	2971M	3941M	5610M
Vancouver (BC)	7778*	8647*	7338*	8884*	8981*	9071*	8101*	10099*
Victoria (Vanc Is)	7711*	8580M	7271*	8817*	8914*	9004*	8034*	10032*

AREA D

AREA D	Abidjan	Azores (Ponta Delgada)	Banjul	Cape Town	Conakry	Dar es Salaam	Diego Suarez	Douala
Bahia Blanca	4188	5250	4118	3804	4030	6114	6062	4737
Beira	4162	6494	5037	1492	4680	1012	1005	3860
Belem	2740	2678	2124	4337	2222	6675	6623	3554
Buenos Aires	3933	4975	3839	3718	3742	6028	5976	4501
Cape Town	2679	5040	3558	–	3201	2369	2317	2374
Dakar	1166	1459	96	3604	450	5954	5902	1987
Durban	3462	5801	4337	800	3980	1580	1527	3160
Fortaleza	2163	2590	1677	3660	1699	5998	5946	2940
Lagos	457	3099	1566	2566	1205	4924	4872	439
Las Palmas	1989	777	924	4427	1272	6777	6725	2814
Lobito	1500	3943	2502	1406	2140	3764	3712	1059
Luanda	1345	3863	2369	1600	2007	3960	3908	858
Madeira	2243	550	1179	4682	1527	5660†	5760†	3069
Mauritius	4962	6638†	5837	2295	5480	1354	674	4660
Mogadiscio	5567	5408†	6442	2900	6085	643	901	5265
Monrovia	470	2143	658	2933	297	5289	5237	1285
Montevideo	3836	4872	3742	3621	3645	5931	5879	4404
Namibe	1558	4023	2531	1205	2169	3563	3511	1192
Nouadhibou	1547	1050	484	3985	830	6335	6283	2372
Paranagua	3202	4188	3058	3500	2964	5820	5768	3822
Pepel	732	1963	478	3170	83	5526	5474	1547
Pointe Noire	1118	3677	2186	1810	1824	4168	4116	616
Port Elizabeth	3089	5427	3964	422	3607	1960	1908	2787
Port Harcourt	702	3300	1808	2428	1444	4786	4734	205
Rio de Janeiro	2891	3875	2741	3272	2649	5595	5543	3509
Santos	3072	4058	2928	3400	2834	5726	5674	3694
Sao Vicente Island	1535	1253	527	3944	823	6294	6242	2355
Tema	243	2899	1352	2592	991	4949	4897	613
Tubarao	2668	3619	2487	3201	2412	5524	5472	3310
Vitoria (Brazil)	2653	3604	2472	3204	2397	5527	5475	3293

AREA D

AREA D	East London	Las Palmas	Lobito	Maputo	Mombasa	Porto Alegre	Recife	Rio de Janeiro
Bahia Blanca	4280	4903	4301	4830	6245	860	2455	1423
Beira	953	5900	2890	485	1150	5075	4780	4721
Belem	4851	2624	3818	5400	6816	3018	1089	2160
Buenos Aires	4204	4623	4117	4754	6165	579	2177	1142
Cape Town	544	4427	1406	1095	2510	3636	3318	3272
Dakar	4130	839	2547	4680	6095	3620	1717	2761
Durban	261	5208	2190	305	1720	4375	4080	4021
Fortaleza	4173	2341	3142	4723	6138	2342	410	1484
Lagos	3100	2430	1285	3650	5065	4087	2453	3268
Las Palmas	4952	–	3374	5502	6917	4384	2469	3525
Lobito	1940	3374	–	2490	3905	3946	3551	3297
Luanda	2136	3241	234	2686	4101	4037	2861	3357
Madeira	5208	282	3629	5758	5560†	4580	2654	3722
Mauritius	1758	6703	3690	1445	1425	5875	5580	5521
Mogadiscio	2631	7308	4295	1890	500	6470	6185	6126
Monrovia	3465	1521	1847	4015	5430	3462	1680	2614
Montevideo	4104	4526	4020	4654	6069	482	2080	1045
Namibe	1738	3401	207	2288	3703	3786	2794	3160
Nouadhibou	4510	442	2932	5060	6475	4065	2136	3204
Paranagua	3995	3840	3592	4545	5960	654	1395	344
Papel	3702	1341	2109	4252	5667	3484	1649	2627
Pointe Noire	2343	2655	453	2893	4308	4089	2791	3375
Port Elizabeth	135	4830	1817	685	2100	4005	3710	3651
Port Harcourt	2962	2678	1142	3512	4927	4215	2660	3420
Rio de Janeiro	3771	3525	3297	4321	5736	900	1080	–
Santos	3901	3710	3478	4451	5866	758	1265	210
Sao Vicente Island	4470	869	2912	5020	6435	3545	1616	2684
Tema	3125	2216	1353	3675	5090	3888	2235	3063
Tubarao	3699	3270	3148	4249	5664	1128	824	263
Vitoria (Brazil)	3703	3256	3133	4253	5668	1145	810	280

AREA D

AREA D	Saco (Mocamedes)	Salvador	Santos	Sao Vicente Island	Takoradi	Tramandai	Tubarao	Walvis Bay
Bahia Blanca	4115	2126	1280	4065	4274	710	1648	3955
Beira	2686	4793	4852	5420	4077	4925	4647	2189
Belem	3744	1474	2345	1790	2868	2868	1906	3958
Buenos Aires	3946	1848	998	3782	4016	429	1367	3828
Cape Town	1205	3336	3400	3944	2593	3486	3201	700
Dakar	2574	2100	2950	465	1297	3470	2507	2982
Durban	1994	4093	4152	4720	3385	4125	3955	1489
Fortaleza	3068	798	1690	1477	2270	2192	1230	3283
Lagos	1396	2770	3454	1976	320	3937	3053	1880
Las Palmas	3401	2845	3710	869	2120	4234	3270	3809
Lobito	207	3068	3478	2912	1380	3796	3146	720
Luanda	407	3069	3538	2779	1218	3887	3192	915
Madeira	3656	3040	3907	1044	2374	4430	3468	4065
Mauritius	3489	5593	5652	6220	4880	5725	5450	2989
Mogadiscio	4094	6198	6257	6825	5485	6330	6055	3594
Monrovia	1882	2030	2799	1068	601	3312	2381	2300
Montevideo	3849	1751	901	3685	3919	332	1270	3731
Namibe	–	2954	3338	2939	1462	3636	2990	518
Nouadhibou	2959	2518	3391	520	1678	3915	2941	3367
Paranagua	3447	1066	163	3001	3285	504	565	3427
Pepel	2140	2013	2810	890	863	3334	2360	2550
Pointe Noire	618	3040	3556	2596	997	3939	3163	1122
Port Elizabeth	1616	3723	3782	4350	3007	3855	3577	1119
Port Harcourt	1253	2975	3600	2220	571	4065	3185	1740
Rio de Janeiro	3160	750	210	2685	2968	753	263	3167
Santos	3338	936	–	2871	3155	608	435	3330
Sao Vicente Island	2939	2000	2871	–	1666	3395	2400	3340
Tema	1443	2555	3247	1762	102	3738	3045	1911
Tubarao	2990	465	435	2400	2951	978	–	3085
Vitoria (Brazil)	3004	480	450	2415	2730	993	15	3085

Area E

Distances between principal ports in the Red Sea, The Gulf, the Indian Ocean and the Bay of Bengal.

and

Area F Malaysia, Indonesia, South East Asia, the China Sea and Japan.

Area G Australasia, New Guinea and the Pacific Islands.

Area H The West Coast of North and South America.

Area E Other ports in the Red Sea, The Gulf, the Indian Ocean, and the Bay of Bengal.

AREA E

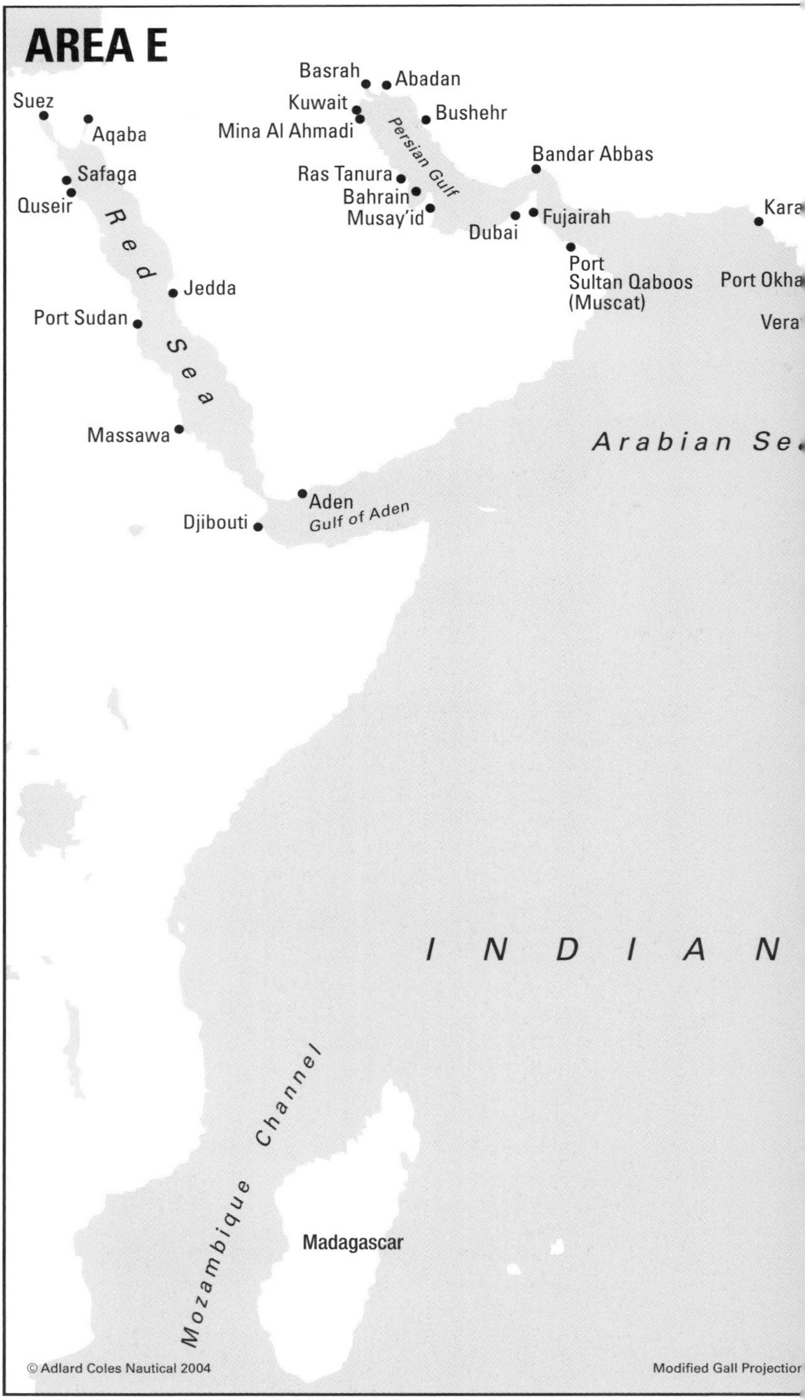
Basrah
Abadan
Suez
Kuwait
Bushehr
Aqaba
Mina Al Ahmadi
Persian Gulf
Bandar Abbas
Safaga
Ras Tanura
Quseir
Bahrain
Musay'id
Dubai
Fujairah
Kara
Red Sea
Port
Sultan Qaboos
(Muscat)
Port Okha
Jedda
Port Sudan
Vera
Massawa
Arabian Se
Aden
Gulf of Aden
Djibouti
I N D I A N
Mozambique Channel
Madagascar
Modified Gall Projectior

AREA E

Reed's Marine Distance Tables

THE RED SEA, THE GULF & INDIAN OCEAN

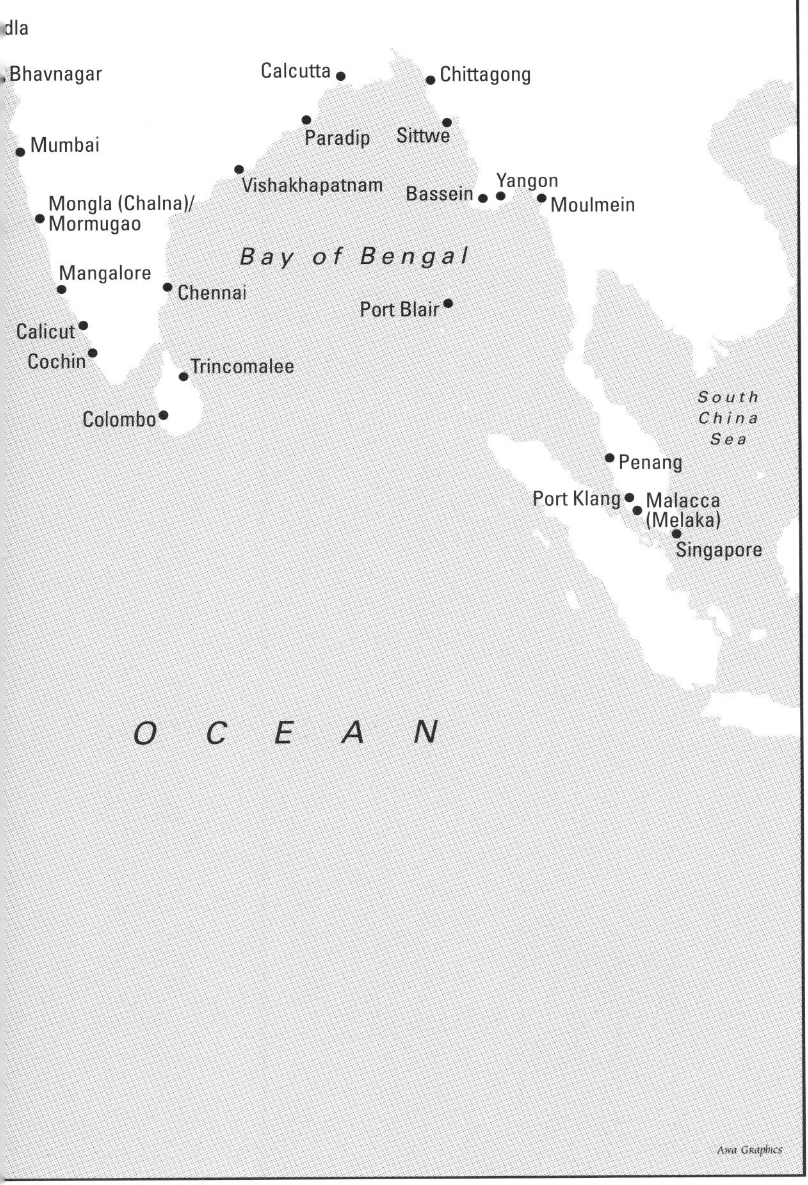

AREA F

AREA E	Abadan	Aden	Aqaba	Bahrain	Bandar Abbas	Basrah	Bassein	Bhavnagar	Bushehr
Balikpapan	4899	4675	5882	4688	4409	4929	2210	3694	4805
Bangkok	4696	4475	5698	4491	4212	4708	2000	3485	4555
Basuo (Hainan Is)	5165	4935	6167	4960	4681	5196	2460	3945	5025
Cam-Pha	5287	5049	6289	5082	4803	5306	2620	4105	5145
Cebu	5220	5000	6222	5015	4736	5271	2515	4000	5080
Dalian	6484	6243	7476	6279	6000	6528	3800	5253	6335
Haiphong	5187	5010	6189	4982	4705	5206	2520	4005	5045
Ho Chi Minh City	4511	4280	5513	4306	4027	4565	1805	3290	4360
Hong Kong	5325	5080	6527	5120	4841	5350	2615	4100	5180
Hungnam	6610	6390	7612	6405	6126	6645	3919	5290	6464
Inchon	6417	6205	7419	6212	5933	6470	3720	5225	6275
Kampong Saom	4396	4158	5398	4191	3912	4426	1700	3185	4251
Kaohsiung (Taiwan)	5486	5260	6488	5281	5002	5501	2785	4270	5340
Keelung (Taiwan)	5677	5436	6679	5472	5193	5721	2965	4446	5530
Kobe	6556	6300	7658	6351	6072	6509	3820	5305	6415
Makassar	4897	4655	5881	4697	4408	4926	2150	3655	4745
Manila	5206	4960	6208	5001	4722	5246	2495	3970	5060
Masinloc	5246	5000	6248	5041	4762	5286	2535	4010	5100
Menado	5358	5128	6360	5153	4874	5389	2653	4138	5218
Moji	6405	6180	7407	6200	5921	6437	3715	5200	6260
Muroran	7104	6873	8106	6899	6620	7134	4398	5883	6953
Nagasaki	6282	6046	7284	6077	5798	6301	3580	5056	6135
Nagoya	6655	6405	7657	6450	6171	6870	4014	5495	6509
Nampo	6494	6253	7496	6289	6010	6538	3810	5263	6365
Osaka	6560	6302	7562	6355	6076	6587	3831	5312	6396
Otaru	7142	6911	8144	6937	6658	7192	4436	5921	7001
Palembang	4165	3917	5167	3960	3681	4198	1350	2827	4020
Pusan	6368	6138	7370	6163	5884	6419	3673	5148	6238
Qingdao	6328	6097	7330	6123	5844	6382	3626	5107	6201
Qinhuangdao	5590	6370	7592	6385	6106	6625	3899	5380	6444
Sabang	3274	3036	4276	3069	2790	3304	655	2045	3155
Shanghai	6057	5845	7059	5852	5573	6086	3370	4855	5905
Shimonoseki	6404	6170	7406	6199	5920	6434	3705	5190	6260
Singapore	3865	3635	4867	3660	3381	3896	1160	2645	3725
Surabaya	4508	4260	5510	4303	4024	4531	1880	3278	4365
Tanjung Priok	4138	3900	5127	3933	3654	4168	1625	2940	4260
Tokyo	6769	6538	7771	6564	6285	6799	4073	5553	6628
Toyama	6855	6630	7857	6650	6371	6887	4165	5650	6700
Vladivostok	6872	6635	7874	6667	6388	6820	4164	5650	6739
Yokohama	6757	6520	7759	6552	6273	6789	4055	5535	6612

AREA F

AREA E	Calcutta	Chennai	Chittagong	Cochin	Colombo	Djibouti	Dubai	Fujairah	Jedda
Balikpapan	2691	2638	2585	2935	2625	4795	4487	4321	5355
Bangkok	2475	2430	2375	2725	2415	4595	4290	4124	5155
Basuo (Hainan Is)	2935	2885	2835	3175	2865	5055	4759	4593	5615
Cam-Pha	3105	3045	2995	3345	3035	5230	4881	4715	5790
Cebu	3005	2925	2890	3245	2935	5120	4814	4648	5680
Dalian	4250	4197	4175	4494	4184	6363	6078	5912	6923
Haiphong	3005	2945	2895	3245	2935	5130	4783	4617	5690
Ho Chi Minh City	2290	2230	2180	2530	2220	4400	4105	3939	4160
Hong Kong	3100	3039	2990	3336	3026	5300	4919	4753	5760
Hungnam	4285	4355	4294	4645	4335	6510	6204	6038	7070
Inchon	4225	4135	4095	4435	4125	6345	6011	5845	6905
Kampong Saom	2175	2130	2075	2425	2115	4295	3990	3824	4855
Kaohsiung (Taiwan)	3260	3210	3160	3500	3190	5380	5080	4914	5940
Keelung (Taiwan)	3443	3390	3340	3687	3377	5556	5271	5105	6116
Kobe	4305	4250	4195	4545	4235	6420	6150	5984	6980
Makassar	2655	2765	2525	2865	2555	4775	4486	4320	5335
Manila	2950	2910	2870	3210	2900	5080	4800	4634	5640
Masinloc	2990	2950	2910	3250	2940	5120	4840	4674	5680
Menado	3128	3078	3028	3368	3058	5248	4952	4786	5808
Moji	4200	4136	4090	4430	4120	6300	5999	5833	6860
Muroran	4873	4823	4773	5113	4803	6993	6698	6532	7553
Nagasaki	4050	4000	3955	4300	3990	6166	5876	5710	6726
Nagoya	4492	4439	4389	4736	4426	6605	6249	6083	7165
Nampo	4260	4207	4185	4504	4194	6373	6088	5922	6933
Osaka	4309	4256	4206	4553	4243	6422	6154	5988	6982
Otaru	4911	4861	4811	5151	4841	7031	6736	6570	7591
Palembang	1817	1767	1725	2057	1747	3937	3759	3593	4497
Pusan	4138	4088	4038	4378	4068	6258	5962	5796	6818
Qingdao	4104	4051	4001	4348	4038	6217	5922	5756	6777
Qinhuangdao	4377	4324	4274	4621	4311	6490	6184	6018	7050
Sabang	1130	990	1025	1275	965	3155	2868	2702	3715
Shanghai	3850	3800	3745	4095	3785	5965	5651	5485	6525
Shimonoseki	4190	4126	4080	4420	4110	6290	5998	5832	6850
Singapore	1635	1585	1535	1875	1565	3755	3459	3293	4315
Surabaya	2291	2380	2160	2496	2230	4420	4102	3936	4980
Tanjung Priok	2160	2008	2055	2120	1860	4020	3732	3566	4580
Tokyo	4548	4498	4448	4794	4484	6658	6363	6197	7218
Toyama	4650	4586	4540	4880	4570	6750	6449	6283	7310
Vladivostok	4645	4600	4539	4890	4580	6755	6466	6300	7315
Yokohama	4530	4480	4430	4776	4466	6640	6351	6185	7200

AREA F

AREA E	Karachi	Kuwait	Malacca	Mangalore	Massawa	Mina Al Ahmadi	Mongla	Mormugao
Balikpapan	3935	4883	1180	3073	5075	4863	2656	3242
Bangkok	3724	4676	970	2866	4875	4656	2446	3059
Basuo (Hainan Is)	4185	5145	1430	3335	5335	5125	2906	3520
Cam-Pha	4342	5267	1590	3455	5510	5247	3066	3677
Cebu	4237	5200	1485	3390	5400	5180	2961	3572
Dalian	5494	6464	2770	4654	6643	6444	4246	4829
Haiphong	4242	5167	1490	3357	5410	5147	2966	3577
Ho Chi Minh City	3531	4491	775	2671	4680	4471	2251	2866
Hong Kong	4336	5305	1585	3495	5480	5285	3061	3671
Hungnam	5641	6590	2889	4780	6790	6570	4365	4976
Inchon	5437	6397	2690	4587	6625	6377	4165	4775
Kampong Saom	3424	4376	670	2566	4575	4356	2146	2759
Kaohsiung (Taiwan)	4510	5466	1755	3656	5660	5446	3231	3845
Keelung (Taiwan)	4687	5657	1935	3847	5836	5637	3411	4022
Kobe	5545	6536	2790	4726	6700	6516	4266	4880
Makassar	3875	4872	1220	3062	5055	4852	2596	3210
Manila	4212	5186	1465	3376	5360	5166	2931	3547
Masinloc	4252	5226	1505	3416	5400	5206	2971	3587
Menado	4378	5338	1623	3525	5525	5315	3099	3705
Moji	5433	6385	2685	4575	6580	6365	4161	4768
Muroran	6123	7084	3368	5264	7273	7064	4844	5458
Nagasaki	5297	6262	2550	4452	6446	6242	4026	4632
Nagoya	5736	6635	2984	4825	6885	6615	4460	5071
Nampo	5504	6474	2780	4664	6653	6454	4256	4839
Osaka	5553	6540	2801	4730	6702	6520	4277	4888
Otaru	6161	7122	3406	5312	7311	7102	4882	5496
Palembang	3067	4145	320	2335	4217	4125	1796	2402
Pusan	5388	6348	2633	4538	6538	6328	4109	4723
Qingdao	5348	6308	2596	4498	6497	6288	4072	4683
Qinhuangdao	5621	6570	2869	4860	6770	6550	4346	4956
Sabang	2285	3254	480	1444	3428	3234	1066	1624
Shanghai	5092	6037	2340	4227	6245	6017	3816	4427
Shimonoseki	5423	6384	2675	4574	6570	6364	4151	4758
Singapore	2885	3845	130	2035	4035	3825	1606	2220
Surabaya	3875	4488	890	2678	4700	4468	2221	2855
Tanjung Priok	3170	4118	650	2308	4300	4098	2126	2500
Tokyo	5794	6749	3043	4939	6938	6729	4519	5129
Toyama	5883	6835	2135	5025	7030	6815	4611	5218
Vladivostok	5886	6852	3134	5042	7035	6832	4610	5221
Yokohama	5776	6737	3025	4927	6920	6717	4501	5111

AREA F

AREA E	Moulmein	Mumbai	Musay'td	Penang	Port Blair	Port Kelang	Port Okha	Port Sudan
Balikpapan	2185	3494	4668	1420	1984	1269	3770	5310
Bangkok	1975	3285	4461	1199	1760	1058	3563	5126
Basuo (Hainan Is)	2435	3745	4930	1668	2229	1515	4032	5584
Cam-Pha	2595	3905	5052	1830	2351	1676	4154	5744
Cebu	2490	3800	4985	1730	2284	1571	4087	5639
Dalian	3775	5053	6249	2979	3548	2828	5351	6896
Haiphong	2495	3805	4952	1730	2251	1576	4054	5644
Ho Chi Minh City	1780	3090	4276	1005	1675	865	3378	4933
Hong Kong	2590	3900	5090	1815	2389	1670	4192	5738
Hungnam	3894	5090	6375	3025	3674	2975	5477	7043
Inchon	3695	5025	6182	2940	3481	2770	5284	6839
Kampong Saom	1675	2985	4161	899	1460	758	3263	4826
Kaohsiung (Taiwan)	2760	4070	5251	1993	2550	1840	4353	5909
Keelung (Taiwan)	2940	4246	5442	2172	2741	2020	4544	6089
Kobe	3705	5105	6321	3030	3620	2879	5423	6947
Makassar	2125	3455	4657	1370	2031	1305	3759	5274
Manila	2470	3770	4971	1700	2270	1546	4073	5614
Masinloc	2510	3810	5011	1740	2310	1586	4113	5654
Menado	2584	3938	5120	1866	2422	1705	4222	5768
Moji	3690	5000	6170	2920	3469	2767	5272	6835
Muroran	4373	5683	6869	5606	4168	3453	5971	7522
Nagasaki	3555	4856	6047	2785	3346	2631	5149	6698
Nagoya	3989	5295	6420	3221	3719	3070	5522	7138
Nampo	3785	5063	6259	2989	3558	2838	5361	6906
Osaka	3806	5112	6325	3038	3614	2887	5427	6955
Otaru	4411	5721	6907	4644	4206	3491	6009	7560
Palembang	1325	2627	3930	550	1229	397	3032	4466
Pusan	3638	4948	6133	2871	3432	2718	5235	6787
Qingdao	3601	4907	6093	2833	3392	2682	5195	6750
Qinhuangdao	3874	5180	6355	3106	3654	2955	5457	7023
Sabang	660	1845	3039	210	381	410	2141	3684
Shanghai	3345	4655	5822	2580	3121	2426	4924	6494
Shimonoseki	3680	4990	6169	2910	2468	2757	5271	6825
Singapore	1135	2445	3630	368	929	215	2732	4284
Surabaya	1895	3080	4273	1130	1572	979	3375	4899
Tanjung Priok	1650	2740	3903	900	1419	741	3005	4550
Tokyo	4048	5353	6534	3283	3833	3128	5636	7196
Toyama	4140	5450	6620	3370	3919	3217	5722	7285
Vladivostok	4139	5450	6637	3370	3936	3220	5739	7288
Yokohama	4030	5335	6522	3265	3821	3110	5624	7178

AREA F

AREA E	Quseir	Singapore	Sittwe	Suez	Trincomalee	Veraval	Vishakhapatnam	Yangon
Balikpapan	5725	1050	2425	5967	2565	3642	2523	2163
Bangkok	5525	840	2215	5772	2286	3446	2412	1960
Basuo (Hainan Is)	5985	1300	3675	6241	2755	3915	2870	2400
Cam-Pha	6160	1460	2785	6349	2877	4037	3030	2600
Cebu	6050	1355	2730	6296	2810	3970	2925	2460
Dalian	7293	2640	3975	7553	4074	5234	4182	3722
Haiphong	6060	1360	2685	6251	2777	3937	2930	2500
Ho Chi Minh City	5330	645	2020	5590	2101	3261	2219	1760
Hong Kong	6130	1455	2830	6395	2915	4075	3024	2565
Hungnam	6440	2759	4134	7700	4200	5360	4329	3864
Inchon	7275	2560	3935	7496	4007	5167	4125	3700
Kampong Saom	5225	540	1896	5458	1986	3146	2112	1660
Kaohsiung (Taiwan)	6310	1625	3000	6566	3076	4236	3195	2725
Keelung (Taiwan)	6486	1805	3180	6746	3267	4427	3375	2915
Kobe	7350	2660	4035	7604	4146	5306	4233	3780
Makassar	5705	1102	2465	5731	2554	3610	2660	2200
Manila	6010	1335	2710	6271	2796	3956	2900	2435
Masinloc	6050	1375	2750	6311	2836	3996	2940	2475
Menado	6178	1490	2868	6431	2945	4105	3060	2490
Moji	7230	2555	3930	7465	3995	5155	4121	3665
Muroran	7923	3238	4613	8179	4694	5854	4808	4338
Nagasaki	7096	2420	3795	7355	3872	5032	3985	3525
Nagoya	7535	2854	4155	7705	4245	5405	4424	3964
Nampo	7303	2650	4035	7563	4084	5244	4192	3732
Osaka	7352	2671	4046	7625	4150	5310	4241	3781
Otaru	7961	3276	4651	8217	4732	5892	4846	4376
Palembang	4867	190	1665	5223	1755	2915	1752	1282
Pusan	7188	2503	3878	7444	3958	5118	4073	3603
Qingdao	7147	2466	3841	7407	3970	5078	4036	3576
Qinhuangdao	7420	2739	4114	7680	4180	5340	4309	3849
Sabang	4085	600	900	4340	859	2024	995	665
Shanghai	6895	2210	3585	7151	3647	4807	3780	3320
Shimonoseki	7220	2545	3920	7455	3994	5154	4110	3655
Singapore	4685	–	1375	4941	1455	2615	1570	1100
Surabaya	5350	760	2005	5580	2098	3258	2411	1880
Tanjung Priok	4950	520	1855	5207	1800	2902	2078	1630
Tokyo	7588	2913	4288	7853	4359	5519	4482	4023
Toyama	7680	3005	4380	7915	4445	5605	4571	4115
Vladivostok	7685	3004	4379	7945	4859	5622	4574	4109
Yokohama	7570	2895	4270	7835	4350	5507	4464	4005

AREA G

AREA E	Abadan	Aden	Aqaba	Bahrain	Bandar Abbas	Basrah	Bassein	Bhavnagar
Adelaide	6647	6100	7353	6438	6163	6725	4518	5430
Albany	5643	5125	6359	5444	5169	5728	3522	4430
Apia	9064	8809	10049	8859	8580	9094	6426	7834
Auckland	8506	8000	8212	8287	8022	8589	6204	7288
Banaba	7976	7719	8956	7771	7492	8006	5337	6742
Bluff	7968	7440	8674	7759	7484	8079	5837	6740
Brisbane	7624	7375	8609	7419	7145	7627	4986	6398
Cairns	6794	6539	7779	6589	6310	6824	4156	5564
Cape Leeuwin	5484	4944	6189	5275	4990	5505	3353	4257
Darwin	5610	5355	6595	5405	5126	5640	3019	4380
Esperance	5864	5385	6570	5655	5380	5988	3733	4630
Fremantle	5411	4900	6154	5206	4927	5440	3242	4200
Geelong	6990	6460	7696	6781	6506	7057	4859	5756
Geraldton	5238	4780	6020	5030	4755	5290	3050	4008
Hobart	7110	6595	7816	6901	6626	7271	4979	5900
Honolulu	9742	9512	10744	9537	9258	9797	7014	8722
Launceston	7061	6570	7787	6852	6577	7062	4930	5870
Lyttleton	8276	7700	8982	8067	7792	8276	6145	7045
Mackay	7134	6879	8119	6929	6650	7164	4496	5904
Madang	6678	6427	7667	6460	6181	6695	3937	5435
Makatea	10274	10100	11356	10171	9892	10406	7745	9165
Melbourne	6984	6480	7690	6775	6500	7057	4853	5756
Napier	8548	7959	9254	8339	8064	8572	6417	7280
Nauru Island	7817	7559	8796	7611	7332	7846	5175	6582
Nelson	8274	7769	8984	8069	7794	8282	6147	7040
Newcastle (NSW)	7499	6995	8205	7290	7015	7507	5356	6295
New Plymouth	8268	7734	8974	8059	7784	8284	6137	7034
Noumea	7947	7686	8926	7741	7462	8000	5345	6671
Otago Harbour	8106	7500	8812	7897	7622	8239	5975	6950
Papeete	10324	10029	11306	10121	9842	10356	7695	9092
Portland (Victoria)	6788	6254	7494	6579	6304	6804	4657	5554
Port Hedland	5133	4800	6040	4928	4649	5163	2810	3902
Port Kembla	7389	6900	8105	7290	6915	7500	4768	6200
Port Lincoln	6584	6050	7290	6375	6100	6600	4453	5350
Port Moresby	6624	6369	7609	6419	6140	6654	3986	5394
Port Pirie	6307	6200	7413	6498	6223	6790	4576	5488
Rockhampton	7314	7059	8299	7109	6830	7344	4676	6084
Suva	8515	8276	9499	8309	8030	8550	5876	7281
Sydney	7444	6925	8150	7235	6960	7525	5313	6225
Wellington	8384	7809	9054	8139	7864	8422	6217	7130

AREA G

AREA E	Bushehr	Calcutta	Chennai	Chittagong	Cochin	Colombo	Djibouti	Dubai	Fujairah
Adelaide	6498	4970	4650	4945	4670	4360	6220	6241	6075
Albany	5504	3960	3645	3951	3685	3375	5245	5247	5081
Apia	8919	6939	6875	6806	7052	6766	8918	8658	8492
Auckland	8357	6655	6509	6584	6540	6230	8120	8100	7934
Banaba	7831	5850	5786	5717	5960	5674	7825	7570	7404
Bluff	7819	6440	6105	6266	6135	5825	7560	7562	7396
Brisbane	7479	5520	5450	5366	5635	5325	7495	7223	7057
Cairns	6649	4660	4605	4536	4782	4496	6648	6388	6222
Cape Leeuwin	5330	3794	3480	3782	3475	3200	5060	5068	4902
Darwin	5465	3532	3468	3399	3598	3312	5464	5204	5038
Esperance	5715	4220	3905	4162	3945	3635	5505	5458	5292
Fremantle	5226	3695	3390	3582	3440	3130	5020	5005	4839
Geelong	6841	5293	4977	5288	5010	4697	6580	6584	6418
Geraldton	5093	3489	3204	3387	3220	2980	4870	4833	4667
Hobart	6961	5430	5115	5408	5135	4825	6715	6704	6538
Honolulu	9597	7519	7466	7394	7763	7453	9632	9336	9170
Launceston	6912	5407	5091	5359	5121	4811	6690	6655	6489
Lyttleton	8127	6712	6396	6574	6426	6116	7820	7870	7704
Mackay	6989	5009	4945	4876	5122	4836	6988	6728	6562
Madang	6520	4450	4386	4317	4653	4367	6535	6259	6093
Makatea	10231	8275	8225	8125	8405	8095	10220	9970	9804
Melbourne	6835	5295	5000	5282	5008	4698	6600	6578	6412
Napier	8399	6809	6490	6836	6520	6210	8079	8142	7976
Nauru Island	7671	5688	5664	5555	5800	5514	7665	7410	7244
Nelson	8129	6619	6300	6576	6330	6020	7889	7872	7706
Newcastle (NSW)	7350	5830	5520	5736	5545	5235	7115	7093	6927
New Plymouth	8119	6589	6263	6566	6262	5985	7842	7862	7696
Noumea	6801	5784	5731	5644	5910	5600	7806	7540	7374
Otago Harbour	7957	6500	6165	6404	6195	5885	7620	7700	7534
Papeete	10181	8205	8152	8075	8331	8021	10149	9920	9754
Portland (Victoria)	6639	5094	4779	5086	4775	4501	6358	6382	6216
Port Hedland	4989	3256	3025	3154	3125	2833	4909	4727	4561
Port Kembla	7250	5735	5420	5692	5450	5140	7020	6993	6827
Port Lincoln	6435	4894	4579	4882	4575	4301	6158	6178	6012
Port Moresby	6479	4499	4435	4366	4612	4326	6478	6218	6052
Port Pirie	6558	5055	4509	5005	4540	4230	6120	6301	6135
Rockhampton	7169	5189	3218	5056	5302	5016	7168	6908	6742
Suva	8369	6384	6321	6256	6500	6190	8368	8108	7742
Sydney	7295	5760	5445	5742	5475	5165	7045	7038	6872
Wellington	8199	6659	6340	6636	6370	6060	7929	7942	7776

AREA G

AREA E	Jedda	Karachi	Kuwait	Malacca	Mangalore	Massawa	Mina Al Ahmadi	Mongla	Mormugao
Adelaide	6780	5680	6627	3639	4813	6500	6607	4999	5006
Albany	5805	4685	5623	2650	3819	5525	5603	4005	4009
Apia	9503	8086	9044	5411	7134	9201	9024	6867	7414
Auckland	8680	7540	8486	5145	6672	8400	8466	6645	6870
Banaba	8410	6994	7936	4322	6142	8108	7936	5778	6322
Bluff	8120	7140	7948	5100	6134	7840	7928	6320	6466
Brisbane	8055	6685	7604	4005	5794	7775	7584	5427	5943
Cairns	7233	5816	6774	3141	4964	6931	6754	4597	6144
Cape Leeuwin	5645	4510	5460	2420	3657	5340	5440	3836	3840
Darwin	6049	4632	5590	2000	3780	5747	5570	3460	3960
Esperance	6065	4945	5844	2910	4030	5785	5824	4216	4269
Fremantle	5580	4446	5391	2369	3582	5300	5371	3636	3766
Geelong	7140	6009	6970	3980	5156	6860	6950	5342	5338
Geraldton	5480	4286	5218	2090	3408	5150	5198	3441	3616
Hobart	7275	6145	7090	4110	5276	6995	7070	5462	5469
Honolulu	10192	8763	9722	6011	7912	9912	9702	7455	8098
Launceston	7250	6125	7041	4094	5227	6970	7021	5413	5452
Lyttleton	8380	7426	8256	5399	6442	8100	8236	6628	6757
Mackay	7573	6156	7114	3481	5304	7271	7094	4937	5484
Madang	7121	5687	6645	2922	4835	6819	6625	4378	5015
Makatea	10780	9410	10356	6767	8542	10500	10336	8186	8710
Melbourne	7160	6009	6964	3980	5150	6880	6944	5336	5318
Napier	8639	7530	8528	5480	3714	8359	8508	6900	6854
Nauru Island	8250	6834	7796	4160	5982	7948	7776	5616	6162
Nelson	8449	7340	8254	5290	6444	8169	8234	6630	6664
Newcastle (NSW)	7675	6545	7479	4345	5665	7395	7459	5797	5878
New Plymouth	8427	7286	8248	5206	6434	8125	8228	6620	6621
Noumea	8366	6920	7926	4276	6112	8086	7906	5705	6216
Otago Harbour	8180	7200	8086	5160	6272	7900	8066	6458	6526
Papeete	10709	9341	10306	6697	8492	10429	10286	8136	8637
Portland (Victoria)	6943	5809	6768	3722	4954	6641	6748	5140	5137
Port Hedland	5494	4157	5113	1795	3104	5192	5093	3213	3485
Port Kembla	7580	6450	7379	4390	5565	7300	7359	5751	5781
Port Lincoln	6743	5609	6564	3522	4750	6441	6544	4936	4937
Port Moresby	7063	5646	6604	2971	4794	6761	6584	4427	4974
Port Pirie	6680	5540	6287	3145	4873	6400	6267	5059	4870
Rockhampton	7755	6336	7294	1991	5484	7455	7274	5117	5664
Suva	8956	7492	8494	4866	6684	8676	8474	6317	6866
Sydney	7605	6475	7424	4415	5610	7325	7404	5796	5806
Wellington	8489	7380	8328	5330	6514	8209	8308	6700	6704

AREA G	AREA E: Moulmein	Mumbai	Musay'td	Penang	Port Blair	Port Kelang	Port Okha	Port Sudan
Adelaide	4521	5230	6408	3997	4223	3734	5513	6776
Albany	3525	4230	5414	2888	3229	2737	4519	5779
Apia	6383	7634	8829	5665	6218	5499	7931	9460
Auckland	6161	7088	8267	5384	5996	5233	7372	8640
Banaba	5294	6542	7741	4576	5129	4410	6839	8367
Bluff	3840	6540	7729	5339	5544	5154	6834	8086
Brisbane	4943	6198	7389	4240	4778	4089	6491	8052
Cairns	4113	5364	6559	3395	3948	3229	5661	7190
Cape Leeuwin	3355	4057	5245	2676	3060	2510	4354	5600
Darwin	2976	4180	5375	2258	2811	2092	4477	6006
Esperance	3736	4430	5625	3148	3440	2997	4730	6039
Fremantle	3246	4000	5176	2596	2950	2445	4279	5574
Geelong	4862	5556	6751	4211	4566	4026	5856	7109
Geraldton	3051	3808	5003	2352	2755	2186	4105	5424
Hobart	4982	5700	6871	4342	4686	4157	5976	7251
Honolulu	6971	8322	9507	6248	6806	6097	8609	10165
Launceston	4933	5670	6822	4325	4637	4140	5927	7222
Lyttleton	6148	6845	8037	5630	5852	5445	7142	8353
Mackay	4453	5704	6899	3735	4288	3569	6000	7530
Madang	3894	5235	6430	3176	3729	3010	5532	7078
Makatea	7702	8965	10141	7005	7537	7853	9239	10710
Melbourne	4856	5556	6745	4211	4560	4026	5850	7123
Napier	6420	7080	8309	5701	6124	5550	7414	8617
Nauru Island	5132	6382	7581	4414	4967	4248	6679	8207
Nelson	6150	6840	8039	5511	5854	5360	7144	8427
Newcastle (NSW)	8348	6095	7260	4585	5148	4434	6365	7520
New Plymouth	6140	6834	8029	5460	5844	5294	7134	8384
Noumea	5220	6471	7711	4513	5056	4362	6809	8339
Otago Harbour	5978	6750	7867	5399	5682	5214	6972	8146
Papeete	7652	8892	10091	6934	7487	6783	9189	10640
Portland (Victoria)	4660	5354	6549	3976	4364	3810	5654	6900
Port Hedland	2765	3702	4898	2049	2525	1883	4000	5451
Port Kembla	5271	6000	6160	4627	4975	4476	6265	7510
Port Lincoln	4456	5150	6345	3776	4160	3510	5450	6700
Port Moresby	3943	5194	6389	3225	3778	3059	5491	7020
Port Pirie	4579	5288	6468	3384	4283	3233	5573	6640
Rockhampton	4633	5884	7079	3915	4468	3749	6181	7710
Suva	5833	7081	8279	5103	5668	4952	7381	8929
Sydney	5316	6025	7205	4652	5020	4501	6310	7535
Wellington	6220	6930	8109	5551	5924	5400	7214	8467

AREA G

AREA E	Quseir	Singapore	Sittwe	Suez	Trincomalee	Veraval	Vishakhapatnam	Yangon
Adelaide	7150	3509	4823	7433	4393	5406	4750	4525
Albany	6175	2520	3829	6436	3399	4409	3753	3526
Apia	9863	5294	6654	10109	6728	7814	6862	6406
Auckland	9050	5015	6432	9297	6252	7270	6614	6125
Banaba	8770	4200	5560	9016	6634	6646	5773	5317
Bluff	8490	4970	6144	8743	5714	6866	6210	5980
Brisbane	8425	3875	5214	8709	5288	6343	5443	4985
Cairns	7593	3024	4384	7839	4458	6544	4592	4136
Cape Leeuwin	6000	2340	3655	6250	3230	3755	3612	3360
Darwin	6409	1900	3247	6655	3274	4360	3460	3000
Esperance	6435	2780	4030	6696	5610	4669	4013	3886
Fremantle	5950	2239	3452	6231	3141	4166	3508	3245
Geelong	7510	3850	5156	7766	4736	5738	5082	4855
Geraldton	5830	2009	3257	6081	2961	4016	3328	3095
Hobart	7645	3980	5276	7908	4856	5869	5213	4960
Honolulu	10562	5881	7242	10822	7332	8498	7451	6991
Launceston	7620	3964	5226	8053	4807	5852	5196	4969
Lyttleton	8750	5269	6447	9010	6022	7157	6501	6274
Mackay	7933	3364	4724	8179	4798	5884	4932	4476
Madang	7481	2800	4165	7727	4255	5415	4373	3917
Makatea	11150	6637	7973	10806	8034	9110	8725	7747
Melbourne	7530	3850	5153	7780	4730	5718	5082	4825
Napier	9010	5350	6714	9274	6294	7254	6598	6375
Nauru Island	8610	4035	5400	8856	5474	6562	5611	5155
Nelson	8819	5160	6444	9084	6024	7064	6408	6185
Newcastle (NSW)	8045	4215	5586	8304	5245	6278	5622	5380
New Plymouth	8787	5125	6454	9033	6014	7021	6396	6146
Noumea	8735	4146	5537	8996	6604	6616	5716	5256
Otago Harbour	8550	5030	6274	8803	5852	6926	6270	6040
Papeete	11079	6567	7923	11364	7984	9037	8655	7677
Portland (Victoria)	7303	3641	4954	7549	4534	5537	4912	4662
Port Hedland	5854	1678	3029	6100	2807	3885	3106	2790
Port Kembla	7950	4260	5567	8208	5145	6181	5525	5300
Port Lincoln	7103	3441	4750	7349	4330	5337	4712	4462
Port Moresby	7423	2854	4214	7669	4288	5374	4422	3966
Port Pirie	7050	3815	4873	7297	4453	5270	4614	4125
Rockhampton	8125	3544	4904	8359	4978	6064	5112	4656
Suva	9326	4736	6104	9632	6178	7266	6306	5846
Sydney	7945	4285	5612	8233	5190	6206	5550	5325
Wellington	8859	5200	6516	9124	6094	7104	6448	6225

AREA H

AREA E	Abadan	Aden	Aqaba	Bahrain	Bandar Abbas	Basrah	Bassein
Antofagasta	9801*	9831*	8823*	10223M	10944M	11458M	11373
Arica	9582*	9612*	8604*	11363*	11084*	11598*	11643
Astoria	10657	10687	10466*	10737	10458	10972	8186
Balboa *	9622	7692	6672	9406	9127	9678	10977
Buenaventura *	8013	8043	7035	9794	9515	10029	11331
Cabo Blanco *	10372	8442	7422	10156	9877	10428	11789
Caldera	9877M	9907M	8974*	9936M	10759M	11270M	11240
Callao	9007*	9037*	8029*	10788*	10509*	11023*	11806
Cape Horn	9344	8114	9354	9139	8860	9374	9583
Chimbote *	8801	8831	7823	10582	10303	10817	11843
Coos Bay	10545	10575	10282	10625	10346	10860	8074
Corinto *	10305	8375	7355	10089	8910	10361	11660
Eureka	10839	10869	10141*	10919	10640	11154	8368
Guayaquil	10486	8516	9508	10265	9986	10500	11856
Guaymas	10017*	10047*	9039*	11798*	11519*	12033*	10211
Honolulu	9482	9512	10757	9562	9283	9797	7011
Iquique	9648*	9678*	8670*	11428M	11049M	11663M	11387
Los Angeles	10574*	10604*	9596*	11548	11269	11783	8997
Manzanillo (Mex)	9379*	9409*	8401*	11048*	10879*	11393*	10039
Mazatlan	9667*	9697*	8689*	11448*	11169*	11683*	9861
Nanaimo	10673	10703	10723*	10753	10474	10988	8202
New Westminster	10689	10719	10739*	10769	10490	11004	8218
Portland (Oreg)	10743	10773	10552*	10823	10544	11058	8272
Port Alberni	10580	10610	10630*	10660	10381	10895	8109
Port Isabel	10247*	10277*	9269*	12028*	11749*	12263*	10441
Port Moody	10676	10706	10726*	10756	10477	10991	8205
Prince Rupert	9548	9420	10550	9335	9064	9599	6820
Puerto Montt M	10346	9116	10356	10140	9862	10376	10585
Puntarenas (CR) *	10093	8163	7143	9877	9598	10159	11448
Punta Arenas (Ch) M	9386	8156	9396	9180	8902	9416	9625
Salina Cruz	10792*	8862*	7842*	10576*	10297*	10848*	11304
San Francisco	10906*	10936*	9928*	11034	10755	11269	8483
San Jose *	10508	8678	7558	10292	10013	10564	11863
Seattle	10663	10693	10404*	10743	10464	10978	8192
Tacoma	10685	10715	10735*	10765	10486	11000	8214
Talcahuano	9293M	9323M	9488*	10452M	10173M	10687M	10623
Tocopilla	9729	9759	8751*	11407M	11128M	11642M	11403
Valparaiso	9497M	9527	9299*	9556M	10377M	10891	11082
Vancouver (BC)	10672	10702	10722*	10751	10473	10987	8201
Victoria (Vanc Is)	10605	10635	10655*	10685	10406	10920	8134

AREA H

AREA E	Bhavnagar	Bushehr	Calcutta	Chennai	Chittagong	Cochin	Colombo
Antofagasta	11060M	11283M	11762M	11108M	11711M	10627M	10627M
Arica	11365M	11423*	12067M	11413M	11961M	10932M	10932M
Astoria	9697	10979	8694	8641	8561	8915	8628
Balboa *	9302	9462	10997	10349*	11132	9488	9788*
Buenaventura *	9793	9854	11348	10700*	11484	9892	10139*
Cabo Blanco *	10052	10212	11747	11099*	11882	10238	10538*
Caldera	11604*	11096M	11575M	11921M	11695	10440M	10440M
Callao	10787*	10848*	12296	11694*	12284	10887*	11133*
Cape Horn	8955	9199	9644	8990	9692	8517	8517
Chimbote	10581*	10642*	12363	11488	12280	10681*	10927*
Coos Bay	9585	10685	8582	8529	8449	8803	8516
Corinto *	9985	10145	11680	11032*	11815	10171	10471*
Eureka	9879	10979	8876	8823	8743	9097	8810
Guayaquil	10266*	10325*	11821*	11173*	11956*	10366*	10612*
Guaymas	11700	11858*	10697	10644	10564	10918	10631
Honolulu	8522	9622	7519	7466	7386	7740	7453
Iquique	11265M	11488M	11967M	11798	11851M	10832M	10832M
Los Angeles	10508	11608	9505	9452	9372	9826	9439
Manzanillo (Mex)	11559*	11281*	10457	10494	10426	11259*	10481
Mazatlan	11372	11508*	10369	10316	10236	10590	10303
Nanaimo	9713	10183	8710	8657	8577	8931	8644
New Westminster	9729	10829	8728	8673	8593	8947	8660
Portland (Oreg)	9783	10883	8780	8727	8647	9001	8714
Port Alberni	9620	10720	8617	8564	8484	8838	8551
Port Isabel	11930	12088*	10927	10874	10794	11148	10861
Port Moody	9716	10816	8713	8660	8580	8934	8647
Prince Rupert	8324	9420	7332	7266	7200	7536	7264
Puerto Montt	10003M	10275M	10827M	10177	10694M	6090M	9520
Puntarenas (CR) *	9773	9933	11468	10820*	11603	9959	10259*
Punta Arenas (Ch)	9043M	9315M	9867M	9217	9734M	8560M	8560
Salina Cruz	10472*	10632*	11816	11423*	11634	10658*	10950*
San Francisco	9994	11094	8991	8938	8858	9212	8925
San Jose *	10188	10348	11883	11235*	12018	10374	10674*
Seattle	9703	10803	8700	8647	8567	8921	8634
Tacoma	9725	10825	8722	8669	8589	8943	8656
Talcahuano	10289M	10512M	10991M	10337M	11003M	9856M	9856M
Tocopilla	11244M	11467M	11850	11292M	11838	10811M	10811M
Valparaiso	10493M	10716M	11195M	11541M	11166M	10060M	10060M
Vancouver (BC)	9712	10812	8709	8656	8576	8930	8643
Victoria (Vanc Is)	9645	10745	8642	8589	8509	8863	8576

AREA H	AREA E Djibouti	Dubai	Fujairah	Jedda	Karachi	Kuwait	Malacca
Antofagasta	9814*	11022M	10856M	9160*	10902M	11408M	10646
Arica	9595*	11162*	10996*	9841*	11083*	11548*	10853
Astoria	10792	10536	10370	10798*	9938*	10922	7178
Balboa	7572*	9205	9037	7012*	9163*	9592*	10626
Buenaventura	8026*	9593	9427	7372*	9514*	9979*	10497
Cabo Blanco	8322*	9955	9789	7762*	9913*	10342*	10734
Caldera	9874*	10837M	10671M	9314*	10715M	11220M	10300
Callao	9020*	10587*	10421*	8362*	10508*	10973*	10798
Cape Horn	8223	8938	8772	8808	8826	9324	9643
Chimbote *	8814*	10381	10215	8156*	10302*	10767	10766
Coos Bay	10680	10424	10258	10654*	9826	10810	7066
Corinto *	8255*	8988	8822	7695*	9846	10275*	11009
Eureka	10974	10718	10552	10513*	10120	11104	7360
Guayaquil *	8494*	10064	9898	7845*	9987*	10450*	10848
Guaymas	10030*	11597*	11431*	9376*	11718*	11983*	9181
Honolulu	9617	9901	9195	10202	8763	9747	6003
Iquique	9661*	11127M	10961M	9007*	11149*	11613M	10379
Los Angeles	10587*	11347	11181	9933*	10749	11733	7989
Manzanillo (Mex)	9392*	10957*	10791*	8738*	10880*	11343*	9031
Mazatlan	9680*	11247*	11081*	9026*	11168*	11633*	8853
Nanaimo	10808	10552	10386	11393	9954	10938	7194
New Westminster	10824	10568	10402	11409	9970	10954	7210
Portland (Oreg)	10878	10622	10456	10881*	10024	11008	7264
Port Alberni	10715	10459	10293	11300	9861	10845	7101
Port Isabel	10260*	11827*	11661*	9606*	11948*	12213*	9411
Port Moody	10812	10555	10389	11396	9957	10941	7197
Prince Rupert	9452	9142	8976	10993	8565	9516	5800
Puerto Montt M	9311	9940	9774	9810	9890	10363	10686
Puntarenas (CR)	8043*	9676	9510	7483*	9634*	10063*	11030
Punta Arenas (Ch) M	8351	8980	8814	8850	8930	9403	9726
Salina Cruz	8742*	10375*	10209*	8182*	10333*	10762*	10289
San Francisco	10919*	10833	10667	10265*	10235	11219	7475
San Jose *	8458*	10091	9925	7898*	10049*	10478*	9745
Seattle	10798	10542	10376	11383	9944	10928	7184
Tacoma	10820	10564	10398	11405	9966	10950	7206
Talcahuano	9620M	10251M	10085M	10119M	10131M	10637M	9615
Tocopilla	9742*	11206M	11040M	9088*	11086M	11592M	10534
Valparaiso	9783M	10455M	10289M	10282M	10335M	10841M	10067
Vancouver (BC)	10808	10551	10385	11392	9953	10937	7193
Victoria (Vanc Is)	10740	10484	10318	11325	9886	10870	7126

AREA H

AREA E	Mangalore	Massawa	Mina Al Ahmadi	Mongla	Mormugao	Moulmein	Mumbai
Antofagasta	10620M	9497*	11388M	11677M	10695M	11376	10860M
Arica	10925M	9278*	11528*	11927M	11000M	11646M	11165M
Astoria	9097	11140*	10902	8622	9273	8143	9497
Balboa *	9452	7292	9572	11102	9402	11062	9349
Buenaventura	9791*	7709*	9959*	11454	9753*	11393*	9700
Cabo Blanco	10202*	8042*	10322*	11852	10152*	11699	10099
Caldera	11754*	9594*	11201M	11756	10508M	11613M	10673M
Callao	10802*	8703*	10953*	12338	10747*	11763	10694*
Cape Horn	8571	8488	9304	9658	8646	9681	8754
Chimbote	10596*	8497*	10747*	12250	10541*	11792	10488*
Coos Bay	8985	10956*	10790	8510	9161	8031	9385
Corinto	10135*	7975*	10255*	11785	10085*	11725*	10032
Eureka	9279	10815*	11084	8804	9455	8325	9679
Guayaquil	10264*	8182*	10430*	11926*	10226*	11813	10173*
Guaymas	11100	9713	11963*	10425	11266	10146	11500
Honolulu	7922	9888	9727	7447	8098	6968	8322
Iquique	11438*	9344*	11593M	11817M	11388*	11344	11065M
Los Angeles	10008	10270*	11713	9433	10084	8954	10308
Manzanillo (Mex)	11157*	9075*	11323*	10487	11119*	9996	11066*
Mazatlan	10772	9363	11613*	10297	10948	9818	11172
Nanaimo	9113	10188	10918	8638	9289	8159	9513
New Westminster	9129	10204	10934	8654	9305	8175	9529
Portland (Oreg)	9183	11143	10988	8708	9359	8229	9583
Port Alberni	9020	10095	10825	8545	9196	9766	9420
Port Isabel	11330	9943*	12193*	10655	11496	10376	11730
Port Moody	9116	10191	10921	8641	9292	8162	9516
Prince Rupert	7720	9755	9496	7261	7900	6769	8124
Puerto Montt M	9574	9490	10343	10660M	9649	10853	9803M
Puntarenas (CR)	9923*	7763*	10043*	11573	9873*	11533*	9820
Punta Arenas (Ch) M	8614	8629	9383	9700M	8689	9893	8843M
Salina Cruz	10622*	8462*	10742*	11745	10572*	11254	10519*
San Francisco	9394	10602*	11199	8919	9570	8440	9794
San Jose	10338	8178*	10458*	11988	10288*	11948*	10235
Seattle	9103	10178	10908	8628	9279	8149	9503
Tacoma	9125	10200	10930	8650	9301	8171	9525
Talcahuano	9849M	10162*	10617M	10969M	9924M	10580	10089M
Tocopilla	10804M	9425*	11572M	11892	10879M	11406	11044M
Valparaiso	10053M	9973*	10821M	11132M	10128M	11233M	10293M
Vancouver (BC)	9112	10187	10917	8637	9288	8158	9512
Victoria (Vanc Is)	9045	10120	10850	8570	9221	8091	9445

AREA H

AREA E	Musay'td	Penang	Port Blair	Port Kelang	Port Okha	Port Sudan	Quseir
Antofagasta	11193M	10891	11194	10740	10902M	9220*	8778*
Arica	11333	11098	11464	10947	11207M	9001 *	8559*
Astoria	10707	7423	8078	7272	9794	10863*	10421*
Balboa *	9372	10871	10638	10720	9189	7081	6612*
Buenaventura	9764*	10742	11005	10591	9540*	7432*	6990*
Cabo Blanco	10122*	10988	11388	10822	9922*	7831*	7392*
Caldera	11006M	10554	11207M	10388	11474*	9383*	8944*
Callao	10758*	11043	11598	10892	10534*	8426*	7984*
Cape Horn	9109	9232	9275	9313	8594	8765	9168
Chimbote	10552*	11020	11796	10854	10328 *	8220 *	7778*
Coos Bay	10595	7311	7866	7160	9682	10679*	10237*
Corinto	10055*	10233	11321	10067	9855*	7764*	7325*
Eureka	10879	7605	8160	7454	9976	10538*	10096*
Guayaquil	10235*	11093	11462	10942	10013*	7905	9463*
Guaymas	11768*	9426	10003	9275	11797	9436*	8994*
Honolulu	9532	6248	6803	6097	8619	10165	10562
Iquique	11398M	10625	11179	10473	11107M	9067*	8625*
Los Angeles	11518	8234	8789	8083	10605	9993*	9551*
Manzanillo (Mex)	11128*	9276	9831	9125	10906*	8798*	8356*
Mazatlan	11418*	9098	9653	8947	11469	9086*	8644*
Nanaimo	10723	7439	7994	7288	9810	10465	10678*
New Westminster	10739	7455	8010	7304	9826	10481	10694*
Portland (Oreg)	10793	7509	8064	7358	9880	10949*	10507*
Port Alberni	10630	7346	7901	7195	9717	10372	10585*
Port Isabel	11998*	9656	10233	9505	12027	9666*	9224*
Port Moody	10726	7442	7997	7291	9813	10468	10681*
Prince Rupert	9313	6050	6612	5893	8421	9961	10364
Puerto Montt M	10111M	10151	10277	10232M	9845	9767	10170
Puntarenas (CR)	9843*	10256	11109	10090	9643*	7552*	7113*
Punta Arenas (Ch) M	9151M	9191	9317	9272	8835	8807	9210
Salina Cruz	10542*	10543	11103	10377	10342*	8251*	7812*
San Francisco	11004	7720	8275	7569	10091	10325*	9883*
San Jose	10258*	9999	11524	9833	10058*	7967*	7528*
Seattle	10713	7429	7984	7278	9800	11455	10659*
Tacoma	10735	7451	8006	7300	9822	10477	10690*
Talcahuano	10422M	9860	10415	9709	10131M	9885*	9443*
Tocopilla	11377M	10768	11224	10583	11086M	9148*	8706*
Valparaiso	10626M	10301	10827M	10116	10335M	9696*	9254*
Vancouver (BC)	10722	7438	7993	7287	9809	11464	10677*
Victoria (Vanc Is)	10655	7371	7926	7220	9742	11397	10610*

AREA H

AREA E	Singapore	Sittwe	Suez	Trincomalee	Veraval	Vishakhapatnam	Yangon
Antofagasta	10524	11672	8523*	10830M	10860M	11419M	11382
Arica	10731	11942	8304*	11135M	11165M	11724M	11652
Astoria	7059	8416	10166*	8740	9673	8626	8166
Balboa	10504	11032	6384*	9972*	9162	10664	10997
Buenaventura	10375	11382	6735*	10417*	9600*	11016*	11348
Cabo Blanco	10612	11782	7134*	10722*	9912*	11414*	11722
Caldera	10178	11809	8686*	10643M	10673M	11751	11575M
Callao	19676	12036	7729*	11411*	10594*	12009*	11786
Cape Horn	9523	9625	8409†	8720	8754	9254	9643
Chimbote	10644	12078	7523*	11205*	10388*	11803*	11754
Coos Bay	6944	8304	9982*	8404	9561	8514	8054
Corinto	9857	11715	7067*	10655*	9845*	11347	11680*
Eureka	7238	8598	9841*	8698	9855	8808	8348
Guayaquil	10726	11886	9208*	10890*	10073*	11488*	11836
Guaymas	9059	10441	8739*	10519	11676	10629	10169
Honolulu	5880	7241	10822	7341	8498	7451	6991
Iquique	10257	11617	8370*	11035M	11065M	11903	11367
Los Angeles	7867	9227	9296*	9327	10484	9437	8977
Manzanillo (Mex)	8909	10269	8101*	10369	10966	10479	10019
Mazatlan	8731	10091	8389*	10191	11348	10301	9841
Nanaimo	7072	10432	10423*	8532	9689	8642	8182
New Westminster	7088	8448	10439*	8548	9705	8658	8198
Portland (Oreg)	7142	8502	10252*	8602	9759	8712	8252
Port Alberni	6981	8339	10330*	8439	9596	8549	8089
Port Isabel	9289	10671	8969*	10749	11906	10859	10399
Port Moody	7075	8435	10426*	8535	9692	8645	8185
Prince Rupert	6683	7048	10613	7138	8300	7256	6792
Puerto Montt	10442M	10627	9333†	9723M	9803M	10256M	10815M
Puntarenas (CR)	9880	11503	6855*	10443*	9633*	11135*	11468*
Punta Arenas (Ch)	9482M	9667	8373†	8763M	8843M	9296M	9855M
Salina Cruz	10167	11539	7454*	11622	10332*	11740	11277
San Francisco	7350	8713	9628*	8813	9970	8923	8463
San Jose	9633	11918	7270*	10858*	10048*	11550*	11883*
Seattle	7062	8422	10404*	8522	9679	8632	8172
Tacoma	7084	8444	10435*	8544	9701	8654	8194
Talcahuano	9493	10853	9188*	10059M	10089M	10648M	10603
Tocopilla	10412	11702	8451*	11014M	11044M	11639	11412
Valparaiso	9945	11299	8999*	10263M	10293M	11172	11195M
Vancouver (BC)	7071	8431	10422*	8531	9688	8641	8181
Victoria (Vanc Is)	7004	8364	10355*	8464	9621	8574	8114

AREA E

AREA E	Aden	Bahrain	Bandar Abbas	Bushehr	Calcutta	Cochin	Colombo	Dubai	Fujairah
Aden	–	1732	1453	1792	3304	1850	2094	1531	1365
Aqaba	1246	2974	2695	3044	4544	3090	3334	2773	2607
Bandar Abbas	1453	341	–	400	3058	1549	1835	135	118
Basrah	1967	322	572	192	3572	2064	2349	520	605
Bassein	3251	3284	3005	3344	643	1477	1194	3083	2917
Bushehr	1792	170	400	–	3397	1888	2174	312	425
Calcutta	3304	3337	3058	3397	–	1530	1244	3136	2970
Calicut	1815	1754	1475	1814	1612	84	389	1553	1387
Chennai	2650	2683	2404	2743	775	876	590	2482	2316
Chittagong	3352	3385	3106	3445	367	1578	1292	3264	3018
Cochin	1850	1828	1549	1888	1530	–	307	1627	1461
Colombo	2094	2114	1835	2174	1244	307	–	1913	1747
Dubai	1531	298	135	312	3136	1627	1913	–	149
Fujairah	1365	400	128	425	2970	1461	1747	149	–
Jedda	701	2428	2149	2488	3998	2544	2788	2227	2061
Kandla	1567	1136	857	1196	2478	953	1255	935	769
Karachi	1470	922	643	982	2564	1039	1341	721	555
Kuwait	1917	263	518	154	3522	2013	2299	462	583
Mormugao	1687	1505	1226	1565	1892	365	669	1304	1216
Mumbai	1657	1352	1073	1412	2112	585	889	1151	985
Paradip	3154	3187	2908	3247	154	1380	1194	2986	2820
Penang	3336	3369	3090	3429	1301	1562	1276	3168	3002
Port Sudan	658	2385	2106	2445	3955	2501	2745	2184	2018
Port Sultan Qaboos	1203	532	253	592	2819	1301	1596	283	153
Quseir	1061	2788	2509	2848	4358	2904	3148	2587	2421
Ras Tanura	1773	122	382	145	3378	1869	2155	290	447
Safaga	1109	2836	2557	2896	4406	2952	3196	2635	2469
Singapore	3627	3660	3380	3720	1650	1853	1567	3458	3292
Sittwe	3285	3318	3039	3378	402	1511	1225	3117	2951
Suez	1307	3034	2755	3094	4604	3150	3394	2833	2667
Vishakhapatnam	2914	2947	2668	3007	442	1140	866	2746	2580
Yangon	3309	3342	3063	3402	779	1535	1249	3141	2975

AREA E

AREA E	Jedda	Kakinada	Massawa	Mina Al Ahmadi	Mongla	Mormugao	Mumbai	Penang	Port Okha
Aden	701	2869	399	1897	3318	1687	1657	3336	1498
Aqaba	574	4109	896	3139	4558	2929	2899	4576	2740
Bandar Abbas	2149	2623	1847	497	3072	1226	1073	3090	791
Basrah	2663	3137	2361	140	3586	1740	1587	3604	1305
Bassein	3363	766	3643	3449	557	1839	2059	786	2356
Bushehr	2488	2962	2186	140	3411	1565	1412	3429	1130
Calcutta	3998	529	3696	3502	288	1892	2112	1301	2409
Calicut	2509	1177	2207	1919	1626	286	506	1644	805
Chennai	3344	272	3042	2848	806	1238	1458	1277	1755
Chittagong	4046	645	3744	3550	248	1940	2160	1167	2457
Cochin	2544	1095	2242	1993	1544	365	585	1562	884
Colombo	2788	809	2486	2279	1258	669	889	1276	1186
Dubai	2227	2701	1925	451	3150	1304	1151	3168	869
Fujairah	2061	2535	1759	541	2984	1138	985	3002	703
Jedda	–	3563	360	2593	4012	2383	2353	4030	2194
Kandla	2266	2043	1961	1301	2492	602	415	2510	79
Karachi	2166	2129	1864	1087	2578	688	501	2596	195
Kuwait	2590	3087	2311	30	3536	1690	1537	3554	1255
Mormugao	2383	1457	2081	1670	1906	–	232	1924	533
Mumbai	2353	1677	2051	1517	2126	232	–	2144	346
Paradip	3263	378	3546	3352	230	1742	1962	1225	2259
Penang	4030	1267	3728	3534	1228	1924	2144	–	2441
Port Sudan	155	3520	297	2550	3969	2340	2310	3987	2151
Port Sultan Qaboos	1899	2384	1597	697	2833	990	853	2851	611
Quseir	1044	3923	739	2953	4372	2743	2713	4390	2554
Ras Tanura	2469	2943	2167	222	3392	1546	1393	3410	1111
Safaga	437	3971	754	3001	4420	2791	2761	4438	2602
Singapore	4321	1594	4019	3825	1578	2215	2435	376	2732
Sittwe	3979	636	3677	3483	288	1873	2093	1015	2390
Suez	636	4169	973	3199	4618	2989	2959	4636	2800
Vishakhapatnam	3608	73	3306	3112	480	1502	1722	1246	2019
Yangon	4003	867	3701	3507	704	1897	2117	766	2414

AREA E

AREA E	Port Sudan	Quseir	Safaga	Singapore	Sittwe	Suez	Vishakhapatnam	Yangon
Aden	658	1061	1109	3627	3285	1307	2914	3309
Aqaba	639	212	183	4867	4525	300	4154	4549
Bandar Abbas	2106	2509	2557	3381	3039	2755	2668	3063
Basrah	2620	3023	3071	3895	3553	3269	3182	3577
Bassein	3902	4305	4353	1137	322	4551	711	250
Bushehr	2445	2848	2896	3720	3378	3094	3007	3402
Calcutta	3955	4358	4406	1650	402	4604	442	779
Calicut	2466	2869	2917	1935	1593	3115	1221	1617
Chennai	3301	3704	3752	1586	844	3950	328	998
Chittagong	4003	4406	4454	1517	175	4652	578	600
Cochin	2501	2904	2952	1853	1511	3150	1140	1535
Colombo	2745	3148	3196	1567	1225	3394	866	1249
Dubai	2184	2587	2635	3459	3117	2833	2746	3141
Fujairah	2018	2421	2469	3293	2951	2667	2580	2975
Jedda	155	390	437	4321	3979	636	3608	4003
Kandla	2220	2623	2671	2801	2459	2869	2088	2483
Karachi	2123	2526	2574	2887	2545	2772	2174	2569
Kuwait	2570	2973	3021	3845	3503	3219	3132	3527
Mormugao	2340	2743	2791	2215	1873	2989	1502	1897
Mumbai	2310	2713	2761	2435	2093	2959	1722	2117
Paradip	3805	4208	4256	1600	335	4454	298	700
Penang	3987	4390	4438	376	1015	4636	1246	766
Port Sudan	–	460	508	4278	3936	694	3565	3960
Port Sultan Qaboos	1856	2259	2307	3142	2800	2505	2429	2824
Quseir	460	–	42	4681	4339	255	3968	4363
Ras Tanura	2426	2829	2877	3701	3359	3075	2988	3383
Safaga	508	42	–	4729	4387	223	4016	4411
Singapore	4278	4681	4729	–	1365	4927	1573	1117
Sittwe	3936	4339	4387	1365	–	4585	599	479
Suez	694	255	223	4927	4585	–	4214	4609
Vishakhapatnam	3565	3968	4016	1573	599	4214	–	818
Yangon	3960	4363	4411	1117	479	4609	818	–

Area F

Distances between principal ports in Malaysia, Indonesia, South East Asia, the China Sea and Japan.

and

Area G Australasia, New Guinea and the Pacific Islands.

Area H The West Coast of North and South America.

Area F Other ports in Malaysia, Indonesia, South East Asia, the China Sea and Japan.

AREA F
Reed's Marine Distance Tables
THE FAR EAST

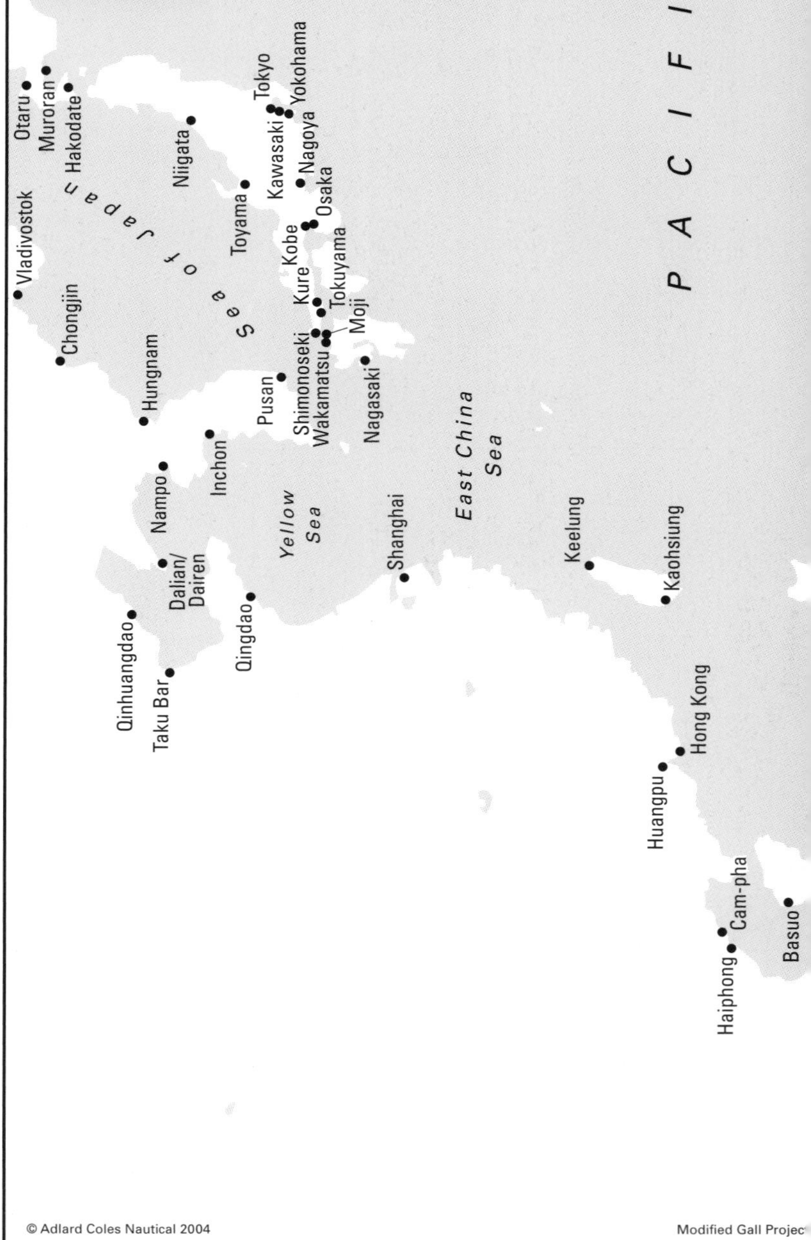

Modified Gall Projec

AREA F

Reed's Marine Distance Tables

THE FAR EAST

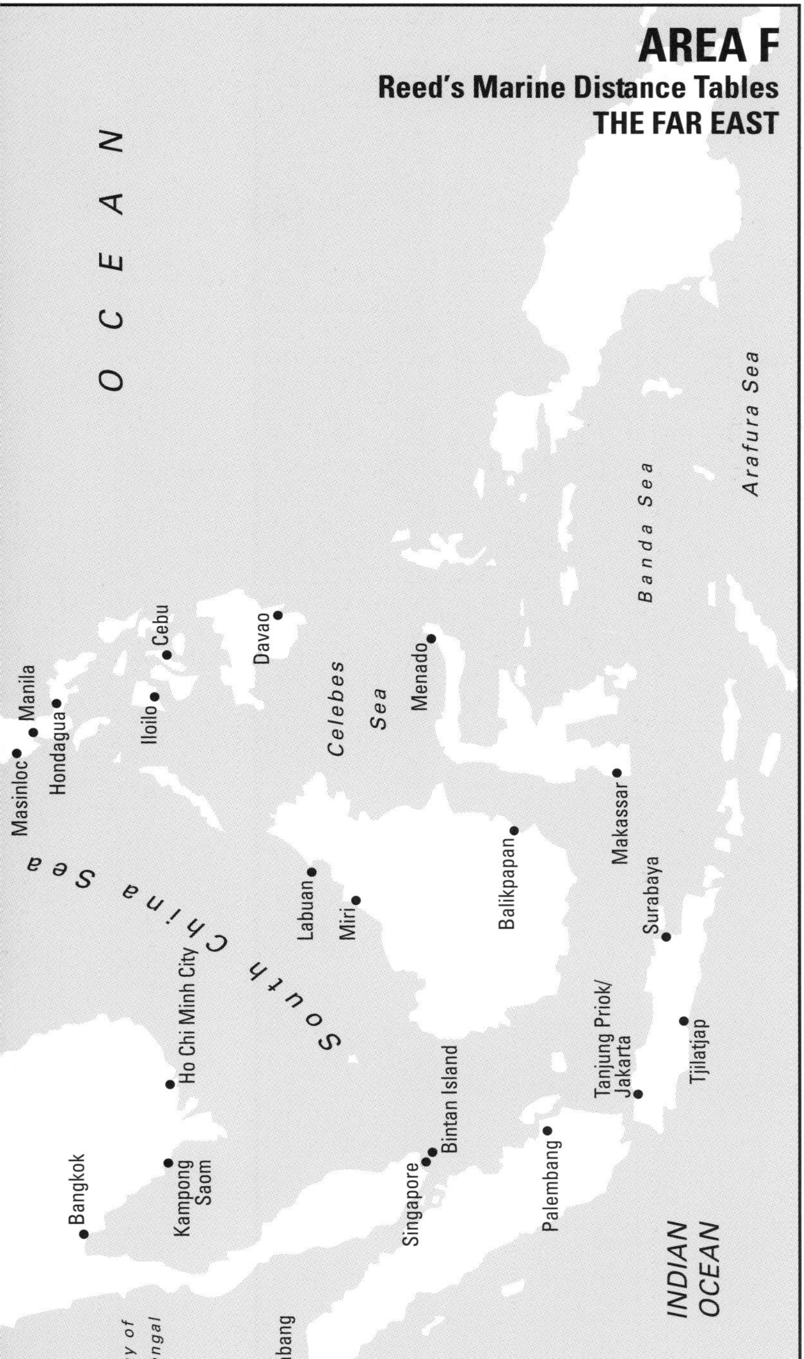

AREA G	AREA F							
	Balikpapan	Bangkok	Basuo (Hainan Is)	Cam-Pha	Cebu	Dalian	Haiphong	Ho Chi Minh City
Adelaide	3817	4272	4530	4780	4014	6099	4730	4060
Albany	2820	3275	3533	3783	3018	5102	3733	3063
Apia	4473	5715	5159	5409	4118	4943	5359	5237
Auckland	4244	5819	5291	5541	4413	5469	5491	5122
Banaba	3242	4469	3876	4126	2860	3696	4076	4031
Bluff	4625	5700	5880	6130	4995	5985	6080	5430
Brisbane	3100	4675	4099	4349	3469	4486	4299	3977
Cairns	2265	3723	3286	3536	2318	3936	3486	3294
Cape Leeuwin	2047	3121	3300	3550	2831	4531	3500	2863
Darwin	1169	2612	2405	2655	1550	3175	2605	2327
Esperance	3080	3525	3793	4043	3878	5362	3993	3323
Fremantle	2528	2983	3241	3491	3326	4425	3441	2771
Geelong	4078	4604	4862	5112	4346	5556	5062	4392
Geraldton	2343	2798	3056	3306	3141	4200	3256	2586
Hobart	4022	4735	4943	5193	4391	5534	5143	4523
Honolulu	5230	6319	5127	5357	4610	4470	5327	5542
Launceston	3971	4718	4899	5149	4340	5420	5099	4506
Lyttleton	4558	6023	5608	5858	4947	5914	5808	6007
Mackay	2609	4067	3630	3880	2662	4280	3830	3638
Madang	2000	3268	2785	3035	1718	3045	2985	2830
Makatea	5816	7062	6400	6735	5470	6155	6685	6574
Melbourne	4078	4604	4862	5112	4345	5507	5062	4392
Napier	4596	6171	5646	5896	4957	5862	5846	6008
Nauru Island	4391	5915	3750	4000	2700	3573	3950	3873
Nelson	4333	5791	5390	5640	4353	5630	5590	5423
Newcastle (NSW)	3445	4925	4461	4711	3520	4894	4661	4496
New Plymouth	4281	5856	5331	5381	4642	5547	5531	5393
Noumea	3373	4948	4409	4659	3380	4531	4609	4782
Otago Harbour	4723	5792	5980	6230	5097	6089	6180	5530
Papeete	5794	6860	6427	6652	5594	6068	6602	6422
Portland (Victoria)	4238	4444	4702	4952	4186	6416	4902	4232
Port Hedland	1185	2403	2535	2785	1969	3669	2735	2118
Port Kembla	2537	5097	4587	4837	3899	5001	4787	4839
Port Lincoln	3147	4221	4399	4649	3931	5631	4599	3963
Port Moresby	2093	3551	3114	3364	2146	3764	3314	3122
Port Pirie	3270	4344	4522	4772	4054	5754	4722	4086
Rockhampton	2780	4238	2972	3222	2833	4451	3172	3859
Suva	3963	5538	4689	4939	3893	4681	4889	4679
Sydney	3512	5072	4562	4812	3874	4976	4762	4814
Wellington	4459	5986	5461	5711	4402	5677	5661	5823

AREA G

AREA F	Hong Kong	Hungnam	Inchon	Kampong Saom	Kaohsiung (Taiwan)	Keelung (Taiwan)	Kobe	Makassar
Adelaide	4788	6092	5625	3970	4679	5164	5325	3052
Albany	3785	5095	4631	2975	3685	4167	4920	2058
Apia	4865	4422	4790	5415	4571	4549	4228	4244
Auckland	5060	5271	5305	5515	4802	4780	4880	4023
Banaba	3554	3177	3574	4169	3261	3226	2907	3154
Bluff	5600	5705	5690	5400	5168	5435	5500	4185
Brisbane	4080	4346	4410	4372	3888	4342	3880	2805
Cairns	3237	3921	3824	3423	3021	3139	3652	1975
Cape Leeuwin	3575	4610	4462	2821	3516	3698	4435	1889
Darwin	2341	3183	3068	2312	2249	2368	2935	871
Esperance	4045	5355	4842	3225	3896	4427	5180	2269
Fremantle	3500	4803	4330	2683	3384	3582	4625	1757
Geelong	5119	5446	5381	4304	4852	5496	4950	3395
Geraldton	3315	4618	4127	2498	3181	3397	4440	1554
Hobart	5015	5495	5428	4435	4899	4850	5022	3515
Honolulu	4857	3480	4312	6020	4539	4350	3669	5193
Launceston	5224	5390	5308	4415	4779	5463	4889	3466
Lyttleton	5334	5655	5674	5723	5152	5546	5584	4304
Mackay	3581	4265	4168	3767	3365	3483	4031	2319
Madang	2636	2982	2803	2968	2281	2336	2641	1824
Makatea	6182	5463	5975	6762	5850	5798	5396	5532
Melbourne	4875	5395	5376	4304	4847	5246	5275	3390
Napier	5335	5740	5594	5871	5091	5550	5585	4308
Nauru Island	3431	3082	3451	5615	3138	3103	2787	2995
Nelson	5217	5437	5488	5491	4966	5021	5045	4101
Newcastle (NSW)	4439	4822	4752	4720	4223	4270	4320	3177
New Plymouth	5020	5325	5389	5556	4867	5236	5370	4043
Noumea	4105	4345	4343	4645	3857	3911	3870	3135
Otago Harbour	5700	5805	5828	5492	5306	5535	5600	4327
Papeete	6132	5418	5955	6560	5830	5778	4912	5512
Portland (Victoria)	4959	5606	5458	4144	5556	4990	5110	3193
Port Hedland	2712	3713	3600	2103	2654	2836	3475	1027
Port Kembla	4505	4884	4847	4797	4318	4382	4405	3272
Port Lincoln	4674	5808	5562	3921	4616	4798	5408	2992
Port Moresby	3065	3749	3652	3251	2849	2967	3479	1803
Port Pirie	4797	5900	5685	4044	4739	4921	5509	3115
Rockhampton	3750	4336	4339	3938	3536	3654	4150	2490
Suva	4545	4381	4582	5238	4225	4179	4112	3696
Sydney	4480	4859	4811	4772	4282	4307	4380	3236
Wellington	5250	5555	5537	5685	5015	5075	5090	4169

AREA G

AREA F	Manila	Masinloc	Menado	Moji	Muroran	Nagasaki	Nagoya	Nampo
Adelaide	4210	4250	3731	5401	5737	5490	5247	6059
Albany	3565	3605	2732	4748	5492	4765	5177	5062
Apia	4436	4476	3957	4371	4475	4400	4165	4903
Auckland	4650	4690	3958	4944	5200	4935	4879	5429
Banaba	3100	3140	2725	3018	3072	3067	2862	3656
Bluff	2115	2155	4130	5550	5665	5560	5445	5945
Brisbane	3550	3590	2750	3939	4330	3925	3990	4446
Cairns	2671	2711	1920	3637	4143	3538	3703	3896
Cape Leeuwin	3057	3097	2568	4359	4992	4234	4514	4491
Darwin	1800	1840	990	2913	3425	2800	2985	4135
Esperance	3825	3865	2948	5008	5758	5750	5507	5322
Fremantle	2920	2960	2436	4456	5206	4480	4885	4385
Geelong	4542	4582	3751	5010	5316	5000	4856	6216
Geraldton	2735	2775	2233	4271	5021	4295	4700	4200
Hobart	4464	4504	3798	5091	5327	5069	5028	6194
Honolulu	4767	4807	4664	3856	3392	3986	3527	4430
Launceston	4388	4428	3678	4983	5260	4969	4820	6180
Lyttleton	4340	4380	4249	5444	5572	5291	5235	5874
Mackay	3015	3055	2264	3981	4487	3992	4047	4240
Madang	2121	2161	1433	2663	2855	2593	2479	3005
Makatea	5773	5813	5296	5554	5440	5625	5313	6115
Melbourne	4505	4545	3746	5000	5320	4850	4856	6067
Napier	4685	4725	4217	5445	5625	5160	5146	5822
Nauru Island	3053	3093	2532	2892	2949	2944	2739	3533
Nelson	4706	4746	4046	5119	5380	5105	5025	5590
Newcastle (NSW)	3873	3730	3122	4388	4668	4371	4311	5026
New Plymouth	4370	4410	3988	5130	5310	4845	4831	5507
Noumea	3616	3656	3013	3979	4240	3970	3882	4491
Otago Harbour	5215	5225	4262	5656	5765	5659	5545	6049
Papeete	5728	5768	5246	5533	5440	5572	5297	6028
Portland (Victoria)	4382	4422	3829	5170	5476	5160	5016	6376
Port Hedland	2195	2235	1524	3445	4004	3328	3526	3629
Port Kembla	3975	4015	3217	4623	4755	4464	4275	4961
Port Lincoln	4157	4197	3671	5481	5761	5460	5400	5591
Port Moresby	2499	2539	1760	3465	3832	3378	3471	3724
Port Pirie	4280	4320	3794	5582	5862	5561	5501	5714
Rockhampton	2950	2990	2435	4152	4775	4150	4200	4411
Suva	4048	4088	3465	4137	4367	4260	3875	4641
Sydney	3950	3990	3181	4598	4730	4439	4250	4936
Wellington	4750	4790	4114	5260	5440	4975	4961	5637

AREA G

AREA F	Osaka	Otaru	Palembang	Pusan	Quingdao	Qinhuangdao	Sabang	Shanghai
Adelaide	5349	5809	3338	5529	5839	6031	4118	5515
Albany	4924	5532	2344	4527	4842	5034	3120	4518
Apia	4232	4597	5160	4481	4877	5049	5881	4708
Auckland	4849	5322	4939	5058	5378	5574	5615	5148
Banaba	2911	3194	4098	3140	3617	3802	4795	3434
Bluff	5510	5787	4659	5452	6010	5945	5530	5810
Brisbane	3878	4452	3721	4172	4376	4588	4475	4250
Cairns	3657	4265	2891	3673	3796	4042	3613	3522
Cape Leeuwin	4438	5114	2175	4358	4389	4637	2942	4100
Darwin	2940	3547	1773	2934	3027	3281	2480	2755
Esperance	5607	5792	2555	4738	5102	5294	3380	4778
Fremantle	4632	5240	2054	4226	4550	4542	2825	4225
Geelong	4958	5438	3681	5143	5458	5622	4450	5247
Geraldton	4447	5055	1851	4023	4365	4307	2640	4040
Hobart	5032	5449	3801	5190	5509	5783	4600	5286
Honolulu	3684	3534	5997	3970	4410	4600	6481	4436
Launceston	4824	5382	3752	5070	5978	5633	4564	5654
Lyttleton	5592	5694	4967	5427	5711	5902	5869	5561
Mackay	4000	4609	3235	4017	4140	4386	3957	3866
Madang	2645	2977	2837	2800	2957	3151	3413	2724
Makatea	5400	5562	6478	5672	6092	6261	7200	5955
Melbourne	5280	5442	3676	5138	5406	5662	4455	5175
Napier	5593	5747	5224	5347	5841	5842	5970	5565
Nauru Island	2791	3071	3939	3014	3494	3679	4636	3311
Nelson	5049	5502	4969	5241	5542	5736	5736	5309
Newcastle (NSW)	4323	4790	4093	4515	4811	5000	4815	4590
New Plymouth	5278	5432	4959	5140	5526	5638	5655	5250
Noumea	3915	4362	4051	4096	4416	4621	4746	4185
Otago Harbour	5610	5887	4797	5589	6108	6042	5630	5910
Papeete	4922	5562	6428	5622	6046	6251	7167	5907
Portland (Victoria)	5118	5598	3479	5220	5618	5822	4290	5387
Port Hedland	3479	4126	1564	3465	3527	3775	2279	3239
Port Kembla	4833	5877	4090	4609	4896	5170	4900	4661
Port Lincoln	5412	5883	3275	5603	5489	6108	4041	5201
Port Moresby	3483	3954	2719	3501	3624	3737	3441	3350
Port Pirie	5513	5984	3398	5704	5612	6231	4165	5324
Rockhampton	4210	4897	3406	4153	4361	4557	4176	4085
Suva	4122	3489	4612	4298	4662	4877	5336	4467
Sydney	4308	4852	4135	4573	4871	5145	4875	4636
Wellington	5408	5562	5039	5290	5656	5782	5785	5380

AREA G

AREA F	Shimonoseki	Singapore	Surabaya	Tanjung Priok	Tokyo	Toyama	Vladivostok	Yokohama
Adelaide	5408	3518	2968	3055	5293	5851	6337	5275
Albany	4527	2520	1971	2060	5208	5198	5340	5190
Apia	4372	5281	4550	4926	4093	4821	4667	4075
Auckland	4929	5015	4294	4670	4818	5394	5516	4800
Banaba	3019	4194	3420	3879	2784	3468	3422	2772
Bluff	5331	4930	4675	4480	5283	6000	5950	5265
Brisbane	4051	3875	3150	3525	3948	4389	4591	3930
Cairns	3638	3012	2280	2657	3755	4087	4166	3743
Cape Leeuwin	4358	2341	1802	1884	4603	4809	4955	4592
Darwin	2914	1888	1149	1530	3033	3363	3426	3025
Esperance	4738	2780	2231	2320	5468	5458	5600	5450
Fremantle	4226	2225	1627	1770	4918	4906	5048	4900
Geelong	5022	3850	3300	3389	4934	5460	5691	4916
Geraldton	4023	2040	1442	1585	4733	4721	4863	4715
Hobart	5069	4000	3431	3520	4945	5531	5740	4927
Honolulu	3848	5880	5598	5934	3415	3566	3725	3397
Launceston	4949	3964	3414	3503	4878	5433	5635	4860
Lyttleton	5306	5269	4608	4808	5190	5894	5900	5172
Mackay	3982	3356	2624	3000	4100	4431	4510	4087
Madang	2714	2813	2450	2600	2467	3113	3227	2455
Makatea	5555	6599	5872	6244	5204	6004	5708	5192
Melbourne	5017	3855	3300	3390	4938	5450	5640	4920
Napier	5218	5370	4851	4940	5243	5895	5985	5225
Nauru Island	2893	4035	3260	3720	2662	3342	3327	2649
Nelson	5120	5135	4406	4678	4992	5569	5682	4980
Newcastle (NSW)	4393	4215	3495	3869	4286	4838	4955	4268
New Plymouth	5021	5055	4536	4625	4928	5580	5670	4910
Noumea	3975	4146	3423	3797	3858	4429	4590	3840
Otago Harbour	5469	5030	4773	4580	5383	6106	6050	5365
Papeete	5505	6567	5844	6218	5158	5983	5663	5140
Portland (Victoria)	5100	3690	3140	3229	5094	5620	5851	5076
Port Hedland	3446	1678	940	1274	3616	3895	3958	3604
Port Kembla	4488	4300	3587	3961	4373	5073	5129	4355
Port Lincoln	5482	3441	2902	2984	5373	5931	6053	5361
Port Moresby	3466	2840	2108	2485	3444	3915	3994	3432
Port Pirie	5583	3564	3025	3107	5474	6032	6145	5462
Rockhampton	4153	3527	2795	3075	4393	4602	4681	4375
Suva	4179	4736	4013	4387	3985	4587	4626	3967
Sydney	4452	4275	3562	3936	4348	5048	5104	4330
Wellington	5169	5185	4666	4755	5058	5710	5800	5040

AREA H

AREA F	Balikpapan	Bangkok	Basuo (Hainan Is)	Cam-Pha	Cebu	Dalian	Haiphong	Ho Chi Minh City
Antofagasta	9751	11131	10776	10061	9778	10232	11001	10629
Arica	9958	11401	10724	10809	8969	10119	10849	10049
Astoria	6609	7045	6061	6146	5918	5157	6185	6806
Balboa	9218	10721	9543	9628	9212	8641	9668	10017
Buenaventura	9985	10853	9561	9646	9322	8747	9686	10416
Cabo Blanco	9984	10784	9888	9972	9291	8853	10012	10217
Caldera	9768	10701	10749	10834	9259	10270	10874	11124
Callao	9903	11155	10343	10428	8530	9631	10468	10781
Cape Horn	9024	10303	10030	10115	8893	10096	10155	10045
Chimbote	9893	10919	10065	10150	8860	9192	10190	10449
Coos Bay	6695	7531	6365	6450	5953	5370	6490	6638
Corinto	9237	9945	9057	9142	8577	7978	9182	9380
Eureka	6740	7829	6439	6524	6006	5276	6564	6719
Guayaquil	9906	10995	9855	9940	9463	9226	9980	10321
Guaymas	8131	8822	7921	8008	7450	6851	8046	8490
Honolulu	5230	6319	5202	5287	4609	4470	5327	5542
Iquique	9771	10546	10765	10850	8973	10216	10890	10943
Los Angeles	7408	7948	6715	6800	6423	6022	6840	7291
Manzanillo (Mex)	8220	9249	7778	7863	7417	6989	7903	8307
Mazatlan	8075	9048	7603	7688	7285	6837	7728	8140
Nanaimo	6715	7911	6107	6192	5915	5207	6232	6479
New Westminster	6723	7919	6115	6200	5923	5215	6240	6673
Portland (Oreg)	6719	7823	6144	6229	6001	5240	6269	6889
Port Alberni	6624	7820	6016	6101	5824	5116	6141	6574
Port Isabel	8361	9052	8151	8238	7680	7081	8276	8720
Port Moody	6718	7914	6110	6195	5918	5210	6235	6668
Prince Rupert	6264	7460	5656	5741	5464	4756	5781	6214
Puerto Montt	9324	10509	10336	10421	9203	10139	10411	10654
Puntarenas (CR)	9127	10630	9452	9537	9121	8550	9577	9926
Punta Arenas (Ch)	8983	10262	9939	10024	8862	10055	10064	10004
Salina Cruz	8728	9597	8417	8502	7997	7483	8542	8843
San Francisco	6972	8061	6471	6456	6146	5456	6496	6880
San Jose	9031	9998	8575	8640	8235	7862	8725	9090
Seattle	6705	7901	6097	6182	5905	5197	6222	6834
Tacoma	6727	7923	6119	6204	5927	5219	6244	6677
Talcahuano	9276	10680	10148	10433	9100	10295	10473	10154
Tocopilla	9781	11374	10680	10765	9013	10240	10805	10696
Valparaiso	9766	10857	10733	10818	9545	10324	10858	11305
Vancouver (BC)	6714	7910	6106	6191	5914	5206	6231	6664
Victoria (Vanc Is)	6647	7843	6039	6124	5847	5139	6164	6597

AREA H

AREA F	Hong Kong	Hungnam	Inchon	Kampong Saom	Kaohsiung (Taiwan)	Keelung (Taiwan)	Kobe	Makassar
Antofagasta	10532	9534	10002	10831	10295	10131	9374	9613
Arica	10425	9382	9767	11101	10138	9978	9241	9745
Astoria	5739	4439	4984	6745	5473	5335	4507	6813
Balboa	9194	7841	9034	10421	8949	8723	7960	9855
Buenaventura	9317	8053	8625	10553	9085	8444	8086	9938
Cabo Blanco	9403	8067	8724	10484	9156	8946	8168	9631
Caldera	10391	9564	10026	10401	10093	10014	9422	9469
Callao	10018	8986	9230	10855	9674	9508	8830	9665
Cape Horn	9745	9877	9961	10003	9494	9537	9450	8734
Chimbote	9660	8476	8927	10619	9363	9177	8449	9598
Coos Bay	5811	4452	5203	7231	5510	5371	4607	6848
Corinto	8573	7772	7849	9645	8310	8107	7331	9250
Eureka	5984	4601	5380	7529	5612	5435	4567	6817
Guayaquil	9505	8144	8804	10695	9267	8932	8182	9771
Guaymas	7437	6407	6722	8522	7005	7245	6438	8170
Honolulu	4857	3826	4300	6019	4539	4350	3669	5298
Iquique	10563	9423	9862	10246	10238	10078	9311	9754
Los Angeles	6380	5091	5634	7648	6111	5930	5185	7280
Manzanillo (Mex)	7465	6239	6742	8949	7218	7070	6238	8215
Mazatlan	7290	6057	6582	8748	7043	6895	6088	8030
Nanaimo	5778	4352	5028	7611	5517	5348	4531	6881
New Westminster	5786	4487	5036	7619	5525	5356	4550	6889
Portland (Oreg)	5853	4522	5067	7523	5556	5418	4590	6906
Port Alberni	5688	4388	4937	7520	5426	5257	4451	6790
Port Isabel	7667	6637	6952	8752	7235	7475	6668	8400
Port Moody	5781	4482	5031	7614	5520	5351	4545	6884
Prince Rupert	5286	4028	4577	7160	5066	4897	4091	5800
Puerto Montt	9913	9771	10050	10259	9701	9723	9468	8938
Puntarenas (CR)	9103	7750	8943	10330	8858	8632	7869	9764
Punta Arenas (Ch)	9708	9836	9920	9962	9453	9496	9403	8693
Salina Cruz	8019	7005	7295	9297	7764	7588	6784	8732
San Francisco	6050	4666	5586	7761	5807	5630	4820	7009
San Jose	8285	7082	7623	9698	8084	7920	7113	9018
Seattle	5768	4310	5011	7601	5500	5338	4527	6864
Tacoma	5790	4331	5031	7623	5520	5360	4549	6884
Talcahuano	10025	9734	10151	10380	10021	10056	9526	9491
Tocopilla	10335	9399	9891	11074	10211	10090	9363	9694
Valparaiso	10218	9706	10190	10557	9949	9950	9534	9185
Vancouver (BC)	5777	4478	5027	7610	5516	5347	4541	6880
Victoria (Vanc Is)	5710	4438	4957	7543	5440	5280	4469	6804

AREA H

AREA F	Manila	Masinloc	Menado	Moji	Muroran	Nagasaki	Nagoya	Nampo
Antofagasta	9943	9983	9493	9825	9017	9685	9289	10175
Arica	10162	10202	9488	9421	8815	9547	9111	10061
Astoria	5940	5840	6342	4702	3783	4706	4375	5100
Balboa	9346	9386	9352	8209	7438	8200	7716	8584
Buenaventura	9497	9537	9466	8275	7631	8366	7956	8690
Cabo Blanco	9500	9540	9263	8320	7732	8437	8062	8794
Caldera	9285	9325	9364	9632	9076	9723	9281	10213
Callao	9785	9825	9433	9015	8238	9147	8633	9574
Cape Horn	9250	9290	8679	9556	9535	9562	9393	10039
Chimbote	9592	9632	9298	8617	7935	8742	8297	9134
Coos Bay	6098	5998	6197	4753	4073	4901	4418	5313
Corinto	8720	8760	8719	7451	6857	7566	7187	7929
Eureka	6067	5967	6242	4832	4138	4968	4495	5219
Guayaquil	9615	9655	9400	8325	7812	8487	8016	9189
Guaymas	6940	6980	7613	6633	5730	6769	6286	6794
Honolulu	4768	4808	4664	3860	3392	3986	3527	4413
Iquique	10171	10211	9615	9482	8877	9640	9163	10159
Los Angeles	6530	6430	6651	5507	4649	5337	4955	5965
Manzanillo (Mex)	7680	6820	7670	6442	5750	6592	6105	6932
Mazatlan	6590	6630	7483	6283	5590	6419	5936	6780
Nanaimo	5977	5877	6218	4577	4036	4584	4303	5150
New Westminster	5985	5885	6226	4696	4044	4755	4462	5158
Portland (Oreg)	6023	5923	6425	4785	3866	4789	4458	5183
Port Alberni	5733	5633	6127	4597	3941	4656	4363	5059
Port Isabel	7170	7210	7843	6863	5960	6999	6516	7024
Port Moody	5827	5727	6221	4691	4039	4750	4437	5153
Prince Rupert	5493	5426	5767	4237	3575	4296	4003	4699
Puerto Montt	8802	8846	8876	9647	9394	9670	9378	10186
Puntarenas (CR)	9255	9295	9261	8118	7404	8109	7625	5493
Punta Arenas (Ch)	9202	9242	8638	9515	9520	9522	9352	9998
Salina Cruz	7750	7790	8194	6946	6303	7079	6646	7430
San Francisco	6230	6130	6432	5021	4328	5030	4666	5399
San Jose	7540	7580	8513	7308	6631	6444	6961	7805
Seattle	5959	5859	6201	4734	4020	4705	4313	5140
Tacoma	5989	5889	6221	4700	4040	4759	4425	5162
Talcahuano	9693	9733	9436	9701	9318	9802	9381	10238
Tocopilla	10990	11030	9553	10180	8918	10206	9680	10183
Valparaiso	8400	8440	9114	9782	9275	9806	9400	10267
Vancouver (BC)	5976	5876	6217	4687	4035	4746	4453	5149
Victoria (Vanc Is)	5760	5660	6141	4620	3959	4679	4255	5082

AREA H	AREA F							
	Osaka	Otaru	Palembang	Pusan	Qingdao	Qinhuangdao	Sabang	Shanghai
Antofagasta	9376	9129	10186	9598	10152	10332	11120	10039
Arica	9246	8928	10456	9363	10154	10272	11335	9912
Astoria	4515	4104	7602	4580	5010	5250	7659	5062
Balboa	7968	7612	10192	9140	8573	8892	11105	8649
Buenaventura	8091	7743	10766	8219	8697	8877	10975	8770
Cabo Blanco	8172	7844	10682	8320	8812	8959	11213	8802
Caldera	9447	9185	10462	9643	10213	10413	10700	10309
Callao	8838	8350	10597	8826	9617	9821	11276	9557
Cape Horn	9454	9874	9299	9665	10031	10202	9180	9870
Chimbote	8455	8047	10589	8523	9164	9340	11194	9129
Coos Bay	4560	4175	7753	4895	5150	5541	7544	5256
Corinto	7335	6969	10025	7445	7937	8084	10458	7927
Eureka	4645	4250	7798	4732	5221	5608	7840	5323
Guayaquil	8151	7924	10715	8400	8880	9453	11326	8872
Guaymas	6436	5842	8867	6318	7021	6957	9680	7121
Honolulu	3684	3500	6204	3970	4456	4600	6480	4340
Iquique	9308	8989	10465	9458	10153	10332	10855	10200
Los Angeles	5193	4754	7626	5230	6025	6097	8467	5810
Manzanillo (Mex)	6255	5702	8718	6582	6658	7243	9710	6942
Mazatlan	6086	5540	8517	6178	6671	7053	9330	6771
Nanaimo	4442	4148	7631	4624	5130	5275	7672	5086
New Westminster	4553	4156	7639	4632	5096	5283	7680	5101
Portland (Oreg)	4598	4187	7685	4663	5093	5601	7742	5145
Port Alberni	4454	4045	7540	4533	4927	5184	7581	5002
Port Isabel	6666	6072	9090	6548	7251	7187	9910	7351
Port Moody	4548	4151	7634	4627	4421	5278	7675	5096
Prince Rupert	4094	3697	5885	4173	3967	4824	6285	4642
Puerto Montt	9496	9508	9859	9726	10132	10277	9883	10093
Puntarenas (CR)	7877	7521	10821	9049	8482	8801	11014	8558
Punta Arenas (Ch)	9407	9635	9258	9624	9990	10161	9222	9768
Salina Cruz	6795	6335	9371	7013	7397	7663	10084	7434
San Francisco	4826	4440	7911	4922	5403	5827	7950	5500
San Jose	7110	6743	9467	7221	7696	8078	10280	7796
Seattle	4635	4131	7621	4607	5109	5265	7665	5101
Tacoma	4557	4151	7643	4627	5130	5287	7684	5105
Talcahuano	9531	9460	9970	9962	10225	10499	10090	10061
Tocopilla	9382	9030	10475	9510	10207	10350	11010	9963
Valparaiso	9586	9382	10460	9828	10274	10494	10545	10418
Vancouver (BC)	4544	4147	7630	4623	5115	5274	7671	5092
Victoria (Vanc Is)	4477	4071	7563	4547	5039	5207	7604	5025

AREA H

AREA F	Shimonoseki	Singapore	Surabaya	Tanjung Priok	Tokyo	Toyama	Vladivostok	Yokohama
Antofagasta	9850	10524	9801	9916	9172	10275	9434	9154
Arica	9446	10731	10008	10186	8999	9871	9282	8981
Astoria	4727	7059	7126	7332	4258	4352	4339	4240
Balboa	8234	10504	10269	10642	7699	8659	7741	7681
Buenaventura	8300	10375	10122	10496	7822	8725	7953	7804
Cabo Blanco	8319	10612	9936	10313	7928	8770	7967	7916
Caldera	9657	10178	9818	10192	9171	10082	9464	9153
Callao	9040	10676	9953	10327	8576	9465	6886	8558
Cape Horn	9557	9557	8984	9066	9319	10006	9906	9301
Chimbote	8629	10644	9894	10270	8202	9067	8376	8187
Coos Bay	4778	6944	7262	7483	4301	4403	4352	4283
Corinto	7450	9857	9672	9963	7053	7901	7105	7041
Eureka	4857	7238	7257	7528	4378	4482	4501	4360
Guayaquil	8350	10726	10071	10445	8005	8775	8044	7987
Guaymas	6658	9059	8980	8858	6150	7083	6307	6132
Honolulu	3885	5880	5600	5934	3413	4310	3726	3397
Iquique	9507	10257	9821	10195	9044	9932	9323	9026
Los Angeles	5532	7867	7622	7356	4857	5157	4991	4839
Manzanillo (Mex)	6467	8909	8788	8448	6002	6892	6139	5984
Mazatlan	6308	8731	8630	8247	5800	6733	5957	5782
Nanaimo	4602	7072	7172	7361	4218	4227	4252	4200
New Westminster	4721	7088	7180	7369	4289	4346	4387	4271
Portland (Oreg)	4810	7142	7209	7415	4341	4435	4422	4323
Port Alberni	4622	6981	7081	7270	4190	4247	4288	4172
Port Isabel	6888	9289	9210	9088	6380	7313	6537	6362
Port Moody	4716	7075	7175	7364	4284	4341	4382	4266
Prince Rupert	4762	6683	5783	7810	3830	3887	3928	3812
Puerto Montt	9661	10442M	9379	9557	9284	10089	9733	9269
Puntarenas (CR)	8143	10413	10178	10551	7608	8568	7650	7590
Punta Arenas (Ch)	9515	9482M	8943	9025	9271	9965	9861	9259
Salina Cruz	6958	9383	9230	9205	6527	7396	6622	6512
San Francisco	5046	7350	7343	7641	4554	4671	4566	4536
San Jose	7333	9633	9580	9197	6825	7758	6982	6807
Seattle	4759	7062	7162	7351	4272	4384	4210	4254
Tacoma	4725	7084	7184	7373	4293	4350	4231	4275
Talcahuano	9726	9493	9326	9700	9290	10151	9634	9272
Tocopilla	10205	10412	9831	10205	9109	10630	9299	9091
Valparaiso	9807	9945	9816	10190	9298	10232	9606	9280
Vancouver (BC)	4712	7071	7171	7360	4280	4337	4378	4262
Victoria (Vanc Is)	4645	7004	7104	7293	4212	4270	4338	4194

AREA F

AREA F	Bangkok	Dalian	Haiphong	Hong Kong	Huangpu	Inchon	Kawasaki	Keelung
Bangkok	–	2679	1374	1489	1560	2620	2983	1879
Bintan Island	810	2598	1301	1439	1491	2531	2875	1792
Cebu	1704	1750	1263	963	1033	1655	1770	932
Chongjin	2989	971	2172	1562	1643	818	1006	1144
Dalian	2679	–	1866	1256	1323	280	1153	851
Davao	1907	2090	1612	1375	1446	1995	1991	1286
Haiphong	1374	1866	–	637	708	1800	2198	1082
Hakodate	3240	1217	2419	1812	1883	1069	532	1378
Ho Chi Minh City	681	2119	803	927	998	2052	2422	1312
Hondagua	1935	1562	1332	844	915	1468	1607	746
Hong Kong	1489	1256	637	–	71	1190	1588	471
Huangpu	1560	1323	708	71	–	1261	1659	542
Iloilo	1600	1769	1170	894	965	1678	1788	956
Inchon	2620	280	1800	1190	1261	–	1008	783
Kaohsiung	1685	1029	940	342	412	965	1341	224
Kure	2698	725	1894	1283	1354	580	519	840
Manila	1465	1556	952	632	703	1492	1762	728
Miri	1050	2188	1351	1189	1260	2124	2394	1359
Moji	2599	617	1781	1170	1238	467	540	740
Nagasaki	2495	577	1678	1066	1137	430	687	630
Osaka	2784	859	1986	1376	1447	714	361	921
Pusan	2569	543	1749	1140	1211	396	673	716
Qingdao	2527	356	1709	1100	1171	328	1106	697
Qinhuangdao	2785	142	1972	1362	1429	392	1259	957
Shanghai	2251	551	1433	824	895	502	1040	421
Singapore	831	2619	1322	1460	1445	2552	2896	1812
Surabaya	1486	2980	1820	1939	2010	2914	3050	2150
Tjilatjap	1648	3308	2026	2146	2217	3298	3432	2518
Vladivostok	3066	1048	2249	1639	1710	895	941	1221
Wakamatsu	2597	615	1779	1168	1239	465	551	738
Yokohama	2979	1149	2194	1584	1655	1004	5	1134

AREA F

AREA F	Kobe	Labuan	Manila	Moji	Nagoya	Niigata	Osaka	Qinhuangdao
Bangkok	2780	1128	1465	2599	2885	3050	2784	2785
Bintan Island	2671	700	1306	2520	2770	2965	2675	2704
Cebu	1604	727	400	1526	1684	1984	1608	1856
Chongjin	707	2419	1832	467	900	495	714	1077
Dalian	852	2146	1556	617	1047	1041	859	142
Davao	1801	884	829	1791	1912	2283	1805	2196
Haiphong	1982	1309	952	1781	2090	2165	1986	1972
Hakodate	813	2654	2064	682	674	247	817	1323
Ho Chi Minh City	2213	698	907	2035	2322	2489	2217	2225
Hondagua	1446	931	593	1346	1528	1802	1450	1668
Hong Kong	1372	1147	632	1170	1483	1622	1376	1362
Huangpu	1443	1218	703	1238	1554	1693	1447	1429
Iloilo	1632	648	345	1554	1709	2010	1636	1875
Inchon	707	2082	1492	467	901	894	714	392
Kaohsiung	1121	1132	543	933	1234	1385	1125	1135
Kure	184	2081	1491	117	412	604	191	831
Manila	1563	701	–	1426	1663	1880	1567	1662
Miri	2195	115	743	2055	2294	2511	2199	2294
Moji	244	2015	1426	–	433	493	251	723
Nagasaki	398	1893	1305	156	577	610	402	683
Osaka	11	2157	1567	251	249	738	–	965
Pusan	362	1997	1410	122	556	516	369	649
Qingdao	805	1996	1404	565	999	999	817	373
Qinhuangdao	958	2252	1662	723	1153	1147	965	–
Shanghai	783	1720	1128	543	933	989	790	657
Singapore	2691	735	1341	2540	2790	2985	2695	2725
Surabaya	2890	1079	1498	2811	2968	3265	2894	3086
Tjilatjap	3271	1293	1893	3195	3350	3649	3274	3473
Vladivostok	806	2496	1909	566	999	453	812	1154
Wakamatsu	255	2013	1424	9	444	491	263	721
Yokohama	353	2348	1758	536	214	758	357	1255

AREA F

AREA F	Shanghai	Shimonoseki	Taku Bar (Hsinkang)	Tanjung Priok	Tokuyama	Tokyo	Yokohama
Bangkok	2251	2598	2824	1291	2647	2991	2979
Bintan Island	2172	2519	2744	487	2563	2884	2872
Cebu	1322	1527	1895	1565	1515	1778	1766
Chongjin	914	466	1116	3261	515	1014	1002
Dalian	551	616	198	2956	765	1161	1149
Davao	1676	1792	2235	1510	1765	1999	1987
Haiphong	1433	1780	2011	1668	1829	2206	2194
Hakodate	1164	681	1362	3509	730	540	528
Ho Chi Minh City	1697	2034	2264	1032	2099	2430	2418
Hondagua	1137	1345	1707	1770	1318	1615	1603
Hong Kong	824	1169	1401	1789	1218	1596	1584
Huangpu	895	1240	1468	1860	1289	1667	1655
Iloilo	1345	1553	1914	1490	1539	1796	1784
Inchon	502	466	444	2888	515	1016	1004
Kaohsiung	600	932	1174	1957	1011	1349	1337
Kure	656	116	870	2949	76	527	515
Manila	1128	1425	1700	1562	1458	1770	1758
Miri	1762	2056	2333	835	2090	2402	2390
Moji	543	1	762	2865	49	548	536
Nagasaki	462	155	722	2746	204	695	683
Osaka	790	252	1004	3024	218	369	357
Pusan	492	121	688	2839	170	681	659
Qingdao	399	564	412	2799	613	1114	1102
Qinhuangdao	657	722	139	3062	871	1267	1255
Shanghai	–	542	696	2523	591	1048	1036
Singapore	2192	2539	2764	527	2583	2904	2892
Surabaya	2553	2810	3125	384	2796	3058	3046
Tjilatjap	2937	3194	3512	413	3181	3440	3428
Vladivostok	991	565	1193	3338	614	949	937
Wakamatsu	541	10	760	2863	59	559	547
Yokohama	1036	537	1294	3221	510	18	–

Area G

Distances between principal ports in Australasia, New Guinea and the Pacific Islands.

and

Area H The West Coast of North and South America.

Area G Other ports in Australasia, New Guinea and the Pacific Islands.

also

Distances between principal ports on the West Coast of North and South America, and other ports on the West Coast of North and South America.

AREA G
Reed's Marine Distance Tables
AUSTRALASIA & OCEANIA
Apra Harbour
South China Sea
Celebes Sea
Banda Sea
Madang
Lae
Port Moresby
Milner B
Arafura Sea
Port Darwin
Darwin
Weipa
INDIAN OCEAN
Cora
Cairns
Townsville
Port Hedland
Dampier
Mackay
Rockhampton
Gladstone
Brisbane
Geraldton
Fremantle
Kwinana
Bunbury
Cape Leeuwin
Albany
Esperance
Whyalla
Port Pirie
Wallaroo
Port Lincoln
Adelaide
Newcastle (NSW)
Port Kembla
Sydn
Great Australian Bight
Portland (Victoria)
Geelong
Melbourne
Port Latta
Launceston
Hobart
© Adlard Coles Nautical 2004
Modified Gall Projec

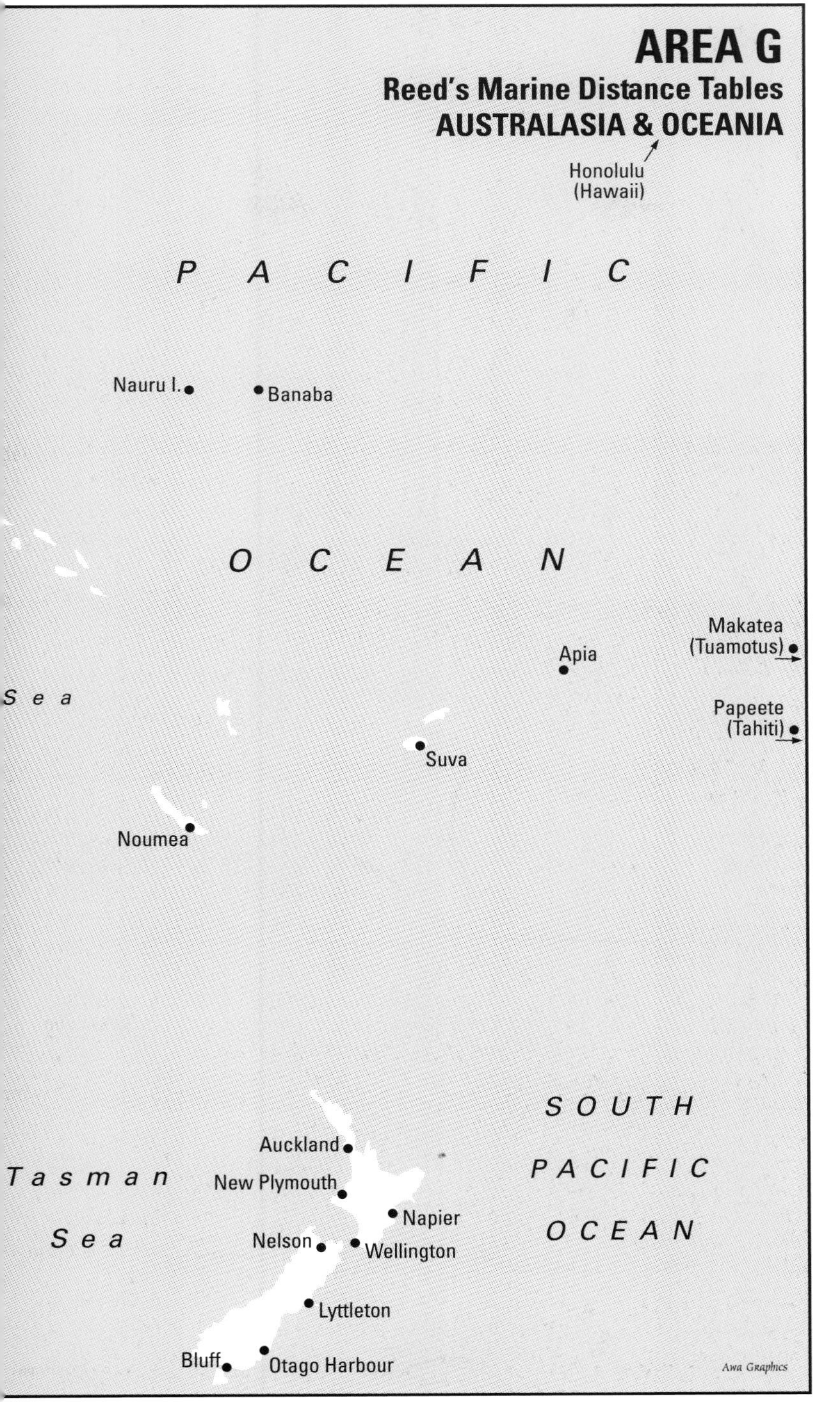
AREA G
Reed's Marine Distance Tables
AUSTRALASIA & OCEANIA
Honolulu
(Hawaii)
P A C I F I C
Nauru I.
Banaba
O C E A N
Makatea
(Tuamotus)
Apia
S e a
Papeete
(Tahiti)
Suva
Noumea
S O U T H
P A C I F I C
O C E A N
Auckland
T a s m a n
New Plymouth
Napier
S e a
Nelson
Wellington
Lyttleton
Bluff
Otago Harbour
Awa Graphics

AREA H

AREA G	Adelaide	Albany	Apia	Auckland	Banaba	Bluff	Brisbane	Cairns
Antofagasta	7037	7855	5697	5631	7047	5600	6904	7638
Arica	7307	8125	5727	5847	7157	5749	7024	7826
Astoria	7572	8390	4440	5989	4505	6650	6338	6864
Balboa	8266	9084	5740	6509	6763	6714	7680	8478
Buenaventura	8177	8995	5730	6411	6800	6580	7568	8424
Cabo Blanco	7603	8361	5374	5977	6537	6068	7177	7939
Caldera	7051	7839	5527	5430	6888	5432	6767	7503
Callao	7509	8331	5500	5830	6755	5866	7050	7868
Cape Horn	6297	7055	5244	4800	6589	4737	5900	6792
Chimbote	7506	8296	5387	5853	6596	5917	7063	7853
Coos Bay	7685	8403	4300	5840	4365	6510	6248	6725
Corinto	8127	8887	5271	6240	6187	6538	7380	8142
Eureka	7379	8197	4141	5705	4401	6601	6198	6799
Guayaquil	7781	8599	5517	6087	6664	6208	7045	8108
Guaymas	7738	8583	4580	5900	5252	6432	6753	7515
Honolulu	5330	6147	2260	3850	2364	4520	4120	4718
Iquique	7330	8148	5750	5797	7107	5772	7089	7851
Los Angeles	7416	8234	4184	5658	4600	6256	6274	6939
Manzanillo (Mex)	7534	8352	4425	5661	5160	6182	6573	7340
Mazatlan	7594	8412	4430	5719	5112	6256	6574	7352
Nanaimo	7733	8553	4634	6179	4630	6842	6483	7002
New Westminster	7747	8565	4646	6191	4642	6854	6495	7014
Portland (Oreg)	7658	8476	4523	6075	4588	6733	6421	6947
Port Alberni	7642	8460	4541	6086	4537	6749	6390	6909
Port Isabel	7968	8813	4810	6130	5482	6662	6983	7745
Port Moody	7734	8556	4646	6204	4642	6854	6504	7014
Prince Rupert	7585	8407	4651	6209	4647	6859	6355	6865
Puerto Montt	6428	7216	5327	4945	6682	4938	6100	7006
Puntarenas (CR)	8096	8909	5565	6334	6375	6539	7505	8303
Punta Arenas (Ch)	6256	7014	5200	4650	6548	4685	5750	6751
Salina Cruz	7830	8619	4848	5951	5673	6360	6976	7741
San Francisco	7400	8216	4160	5680	4404	6311	6200	6795
San Jose	8013	8800	5087	6120	5926	6456	7220	4982
Seattle	7740	8543	4626	6170	4622	6834	6471	6994
Tacoma	7747	8565	4646	6191	4642	6854	6500	7014
Talcahuano	6687	7505	5353	5001	6755	5025	6388	7097
Tocopilla	7067	7885	5723	5678	7052	5718	6495	7768
Valparaiso	6600	7418	5455	5240	6817	5191	6450	7261
Vancouver (BC)	7730	8552	4642	6200	4638	6850	6500	7010
Victoria (Vanc Is)	7667	8485	4566	6111	4562	6774	6415	6934

AREA H

AREA G	Cape Leeuwin	Darwin	Esperance	Fremantle	Geelong	Geraldston	Hobart	Honolulu
Antofagasta	8066	8989	7845	8205	6646	8422	6771	5709
Arica	8210	9107	7991	8475	6916	8568	6576	5744
Astoria	8559	6838	8297	8003	7181	8145	7285	2249
Balboa	9177	9318	8957	9434	7875	9533	7629	4688
Buenaventura	9042	9349	8821	9345	7786	9398	7513	4798
Cabo Blanco	8488	9007	8267	8668	7232	8844	9647	4731
Caldera	7893	8784	7672	8168	6670	8249	6331	5739
Callao	8321	9041	8100	8681	7122	8677	7009	5161
Cape Horn	7182	8110	6961	7362	5962	7538	5200	6477
Chimbote	8354	8974	8133	8624	7127	8710	8278	4896
Coos Bay	8420	6680	8147	7953	6994	7995	7096	2161
Corinto	9014	8838	8793	9194	7741	9370	7481	4070
Eureka	8404	6515	7982	8117	7158	7830	6959	2081
Guayaquil	8668	9147	8447	8949	7380	8024	7086	4853
Guaymas	8726	8125	8463	8905	7352	9081	7226	3000
Honolulu	6323	5122	6061	6497	4938	6679	4930	–
Iquique	8235	9130	8014	8499	6939	8591	6540	5812
Los Angeles	8385	7236	8123	8550	7025	8543	6947	2228
Manzanillo (Mex)	8502	7376	8275	8702	7143	8690	7110	3160
Mazatlan	8562	7985	8300	8762	7203	8918	7215	2845
Nanaimo	8548	6906	8458	8800	7344	8213	7300	2417
New Westminster	8560	6918	8470	8915	7356	8225	7312	2429
Portland (Oreg)	8642	6921	8380	8086	7267	8228	7367	2332
Port Alberni	8455	6813	8365	8810	7251	8120	7207	2324
Port Isabel	8956	8355	8693	9135	7582	9311	7456	3230
Port Moody	8560	6918	8470	8906	7347	8225	7303	2427
Prince Rupert	8411	6769	8321	8757	7198	8076	7308	2393
Puerto Montt	7394	8315	7173	7544	6047	7750	5801	6144
Puntarenas (CR)	9002	9143	8782	6259	7700	9358	7454	4509
Punta Arenas (Ch)	7141	8069	6920	7321	5885	7497	5603	6370
Salina Cruz	8758	8107	8534	8948	7442	9030	7295	3615
San Francisco	8344	6991	8082	8501	7007	8298	6958	2095
San Jose	8927	8973	8706	9107	7627	9283	7374	3845
Seattle	8540	6898	8450	8893	7334	8205	7290	2407
Tacoma	8560	6918	8470	8915	7356	8225	7312	2429
Talcahuano	7485	8406	7264	7855	6296	7841	5902	5926
Tocopilla	8135	9070	7914	8235	6676	8491	6380	5750
Valparaiso	7647	8561	7426	7768	6209	8003	6000	5919
Vancouver (BC)	8556	6914	8466	8902	7343	8221	7299	2434
Victoria (Vanc Is)	8480	6838	8390	8835	7276	8145	7232	2349

AREA H

AREA G	Launceston	Lyttelton	Mackay	Madang	Makatea	Melbourne	Napier	Nauru Island
Antofagasta	6761	5474	7304	7941	3952	6646	5464	7203
Arica	6738	5731	7540	8090	4488	6900	5703	7260
Astoria	7167	6424	6763	5800	3923	7181	6068	4574
Balboa	7811	6574	8144	8080	4442	7880	6397	6918
Buenaventura	7743	6519	8090	8138	4425	7786	6298	6985
Cabo Blanco	7045	5913	7605	7985	4119	7228	5784	6695
Caldera	6369	5306	7169	7847	4324	6668	5281	7022
Callao	7086	5861	7534	7954	4170	7120	5660	6915
Cape Horn	5739	4620	6458	7105	4331	5250	4603	6680
Chimbote	7015	5837	7519	7919	4094	7124	5672	6755
Coos Bay	7011	6252	6435	5680	3783	6394	5908	4425
Corinto	7569	6370	7808	7564	4152	7736	6147	6336
Eureka	6840	6106	6299	5534	3652	6988	5762	4289
Guayaquil	7220	6052	7774	7965	4212	7390	5946	6822
Guaymas	7209	6163	7181	6626	3595	7347	5880	5388
Honolulu	4895	4278	4544	3558	2258	4940	3936	2433
Iquique	6983	5646	7517	8063	4469	7111	5618	7263
Los Angeles	6929	5924	6715	5928	3448	7025	5684	4669
Manzanillo (Mex)	7031	5885	6958	6425	3384	7143	5643	5185
Mazatlan	7072	5958	7018	6486	3466	7203	5703	5248
Nanaimo	7345	6607	6916	5923	4194	7344	6269	4699
New Westminster	7357	6619	6928	5935	4206	7356	6281	4711
Portland (Oreg)	7267	6571	6846	5883	4051	7274	6151	4657
Port Alberni	7252	6519	6823	5830	4101	7251	6176	4606
Port Isabel	7439	6393	7411	6856	3825	7577	6110	5618
Port Moody	7348	6610	6928	5935	4197	7354	6281	4711
Prince Rupert	7353	6615	6779	5786	4205	7359	6286	4716
Puerto Montt	6022	4742	6672	7313	4324	6095	4804	6791
Puntarenas (CR)	7636	6399	7969	7905	4267	7705	6222	6743
Punta Arenas (Ch)	5698	4570	6417	7064	4362	5881	4562	6639
Salina Cruz	7300	6127	7383	6994	3768	7439	5895	5760
San Francisco	6951	5971	6628	5767	3625	7000	5731	4509
San Jose	7484	6254	7648	7352	3966	7622	6039	6077
Seattle	7335	6597	6908	5915	4173	7334	6261	4691
Tacoma	7357	6619	6928	5935	4206	7356	6281	4711
Talcahuano	5881	4886	6763	7478	4186	6296	4885	6864
Tocopilla	6546	5901	7434	8001	4412	6676	5539	7208
Valparaiso	6346	4914	6927	7562	4286	6300	5046	6944
Vancouver (BC)	7344	6606	6924	5931	4193	7350	6277	4707
Victoria (Vanc Is)	7277	6539	6848	5855	4126	7276	6201	4631

AREA H

AREA G	Nelson	Newcastle (New South Wales)	New Plymouth	Noumea	Otago Harbour	Papeete	Portland (Victoria)	Port Hedland
Antofagasta	5581	6707	5638	6638	5472	3920	6876	9170
Arica	5803	6899	5860	6714	5720	4456	7095	9389
Astoria	6350	6750	6407	5648	6542	4046	7253	7493
Balboa	6596	7650	6653	7000	6751	4492	8000	10110
Buenaventura	6486	7603	6543	6972	6734	4475	7852	10143
Cabo Blanco	5970	7068	6027	6549	5974	4144	7298	9592
Caldera	5423	6548	5483	6290	5278	4292	6703	8997
Callao	5821	6925	5878	6550	5996	4192	7131	9425
Cape Horn	4711	5890	4768	5660	4652	4299	5992	8286
Chimbote	5845	6946	5902	6499	5935	4118	7164	9458
Coos Bay	6210	6490	6267	5501	6420	3906	7113	7353
Corinto	6371	7368	6428	6590	6453	4177	7818	9632
Eureka	6235	6506	6307	5537	6255	3775	7139	7379
Guayaquil	6134	7258	6191	6686	6097	4237	7478	9772
Guaymas	6149	6880	6206	5932	6310	3718	7429	8780
Honolulu	4218	4360	4275	3369	4389	2381	5027	5796
Iquique	5753	6811	5810	6617	5642	4439	7045	9339
Los Angeles	5965	6456	6022	5521	6127	3571	7089	7891
Manzanillo (Mex)	5955	6703	6012	5827	6009	3507	7249	8680
Mazatlan	5972	6720	6029	5775	6083	3589	7266	8640
Nanaimo	6551	6623	6608	5777	6735	4317	7416	7561
New Westminster	6563	6797	6620	5789	6747	4329	7428	7573
Portland (Oreg)	6433	6683	6490	5660	6627	4174	7346	7576
Port Alberni	6458	6692	6515	5684	6642	4224	7323	7468
Port Isabel	6379	7110	6436	6162	6540	3948	7659	9010
Port Moody	6563	6788	6620	5790	6738	4320	7428	7573
Prince Rupert	6568	6793	6625	5795	6743	4325	7433	7424
Puerto Montt	4921	6064	4985	5872	4760	4292	6204	8498
Puntarenas (CR)	6383	7409	6441	6695	6576	4234	7809	9771
Punta Arenas (Ch)	4670	5849	4727	5624	4811	4331	5951	8245
Salina Cruz	6163	7035	6220	6208	6231	3842	7533	9156
San Francisco	6013	6467	6070	5420	6175	3748	7048	7646
San Jose	6271	7222	6328	6419	6371	4016	7704	9628
Seattle	6543	6775	6600	5760	6725	4296	7408	7553
Tacoma	6563	6797	6620	5789	6747	4329	7428	7573
Talcahuano	5012	6163	5075	5931	4786	4154	6295	8589
Tocopilla	5680	6705	5737	6495	5654	4380	6945	9239
Valparaiso	5173	6280	5243	6120	4910	4254	6457	8751
Vancouver (BC)	6559	6784	6616	5786	6734	4316	7424	7569
Victoria (Vanc Is)	6483	6717	6540	5709	6667	4249	7348	7493

AREA H

West Coast of North and South America

AREA G	Port Kembla	Port Lincoln	Port Moresby	Port Pirie	Rockhampton	Suva	Sydney	Wellington
Antofagasta	6724	7255	7824	7356	7106	6072	6717	5483
Arica	7002	7509	8077	7610	7432	6263	6929	5735
Astoria	6671	7646	6061	7747	6563	5018	6654	6244
Balboa	7672	8410	8199	8511	7946	6300	7680	6500
Buenaventura	7591	8231	8187	8332	7892	4658	7603	6369
Cabo Blanco	7075	7677	7849	7778	7407	5927	7081	5866
Caldera	6527	7082	7626	7183	6969	5874	6542	5288
Callao	6926	7510	7883	7611	7336	5995	7000	5721
Cape Horn	5840	6371	6957	6472	6260	5402	5823	4500
Chimbote	6950	7543	7816	7645	7321	5911	6990	5744
Coos Bay	6567	7542	5900	7643	6401	4856	6550	6071
Corinto	7408	8201	7680	8302	7610	5898	7398	6276
Eureka	6486	7461	6031	7562	6532	4987	6469	5981
Guayaquil	7239	7857	7989	7958	7576	6067	7268	5998
Guaymas	6943	7812	6802	7913	6983	5218	6920	6045
Honolulu	4447	5410	3857	5511	4346	2776	4425	4113
Iquique	6893	7424	7965	7525	7319	6151	6820	5650
Los Angeles	6540	7472	6136	7573	6517	4788	6511	5858
Manzanillo (Mex)	6793	7655	6678	7756	6836	5067	6774	5770
Mazatlan	6787	7649	6662	7750	6820	5051	6768	5860
Nanaimo	6830	7807	6183	7908	6718	5172	6818	6415
New Westminster	6842	7819	6195	7920	6730	5192	6830	6427
Portland (Oreg)	6754	7729	6144	7830	6646	5108	6737	6327
Port Alberni	6737	7714	6095	7815	6625	5087	6725	6322
Port Isabel	7173	8042	7032	8143	7213	7448	7150	6275
Port Moody	6842	7819	6195	7920	6730	5175	6824	6451
Prince Rupert	6683	7670	6046	7771	6581	5180	6671	6456
Puerto Montt	6037	6583	7218	6684	6474	5564	5720	4693
Puntarenas (CR)	7497	8235	8024	8336	7771	6125	7505	6325
Punta Arenas (Ch)	5799	6330	7034	6431	6219	5369	5150	4350
Salina Cruz	7101	7928	7179	8029	7223	5482	7086	6023
San Francisco	6481	7430	5992	7531	6430	4749	6450	5900
San Jose	7262	8087	7471	8188	7450	5708	7252	4570
Seattle	6822	7799	6175	7900	6710	5162	6810	6433
Tacoma	6842	7819	6195	7920	6730	5184	6830	6454
Talcahuano	6115	6674	7248	6775	6569	5606	6157	4846
Tocopilla	6783	7324	7912	7425	7236	6105	6684	5663
Valparaiso	6275	6836	7403	6937	6729	5759	6290	5036
Vancouver (BC)	6838	7815	6191	7916	6726	5171	6820	6447
Victoria (Vanc Is)	6762	7739	6115	7840	6650	5112	6750	6347

AREA G	Apra Harbour	Auckland	Banaba	Brisbane	Cairns	Dampier	Esperance	Fremantle
Adelaide	3961	2035	3243	1471	2233	2172	889	1343
Albany	3765	2880	4088	2316	3078	1178	224	349
Apia	3068	1583	1363	2173	2935	4486	3953	4395
Bunbury	3529	3119	4327	2555	3115	941	477	100
Cairns	2674	2120	2467	846	–	2217	2958	3050
Dampier	2664	4031	3688	3047	2217	–	1389	877
Fremantle	3464	3202	4410	2638	3050	877	560	–
Geelong	3575	1651	2857	1084	1846	2515	1243	1686
Geraldton	3261	3378	4318	2814	2847	674	736	213
Gladstone	2834	1588	2118	314	581	2782	2426	2868
Hobart	3622	1520	2904	1132	1894	2635	1396	1806
Mackay	3018	1786	2316	512	361	2561	2624	3066
Milner Bay	2561	2963	2386	1745	915	1613	2958	2446
Napier	3781	377	2449	1648	2410	4073	2802	3244
Nauru	1627	2235	160	1941	2325	3546	4012	4379
Newcastle (NSW)	2946	1245	2228	456	1218	3024	1752	2195
Noumea	2530	990	1496	825	1587	3377	2713	3155
Otago Harbour	4022	847	2824	1606	2368	3631	2397	2802
Papeete	4332	2215	2623	3259	4021	5754	4811	5253
Port Darwin	1954	3399	2822	2181	1351	996	2353	1841
Port Hedland	2609	4126	3616	2975	2145	102	1484	972
Port Kembla	3041	1285	2323	529	1313	2924	1653	2095
Port Latta (Tas)	3592	1518	2784	1012	1774	2531	1261	1702
Port Pirie	4136	2210	3418	1639	2401	2232	949	1403
Rabaul	1190	2357	1111	1443	1748	2804	3525	3615
Sydney	3005	1275	2287	515	1277	2969	1698	2140
Townsville	2832	1972	2502	698	174	2375	2810	3208
Weipa	2331	2733	2156	1515	685	1729	3064	2552
Wellington	3727	561	2515	1448	2210	3873	2607	3044
Whyalla	4118	2192	3400	1621	2383	2214	931	1385

AREA G

AREA G	Gladstone	Honolulu	Kwinana	Lae	Melbourne	Nelson	Newcastle (New South Wales)	New Plymouth
Adelaide	1701	5336	1352	2899	514	1814	1028	1804
Albany	2546	6181	358	3744	1359	2652	1872	2642
Apia	2043	2262	4404	2520	2837	1992	2310	1807
Bunbury	2785	6420	109	3637	1598	2891	2112	2881
Cairns	581	4718	3059	1847	1842	2142	1218	2084
Dampier	2782	5851	886	2682	2510	3803	3024	3793
Fremantle	2868	6503	14	3572	1681	2974	2195	2964
Geelong	1314	4950	1695	2513	36	1425	642	1415
Geraldton	3044	6679	222	3369	1857	3150	2371	3140
Gladstone	–	4346	2877	1772	1310	1610	686	1552
Hobart	1362	4931	1815	2560	470	1223	693	1213
Mackay	247	4544	3075	1970	1508	1808	884	1750
Milner Bay	1480	4686	2455	1766	2741	3041	2117	2983
Napier	1878	3936	3253	2745	1690	325	1423	382
Nauru	2171	2433	4388	1334	2905	2520	2281	2410
Newcastle (NSW)	686	4397	2204	1884	637	1154	–	1167
Noumea	1055	3370	3164	1511	1599	1194	1016	1095
Otago Harbour	1836	4400	2811	2960	1346	435	1297	489
Papeete	3489	2380	5262	3814	3695	2452	3253	2509
Port Darwin	1916	5122	1850	1972	3177	3477	2553	3419
Port Hedland	2710	5796	981	2627	2605	3898	3119	3888
Port Kembla	781	4447	2104	1979	537	1161	107	1152
Port Latta (Tas)	1242	4875	1711	2440	186	1268	569	1258
Port Pirie	1869	5511	1412	3074	689	1989	1203	1979
Rabaul	1673	3359	3624	420	2409	2521	1785	2422
Sydney	745	4427	2149	1943	582	1166	71	1124
Townsville	433	4730	3217	2005	1694	1994	1070	1936
Weipa	1250	4456	2561	1536	2511	2811	1887	2753
Wellington	1678	4114	3053	2669	1490	126	1223	180
Whyalla	1851	5493	1394	3056	671	1871	1185	1961

AREA G

AREA G	Port Kembla	Port Latta (Tasmania)	Port Moresby	Portland (Victoria)	Suva	Sydney	Wallaroo	Whyalla
Adelaide	928	545	2694	321	2626	973	210	256
Albany	1773	1381	3191	1166	3469	1818	1012	1058
Apia	2381	2730	2462	2919	644	2357	3339	3385
Bunbury	2012	1619	2943	1401	3712	2057	1256	1302
Cairns	1313	1774	424	1925	2310	1277	2337	2383
Dampier	2924	2531	1878	2313	3938	2969	2168	2214
Fremantle	2095	1702	2878	1484	3795	2140	1339	1385
Geelong	542	191	2308	211	2240	587	630	676
Geraldton	2271	1878	2675	1660	3971	2316	1515	1561
Gladstone	781	1242	1389	1393	1778	745	1805	1851
Hobart	593	300	2351	540	2195	638	867	913
Mackay	979	1440	1168	1591	1976	943	2003	2049
Milner Bay	2222	2673	743	2824	2636	2176	3236	3282
Napier	1430	1505	2526	1772	1341	1436	2195	2241
Nauru	2376	2837	1522	2987	1336	2340	3407	3453
Newcastle (NSW)	107	570	1679	719	1688	71	1139	1185
Noumea	1105	1530	1360	1681	735	1069	2099	2145
Otago Harbour	1247	1176	2700	1416	1785	1243	1832	1878
Papeete	3316	3571	3730	3777	1835	3306	4197	4243
Port Darwin	2648	3110	1179	3260	3072	2612	3132	3178
Port Hedland	3019	2626	1973	2408	3866	3064	2263	2309
Port Kembla	–	470	1774	619	1755	50	1039	1085
Port Latta (Tas)	470	–	2236	259	2144	515	656	720
Port Pirie	1103	720	2754	496	2801	1148	72	29
Rabaul	1880	2341	945	2491	1786	1844	2911	2957
Sydney	50	515	1738	664	1735	–	1084	1130
Townsville	1165	1626	598	1777	2162	1129	2189	2235
Weipa	1982	2443	513	2594	2406	1946	3006	3052
Wellington	1230	1338	2440	1572	1476	1236	1995	2041
Whyalla	1085	720	2736	478	2783	1130	57	–

Area H

Distances between principal ports on the West coast of North and South America.

AREA H

Reed's Marine Distance Tables

WEST COAST OF NORTH & SOUTH AMERICA

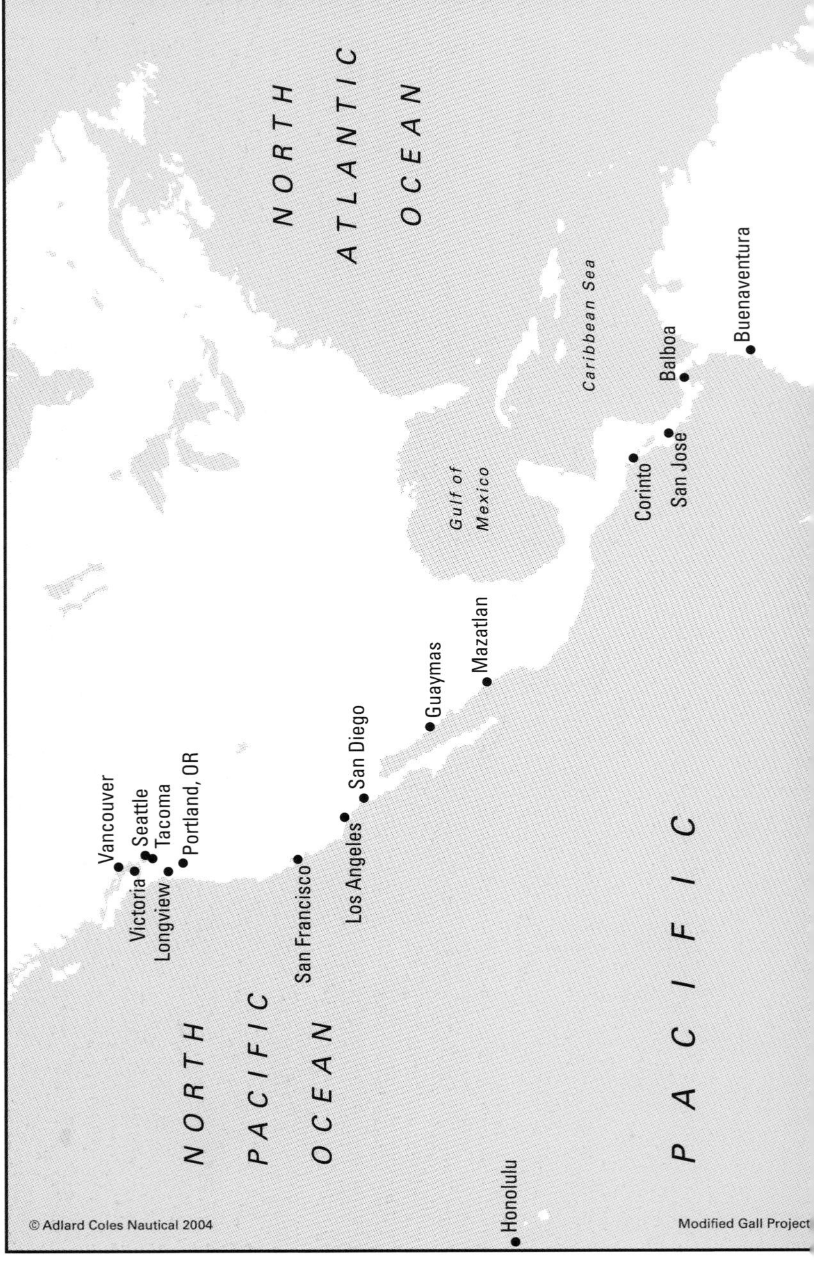

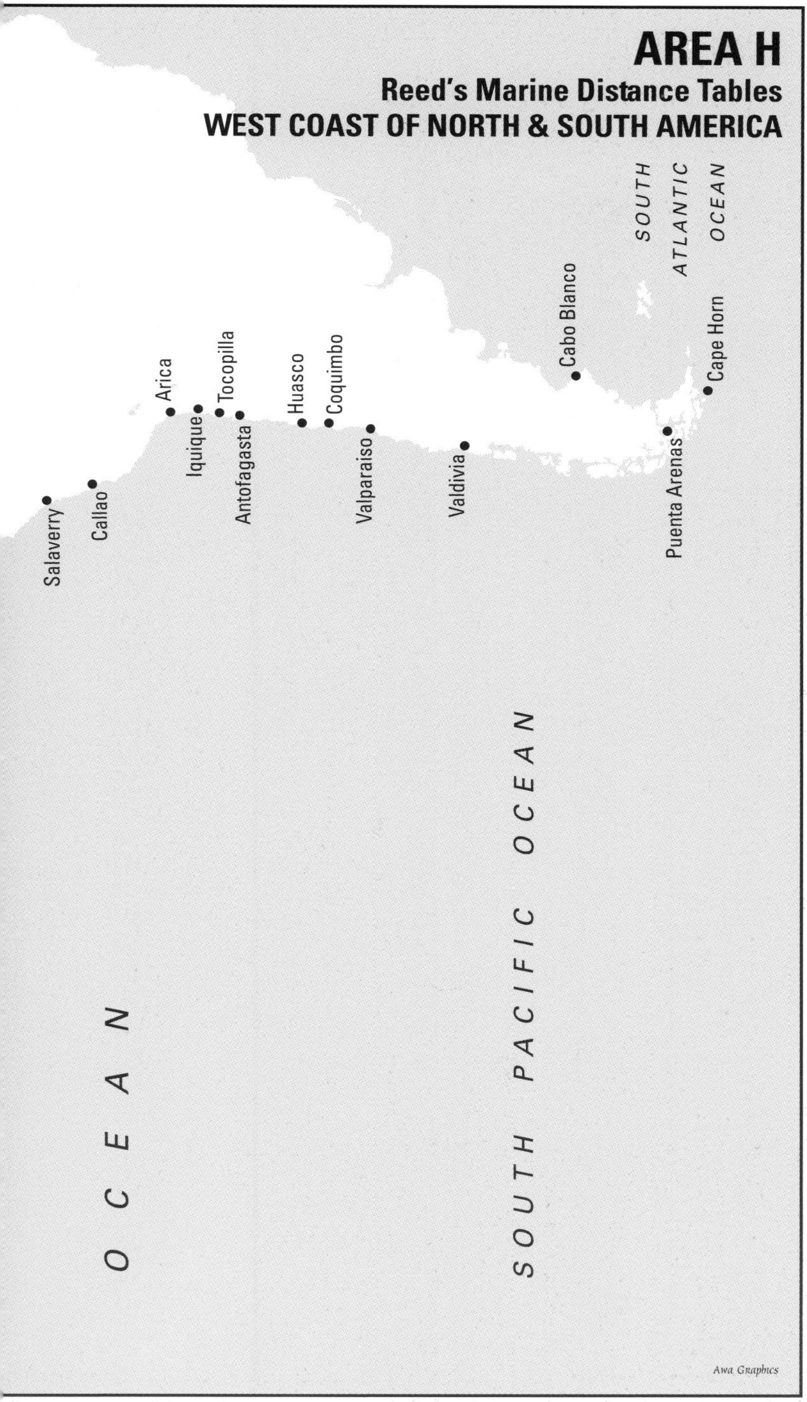
AREA H
Reed's Marine Distance Tables
WEST COAST OF NORTH & SOUTH AMERICA
SOUTH ATLANTIC OCEAN
Cabo Blanco
Cape Horn
Puenta Arenas
Valdivia
Valparaiso
Coquimbo
Huasco
Antofagasta
Tocopilla
Iquique
Arica
Callao
Salaverry
SOUTH PACIFIC OCEAN
OCEAN
Awa Graphics

AREA H

AREA H	Antofagasta	Arica	Balboa	Buenaventura	Callao	Cape Horn	Corinto	Guaymas
Antofagasta	–	339	2125	1909	795	2130	2390	3895
Balboa	2125	1911	–	354	1340	4085	681	2369
Buenaventura	1909	1697	354	–	1124	3867	817	2501
Cabo Blanco	1241	1129	812	596	556	3299	1093	2603
Callao	795	579	1340	1124	–	2814	1604	3113
Cape Horn	2130	2450	4085	3867	2814	–	4330	5539
Coquimbo	390	703	2425	2233	1130	1762	2717	4157
Corinto	2390	2180	681	817	1604	4330	–	1730
Guayaquil	1491	1282	837	621	706	3449	1120	2683
Guaymas	3895	3680	2369	2501	3113	5539	1730	–
Honolulu	5777	5683	4688	4808	5157	6477	4070	2999
Huasco	288	624	2410	2194	1080	1845	2675	4180
Iquique	234	108	1980	1764	650	2345	2245	3750
Longview	5333	5123	3814	3951	4556	6926	3175	2048
Los Angeles	4433	4219	2912	3047	3654	6010	2275	1150
Mazatlan	3533	3320	2010	2138	2750	5206	1367	385
Portland (Oreg)	5375	5165	3856	3993	4598	6968	3217	2090
Punta Arenas (Ch)	1979	2296	3937	3716	2655	417	4170	5400
Salaverry	1040	824	1095	879	246	3059	1319	2868
San Diego	4358	4146	2844	2974	3581	5945	2207	1075
San Francisco	4768	4559	3246	3381	3988	6338	2609	1480
San Jose	2550	2340	889	1022	1763	4440	232	1501
Seattle	5529	5312	4005	4140	4747	7095	3371	2242
Tacoma	5549	5332	4025	4160	4767	7115	3391	2262
Tocopilla	113	235	2060	1844	726	2218	2325	3830
Valdivia	990	1305	2980	2766	1684	1150	3240	4576
Valparaiso	571	888	2615	2399	1299	1573	2282	4290
Vancouver (BC)	5545	5328	4021	4156	4763	7111	3387	2258
Victoria (Vanc Is)	5469	5252	3945	4080	4687	7035	3311	2182

AREA H

AREA H	Honolulu	Iquique	Longview	Los Angeles	Mazatlan	Portland (Oregon)	Punta Arenas (Chile)	San Diego
Antofagasta	5777	234	5333	4433	3533	5375	1979	4358
Balboa	4688	1980	3814	2912	2010	3856	3937	2844
Buenaventura	4808	1764	3951	3047	2138	3993	3716	2974
Cabo Blanco	4731	1196	4050	3148	2240	4092	3148	3075
Callao	5157	650	4556	3654	2750	4598	2655	3581
Cape Horn	6477	2345	6926	6010	5206	6968	417	5945
Coquimbo	5871	598	5578	4680	3790	5620	1612	4615
Corinto	4070	2245	3175	2275	1367	3217	4170	2207
Guayaquil	4865	1346	4130	3228	2323	4172	3298	3158
Guaymas	2999	3750	2048	1150	385	2090	5400	1075
Honolulu	–	5720	2287	2231	2859	2329	6370	2275
Huasco	6060	519	5618	4718	3818	5660	1694	4643
Iquique	5720	–	5188	4288	3388	5230	2191	4213
Longview	2287	5188	–	937	1910	42	6781	1020
Los Angeles	2231	4288	937	–	1006	979	5865	95
Mazatlan	2859	3388	1910	1006	–	1952	5051	935
Portland (Oreg)	2329	5230	42	979	1952	–	6823	1062
Punta Arenas (Ch)	6370	2191	6781	5865	5051	6823	–	5792
Salaverry	4910	895	4311	3369	2505	4353	2900	3336
San Diego	2275	4213	1020	95	935	1062	5792	–
San Francisco	2095	4623	603	369	1345	645	6201	453
San Jose	3845	2405	2950	2047	1140	2992	4290	1974
Seattle	2403	5384	305	1128	2099	347	6988	1209
Tacoma	2423	5404	325	1148	2119	367	7008	1229
Tocopilla	5757	130	5268	4368	3468	5310	2067	4293
Valdivia	5975	1200	4920	5075	4215	4962	1006	5008
Valparaiso	5917	783	5708	4806	3930	5750	1427	4733
Vancouver (BC)	2419	5400	321	1144	2115	363	7004	1225
Victoria (Vanc Is)	2343	5324	245	1068	2039	287	6928	1149

AREA H

AREA H	San Francisco	San Jose	Seattle	Tocopilla	Valdivia	Valparaiso	Vancouver	Victoria (British Columbia)
Antofagasta	4768	2550	5529	113	990	571	5545	5469
Balboa	3246	889	4005	2060	2980	2615	4021	3945
Buenaventura	3381	1022	4140	1844	2766	2399	4156	4080
Cabo Blanco	3482	1259	4241	1276	2198	1831	4257	4181
Callao	3988	1763	4747	726	1684	1299	4763	4687
Cape Horn	6338	4440	7095	2218	1150	1573	7111	7035
Coquimbo	5022	2864	5776	478	622	203	5792	5716
Corinto	2609	232	3371	2325	3240	2882	3387	3311
Guayaquil	3562	1290	4324	1426	2350	1984	4340	4264
Guaymas	1480	1501	2242	3830	4576	4290	2258	2182
Honolulu	2095	3845	2403	5757	5975	5917	2419	2343
Huasco	5053	2835	5814	398	705	286	5830	5754
Iquique	4623	2405	5384	130	1200	783	5400	5324
Longview	603	2950	305	5268	4920	5708	321	245
Los Angeles	369	2047	1128	4368	5075	4806	1144	1068
Mazatlan	1345	1140	2099	3468	4215	3930	2115	2039
Portland (Oreg)	645	2992	347	5310	4962	5750	363	287
Punta Arenas (Ch)	6201	4290	6988	2067	1006	1427	7004	6928
Salaverry	3743	1518	4502	4522	1929	1544	4518	4442
San Diego	453	1974	1209	4293	5008	4733	1225	1149
San Francisco	–	2385	796	4703	5416	5146	812	736
San Jose	2385	–	3140	2485	3378	3024	3156	3080
Seattle	796	3140	–	5464	6169	5899	126	70
Tacoma	816	3160	20	5484	6189	5919	146	90
Tocopilla	4703	2485	5464	–	1080	663	5480	5404
Valdivia	5416	3378	6169	1080	–	439	6185	6109
Valparaiso	5146	3024	5899	663	439	–	5915	5839
Vancouver (BC)	812	3156	126	5480	6185	5915	–	74
Victoria (Vanc Is)	736	3080	70	5404	6109	5839	74	–

Other ports on West Coasts of North and South America

Ports in the Great Lakes and the St Lawrence Seaway

	Buffalo	Chicago	Cleveland	Detroit	Duluth-Superior	Hamilton	Milwaukee	Montreal	Port Arthur	Toledo	Toronto
Buffalo	–	895	175	260	985	80	830	385	865	255	75
Chicago	895	–	740	635	810	930	85	1240	685	690	930
Cleveland	175	740	–	110	835	215	675	525	710	95	215
Detroit	260	635	110	–	725	300	570	610	605	55	300
Duluth-Superior	985	810	835	725	–	1025	745	1335	195	780	1025
Hamilton	80	930	215	300	1025	–	870	360	905	295	30
Kingston	210	1065	345	430	1155	185	1000	180	1035	425	160
Milwaukee	830	85	675	570	745	870	–	1175	620	620	865
Montreal	385	1240	525	610	1335	360	1175	–	1210	600	340
Port Arthur	865	685	710	605	195	905	620	1210	–	660	905
Sault Ste Marie	590	415	440	330	305	630	350	940	275	385	630
Toledo	255	690	95	55	780	295	620	600	660	–	290
Toronto	75	930	215	300	1025	30	865	340	905	290	–

The above distances are given in statute miles which is usual for this locality.
Note: 1.15 statute miles equals 1 nautical mile.

Turning points

Key: CW = Cape Wrath
DS = Dover Strait

Area		Bishop Rock	Cape Wrath	Dover Strait	Finisterre	North Cape	Skaw	Ushant	Gibraltar
		A	A	A	A	A	A	A	A
A	**Bishop Rock**	–	–	–	–	–	–	–	–
A	**Cape Wrath**	581	–	–	–	–	–	–	–
A	**Dover Strait**	325	583	–	–	–	–	–	–
A	**Finisterre**	424	1005	700	–	–	–	–	–
A	**North Cape**	1667CW	1086	1430	2130	–	–	–	–
A	**Skaw**	860	530	535	1235	1157	–	–	–
A	**Ushant**	95	700	319	378	1746DS	854	–	–
A/B	**Gibraltar**	988	1569	1261	564	2691	1796	942	–
B	**Istanbul**	2783	3364	3059	2330	4486	3545	2737	1795
B	**Port Said**	2913	3494	3186	2455	4616	3670	2867	1925
B	**Valletta, Malta**	1996	2577	2269	1530	3699	2745	1950	1008
C	**Cape Race, NF**	1831	1910	2156	1840	2650	2440	1950	2240
C	**Cristobal**	4325	4655	4665	4166	5465	4989	4400	4340
C	**Key West**	3835	4035	4160	3705	4660	4363	3875	4060
C	**Port of Spain, Trinidad**	3570	3895	3905	3338	5210	4351	3595	3460
D	**Cape Town**	5763	6140	6095	5347	7345	6628	5745	5190
D	**São Vicente, Cape Verde**	2173	2754	2449	1749	3876	2984	2130	1540
D	**Dakar**	2196	2777	2479	1766	3906	3047	2160	1570
D	**Recife**	3765	4105	4060	3360	5315	4630	3775	3150
D/H	**Cape Horn**	7032	7323	7321	6625	8620	7897	7035	6387
E	**Cape Guardafui**	4634†	5165†	4920†	4254†	6365†	5499†	4650†	3670†
E	**Dondra Head, Sri Lanka**	6433†	6970†	6725†	6053†	8165†	7298†	6450†	5469†
E	**Perim Island**	4174†	4705†	4460†	3794†	5905†	5039†	4190†	3210†
E	**Strait of Hormuz**	5690†	6226†	5976†	5310†	7421†	6555†	5706†	4726†
F	**Sabang**	7345†	7870†	7625†	6885†	9035†	8205†	7320†	6375†
F	**Singapore**	7963†	8440†	8236†	7477†	9666†	8805†	7917†	6975†
F	**Tanjung Priok**	8198†	8779†	8471†	7737†	9901†	9040†	8152†	7210†
F	**Yokahama**	10918†	11499†	11191†	10369†	12621†	11760†	10872†	9930†
G	**Torres Strait**	10353†	10884†	10639†	9773†	12069†	11126†	10470†	9417†
G	**Bass Strait**	10670†	11025†	10970†	10265†	12410†	11453†	10701†	9745†
G	**Cape Leeuwin**	9206†	9559†	9503†	8798†	10945†	9985†	9231†	8280†
G/H	**Auckland**	10890*	11155*	11205*	10725*	12020*	11545*	10945*	10865*
G/H	**Honolulu**	9065*	9120*	9380*	8900*	10195*	9720*	9120*	9040*
H	**Balboa**	4390*	4706*	4715*	4205*	5510*	5036*	4445*	4390*
H	**San Francisco**	7630*	7982*	7992*	7482*	8755*	8281*	7685*	7600*

Turning points

Key: CW = Cape Wrath
DS = Dover Strait

Area		Istanbul	Port Said	Valletta, Malta	Cape Race, NF	Cristobal	Key West	Port of Spain Trinidad	Gibraltar
		B	B	B	C	C	C	C	D
A	**Bishop Rock**	–	–	–	–	–	–	–	–
A	**Cape Wrath**	–	–	–	–	–	–	–	–
A	**Dover Strait**	–	–	–	–	–	–	–	–
A	**Finisterre**	–	–	–	–	–	–	–	–
A	**North Cape**	–	–	–	–	–	–	–	–
A	**Skaw**	–	–	–	–	–	–	–	–
A	**Ushant**	–	–	–	–	–	–	–	–
A/B	**Gibraltar**	–	–	–	–	–	–	–	–
B	**Istanbul**	–	–	–	–	–	–	–	–
B	**Port Said**	805	–	–	–	–	–	–	–
B	**Valletta, Malta**	811	925	–	–	–	–	–	–
C	**Cape Race, NF**	4035	4165	3248	–	–	–	–	–
C	**Cristobal**	6115	6240	5310	2615	–	–	–	–
C	**Key West**	5835	5960	5030	1977	1054	–	–	–
C	**Port of Spain, Trinidad**	5235	5360	4430	2211	1140	1472	–	–
D	**Cape Town**	6165†	5360†	6090	6165	6465	6718	5307	–
D	**São Vicente, Cape Verde**	3335	3500	2565	2236	3225	3250	2178	3944
D	**Dakar**	3330	3430	2445	2626	3694	3709	2628	3604
D	**Recife**	4970	5065	4130	3451	3217	3539	2106	3318
D/H	**Cape Horn**	8230	8322	7394	6709	4130*	5148*	5332	4256
E	**Cape Guardafui**	2575†	1760†	2710†	5841†	8008†	7647†	7101†	3620
E	**Dondra Head, Sri Lanka**	4380†	3550†	4515†	7642†	9809†	9448†	8902†	4300
E	**Perim Island**	2115†	1300†	2250†	5421†	7548†	7187†	6641†	4100
E	**Strait of Hormuz**	3597†	2791†	3730†	6880†	9046†	8689†	8133†	4668
F	**Sabang**	5246†	4440†	5379†	8510†	10681†	10316†	9770†	4980
F	**Singapore**	5880†	5065†	6015†	9111†	10548*	10917†	10371†	5630
F	**Tanjung Priok**	6115†	5300†	6250†	9378†	10686*	11184†	10638†	5190
F	**Yokahama**	8835†	8020†	8970†	10377*	7725*	8790*	9187*	8320
G	**Torres Strait**	8285†	7479†	8418†	11130*	8504*	9568*	9662*	6859C
G	**Bass Strait**	8610†	7800†	8750†	10573*	7921*	8986*	9080*	6046C
G	**Cape Leeuwin**	7151†	6345†	7284†	10442†	9293*	10358*	10452*	4675C
G/H	**Auckland**	10190†	9380†	10335†	9207*	6555*	7620*	7714*	7150C
G/H	**Honolulu**	10880*	10906*	10045*	7380*	4728*	5800*	5887*	10820C
H	**Balboa**	6200*	6295*	5360*	2696*	44*	1109*	1203*	6509*
H	**San Francisco**	9419*	9540*	8605*	5940*	3290*	4413*	4464*	9753*

Turning points

Key: CW = Cape Wrath
DS = Dover Strait

Area		São Vicente Cape Verde	Dakar	Recife	Cape Horn	Cape Guardafui	Dondra Head	Perim Island	Strait of Hormuz
		D	D	D	D/H	E	E	E	E
A	**Bishop Rock**	–	–	–	–	–	–	–	–
A	**Cape Wrath**	–	–	–	–	–	–	–	–
A	**Dover Strait**	–	–	–	–	–	–	–	–
A	**Finisterre**	–	–	–	–	–	–	–	–
A	**North Cape**	–	–	–	–	–	–	–	–
A	**Skaw**	–	–	–	–	–	–	–	–
A	**Ushant**	–	–	–	–	–	–	–	–
A/B	**Gibraltar**	–	–	–	–	–	–	–	–
B	**Istanbul**	–	–	–	–	–	–	–	–
B	**Port Said**	–	–	–	–	–	–	–	–
B	**Valletta, Malta**	–	–	–	–	–	–	–	–
C	**Cape Race, NF**	–	–	–	–	–	–	–	–
C	**Cristobal**	–	–	–	–	–	–	–	–
C	**Key West**	–	–	–	–	–	–	–	–
C	**Port of Spain, Trinidad**	–	–	–	–	–	–	–	–
D	**Cape Town**	–	–	–	–	–	–	–	–
D	**São Vicente, Cape Verde**	–	–	–	–	–	–	–	–
D	**Dakar**	465	–	–	–	–	–	–	–
D	**Recife**	1627	1717	–	–	–	–	–	–
D/H	**Cape Horn**	4905	5005	3300	–	–	–	–	–
E	**Cape Guardafui**	5238†	5185†	6823†	7744C	–	–	–	–
E	**Dondra Head, Sri Lanka**	7059†	6986†	7606C	8422C	1779	–	–	–
E	**Perim Island**	4798†	4725†	6363†	8224C	460	2259	–	–
E	**Strait of Hormuz**	6271†	6213†	7953C	8823C	1160	1860	1530	–
F	**Sabang**	7915†	7858†	8310C	9180C	2656	881	3136	2748
F	**Singapore**	8528†	8455†	8934C	9557	3247	1470	3735	3343
F	**Tanjung Priok**	8795†	8722†	8490C	9066	3520	1765	4000	3617
F	**Yokahama**	11422†	11349†	10942*	9301	6140	4371	6620	6236
G	**Torres Strait**	10792C	10452C	10546M	7217	5699	3941	6179	5813
G	**Bass Strait**	9949C	9641C	9212M	5875	6030	4552	6510	6419
G	**Cape Leeuwin**	8568C	8220C	7928C	7182	4564	3105	5044	4953
G/H	**Auckland**	9680M	9742M	8071M	4800	7620	6135	8100	7985
G/H	**Honolulu**	7984*	8422*	7945*	6477	9132	7358	9612	9221
H	**Balboa**	3295*	3738*	3261*	4085	8052*†	9853*†	7592*†	9090*†
H	**San Francisco**	6550*	6982*	6505*	6338	11296*†	8990*†	10836*†	10718

Turning points

Key: CW = Cape Wrath
DS = Dover Strait

Area		Sabang	Singapore	Tanjung Priok	Yokahama	Torres Strait	Bass Strait	Cape Leeuwin	Auckland
		F	F	F	F	G	G	G	G/H
A	**Bishop Rock**	–	–	–	–	–	–	–	–
A	**Cape Wrath**	–	–	–	–	–	–	–	–
A	**Dover Strait**	–	–	–	–	–	–	–	–
A	**Finisterre**	–	–	–	–	–	–	–	–
A	**North Cape**	–	–	–	–	–	–	–	–
A	**Skaw**	–	–	–	–	–	–	–	–
A	**Ushant**	–	–	–	–	–	–	–	–
A/B	**Gibraltar**	–	–	–	–	–	–	–	–
B	**Istanbul**	–	–	–	–	–	–	–	–
B	**Port Said**	–	–	–	–	–	–	–	–
B	**Valletta, Malta**	–	–	–	–	–	–	–	–
C	**Cape Race, NF**	–	–	–	–	–	–	–	–
C	**Cristobal**	–	–	–	–	–	–	–	–
C	**Key West**	–	–	–	–	–	–	–	–
C	**Port of Spain, Trinidad**	–	–	–	–	–	–	–	–
D	**Cape Town**	–	–	–	–	–	–	–	–
D	**São Vicente, Cape Verde**	–	–	–	–	–	–	–	–
D	**Dakar**	–	–	–	–	–	–	–	–
D	**Recife**	–	–	–	–	–	–	–	–
D/H	**Cape Horn**	–	–	–	–	–	–	–	–
E	**Cape Guardafui**	–	–	–	–	–	–	–	–
E	**Dondra Head, Sri Lanka**	–	–	–	–	–	–	–	–
E	**Perim Island**	–	–	–	–	–	–	–	–
E	**Strait of Hormuz**	–	–	–	–	–	–	–	–
F	**Sabang**	–	–	–	–	–	–	–	–
F	**Singapore**	600	–	–	–	–	–	–	–
F	**Tanjung Priok**	1075	527	–	–	–	–	–	–
F	**Yokahama**	3492	2892	3221	–	–	–	–	–
G	**Torres Strait**	3151	2550	2195	3142	–	–	–	–
G	**Bass Strait**	4400	3800	3339	4886	2518	–	–	–
G	**Cape Leeuwin**	2942	2341	1884	4592	2723	1519	–	–
G/H	**Auckland**	5615	5015	4670	4800	2533	1601	3019	–
G/H	**Honolulu**	6481	5880	5934	3397	4256	4888	6323	3850
H	**Balboa**	10729*†	10504	10642	7681	8459	7825	9177	6509
H	**San Francisco**	7950	7350	7641	4536	6252	6957	8344	5680

Rivers and Canals

ST LAWRENCE, RIVER AND GULF

MONTREAL to

Varennes	12
Verchéres	19
Plum Island Light	20
Lavaltrie	26
Sorel	39
Ile de Grace Light	42
Stone Island Light	45
Port St Francis	65
Three Rivers	71
Champlain	81
Cape Charles	96
Richelieu Rapids	104
Cap Santé	110
Quebec	135

QUEBEC to

L'Islet	41
Father Point	157
Matane	199
Cap Chatte	233
Port Cartier	273
Sept Iles	280
West Point (Anticosti)	333
Cape Rosier	346
South Point (Anticosti)	414
Heath Point (Anticosti)	437
Cape Ray (Newfoundland)	551
Cape Race (Newfoundland)	817

RIVER AMAZON

Para/Iquitos	2,400
Para/Manaus	860

RIVER PLATE

BUENOS AIRES to

Martin Garcia	33
San Pedro	129
Obligado	138
San Nicolas	163
Villa Constitucion	172
Rosario	202
San Lorenzo	218
Diamante	261
Colastine	288
Parana	294

ROSARIO to

San Lorenzo	16
Diamante	59
Colastine	86
Parana	92
Curtiembre	127

Las Palmas branch of the River Parana

SAN PEDRO to

Baradero	15
Las Palmas	45
Zarate	58
Campana	64

CANALS

Kiel Canal about	60
Manchester Ship Canal	35½
N Sea Canal (IJmuiden/Amsterdam)	15
Suez Canal	88
Panama Canal	44

Time Zones Based on UT (Universal Time)

Alexandria	+2
Algiers	+1
Amsterdam	+1
Antwerp	+1
Baltimore	−5
Barbados	−4
Beijing	+8
Berlin	+1
Boston	−5
Bremen	+1
Brussels	+1
Buenos Aires	−3
Cadiz	+1
Cairo	+2
Calcutta	+5.5
Callao	−5
Canton	+8
Cape Horn	−4
Cape of Good Hope	+2
Cape Race	−3.5
Charleston	−5
Chennai	+5.5
Chicago	−6
Cincinnati	−6
Copenhagen	+1
Dublin	0
Edinburgh	0
Florence	+1
Galveston	−6
Genoa	+1
Geneva	+1
Gibraltar	+1
Glasgow	0
Greenwich	0
Hamburg	+1
Havana	−5
Havre	+1
Istanbul	+2
Jedda	+3
Kingston, Jamaica	−5
Leghorn	+1
Leipzig	+1
Lima	−5
Lisbon	0
Liverpool	0
Madrid	+1
Malaga	+1
Malta	+1
Manila	+8
Marseilles	+1
Mexico	−6
Montreal	−5
Montevideo	−3
Moscow	+3
Mumbai	+5.5
Naples	+1
New Orleans	−6
New York	−5
Odessa	+3
Palermo	+1
Panama	−6
Paris	+1
Pensacola	−6
Philadelphia	−5
Portland (Maine)	−5
Puerto Rico	−4
Quebec	−5
Rio de Janeiro	−3
Rome	+1
Rotterdam	+1
St Helena	0
St Petersburg	+3
Salt Lake City	−7
Sandy Hook	−5
San Francisco	−8
Santa Cruz	0
Santiago (Cuba)	−5
Savannah	−5
Seville	+1
Sierra Leone	0
Singapore	+8
Smyrna	+2
Stockholm	+1
Suez	+2
Sydney	+10
Thailand	+7
Toronto	−5
Toulon	+1
Tripoli	+2
Tunis	+1
Valparaiso	−4
Venice	+1
Veracruz	−6
Vienna	+1
Warsaw	+1

Time and Speed Conversion Table

Distance in nautical miles	10 knots		11 knots		12 knots		13 knots		14 knots		15 knots		16 knots	
	dys	hrs	dys	hrs	dys	hrs	dys	hrs	dys	hrs	dys	hrs	dys	hrs
250	1	1	–	23	–	21	–	19	–	18	–	17	–	16
300	1	6	1	3	1	1	–	23	–	21	–	20	–	19
350	1	11	1	8	1	5	1	3	1	1	–	23	–	22
400	1	16	1	12	1	9	1	7	1	5	1	3	1	1
450	1	21	1	17	1	14	1	11	1	8	1	6	1	4
500	2	2	1	21	1	18	1	14	1	12	1	9	1	7
550	2	7	2	2	1	22	1	18	1	15	1	13	1	10
600	2	12	2	7	2	2	1	22	1	19	1	16	1	14
650	2	17	2	11	2	6	2	2	1	22	1	19	1	17
700	2	22	2	16	2	10	2	6	2	2	1	23	1	20
750	3	3	2	20	2	14	2	10	2	6	2	2	1	23
800	3	8	3	1	2	19	2	14	2	9	2	5	2	2
900	3	18	3	10	3	3	2	21	2	16	2	12	2	8
1000	4	4	3	19	3	11	3	5	2	23	2	19	2	14
1100	4	14	4	4	3	20	3	13	3	7	3	1	2	21
1200	5	–	4	13	4	4	3	20	3	14	3	8	3	3
1300	5	10	4	22	4	12	4	4	3	21	3	15	3	9
1400	5	20	5	7	4	21	4	12	4	4	3	21	3	16
1500	6	6	5	16	5	5	4	19	4	11	4	4	3	22
1600	6	16	6	1	5	13	5	3	4	18	4	11	4	4
1700	7	2	6	11	5	22	5	11	5	1	4	17	4	10
1800	7	12	6	20	6	6	5	18	5	9	5	–	4	17
1900	7	22	7	5	6	14	6	2	5	16	5	7	4	23
2000	8	8	7	14	6	23	6	10	5	23	5	13	5	5
2250	9	9	8	13	7	20	7	5	6	17	6	6	5	21
2500	10	10	9	11	8	16	8	–	7	11	6	23	6	12
2750	11	11	10	10	9	13	8	19	8	5	7	16	7	4
3000	12	12	11	9	10	10	9	15	8	22	8	8	7	20
3250	13	13	12	8	11	7	10	10	9	16	9	1	8	12
3500	14	14	13	6	12	4	11	5	10	10	9	17	9	3
3750	15	15	14	5	13	1	12	–	11	4	10	10	9	19
4000	16	16	15	4	13	21	12	20	11	22	11	3	10	10
4250	17	17	16	3	14	18	13	15	12	16	11	20	11	2
4500	18	18	17	1	15	15	14	10	13	9	12	12	11	17
4750	19	19	18	–	16	12	15	5	14	3	13	5	12	9
5000	20	20	18	23	17	9	18	1	14	21	13	21	13	1
5500	22	22	20	20	19	2	17	15	16	9	15	7	14	8
6000	25	–	22	17	20	20	19	6	17	21	16	16	15	15
6500	27	2	24	15	22	14	20	20	19	8	18	1	16	22
7000	29	4	26	12	24	7	22	10	20	20	19	11	18	5
7500	31	6	28	10	28	1	24	1	22	8	20	20	19	13
8000	33	8	30	7	27	19	25	15	23	19	22	5	20	20
8500	35	10	32	5	29	12	27	6	25	7	23	15	22	3
9000	37	12	34	2	31	6	28	20	26	19	25	–	23	11
9500	39	14	36	–	33	–	30	11	28	7	26	9	24	18
10000	41	16	37	21	34	17	32	1	29	18	27	18	26	1

Alphabetical Index of Ports and Places

Basuo (Hainan Island), China 32–8, 77–81, 108–12, 135–9, 156–60, 178, 183
Baton Rouge, USA 123
Batumi, Georgia 92
Bayonne, France 53
Beaumont, USA 123–5
Beira, Mozambique 18–24, 67–71, 98–102, 130, 135, 140, 145, 152
Beirut, Lebanon 4–10, 62, 67, 72, 77, 82, 87, 92–4
Belem, Brazil 18–24, 67–71, 98–102, 130, 135, 140, 145, 150–2
Belfast, UK 4, 11, 18, 25, 32, 39, 47
Bergen, Norway 4, 11, 18, 25, 32, 39, 46, 53
Bhavnagar, India 25–31, 72–6, 103–7, 130–4, 156, 161, 167
Bilbao, Spain 4, 11, 18, 25, 32, 39, 46, 53–7
Bintan Island, Indonesia 188–190
Bishop Rock 210–11
Bluff, New Zealand 39–45, 82–6, 113–17, 140–4, 161–5, 178–82, 194
Bordeaux, France 5, 12, 19, 26, 33, 40, 47, 53–7
Boston, USA 11–17, 62–6, 98, 103, 108, 113, 118, 123
Botwood, Canada 123
Bourgas (Burgas), Bulgaria 4–10, 62, 67, 72, 77, 82, 87, 92
Bremen, Germany 5, 12, 19, 26, 33, 40, 47, 53–7
Brest, France 53–7
Brindisi, Italy 4–10, 62, 67, 72, 77, 82, 87, 92
Brisbane, Australia 39–45, 82–6, 113–17, 140–4, 161–5, 178–82, 194, 199
Brownsville, USA 123–5
Buenaventura, Colombia 46–52, 87–91, 118–22, 145–9, 166–71, 183–7, 194–8, 204–6
Buenos Aires, Argentina 18–24, 67–71, 98–102, 130, 135, 140, 145, 150–2, 209
Buffalo, USA 208
Bunbury, Australia 199–201
Bushehr, Iran 25–31, 72–6, 103–7, 130–4, 156, 162, 167, 172–4

Cabo Blanco, Peru 46–52, 87–91, 118–22, 145–9, 166–71, 183–7, 194–8, 204–6
Cagliari, Italy 4–10, 62, 67, 72, 77, 82, 87
Cairns, Australia 39–45, 82–6, 113–17, 140–4, 161–5, 178–82, 194, 199
Calcutta, India 25–31, 72–6, 103–7, 130–4, 157, 162, 167, 172–4
Caldera, Chile 46–52, 87–91, 118–22, 145–9, 166–71, 183–7, 194–8
Calicut, India 172–4
Callao, Peru 46–52, 87–91, 118–22, 145–9, 166–71, 183–7, 194–8, 204–6
Campana, Argentina 209, 214
Cam-Pha (formerly Campha), Indonesia 32–8, 77–81, 108–12, 135–9, 156–60, 178
Cap Santé, Canada 209, 214
Cape Charles, Canada 209, 214
Cape Chatte, Canada 209, 214
Cape Guardafui 210–11
Cape Horn, Chile 18–24, 46–52, 67–71, 87–91, 98–102, 118–22, 130,
.... 135, 140, 145–9, 166–71, 183–7, 194–8, 204–6, 210–11
Cape Leeuwin, Australia 39–45, 82–6, 113–17, 140–4, 161–5, 178–82, 195, 210–11
Cape Town, South Africa 18–24, 67–71, 98–102, 130, 135, 140, 145, 150–2, 210–11
Cape Race, Canada 123–5, 210–11, 214
Cape Ray, Canada 209, 214

Dubrovnik, Croatia 4–10, 63, 68, 73, 78, 83, 88
Duluth–Superior, USA 11–17, 62–6, 99, 104, 109, 114, 119, 208
Dundee, UK 54
Dunkirk, France 5, 12, 19, 26, 33, 40, 47, 53–7
Durban, South Africa 18–24, 67–71, 98–102, 131, 136, 141, 150–2
Durres, Albania 4–10, 63, 68, 73, 78, 83, 88, 92
East London, South Africa 18–24, 67–71, 98–102, 131, 136, 141, 146, 151
Emden, Germany 6, 13, 20, 27, 34, 41, 48, 54
Esbjerg, Denmark 6, 13, 20, 27, 34, 41, 48
Esperance, Australia 39–45, 82–6, 113–17, 140–4, 161–5, 178–82, 195, 199
Eureka, USA 46–52, 87–91, 118–22, 145–9, 166–71, 183–7, 194–8

Famagusta, Cyprus 93
Father Point, Canada 209, 214
Finisterre, Spain 6, 13, 20, 27, 34, 41, 48, 210–11
Flushing, Netherlands 6, 13, 20, 27, 34, 41, 48, 54
Fortaleza, Brazil 150–2
Freeport, Bahamas 99, 104, 109, 114, 119
Fremantle, Australia 39–45, 82–6, 113–17, 140–4, 161–5, 178–82, 195, 199–201
Fujairah 25–31, 72–6, 103–7, 130–4, 157, 162, 168, 172–4

Galatz (formerly Galati), Romania 93
Galveston, USA 11–17, 62–6, 99, 104, 109, 114, 123–5
Gdansk, Poland 6, 13, 20, 27, 34, 41, 48
Gydnia, Poland 53–7
Geelong, Australia 39–45, 82–6, 113–17, 140–4, 161–5, 178–82, 195, 199–201
Genoa, Italy 4–10, 63, 68, 73, 78, 83, 88, 92–4
Georgetown, Guyana 11–17, 62–6, 99, 104, 109, 114, 119, 123–5
Geraldton, Australia 39–45, 82–6, 113–17, 140–4, 161–5, 178–82, 195, 199–201
Ghent, Belgium 54
Gibraltar, Gibraltar 4–10, 13, 20, 27, 34, 41, 48, 53–7, 63, 68, 73, 78, 83, 92–4, 210–11
Gijon, Spain 6, 13, 20, 27, 34, 41, 48
Gladstone, Australia 199–201
Glasgow, UK 6, 13, 20, 27, 34, 41, 48, 53–7
Gothenburg, Sweden 7, 14, 21, 28, 35, 42, 49, 53–7
Grangemouth, UK 55
Guayaquil, Equador 46–52, 87–91, 118–22, 145–9, 166–71, 183–7, 194–8, 204–6
Guaymas, Mexico 46–52, 87–91, 118–22, 145–9, 166–71, 183–7, 194–8, 204–6
Gulf, The (formerly the Persian Gulf)

Haifa, Israel 4–10, 63, 68, 73, 78, 83, 88, 93
Haiphong, Vietnam 32–8, 77–81, 108–12, 135–9, 156–60, 178, 183, 188–90
Hakodate, Japan 188–90
Halifax, Canada 11–17, 62–6, 99, 104, 109, 114, 119, 123–5
Hamburg, Germany 7, 14, 21, 28, 35, 42, 49, 53–7
Hamilton, Canada 208
Havana, Cuba 11–17, 62–6, 99, 104, 109, 114, 119, 123–5
Havre, Le, France 7, 14, 21, 28, 35, 42, 49, 53–7
Heath Point (Anticosti), Canada 209, 214

Lagos, Nigeria 18–24, 67–71, 98–102, 131, 136, 141, 146, 150–2
La Guaira, Venezuela 11–17, 62–6, 100, 105, 115, 120
Land's End, UK 8, 15, 22, 29, 36, 43, 50
La Pallice (La Rochelle), France 53–7
Larvik, Norway 55
Las Palmas, Canary Islands 18–24, 67–71, 98–102, 131, 136, 141, 146, 150–2
Las Palmas (River Parana) 209, 214
La Spezia, Italy 92–4
Latakia, Syria 92–4
Launceston, Australia 39–45, 82–6, 113–17, 140–4, 161–5, 178–82, 196
Lavaltrie, Canada 209, 214
Leith, UK 8, 15, 22, 29, 36, 43, 50, 55
Leixoes, Portugal 8, 15, 22, 29, 36, 43, 50
Limassol, Cyprus 92–4
Lisbon, Portugal 8, 15, 22, 29, 36, 43, 50, 53–7
L'Islet, Canada 209, 214
Liverpool, UK 8, 15, 22, 29, 36, 43, 50, 53–7
Lobito, Angola 18–24, 67–71, 98–102, 132, 137, 142, 147, 150–2
London, UK 8, 15, 22, 29, 36, 43, 50, 53–7
Longview, USA 202–6
Los Angeles, USA 46–52, 87–91, 118–22, 145–9, 166–71, 183–7, 194–8, 202–6
Luanda, Angola 18–24, 67–71, 98–102, 132, 137, 142, 147, 150–2
Lulea, Sweden 8, 15, 22, 29, 36, 43, 50, 53–7
Lyttelton, New Zealand 39–45, 82–6, 113–17, 140–4, 161–5, 178–82, 196

Mackay, Australia 39–45, 82–6, 113–17, 140–4, 161–5, 178–82, 196, 199–201
Madang, Papua New Guinea 39–45, 82–6, 113–17, 140–4, 161–5, 178–82, 196
Madeira, Portugal 18–24, 67–71, 98–102, 132, 137, 142, 147, 150–2
Makassar, Indonesia 32–8, 77–81, 108–12, 135–9, 156–60, 179, 184
Makatea, French Polynesia 39–45, 82–6, 113–17, 140–4, 161–5, 178–82, 196
Malacca (now known as Melaka), Malaysia 25–31, 72–6, 103–7, 130–4, 158, 163, 168
Malmo, Sweden 53–7
Manaus, Brazil 209, 214
Manchester, UK 56
Manchester Ship Canal, UK 209, 214
Mangalore, India 25–31, 72–6, 103–7, 130–4, 158, 163, 169
Manila, Philippines 32–8, 77–81, 108–12, 135–9, 156–60, 180, 185, 188–90
Manzanillo, Mexico 46–52, 87–91, 118–22, 145–9, 166–71, 183–7, 194–8
Maputo, Mozambique 18–24, 67–71, 98–102, 132, 137, 142, 147, 151
Maracaibo, Venezuela 11–17, 62–6, 100, 105, 110, 115, 120
Mariupol, Ukraine 4–10, 64, 69, 74, 79, 84, 89, 92–4
Marseilles, France 4–10, 64, 69, 74, 79, 84, 89, 92–4
Martin Garcia, Argentina 209, 214
Masinloc, Philippines 32–8, 77–81, 108–12, 135–9, 156–60, 180, 185
Massawa, Eritrea 25–31, 72–6, 103–7, 130–4, 158, 163, 169, 173
Matane, Canada 209, 214
Mauritius, Mauritius 18–24, 67–71, 98–102, 132, 137, 142, 147, 151–2
Mazatlan, Mexico 46–52, 87–91, 118–22, 145–9, 166–71, 183–7, 194–8, 202–4
Melaka (see Malacca), Malaysia

Melbourne, Australia 39–45, 82–6, 113–17, 140–4, 161–5, 178–82, 196, 200
Melilla, Spain 93
Menado, Indonesia 32–8, 77–81, 108–12, 135–9, 156–60, 180, 185
Messina, Italy 4–10, 64, 69, 74, 79, 84, 89, 93
Milford Haven, UK 9, 16, 23, 30, 37, 44, 51
Milner Bay, Australia 199–201
Milwaukee, USA 208
Mina al Ahmadi, Kuwait 25–31, 72–6, 103–7, 130–4, 158, 163, 169, 173
Miri, Malaysia 188–90
Mobile, USA 11–17, 62–6, 100, 105, 110, 115, 120
Mogadiscio, Somalia 18–24, 67–71, 98–102, 132, 137, 142, 147, 151–2
Moji, Japan 32–8, 77–81, 108–12, 135–9, 156–60, 180, 185, 188–90
Mombasa, Kenya 18–24, 67–71, 98–102, 132, 137, 142, 147, 151
Mongla, Bangladesh 25–31, 72–6, 103–7, 130–4, 158, 163, 169, 173
Monrovia, Liberia 18–24, 67–71, 98–102, 132, 137, 142, 147, 151–2
Montevideo, Uruguay 18–24, 67–71, 98–102, 133, 138, 143, 148, 151–2
Montreal, Canada 11–17, 62–6, 100, 105, 110, 115, 120, 123–5, 209, 214
Mormugao, India 25–31, 72–6, 103–7, 130–4, 158, 163, 169, 172–4
Morphou Bay, Cyprus 4–10, 64, 69, 74, 79, 84, 89
Moulmein, Myanmar 25–31, 72–6, 103–7, 130–4, 159, 164, 169
Mozambique Island, Mozambique 18–24, 67–71, 98–102, 133, 138, 143, 148
Mumbai, India 25–31, 72–6, 103–7, 130–4, 159, 164, 169, 172–4
Murmansk, Russia 9, 16, 23, 30, 37, 44, 51, 56
Muroran, Japan 32–8, 77–81, 108–12, 135–9, 156–60, 180, 185
Musay'td, Qatar 25–31, 72–6, 103–7, 130–4, 159, 164, 170

Nagasaki, Japan 32–8, 77–81, 108–12, 135–9, 156–60, 180, 185, 188–90
Nagoya, Japan 32–8, 77–81, 108–12, 135–9, 156–60, 180, 185, 189
Namibe, Angola 151–2
Nampo, North Korea 32–8, 77–81, 108–12, 135–9, 156–60, 180, 185
Nanaimo, Canada 46–52, 87–91, 118–22, 145–9, 166–71, 183–7, 194–8
Napier, New Zealand 39–45, 82–6, 113–17, 140–4, 161–5, 178–82, 196, 199–201
Naples, Italy 4–10, 64, 69, 74, 79, 84, 89, 93
Narvik, Norway 9, 16, 23, 30, 37, 44, 51, 56
Nassau, Bahamas 11–17, 62–6, 100, 105, 110, 115, 120, 123–5, 209
Nauru Island, Nauru 39–45, 82–6, 113–17, 140–4, 161–5, 178–82, 196, 199–201
Nelson, New Zealand 39–45, 82–6, 113–17, 140–4, 161–5, 178–82, 197, 199–201
Newcastle, England 9, 16, 23, 30, 37, 44, 51, 53–7
Newcastle (NSW), Australia 39–45, 82–6, 113–17, 140–4, 161–5, 178–82, 197, 199–201
New Orleans, USA 11–17, 62–6, 100, 105, 110, 115, 120, 123–5
New Plymouth, New Zealand 39–45, 82–6, 113–17, 140–4, 161–5, 178–82, 197, 200
Newport News, USA 123–5
New York, USA 11–17, 62–6, 100, 105, 110, 115, 120, 123–5
New Westminster, Canada 46–52, 87–91, 118–22, 145–9, 166–71, 183–7, 194–8
Niigata, Japan 189
Norfolk (Va), USA 11–17, 62–6, 101, 106, 111, 116, 121, 123–5
North Cape 210–11
North Sea Canal, Netherlands 209, 214
Nouadhibou, Mauritania 151–2

Noumea, New Caledonia 39–45, 82–6, 113–17, 140–4, 161–5, 178–82, 197, 199–201
Novorossiysk, Russia 4–10, 64, 69, 74, 79, 84, 89, 93
Nuevitas, Cuba 11–17, 62–6, 101, 106, 111, 116, 121, 124

Obligado, Argentina 209, 214
Odessa, Ukraine 4–10, 65, 70, 75, 80, 85, 90, 94
Oporto (Porto), Portugal 56
Oran, Algeria 92–4
Osaka, Japan 32–8, 77–81, 108–12, 135–9, 156–60, 180, 185, 188–90
Oskarshamn, Sweden 56
Oslo, Norway 9, 16, 23, 30, 37, 44, 51, 52–7
Otago Harbour, New Zealand 39–45, 82–6, 113–17, 140–4, 161–5, 178–82, 197, 199–201
Otaru, Japan 32–8, 77–81, 108–12, 135–9, 156–60, 181, 181, 186

Palembang, Indonesia 32–8, 77–81, 108–12, 135–9, 156–60, 181, 186
Palermo, Italy 4–10, 65, 70, 75, 80, 85, 90
Panama Canal, Panama 210, 214
Papeete, French Polynesia 39–45, 82–6, 113–17, 140–4, 161–5, 178–82, 197, 199–201
Para, Brazil 210
Paradip, India 172–4
Parana, Argentina 209, 214
Paranagua, Brazil 151–2
Patras (Patrai), Greece 92–4
Penang, Malaysia 25–31, 72–6, 103–7, 130–4, 159, 164, 169, 172–4
Pepel, Sierra Leone 151–2
Perim Island 210–11
Philadelphia, USA 11–17, 62–6, 101, 106, 111, 116, 121, 125
Piraeus, Greece 4–10, 65, 70, 75, 80, 85, 90, 92–4
Plum Island Light, Canada 210, 214
Plymouth, UK 53–7
Pointe Noire, Canada 151–2
Port Alberni, Canada 46–52, 87–91, 118–22, 145–9, 166–71, 183–7, 194–8
Port Arthur (Ontario), Canada (Thunder Bay) 209
Port Arthur (Texas), USA 125
Port Au Prince, Haiti 11–17, 62–6, 101, 106, 111, 116, 121
Port Blair, India 25–31, 72–6, 103–7, 130–4, 159, 164, 170
Port Cartier, Canada 210, 214
Port Darwin, Australia 199–201
Port Elizabeth, South Africa 18–24, 67–71, 98–102, 133, 138, 143, 148, 150–2
Port Harcourt, Nigeria 18–24, 67–71, 98–102, 133, 138, 143, 148, 150–2
Port Hedland, Australia 39–45, 82–6, 113–17, 140–4, 161–5, 178–82, 197, 199–201
Port Isabel, USA 46–52, 87–91, 118–22, 145–9, 166–71, 183–7, 194–8
Port Kelang (formerly Port Klang), Malaysia 25–31, 72–6, 103–7, 130–4, 159, 164, 170
Port Kembla, Australia 39–45, 82–6, 113–17, 140–4, 161–5, 178–82, 198, 199–201
Portland (Maine), USA 11–17, 62–6, 101, 106, 111, 116, 121, 123–5
Portland (Oregon), USA 46–52, 87–91, 118–22, 145–9, 166–71, 183–7, 194–8, 202–4
Portland (Victoria), Australia 39–45, 82–6, 113–17, 140–4, 161–5, 178–82, 197, 201
Port Latta (Tasmania), Australia 199–201
Port Lincoln, Australia 39–45, 82–6, 113–17, 140–4, 161–5, 178–82, 198

Port Moody, Canada 46–52, 87–91, 118–22, 145–9, 166–71, 183–7, 194–8
Port Moresby, Papua New Guinea 39–45, 82–6, 113–17, 140–4, 161–5, 178–82, 198, 201
Port Alegre, Brazil 18–24, 67–71, 98–102, 133, 138, 143, 148, 151
Port of Spain, Trinidad & Tobago 11–17, 62–6, 101, 106, 111, 116, 121, 125, 210–11
Port Okha, India 25–31, 72–6, 103–7, 130–4, 159, 164, 170, 173
Port Pirie, Australia 39–45, 82–6, 113–17, 140–4, 161–5, 178–82, 198, 199–201
Port Said, Egypt 4–10, 65, 70, 75, 80, 85, 90, 92–4, 210–11
Port St Francis (St Lawrence Seaway), Canada 209, 214
Port Sudan, Sudan 25–31, 72–6, 103–7, 130–4, 159, 164, 170, 172–4
Port Sultan Qaboos, Oman 172–4
Poti, Georgia 4–10, 65, 70, 75, 80, 85, 90, 92–4
Prince Rupert, Canada 46–52, 87–91, 118–22, 145–9, 166–71, 183–7, 194–8
Puerto Cabello, Venezuela 125
Puerto Limon, Costa Rica 11–17, 62–6, 101, 106, 111, 116, 121
Puerto Montt, Chile 46–52, 87–91, 118–22, 145–9, 166–71, 183–7, 194–8
Puerto Rico 125
Puntarenas, Costa Rica 46–52, 87–91, 118–22, 145–9, 166–71, 183–7, 194–8
Punta Arenas, Chile 46–52, 87–91, 118–22, 145–9, 166–71, 183–7, 194–8, 202–4
Pusan, South Korea 32–8, 77–81, 108–12, 135–9, 156–60, 181, 186, 188–90

Qingdao, China 32–8, 77–81, 108–12, 135–9, 156–60, 181, 186, 188–90
Qinhuangdao, China 32–8, 77–81, 108–12, 135–9, 156–60, 181, 186, 188–90
Quebec, Canada 123–5, 209, 214
Quseir, Egypt 25–31, 72–6, 103–7, 130–4, 160, 165, 170, 172–4

Rabaul, Papua New Guinea 199–201
Ras Tanura, Saudi Arabia 172–4
Recife, Brazil 18–24, 67–71, 98–102, 133, 138, 143, 148, 151, 210–11
Reunion (St Denis) 18–24, 67–71, 98–102, 133, 138, 143, 148
Reykjavik, Iceland 53–7
Richelieu Rapids, Canada 209, 214
Riga, Latvia 57
Rijeka, Croatia 4–10, 65, 70, 75, 80, 85, 90, 94
Rio de Janeiro, Brazil 18–24, 67–71, 98–102, 133, 138, 143, 148, 150–2
Rockhampton, Australia 39–45, 82–6, 113–17, 140–4, 161–5, 178–82, 198
Rosario, Argentina 209, 214
Rostock, Germany 9, 16, 23, 30, 37, 44, 51
Rotterdam, Netherlands 9, 16, 23, 30, 37, 44, 51, 53–7

Sabang, Indonesia 32–8, 77–81, 108–12, 135–9, 156–60, 181, 186, 210–11
Saco, Mocamedes 152
Safaga, Egypt 172–4
St John (New Brunswick), Canada 11–17, 62–6, 101, 106, 111, 116, 121, 123–5
St John's (Newfoundland), Canada 11–17, 62–6, 102, 107, 112, 117, 122, 125
St Petersburg, Russia 9, 16, 23, 30, 37, 44, 51, 53–7
Salaverry, Peru 202–4
Salina Cruz, Mexico 46–52, 87–91, 118–22, 145–9, 166–71, 183–7, 194–8
Salvador, Brazil 18–24, 67–71, 98–102, 134, 139, 144, 149, 152
San Diego, USA 202–4

San Francisco, USA 46–52, 87–91, 118–22, 145–9, 166–71, 183–7, 194–8, 202–4, 210–11
San Jose, Guatemala 46–52, 87–91, 118–22, 145–9, 166–71, 183–7, 194–8, 202–4
San Juan, Puerto Rico 11–17, 62–6, 101, 106, 111, 116, 121
San Nicolas, Argentina 210, 214
San Lorenzo, Argentina 210, 214
San Pedro, Argentina 210, 214
Santa Marta, Colombia 123–5
Santander, Spain 57
Santiago de Cuba, Cuba 11–17, 62–6, 102, 107, 112, 117, 122
Santo Domingo, Dominican Republic 11–17, 62–6, 102, 107, 112, 117, 122
Santos, Brazil 18–24, 67–71, 98–102, 134, 139, 144, 149, 150–2
São Vicente Island, Cape Verde 18–24, 67–71, 98–102, 134, 139, 144, 149, 150–2, 210–11
Sault Ste Marie, USA 208
Savannah, USA 123–5
Savona–Vado, Italy 94
Seattle, USA 46–52, 87–91, 118–22, 145–9, 166–71, 183–7, 194–8, 202–4
Sept Iles, Canada 209, 214
Sfax, Tunisia 4–10, 65, 70, 75, 80, 85, 90, 94
Shanghai, China 32–8, 77–81, 108–12, 135–9, 156–60, 181, 186, 188–90
Shimonoseki, Japan 32–8, 77–81, 108–12, 135–9, 156–60, 182, 187, 188–90
Sidon, Lebanon 94
Singapore 25–31, 72–6, 103–7, 130–4, 156–60, 165, 172–4, 182, 187, 188–90, 210–11
Siracusa, Italy 4–10, 65, 70, 75, 80, 85, 90
Sittwe, Myanmar 25–31, 72–6, 103–7, 130–4, 160, 165, 171, 172–4
Skaw, Denmark 10, 17, 24, 31, 38, 45, 210–11
Southampton, UK 10, 17, 24, 31, 38, 45, 53–7
South Point (Anticosti), Canada 209, 214
Split, Croatia 92–4
Stockholm, Sweden 10, 17, 24, 31, 38, 45, 53–7
Stone Island Light, Canada 209, 214
Strait of Hormuz 210–11
Suez, Egypt 25–31, 72–6, 103–7, 130–4, 160, 165, 171, 172–4
Suez Canal 210, 214
Sunderland, UK 10, 17, 24, 31, 38, 45, 57
Surabaya, Indonesia 32–8, 77–81, 108–12, 135–9, 156–60, 182, 187, 188–90
Suva, Fiji 39–45, 82–6, 113–17, 140–4, 161–5, 178–82, 198, 201
Swansea, UK 57
Sydney, Australia 39–45, 82–6, 113–17, 140–4, 161–5, 178–82, 198, 199–201
Szczecin, Poland 10, 17, 24, 31, 38, 45, 52, 53–7

Tacoma, USA 46–52, 87–91, 118–22, 145–9, 166–71, 183–7, 194–8, 202–4
Takoradi, Ghana 18–24, 67–71, 98–102, 134, 139, 144, 149, 152
Taku Bar, China 190
Talcahuano, Chile 46–52, 87–91, 118–22, 145–9, 166–71, 183–7, 194–8
Tampa, USA 11–17, 62–6, 102, 107, 112, 117, 122, 123–5
Tampico, Mexico 11–17, 62–6, 102, 107, 112, 117, 122, 123–5
Tanjung Priok, Indonesia 32–8, 77–81, 108–12, 135–9, 156–60, 182, 187, 190, 210–11
Tarabulus (formerly Tripoli), Libya 4–10, 66, 71, 76, 81, 86, 91
Taranto, Italy 4–10, 66, 71, 76, 81, 86, 91